VLSI FOR
ARTIFICIAL INTELLIGENCE
AND NEURAL NETWORKS

VLSI FOR
ARTIFICIAL INTELLIGENCE
AND NEURAL NETWORKS

Edited by

JOSÉ G. DELGADO-FRIAS

State University of New York at Binghamton
Binghamton, New York

and

WILLIAM R. MOORE

Oxford University
Oxford, United Kingdom

SPRINGER SCIENCE+BUSINESS MEDIA, LLC

Library of Congress Cataloging-in-Publication Data

International Workshop on VLSI for Artificial Intelligence and Neural
Networks (1990 : Oxford, England)
    VLSI for artificial intelligence and neural networks / edited by
José G. Delgado-Frias and William R. Moore.
        p.   cm.
    "Proceedings of the International Workshop on VLSI for Artificial
Intelligence and Neural Networks, held September 5-7, 1990, in
Oxford, United Kingdom"--T.p. verso.
    Includes bibliographical references and index.
    ISBN 978-0-306-44029-8   ISBN 978-1-4615-3752-6 (eBook)
    DOI 10.1007/978-1-4615-3752-6
    1. Artificial intelligence--Congresses. 2. Neural networks
(Computer science)--Congresses. 3. Integrated circuits--Very large
scale integration--Congresses. I. Delgado-Frias, José G.
II. Moore, Will R. III. Title.
Q335.I575 1990
006.3--dc20   91-24010
                                                                   CIP

Proceedings of the International Workshop on VLSI for Artificial
Intelligence and Neural Networks, held September 5-7, 1990,
in Oxford, United Kingdom

ISBN 978-1-4613-6671-3

© 1991 Springer Science+Business Media New York
Originally published by Plenum Press in 1991

PROGRAMME COMMITTEE

Igor Aleksander, *Imperial College, UK*
Howard Card, *University of Manitoba, Canada*
José Delgado-Frias, *SUNY-Binghamton, USA*
Richard Frost, *University of Winsor, Canada*
Peter Kogge, *IBM, USA*
Will Moore, *University of Oxford, UK*
Alan Murray, *University of Edinburgh, UK*
John Oldfield, *Syracuse University, USA*
Lionel Tarassenko, *University of Oxford, UK*
Philip Treleaven, *University College London, UK*
Benjamin Wah, *University of Illinois, USA*
Michel Weinfield, *EP Paris, France*

PREFACE

This book is an edited selection of the papers presented at the *International Workshop on VLSI for Artificial Intelligence and Neural Networks* which was held at the University of Oxford in September 1990. Our thanks go to all the contributors and especially to the programme committee for all their hard work. Thanks are also due to the ACM-SIGARCH, the IEEE Computer Society, and the IEE for publicizing the event and to the University of Oxford and SUNY-Binghamton for their active support. We are particularly grateful to Anna Morris, Maureen Doherty and Laura Duffy for coping with the administrative problems.

José Delgado-Frias
Will Moore

April 1991

Artificial intelligence and neural network algorithms/computing have increased in complexity as well as in the number of applications. This in turn has posed a tremendous need for a larger computational power than can be provided by conventional scalar processors which are oriented towards numeric and data manipulations. Due to the artificial intelligence requirements (symbolic manipulation, knowledge representation, non-deterministic computations and dynamic resource allocation) and neural network computing approach (non-programming and learning), a different set of constraints and demands are imposed on the computer architectures for these applications.

Research and development of novel machines for artificial intelligence and neural networks has increased in order to meet the new performance requirements. This book presents novel approaches and future trends to VLSI implementations of machines for these applications. For the time being these architectures have to be implemented in VLSI technology with all the benefits and constraints that this implies. Papers have been drawn from a number of research communities; the subjects span VLSI design, computer design, computer architectures, artificial intelligence techniques and neural computing.

This book has five chapters that have been grouped on two major categories: computer architectures for artificial intelligence and hardware support for neural computing. The topics covered here range from symbolic manipulation to connectionism and from programmed systems to learning systems.

Computer architectures for artificial intelligence

In this category there are two chapters, Chapter 1 deals with artificial intelligence impact on computer architecture issues and Chapter 2 covers novel implementations of machines for Prolog processing.

Issues such as architectural approaches for artificial intelligence processing are covered first. There is a wide variety of approaches that range from a co-processor (§1.5) to alleviate the load of the main processor to multiple processor architectures such as single instruction multiple data stream (§1.7), multiple data multiple data stream (§1.1, 1.3, 1.8) and hybrid MIMD/SIMD machines (§1.2). Other issues that are usually found in hardware implementations of AI are also addressed. These topics include: garbage collection (§1.4), parallel matching (§1.6) and path planning (§1.9).

The use of Prolog as a language for artificial intelligence has increased in recent years. As the AI applications grow in complexity, high performance Prolog machines become an urgent requirement. Chapter 2 provides a number of alternatives for Prolog implementations. The alternatives range from extensions to processors (§2.1, 2.2) through specialized VLSI hardware for unification (§2.3) to parallel implementations (§2.4, 2.5, 2.6, 2.7).

Hardware support for neural computing

There are three chapters under this heading; each chapter reflects a different trend in the implementation of neural networks. Chapter 3 deals with pulse stream neural networks that tend to mimic more closely the behavior of biological neurons (§3.1, 3.2, 3.5, 3.6, 3.7) and analogue approaches which may reduce the size of the circuitry involved in the neural network realizations (§3.3, 3.4, 3.8).

Alternatively digital implementation of neural networks hold a promise of higher precision. The approaches, presented in Chapter 4, include: associative methods (§4.2, 4.3), systolic implementations (§4.8, 4.10), bit-serial streams (§4.4), binary networks (§4.5), sparse connections (§4.6) and neuron-parallel layer-serial (§4.7).

Neural network computing is frequently modelled as a matrix/vector computation. Processor arrays for this type of manipulation may be appropriate and five different implementations are presented in Chapter 5. These implementations are DSP like processors (§5.1), a toroidal ring (§5.2), a cellular array (§5.3) and associative processing (§5.4, 5.5).

CONTENTS

Contents

1.1 VLSI Design of a 3-D Highly Parallel Message-Passing Architecture

Jean-Luc Bechennec, Christophe Chanussot,
Vincent Neri, Daniel Etiemble

LRI, Université Paris Sud
91405 ORSAY Cedex, France

Abstract

We study the feasibility of a massively parallel architecture, the Mega machine, intended for demand-driven and message-passing functional programming. Mega holds thousands of Processing Elements (PE) and may execute millions of parallel functional processes.

We present the basic hardware and VLSI concerns of the architecture : the VLSI constraints to implement the PE within 100 mm^2 chip area, the specific MegaPack which is used for a direct 3D interconnection of the machine and the special 4-valued circuits that have been designed for the transmission between MegaPacks.

MACHINES TO EXPLORE GIANT ARCHITECTURES (MEGA)

Message-Passing Architectures

We are studying message-passing massively parallel architectures for special Artificial Intelligence applications (knowledge bases, semantic networks, large dynamic systems...). Message-passing architectures are characterized by an asynchronous MIMD control, distributed local memories and message-passing communications. The Mega project focuses on message-passing MIMD machines with fine-grained parallelism. It aims to define a Demand-driven model of computation relying on functional programming.

The Mega functional computation model

The Mega parallel functional model is based on a paradigm for functional programming embedded in a language named *MegaTalk*. It is a lexical Lisp kernel, derived from Scheme

VLSI for Artificial Intelligence and Neural Networks, Edited by J.G. Delgado-Frias and
W.R. Moore, Plenum Press, New York, 1991

1

(Steele and Sussman 1975). MegaTalk is implemented with a Demand-driven mechanism applied to the users function calls (Fsubrs). The internal functions (subrs) are run in sequential mode, bounding the explosion of parallel evaluations and allowing to adjust the grain of parallelism and the average processes size to the PEs CPU size (Cappello et al 1990b).

The main impact of this model on the PE architecture lies in the very fine granularity of the functional processes : a typical process may be viewed as a 16-byte frame. The parallel functional calls may generate a large number of processes, despite of the limitation of the parallel evaluation to user function calls and even if this growth is bounded by the model (restriction to strict operators) or by the system (limitation by the processors load estimation). As parallel evaluation can create a huge number of small communicating processes, we examine the structural feasibility of machines with up to 10^6 Processing Elements (PE) with a 32-bit process address capability. With a 64 Kbyte local memory, each PE could execute up to 4K processes.

The interconnection network

The interconnection network is a key feature of a massively parallel architecture. In message-passing machines, the most popular interconnection networks have been for a long time hypercubes (iPSCs, FPS, Connection Machine). This choice is based on the geometrical properties, such as diameter, mean distance and number of parallel paths (Saad and Schultz 1988). However, when taking into account the technological constraints such as wiring density (Dally 1987) or available pin number (Reed and Fujimoto 1987), some structural properties, such as link locality, become critical.

In Germain et al (1989), we showed that low-dimensional grids outperform hypercubes for a large number of processors, with byte serial transmission of messages instead of bit serial tranmission with hypercubes. This phenomenon becomes noticeable above 4K PEs, and the optimal grid dimension then is 4 or 5. So the Mega machine is organized as a 3D grid of Processing Elements. The routing mechanisms are implemented by the Communication Unit (CU). They are based on a randomized routing strategy which minimizes contention by a large use of all the shortest paths.

A monochip Processing Element

For VLSI and packaging constraints, a monochip PE including the CPU, the CU and the Local Memory, has several advantages. The machine consists of the interconnection of a single unique VLSI chip. This modular approach minimizes the number of wiring interconnections. A maximum PE chip area of 100 mm^2 has been assumed to get an acceptable yield, with 15 mm^2 devoted to CPU and CU units and 85 mm^2 to the RAM.

VLSI DESIGN OF THE PROCESSING ELEMENT

The block diagram of the Processing Element is shown in Figure 1. We present the basic features of the CPU, the local memory and the Communication Unit.

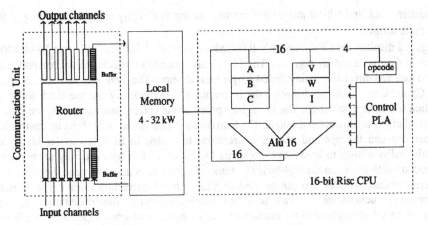

Figure 1 The Processing Element

Table 1 HF3CMOS basic features

CMOS	NPN
NMOS (50/50) Vth : 0.7V	Se : 3.6 x 3.6 µm2
PMOS (50/50) Vth : 1.0V	hfe : 90
BVDSS > 7V	BVCEO : 14V
td (fin=fout) : 220 ps	BVCBO : 25 V
	BVEBO : 5V
	VEA : 50 V
	Ceb : 37.5 fF
	Ccb : 27 fF
	Ccs : 106 fF
	rbb' : 370 Ω
	ft max : 8 GHz

The switching performance have been simulated and the chip areas have been evaluated for the different circuits according to the electrical parameters and the layout design rules of the SGS-Thomson 1.2 µm BiCMOS technology. The basic features of this technology, called HF3CMOS (Mallardeau et al 1990), are given in Table 1.

A 7 mm² RISC CPU for massive parallelism

The small chip area devoted to the CPU is the main reason for a Risc-like architecture. Speeding execution is the most frequent motivation for a Risc architecture (Stallings 1986). For the Mega PE, as for Inmos Transputer, minimizing area and limiting code size are the more decisive. Thus the Mega PE has two similarities with the Transputer : a three registers evaluation stack and a 8-bit instruction format, leading to a highly compact encoding of the processes scripts.

Figure 2 displays the CPU data path. It includes a general 16-bit ALU, an extra 16-bit adder for control purpose and six registers. The 16-bit data path makes possible direct computing on 16-bit data and direct addressing the 64 Kbyte local memory. The three general registers (A, B and C) work as a hardwired stack ; the instructions systematically use the stack top A as implicit source or destination. The W register points to the current process workspace. The V register buffers arguments extensions. The load constant instruction (x,c) shifts its content left 4 positions and the operand part of instructions is loaded in its 4 low order bits. This functionnality allows to load large constants (8, 12, or 16-bit) by executing several load instruction with short constants (4-bit). The same functionality is used to extend the number of different operation codes that can be used with the defined instruction format. The 31 most important instructions only need a byte. 15 instructions, which operation code ranges from 0_H to E_H, have a 4-bit operand in the instruction. For 16 instructions which operation code is F_H, the 4-bit operand is an extra operand code which is loaded in the operand register. To define more than 31 instructions, x,c instruction, which is one of the 15 instructions with explicit operand, is used to load an extra operand code in V.

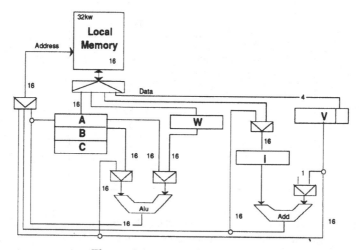

Figure 2 Block Diagram of the CPU

Implementing the local memory on the same VLSI than the CPU severely constraints the silicon area occupation ; conversely, the local memory becomes closely coupled to the CPU and can thus be viewed as a *cache* when considering the access speed. The CPU and assembly language make full use of this cache-effect.

All the instructions, including memory accesses, can be executed in one cycle. The execution of an instruction need two phases. The instruction fetch and decoding use the first phase. It is common to every instruction. The fetch loads the operand code in the Latch Instruction (LI) and the operand part in V. This phase is terminated when the control commands are available at the outputs of the control PLA. The execution part of the instruction uses the second phase. This part of the instruction needs a memory access or not. With HF3CMOS technology, the clock cycle is about 60 ns and the chip area is less than 7 mm^2. The detailed description of the architecture and of its implementation can be found in Cappello et al (1990a).

A large local memory with an ASIC technology

The RAM is an important VLSI issue in the PE design. The static cell approach is chip area consuming. Using a standard layout for the static cell with HF3CMOS technology, a 16 Kbyte memory could be implemented within 100 mm^2, and a 32 Kbyte memory within 90 mm^2 with the next generation 0.8 μm technology. The dynamic approach is difficult without a specific technology for dynamic RAMs. We are now investigating a dynamic approach, with 2 transistors per cell (Yuen et al 1989), by using specific bipolar layers of HF3CMOS technology to increase memory capacitances per area unit, thus decreasing the cell area.

A 7 mm^2 efficient hardwired router for message-passing

Routing performance, both the average message delay and the network throughput, is decisive for a massively parallel architecture (Reed and Fujimoto 1987). A new routing algorithm, Forced routing, is used. It is a tradeoff between the classical greedy algorithms, which are quite easy to hardwire (Lutz 1989), but behave poorly at high network load, and the randomized algorithms (Valiant 1982), which are asymptotically optimal but area-consuming.

Forced Routing may be summarized by the following algorithm :

```
for input_link = 0 to network_degree do
    if there exists a message on input_link
    then
        if shortest path output links are free
        then randomly allocate one
        else
            if output links are free
            then randomly allocate one
            else buffer message
            endif
        endif
    endif
endfor
```

It is adaptative as it insures a large, even though not optimal, occupation of the network channels ; it saves chip area by buffering the messages that cannot progress to their destination on the network instead of using on-chip buffers. It is forced in the sense that, even when there are conflicts between incoming messages, all of them are routed, possibly along directions moving them away from their destination. So the path length, and thus the routing delay, will gracefully degrade with contention. Deadlock is not possible, because messages never stop moving in the network, and starvation is avoiding by giving the highest priority to the internal channel, which serves the routing buffer. A complete descrition of the Forced routing algorithm, with extensive performance simulations, can be found in Germain et al (1989).

Figure 3 shows the CU architecture. There are seven input channels, one-byte wide with 2 extra control bits. Six external channels input the external messages from the 3D-grid interconnection network ; one internal channel is multiplexed between the routing buffer and the processor (for emission). Each channel is associated with a *Channel Controller*. Each controller includes three one-byte registers to buffer the message destination address, a logic circuit to generate the requests on output channels, and a small PLA for error detection purpose. The complete address must actually be known before routing. This address is in relative format (Δx, Δy, Δz) rather than absolute : this format saves time and area, because the sign bit may be directly used.

The *Arbitration Circuit* drives a *Crossbar*, which connects the input channels to the output channels. When passing through the crossbar, the address header is adjusted following the chosen output channel. The *Routing Buffer* is a hardwired FIFO : emission and reception may be pipelined. The *Ejector* stores in the local memory the messages that have reached their final destination. Ejection is not always possible : only one message can be received at a time, the CPU may be in critical section for input/output or the memory stack may be full. In this case, the message will be derouted and will come back later. When ejection is accepted, the CU inhibits the CPU clock, so that the ejection is transparent to the CPU.

A complete description of the CU operations and details on the electrical design of the arbitration circuit can be found in Bechennec et al (1990). With HF3CMOS technology, propagation delay through the arbitration circuit is about 22 ns. Including the possible optimization of the other parts of the CU, a 60 ns cycle time is possible. This performance corresponds to a 16 Megabyte/s link bandwith. CU Chip area is less than 7 mm^2.

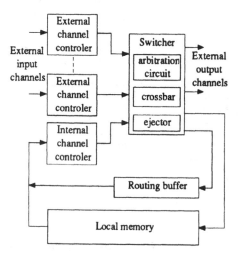

Figure 3 The Hardware Router Block Diagram

THE PACKAGING AND THE INTERCONNECTION SCHEME

The key point of the technological feasability of such a machine is the interconnection of such a large number of processing elements. The classical approach with boards, cards, racks, ... corresponding to different levels of hierarchy, don't allow a total modularity. A big originality of this project is the specification of a special package for a direct and totally modular assembly of the machine. Multivalued signalling allows byte transmission between low-size packages.

A MegaPack for 3D interconnection

We present a special package for the direct 3D interconnection of the machine, without boards and racks. This package, which size is $2 \times 2 \times 1.5$ cm^3 (Figure 4), has been studied for a dense and rigid assembly of the machine. It allows air-cooling to evacuate heat, and a regular distribution of power supply and clock rails. The asynchronous MIMD model of the machine is compatible with a global synchronous clock scheme. The messages are routed through the grid at a byte per clock cycle rate. During a clock cycle, a byte is transmitted from one PE to the next PE in the grid. The clock skew is negligeable for such a short distance.

A 4-valued transmission scheme

As each PE is connected to 6 neighbours, 120 wires should be needed for the byte-serial (plus 2 control bits) binary transmission. As this number is uncompatible with the MegaPack size, either time-multiplexing or multivalued signalling must be used for a reasonnable amount of

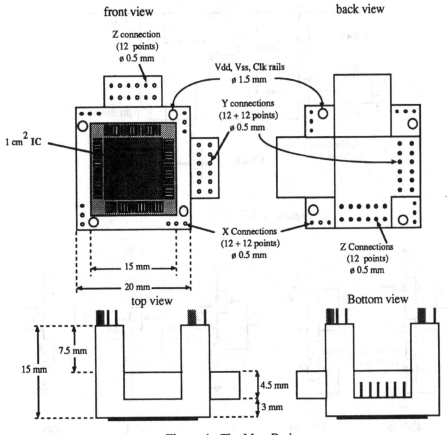

Figure 4 The MegaPack

connectors on the MegaPack (60). Time-multiplexing would mean a more complicated clocking scheme. We thus defined a special 4-valued transmission.

With HF3CMOS technology, two versions have been designed and evaluated : the first one only uses CMOS transistors ; the second one uses the bipolar transistors that can be used in BiCMOS technology to improve drivability. Figure 5 presents the BiCMOS encoder scheme, with 2-valued inputs and a 4-valued output. The precharge phase pulls down Z output to ground. The evaluation phase pulls up Z output to one of the 4 possible levels (V_{dd} - V_{be}, V_{dd} - $|V_{tp}|$, V_{dd} - $|V_{tp}|$ - V_{tn} and ground), according to x and y outputs. Figure 6 shows the threshold detector circuits, that deliver binary outputs according to the comparison between the 4-level input and the different threshold levels. They are used to implement the decoder circuits, as shown in Figure 7. Typical delay times between the input clock transition and the decoded x and y output are shown in Table 2. Assuming a 60 ns clock cycle, the wasted time in coding and decoding multivalued signal is 13 % of the clock cycle. The complete description of the circuits and switching characteristics with worst cases can be found in Etiemble et al (1990). Both switching characteristics and chip area are compatible with the machine requirements.

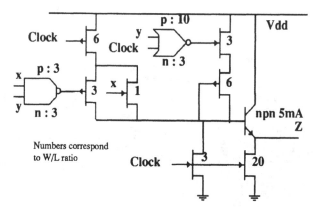

Figure 5 BiCMOS encoder

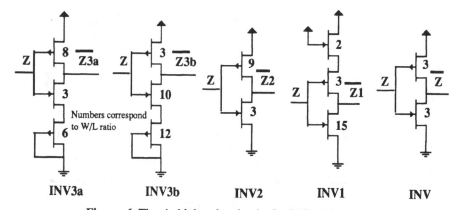

Figure 6 Threshold decoder circuits for BiCMOS version

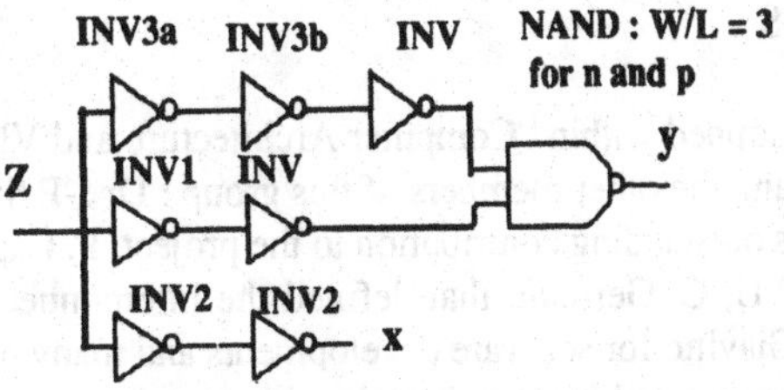

Figure 7 BiCMOS decoder

Table 2 4-valued transmission switching characteristics

INPUTS			EVALUATION		PRECHARGE	
Xin Yin		Z	C-Xout	C-Yout	C-Xout	C-Yout
0 0		0 <--> 1	---	7.8 ns	---	2.6 ns
0 1		0 <--> 0	---	---	---	---
1 0		0 <--> 2	5.6 ns	3.2 ns	1 ns	3.2 ns
1 1		0 <--> 3	3.8 ns	7.7ns	1.4 ns	3.8 ns

CONCLUSION

We have presented some basic features of VLSI and Hardware key points in the design of a massively parallel message-passing architecture for AI applications, based on a functional computational model. A totally modular assembly of the machine is possible by a 3D grid interconnection of monochip Processing Elements. We showed that the CPU and the hardwired router can be implemented within 14 mm^2 with a 1.2 µm CMOS technology, leading to the complete implementation of the Processing Element (CPU, Router and 64 Kbyte Memory) on a single chip with a next generation CMOS technology. A new package has been presented, which suppress the need for boards, cards, racks... A 4-valued transmission has been designed for the transmission between the D packages.

Software and applications concerns have not been considered in this paper. Some VLSI and hardware technical problems must still be solved (Design of the 64 Kbyte local memory with an ASIC technology, actual design of the 3D package...). But the basic features that have been presented in this paper show that there exist solutions that makes giant message-passing architectures feasible.

ACKNOWLEGMENTS

The Mega Project in developped within "Computer Architecture and VLSI Design" Research Group. The authors do thank the other members of this group : Dr J-P Sansonnet, directeur de recherche in CNRS for his outstanding contribution to the project, F. Cappello who worked on the architecture of the CPU, C. Germain that defined the interconnection network and the routing strategy, and J-L Giavitto for software developments and many helpfull discussions.

This work is currently supported by french national research program on New Computer Architectures (PRC-ANM) and by DRET under grant #89342320047050/

REFERENCES

Bechennec J-L., Germain C. and Neri V., "An efficient Hardwired Router for a 3D mesh Interconnection Network", LRI-Archi TR 90-7, *Submitted to COMP EURO 91.*

Cappello F., Bechennec J-L. and Etiemble D., "A RISC Central Processing Unit for a Massively Parallel Architecture", *EUROMICRO 90*, Amsterdam, 1990a.

Cappello F., Germain C. and Sansonnet J-P., " Design of a Reduced Instruction Set for Massively Parallel Functional Programming", *LRI-Archi TR 90-6, Submitted to Fourth International Conference on Architectural Support for Programming Languages and Operating Systems ,* 1990b.

Dally W.J., "Wire-Efficient VLSI Multiprocessor Communication Networks", *1987 Stanford Conference on Advanced Research in VLSI,* pp 391-415, 1987.

Etiemble D., Chanussot C. and Neri V., "4-Valued BiCMOS Circuits for the Transmission System of a Massively Parallel Architecture", *Proceedings International Symposium on Multiple Valued Logic,* Charlotte, pp 348-354, 1990.

Germain C., Bechennec J-L., Etiemble D. and Sansonnet J-P., "A New Communication Design for Massively Parallel Message-Passing Computers", *IFIP Working Conference on Decentralized Systems*, Lyon, 1989.

Lutz C., "Design of the Mosaic Processor", *Caltech Computer Science Technical Report 5129:TR:84*, 1984.

Mallardeau C., Duflos Y., Marin J-C., Roche M., Troster G. and Arndt J., "Esprit Project n° 2268 Combined Analog Digital Integration : CANDI", *Esprit Conference*, 1990.

Reed D.A. and Fujimoto R.M., "Multicomputer Networks - Message based Parallel processing", *MIT Press* - 1987.

Saad Y. and Schultz M.H., "Topological Properties of Hypercubes", *IEEE Trans. on Computers*, vol. C-37, n° 7, 1988, pp 867-870, 1988.

Stallings W. Ed., "Reduced Instruction Set Computers Tutorial", IEEE Computer Society Press, 1986.

Steele G.L. Jr. and Sussman G., "Scheme : An interpreter for the extended lambda calculus", *MIT AI Lab memo 349*, 1975.

Valiant L.G., "A scheme for fast parallel communication", *SIAM journal on Computing*, Vol 11, n° 2, pp 350-361, 1982.

Yuen A., Tsao P., Yin P. and Yuen A.T., "A 32K ASIC Synchronous RAM Using a Two-Transistor Basic Cell", *in IEEE J. Solid-State Circuits*, Vol 24, N° 1, pp 57-61, 1989.

1.2 Architectural Design of the Rewrite Rule Machine Ensemble

Hitoshi Aida,* Sany Leinwand and José Meseguer

SRI International, Menlo Park CA 94025

Abstract

Concurrent rewriting is a very general model of parallel computation based on logic; it directly supports parallel programming in very high level declarative languages ideally suited for AI applications. The Rewrite Rule Machine (RRM) is a massively parallel computer that physically realizes the concurrent rewriting model. The RRM is hierarchical, with SIMD computation performed at the chip level (called an *ensemble*) but the machine as a whole – consisting of thousands of ensemble chips – working in MIMD mode.

After a brief overview of the model of computation and the overall architecture, the paper focuses on the functionality and detailed architectural design of the ensemble chip. Topics discussed include the ensemble's processing elements, topology, instruction set, autonomous processes, and VLSI design.

INTRODUCTION

Two important problems in the field of parallel computing are *programmability* – the programming of parallel machines is generally harder and more expensive than that of sequential machines – and the *full exploitation of parallelism* in *complex, nonhomogeneous problems*. The RRM presents a unified solution to both these problems by means of a parallel model of computation based directly on logic, which supports programming in very high level declarative languages with *implicit parallelism* (Goguen and Meseguer 1988). The RRM exploits the local homogeneity existing in subproblems by executing in SIMD mode at the chip level, while accommodating nonhomogeneous problems by executing in MIMD mode at the level of the entire machine.

RRM Hierarchy

The RRM achieves multigrain concurrency through a hierarchical structure with the following levels:

1. A **cell** holds one data node and its structural links, and also provides basic processing and communication power.

---

*University of Tokyo, Japan; work done at SRI International.

VLSI for Artificial Intelligence and Neural Networks, Edited by J.G. Delgado-Frias and W.R. Moore, Plenum Press, New York, 1991

11

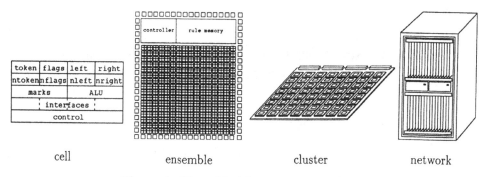

token	flags	left	right
ntoken	nflags	nleft	nright
marks		ALU	
interfaces			
control			

cell   ensemble   cluster   network

Figure 1 Hierarchical Structure of the RRM

2. A **rewrite ensemble** is a regular array of cells on a single VLSI chip, with connections for local data exchange; one ensemble holds several hundred cells plus a shared controller and some interface circuitry. An ensemble performs concurrent rewriting in SIMD mode.

3. A **cluster** might contain about a hundred ensembles placed on a board. The cluster supports MIMD execution, with component ensembles cooperating on a larger task.

4. The **network** (complete RRM prototype) will have about a hundred clusters on a general connection network, and will be capable of solving even larger problems.

A single ensemble yields very fast fine-grain SIMD rewriting, but RRM execution is coarse-grain MIMD at the RRM level, since each ensemble independently executes its own rewrites on its own data, communicating with other ensembles when necessary.

Ensemble Architecture

A preliminary architectural design for the ensemble was reported in (Leinwand *et al* 1988). This paper presents the detailed architectural design for the ensemble and the solutions developed for a variety of issues including the ensemble topology, SIMD rewriting, arbitration of communication conflicts, cell allocation, garbage collection, and autonomous data relocation.

The ensemble design pays attention to long-range trends in VLSI technology, stressing communication performance as the major goal. For this purpose, cells are kept as simple as possible – in order to pack several hundred on a single chip – and are connected on a *regular mesh* structure supporting very fast local data exchanges. Since only local connections are supported, built-in mechanisms for relocating data nodes are provided so that logical links involved in a computation have a chance to become local; such mechanisms exploit the inherent scheduling flexibility of the concurrent rewriting model of computation.

The ensemble design has been validated by extensive simulations, including detailed simulations at the register transfer level. A variety of example programs have been compiled into SIMD code and have been run on the simulators. Our simulation results show that a single ensemble chip is about 50 times faster than a SUN-3/60, which gives about 150 MIPS (Goguen *et al* 1989).

Novel Features

The RRM design exhibits a unique combination of architectural concepts:

1. **Processing, storage, and communication** capabilities are combined in a cell.
2. **SIMD instructions are interpreted in the context of each cell** (e.g., the left and right children need not be allocated in a fixed physical position); this allows very simple and flexible code.
3. **Systematic exploitation of locality,** moving logically connected items next to each other whenever such connections are used, and thus requiring the architecture only to support fast local communications.
4. **Flexible scheduling** due to a model of computation in which the order of rule application is irrelevant.
5. **Autonomous processes** for parallel garbage collection and for data relocation using computational resources not currently engaged in SIMD computation.
6. **Multigrain concurrency** exploits parallelism at all levels, both fine- and coarse-grain.

CONCURRENT REWRITING MODEL OF COMPUTATION

In the *concurrent rewriting* model of computation (Goguen *et al* 1987, Meseguer 1990), data are **terms**, constructed from a given set of constant and function symbols, and a program is a set of **rewrite rules**. The lefthand side (abbreviated LHS) and righthand side (RHS) of a rewrite rule are terms, possibly containing *variables*. A variable can be instantiated with any term of the appropriate sort; a set of instantiations for all variables of a rule is called a **substitution**.

A term rewriting computation starts with a given term as **data** and a given set of rewrite rules as the **program**. Each application of a rewrite rule has two phases: **matching** and **replacement**. The matching phase attempts to find a substitution for the rule's LHS that yields a subterm of the data term. During the replacement phase, the matched subterm – called a **redex** – is replaced by the RHS of the same rewrite rule, instantiated with the same substitution. Rules are applied to the data term until no more matches can be found; the resulting term is called **reduced** and considered to be the final result.

The stated definition of term rewriting does not prescribe an order of rule application. In the **concurrent rewriting** model of computation more than one rule can be applied at once, and each rule can be applied to many subterms of the given term at once. As an example, consider a simple program to compute Fibonacci numbers using basic Peano notation (this inefficient representation is used only for expository purposes):

$$\texttt{fibo(0) = 0} \tag{1}$$
$$\texttt{fibo(s(0)) = s(0)} \tag{2}$$
$$\texttt{fibo(s(s(N))) = fibo(N) + fibo(s(N))} \tag{3}$$

This is the program as a set of rewrite rules. Starting with `fibo(s(s(s(0))))` (i.e. $fibo(3)$) as the initial data term, the top function symbol matches rule (3) by substituting `s(0)` for N in the LHS. In the replacement phase, the initial term is changed to

$$\texttt{fibo(s(0)) + fibo(s(s(0)))} \quad \text{i.e.} \quad fibo(1) + fibo(2).$$

In the next rewrite step the first `fibo` node matches rule (2), and the second `fibo` matches rule (3) again. By concurrent rewriting using both these rules, the data term is changed to

$$\texttt{s(0) + (fibo(0) + fibo(s(0)))} \quad \text{i.e.} \quad 1 + (fibo(0) + fibo(1))$$

A concurrent rewriting computation is **SIMD** when only one rewrite rule is concurrently being applied to the data term; in the RRM, this style of concurrent rewriting is realized by an **ensemble** chip. **MIMD** rewriting is achieved when several rules are applied concurrently, but different rules are applied to different regions of the data term; this is the model for a cluster and RRM network.

THE RRM ENSEMBLE ARCHITECTURE

In the RRM, data terms are represented as binary structures: a function or constant symbol, with two pointers to its argument subterms (called left and right descendents). This is a general model – constants do not need arguments, unary functions only use the left pointer, and n-ary functions for $n > 2$ are decomposed into binary ones. Thus, the most basic unit is a **data node** containing a symbol and up to two functional arguments. In the RRM, data nodes combine processing and memory; they cooperate in executing SIMD instructions to find LHS patterns for a rule, and – when such a pattern is found – to replace a LHS pattern by the corresponding RHS. The architectural unit supporting a data node is called a **cell**. An **ensemble** chip consists of hundreds of such cells obeying SIMD instructions from a single **controller**.

Cell and Tile Architecture

The most basic computational element in the RRM is the **cell** (Leinwand *et al* 1988), which stores one data node, and also provides basic computational and communication capabilities. A cell consists of:

- Several **registers** including:
  - `token`, which encodes the function or constant symbol of the data node;
  - `left` and `right`, which point to the argument nodes;
  - `flags` encoding general rewriting status information (e.g. reduced) and also type information to cope with typed rewrite rules;
  - `marks` holding volatile information (similar to condition codes in conventional computers);
  - four temporary registers: `ntoken`, `nleft`, `nright` and `nflags` used to hold newly created structures (they are capable of holding a "shadow" data node ready to be swapped with the root of the LHS match, thus guaranteeing atomicity of replacement).
- An **ALU** to operate on and test the contents of registers.
- **Interfaces** to communication channels and to the SIMD controller.

The ensemble implementation scheme divides the silicon area into a regular array of **tiles**. Each tile incorporates several cells (4 is the choice currently under evaluation) and several messengers (more on these later). Adjacent tiles are directly connected by short wires, so that placing logically linked nodes in cells located in adjacent tiles permits efficient communication. The inter-tile communication resources are termed **ports**.

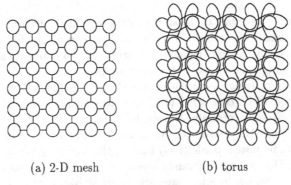

(a) 2-D mesh   (b) torus

Figure 2 Ensemble Topologies

One advantage of mapping several cells onto a single tile is to greatly increase the probability of placing a logically related data node in an adjacent cell. As a result, the occurrence of non-local connections is reduced. A second advantage of using tiles is in making better use of shared communication resources. Inter-tile ports are designed for handling average loads, with requests being dropped when overloading occurs. Due to the properties of the concurrent term rewriting model of computation, abandoning some connection attempts will not affect correctness.

Ensemble Topology

Modern VLSI design practice suggests basing the RRM ensemble implementation on a regular tessellation pattern. The simplest tile interconnection topology (in an RRM ensemble) is a two dimensional mesh, as shown in Figure 2 (a).

The problem with such a mesh is that it has a serious discontinuity at the edges. Whenever a large tree structure is built on such a mesh the structure has to be "folded" or "bent" at the edges. As a result, tiles near the edges become crowded and further replacements may be impossible. If the mesh is large enough, the problem can be tolerated. However, implementation considerations prevent construction of overly large meshes on a single VLSI chip. Simulations using realistic ensemble sizes clearly show that a large load imbalance can occur because of such edge effects.

Our solution to this problem is a torus topology. At first sight, a torus seems to require long wires going all the way across the chip, but this turns out to be unnecessary. As shown in Figure 2 (b) a torus topology can be implemented by connecting tiles to their respective next-to-neighbor tiles. Physically adjacent tiles are completely equivalent, except for being rotated 180 degrees. In this way an ensemble can be implemented as a completely edgeless, uniform structure on a chip, at the cost of having slightly longer wires (and a less planar physical wiring structure).

Instruction Set and SIMD Rewriting

All cells in an ensemble execute the same SIMD instructions broadcast from a common controller. However, the SIMD broadcast is interpreted in the local context of each cell. Using pointers and temporary storage available at the cell level, appropriate cell connections are made according to the abstract data term links. This shields the rewrite process from the details of a specific mapping of data onto ensemble cells and greatly simplifies control. It also permits relocation of data terms to different ensemble cells in order to take advantage of available local communication resources.

In general, when matching a particular LHS of a rule, only subterm structures partially matched need to be considered for further operations (eventually leading to a replacement). Those cells currently of interest for the match are called **active** – only active cells obey the SIMD broadcast. As an implementation mechanism, bits in the **marks** register can be tested to selectively activate those cells that should continue the rule execution. The focus of activity can be passed up and down the data term by placing identifying marks at various locations, and selectively activating only the nodes at specific data term locations. The selective activation of cells greatly reduces communication conflicts.

In addition to being located in "uninteresting" regions of the data term, some cells may become inactive as a result of failing to complete previous SIMD instructions due to communication conflicts. Such cells are deactivated (so they no longer execute SIMD during the current code sequence) and a reserved bit in their **marks** register – called the **failure** bit – is set to indicate the fact that their lack of matching does not necessarily mean the pattern is not present.

Here is a short summary of SIMD instructions for an ensemble chip. More details, including an example of SIMD code for computing Fibonacci numbers, can be found in (Leinwand *et al* 1988, Aida *et al* 1990a).

- **Arithmetic/logic instructions** compare the content of a register against another register, perform addition, subtraction, bitwise boolean operations, or simply move data between registers.
- **Mark instructions** test or modify bits in the **marks** register.
- **Inter-cell communication instructions** get or put the contents of a register (or test / modify a bit in the **marks** register) of a cell pointed at by one of the registers.
- **Allocate instructions** request a new cell in an adjacent tile and store a pointer to it in one of the registers. If no more cells are available, the cell is deactivated and the **failure** bit in the **marks** register is set to indicate the failure.
- **The commit instruction** atomically swaps the contents of `token`, `left`, `right`, and `flags` registers with the temporary registers `ntoken`, `nleft`, `nright`, and `nflags`, respectively. It also starts garbage collection operations.
- **Other instructions** reset the contents of cells, activate all cells, etc.

It is relatively easy to implement rewriting using the SIMD instructions described above. A preliminary version of a compiler has been built, which accepts rewrite rules as input and produces a sequence of SIMD instructions for the RRM ensemble (Aida *et al* 1990a). The instruction sequence to implement rewriting for a specific rule is summarized as follows:

1. Find a match for the LHS pattern of the rewrite rule by using comparisons (arithmetic/logic) instructions, mark instructions and inter-cell mark communication instructions.
2. Build the RHS structure by means of allocate instructions.
3. Copy pointers to the nodes matched by LHS variables into the newly created RHS structure by using inter-cell register communication instructions.
4. Finally, atomically change the structure through the `commit` instruction.

Autonomous Data Relocation and Garbage Collection

Inactive cells use their resources to perform ancillary tasks without SIMD supervision. Among these **autonomous processes**, the most interesting ones are automatic data relocation and garbage collection.

The automatic data relocation mechanism is one of the unique features of the RRM. During the execution of inter-cell communication instructions involving the left or right register, if the cell pointed at is not in an adjacent tile, the original cell is deactivated with the **failure** bit set. As a side effect, an autonomous data relocation operation is initiated that will eventually copy the contents of the cell pointed at to a new cell located in an adjacent tile.

The repeated use of shared substructures is monitored by **reference counters**. When completing a relocation, the data term that supplied a copy decrements its reference counter. If this counter becomes zero, the original term is no longer used and can be garbage collected. Also, after a commit operation the replaced LHS structure (previously pointed at by the left and right registers) becomes garbage if not shared elsewhere. Garbage in the RRM is a more severe problem than in other architectures, because otherwise disconnected cells may remain active and obey SIMD instructions. In this way garbage can create more garbage and make precious resources unavailable for valid cells. Space limitations do not permit a full treatment of the autonomous garbage collection mechanisms used in the RRM; detailed discussion will be found in (Aida *et al* 1990b).

Autonomous cell operations are assisted by **messengers**. A messenger is a resource able to store a cell destination address, request type, and possibly some data. Once created, a messenger tries to allocate a new messenger closer to its destination and, if successful, copies itself into that new location. When a messenger reaches a position adjacent to its cell destination it performs the action appropriate to the encoded request type.

VLSI DESIGN OF THE RRM ENSEMBLE

Technological Considerations

The ensemble design pays attention to long-range trends in VLSI technology, stressing communication performance as the major goal:

- Cells are intentionally kept as simple as possible such that an ensemble composed of several hundred cells can be packed on a **single VLSI chip** avoiding delays associated with off-chip signal propagation.
- Cells within an ensemble are connected by short, dedicated signal wires organized as a **regular mesh** structure; this scheme supports very fast local data exchanges.
- Due to the functional properties of the computation model, communication requests that cannot be accommodated by the ensemble connection structure may be safely aborted. The execution schedule is thus optimized for fastest communication, with a final check to see which requests failed. Only local connections are supported and built-in mechanisms are provided for relocating data nodes on the ensemble till all the logical links needed to apply a rewrite rule have a chance to be local.

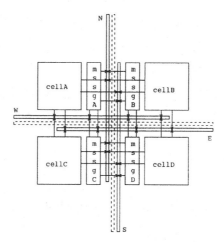

Figure 3 Tile Architecture

- Cell interchanges within an ensemble are independently timed, with handshaking protocols for data transfers. The global clock is only used to synchronize initiation of a SIMD instruction and is relatively slow compared to operations performed within cells. This alleviates the clock distribution problem typical to massively concurrent systems.

Tile Organization

Figure 3 shows the RRM tile organization. Particular to this architecture are the four ports (for simplicity called N, E, W and S) connecting the tile with adjacent ones. In order to support the toroidal ensemble connection structure on a planar VLSI implementation, two orthogonal buses (NS and EW) must also cross the tile. These buses are not connected to the current tile components, but space for their wires must be reserved. To understand the RRM ensemble interconnection structure, picture the N port out of the current tile passing through the NS wires reserved in the tile immediately above it and then connecting to the S port in the second next tile above.

Cell Design

Figure 4 (a) shows the organization of a cell. A register bank supports the storage of tokens and pointers. Twelve bits per register are sufficient to guarantee addressability of any other cell in the ensemble. Addresses show the target cell number and the relative tile position (in both X and Y directions). The unit "decP" decodes such an address and selects an appropriate port (N, E, W, or S) that will attempt the data transfer, or signals a remote connection. Once connected to a port, the cell can transfer the contents of any register (bus D) and a command request (bus C). Acceptance of the request is acknowledged on line "Ack".

The 12 bit ALU uses the accumulator as one of the operands, and any other register as the second operand. The ALU is capable of addition, subtraction, logic operations,

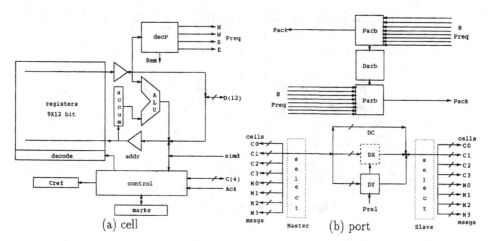

Figure 4 Cell and Port Design

and single bit shifts. The ALU result, or a SIMD broadcast constant, can be written back to any register within the same clock cycle. The control unit contains the marks, the reference counter "Cref" and several counters needed for autonomous operation.

Messengers use only a small subset of the leaf designs composing a cell – in addition to the port decoder, only 2 registers are provided. The messenger control is different, since the SIMD broadcast does not have to be monitored.

Port Design

Figure 4 (b) shows the organization of a port. It consists of arbitration and relative pointer modification units. The arbitration is performed at two levels:

1. requests within each tile are independently arbitrated in "Parb", and
2. since the data connection only supports half-duplex transfers, the top level arbitration "Darb" selects a winning direction.

It is essential that requests be treated fairly, and that repeated rewrite instruction sequences select different winners. Since a completely random selection is impractical, the current implementation uses a round-robin scheme. Some responsibility is delegated to the compiler to occasionally insert spurious instructions in repeated rewrite sequences that might otherwise result in identical round-robin configurations.

The implementation also favors port requests issued by cells over messenger requests. Since messengers operate in autonomous mode, they can wait for the next clock cycle to obtain the port, unlike cells that incur the penalty of missing a whole rule application if the current SIMD instruction fails.

Another port function is to modify relative addresses passing through them. Obviously, only 4 design types are needed: increment or decrement X, increment or decrement Y, respectively, corresponding to ports E, W, N and S. As shown in figure 4 (b), the signal "Prel" selects either unchanged passage of numerical data through the port, or relative address modification.

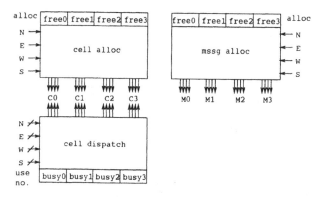

Figure 5 Resource Allocation

Resource Allocation

The last component of an RRM tile deals with resource allocation. Several types of requests (one for each port) can occur:

- allocate a free cell or messenger,
- free a previously occupied cell or messenger,
- use a cell as target of an inter-cell communication instruction.

Figure 5 shows schematically the architecture of the tile resource management. The cell allocation component uses an "iterative array" design. Each of the 4 cells can be occupied or free. Each of the 4 ports connected to the tile may issue an allocation request. The requests are arbitrated in fixed order – the first port with a valid request gets the first free cell, etc. When a cell is allocated to a port, a signal is generated to connect the internal bus D in the corresponding cell to the requesting port bus.

A cell may decide to free itself (when its reference counter reaches zero) by simply resetting its free bit state. That makes it available for the next allocation request. A similar mechanism is used for deleting messengers.

The arbitration between several requests to use an existing cell (dispatch of requests) also uses an iterative array of logic. Each of the 4 ports may request a specific cell by number. Each cell may be busy or available – a cell is busy if it has already initiated some operations under either SIMD or autonomous control. Provided a cell is not busy, the port requests are examined in fixed order, and the cell is allocated as a "slave" to the first port requesting it.

Figure 4 (b) also shows schematically the inter-cell communication. The requesting cell or messenger (termed "master") is connected to the port bus as soon as it wins the port arbitration. Its request type (bus C) is then examined by the resource allocation unit, and, provided the port wins the competition, the desired "slave" cell in the target tile it also connected to the port. That completes the connection master–slave, and the data transfer can proceed. The signal "Ack" signals success to the master.

Instruction Execution

The RRM ensemble has been designed to support execution of a SIMD instruction in one clock cycle. An example of such a SIMD instruction is the fetching of a register from the cell pointed at by the "left" register:

1. read register "left" on the internal cell bus;
2. decode the pointer and locate the appropriate port;
3. the port request passes through the arbitration logic and (assuming it wins) is routed to the cell dispatch unit in the target tile;
4. if the target cell is not busy, and if no port with higher priority also requests that cell, it becomes a "slave" of the port;
5. the slave cell inspects the control bits identifying the request type (bus C); since the request is for fetch-register, the identified register is read and its contents put on the internal bus D;
6. simultaneously, the slave cell connects its internal bus D to the requesting port data bus and sends an acknowledgement;
7. on receipt of the acknowledgement (line Ack), the initiator cell connects the port data to its internal bus D and starts a write operation into the recipient register.

All the above operations are completed within a single clock cycle. As discussed in the "Technological Considerations" section, the VLSI design relies on performing many fast local operations during a single clock cycle, thus alleviating the clock distribution problem. For this instruction example, the inter-cell transfer performs one arbitration and a data word transfer in a single clock cycle.

Projected Size and Speed

The RRM project uses state-of-art commercial technology – the novel architectural features are complex enough to make the use of an overly aggressive technology unadvisable for an RRM prototype. The current experimental chip designs are done in 2 micron CMOS technology. A half size technology (1.2 micron) is also readily available, while a quarter size CMOS (0.6 micron) is expected to be available by the time the RRM prototype will be built.

The RRM ensemble size estimation extrapolates from the size of partially completed mask designs. Considering the additional space needed to complete the cell control, and also the silicon estate allocated to connections and buses, we estimate that 64 tiles (of 4 cells and 2 messengers each) can be fit on a reasonably large chip – 10 mm on a side – fabricated in 0.6 microns CMOS. In other words, we plan on placing 256 cell processors, a regular interconnection network, and ancillary messenger support on a single state-of-art VLSI chip.

Circuit simulations validated by actual chip measurements indicate that a clock rate of 20 MHz would be a realistic target. It is worth repeating that reliance on local connections allows complex data transfers between any two adjacent cells to be completed within a single clock cycle.

CONCLUDING REMARKS

We have presented the architectural design of the rewrite ensemble, the chip level component of the Rewrite Rule Machine that performs concurrent rewriting in SIMD mode. The paper has shown how the abstract model of computation is physically realized in the ensemble, and has discussed VLSI aspects of that realization.

At present, several experimental chips for a cell and for tile components are being designed, fabricated and tested; a tile chip implementation is scheduled for 1991. An ensemble emulator will subsequently be built by placing an array of tile chips on a board, and a series of experiments will be performed on it. Those experiments will provide valuable information for the VLSI implementation of the entire ensemble. We have also started to simulate the inter-ensemble behavior of the prototype RRM.

Acknowledgements: We specially thank Prof. Joseph A. Goguen, who initiated the RRM project and has made many outstanding technical contributions to it, also in the previous design work for the ensemble (Leinwand *et al* 1988) on which this paper is based; we also thank him for his enthusiastic encouragement and his very helpful suggestions. We specially thank Mr. Timothy Winkler for his major contributions to the architecture presented here both in the past and, again very actively, in the present; we also thank him for his many suggestions and his detailed comments. We cordially thank Mr. Patrick Lincoln for his important recent contributions to the RRM architecture and for his suggestions for improving the paper.

REFERENCES

Aida, H., Goguen, J., and Meseguer, J., "Compiling concurrent rewriting onto the rewrite rule machine", in *Intl. Workshop on Conditional and Typed Rewriting Systems*, S.Kaplan and Okada, M., Eds., Concordia U.: pp. 173–182, 1990a.

Aida, H., Lincoln, P., Winkler, T., and Meseguer, J., "Parallel garbage collection in the rewrite rule machine", to appear as a Technical Report in Computer Science Laboratory, SRI International, 1990b.

Goguen, J., Kirchner, C., and Meseguer, J., "Concurrent term rewriting as a model of computation", in *Proc. Workshop on Graph Reduction*, Keller, R. and Fasel, J., Eds., Lecture Notes in Computer Science, No. 279, Santa Fe, New Mexico: Springer-Verlag, pp. 53–93, 1987.

Goguen, J. and Meseguer, J., "Software for the rewrite rule machine", in *Proceedings of the International Conference on Fifth Generation Computer Systems*, Tokyo, Japan: ICOT, pp. 628–637, 1988.

Goguen, J., Meseguer, J., Leinwand, S., Winkler, T., and Aida, H., "The rewrite rule machine", Technical Report SRI-CSL-89-6, Computer Science Laboratory, SRI International, 1989.

Leinwand, S., Goguen, J., and Winkler, T., "Cell and ensemble architecture for the rewrite rule machine", in *Proceedings of the International Conference on Fifth Generation Computer Systems*, Tokyo, Japan: ICOT, pp. 869–878, 1988.

Meseguer, J., "Rewriting as a unified model of concurrency", in *Proceedings of the Concur'90 Conference*, Lecture Notes in Computer Science, No. 458, Amsterdam: Springer-Verlag, pp. 384–400, 1990.

1.3 A Dataflow Architecture for AI

José Delgado-Frias, Ardsher Ahmed and Robert Payne

Department of Electrical Engineering
State University of New York at Binghamton
Binghamton, NY 13902-6000 USA

Abstract

*This paper describes a dataflow architecture for artificial intelligence applications
in particular parallel logic programming. This machine has a decentralized
approach for parallel processing. Dynamic creation of dataflow nodes not only
provides higher performance but also reduces bookkeeping overhead.*

INTRODUCTION

Artificial intelligence (AI) applications have been growing steadily in many fields, such as
computer vision, robotics and natural language understanding. As AI applications grow in
complexity, the need for reliable and high performance computers increases. These computers
would allow AI algorithms to be executed at reasonable speed. The conventional numerically
oriented von Neumann computers might not be appropriate for AI software, since AI has
different computational requirements than numerical applications. These computational
requirements include: *symbolic processing, non-deterministic computations, knowledge
representation and manipulation, parallel and distributed processing, and dynamic resource
allocation* (Wah and Li 1986). Architectures for artificial intelligence applications have been
investigated and developed in order to achieve the performance required (Wah and Li 1986,
Uhr 1987, Delgado-Frias and Moore 1989).

Many AI computations are data dependent, i.e. execution path is determined at run time as
data is processed. Computing resources must be allocated dynamically. For many computer
architectures, this requirement might be handled by having a number of special purpose stacks,
heaps, pointers, and dynamic garbage collection. An architecture based on the dataflow
principle (Dennis 1985) could manage the run-time requirements with little overhead. A
multiprocessor dataflow architecture generates and takes care of tokens that can be executed
independently.

In this paper a novel architecture based on the dataflow principle is presented. This
architecture (called the SUNY dataflow machine) is a special purpose dataflow computer for the
support of artificial intelligence applications. A logic programming application is studied in
order to show the machine potential.

VLSI for Artificial Intelligence and Neural Networks, Edited by J.G. Delgado-Frias and
W.R. Moore, Plenum Press, New York, 1991

23

SUNY DATAFLOW ARCHITECTURE

Previous dataflow architectures (Arvind and Culler 1987, Dennis 1987, Dennis 1985, Gurd *et al* 1985, McGraw 1989, Veen 1986, Watson *et al* 1982) as well as AI application requirements (Ciepielewski and Haridi 1984, DeGroot 1984, Hwang and DeGroot 1989, Uhr 1987, Wah 1986) have been considered for the development of the machine. This system is a medium grained multiprocessing architecture which is connected by means of a five cube interconnection network. The architecture consists of thirty two processing units (PUs). This number of PUs might be sufficient for the purpose of this machine since many AI applications have medium size parallelism. Most of the architectures for AI have few processing elements (around sixteen) (Uhr 1987, Wah and Li 1986). Should a larger dataflow machine be needed, multiple five cube machines can be connected together through a special hardware interface.

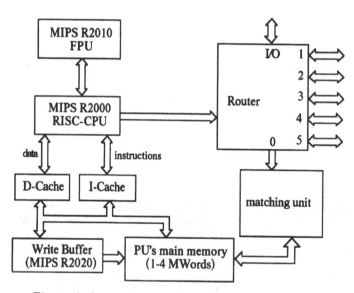

Figure 1. A processing unit of the SUNY dataflow machine

Processing Unit

The processing unit, shown in Figure 1, is the basic computational module in the SUNY dataflow machine. Each PU is homogeneous in design and consists of a high performance RISC processor (MIPS R2000) and floating point coprocessor (MIPS R2010), RAM memory, instruction and data caches memories, matching unit, and router. The matching unit and the router will be custom VLSI units.

Each PU makes up a dataflow processing ring consisting of the router, matching unit and the processor. Each of the three units will operate concurrently providing parallelism within the PU. This processing ring configuration is similar to those found in the MIT and Manchester dataflow computers (Arvind and Culler 1987, Dennis 1987, Dennis 1985, Gurd et al 1985, Watson et al 1982). A token enters the processing ring through the router and passes on to the matching unit. Once all the tokens required by a dataflow node are received, the matching unit forwards them to the processor. The RISC processor executes the dataflow node program and produces new tokens. These tokens are passed to the local router which sends them to the proper PU(s). If a new token is addressed to the local PU, this token is sent into the local matching unit. This cycle makes up the basic dataflow processing ring in the SUNY dataflow machine.

The PUs in the system will operate in a loosely coupled asynchronous manner with message passing being the only means of communication. All communication to and from the PUs will use the five cube network. Initial estimates of the PU's memory requirements indicate that memory size should be between 1 to 4 M-words.

Hybrid Dataflow Computation

Unlike most of the dataflow computers (Arvind and Culler 1987, Dennis 1987, Dennis 1985, Gurd et. al. 1985, Watson et. al. 1982), the SUNY dataflow machine is being designed to facilitate hybrid dataflow computation (Buehrer and Ekanadhm 1987). Each processing unit has the facilities to execute programs in a strictly dataflow mode. However, each dataflow node is executed in a sequential manner. Having a von Neumann RISC processor might not only increase performance (at dataflow node level) but also reduces the design effort.

Matching Unit

Tokens, sent by the router, are first processed in the matching unit. Each token has a destination which is an input to a dataflow node. When a token is received, the matching unit determines if more tokens are required to fire the dataflow node. If the token has as destination a one-input dataflow node, this token is immediately placed in a token pool. When additional tokens are required the matching unit must check if all the required tokens have arrived. If all the inputs of the dataflow node have a token, then these tokens are passed to the token pool. When not all the tokens have arrived, the token that is being processed is stored in the matching unit. For the system to operate efficiently the matching unit must be capable of operating independently of the processor or with only occasional processor interruptions. The need to reduce or eliminate interruption of the processor requires that the matching unit be able write to and read from RAM memory. This feature is used when the matching unit puts tokens in the token pool. The matching unit must therefore handle both simple memory management along with matching functions.

The matching unit (MU) is being designed as a full custom VLSI unit. The MU, shown in Figure 2, consists of several building blocks: CAM, RAM and a matching unit controller. The matching of token tags is accomplished by the use of a content addressable memory (CAM). Each CAM entry has a conventional RAM memory associated with it to store entry status information and a pointer to the token body. The controller manages all matching unit functions with minimal processor interruption.

Many applications would benefit from dataflow nodes with more than one or two input tokens. This is especially true when considering relatively complex sequentially computed dataflow nodes as in hybrid dataflow computation (Buehrer and Ekanadhm 1987). Traditional dataflow computer systems have only allowed unary and binary nodes. Limiting the system to unary and binary nodes simplifies the matching unit design but limits the number of inputs to a node. Therefore, it would be desirable if the matching unit were able to match more than two tokens and determine when all the tokens required to fire a node are present.

THE ROUTER DESIGN AND ANALYSIS

The interconnection scheme in the SUNY dataflow machine is based on a hypercube network. For 32 PUs a 5-*dimensional* hypercube is employed as a routing network. For $n = 5$ dimensions, we have $N = 2^n = 32$ nodes, and $W = n.2^{n-1} = 80$ wires. The router consists of 80 bi-directional wires for communicating tokens, 80 bi-directional links for sending acknowledgment signal between the PU nodes, and router-logic for each of the router nodes. The n-cube topology offers the following key advantages over other communication schemes (Hillis 1985):

- *Small diameter.* The maximum distance in number of hops between the router nodes is $n = log_2 N$.
- *Uniformity.* All the router nodes are identical and equally accessible to any neighboring node in the cube, this ensures a balanced communication and predictable traffic patterns.
- *Extendability.* Hypercube topology allows for the expansion to 2^n number of nodes for any *n-dimension* with some increase in wire-cost, but also providing more redundant paths between the nodes.
- *Fault-Tolerance.* Due to the multiple paths (i.e., $log_2 N$) between any pair of nodes the defective areas of the router can be isolated and bypassed by the network, and the routing process can still be functional.
- *Redundancy.* The messages can be redirected via alternative redundant paths in case of heavy traffic loads or hardware faults.
- *VLSI Implementation.* The uniform and balanced topology of the single node of the n-cube router and its fixed degree (i.e., node connectivity) favors the VLSI design layouts and makes the packaging job easier.
- *Routing algorithm.* The most important aspect of the router design is the routing algorithm. The routing algorithms in dataflow machine is simple and cost-effective, as all the router nodes are controlled locally by the routing logic.

The SUNY dataflow machine was conceived for the artificial intelligent processing, in which the computations are non-deterministic and usually trigger a combinatorial number of data tokens, which are hard to handle and pass around to the PU-nodes in the conventional machines. The 5-cube router addresses such problems as how to receive, deliver, and route the generated tokens in parallel from all the 32 PU-nodes.

Routing algorithm and router model

The routing scheme is based on a packet switched system, where each packet in a router node may be routed through a different path depending on the availability of the non-busy communication line.

Each router node handles tokens generated at a local PU-node as well as those passed from its five neighboring PU-nodes. The addresses of the router nodes depend on their relative position within the 5-cube, and range from 0 to 31. The router node with address i is linked to router node with address j if and only if $i \oplus j = 2^m$ (where m is an integer). The addresses of any two nodes can differ by a maximum of 5 bits, that would mean that the destination is 5 hops away from the source. Whereas the nearest neighboring router nodes differ by only one bit. This relative addressing scheme allows to route the packets along the dimension where the difference bit is 1 in the *exclusive-OR* of the physical addresses of the source and the destination.

Figure 2 shows the 5-cube router model which consists of four types of queues, namely rQs, outQs, inQ, and camQ. The rQs and outQs are the router queues for each of the cube dimensions. The inQ is the port to which tokens are fed by the local PU-node, whereas the camQ serves as the input port for the matching unit. The routing logic determines the destination of the token from its format field PU-address, computes the relative address, and stacks the token on appropriate outQs for routing to their destinations. If the token has reached its destination PU-node then it is appended to the camQ of the local PU-node and eventually sent to the matching unit for further processing.

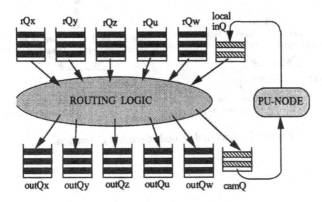

Figure 2. Processing unit router

LOGIC PROGRAMMING IN SUNY DATAFLOW

Parallel logic programming involves either OR-, AND- or AND/OR-parallelism. OR-parallelism allows independent binding in different branches of the execution tree. This feature generates independent processes that might get a solution to a query (Ciepielewski and Haridi 1984). However, to have a large number of OR nodes in a logic program might not be realistic. In AND-parallelism, all the assignments to variables must be checked in order to avoid conflicts. This feature creates the need for interprocess communication which might create bottlenecks. In order to avoid large overheads of communication the AND-parallelism can be restricted to few at the time (DeGroot 1989). A combination of AND- and OR-parallelism could allow this machine to run a number logic programming programs.

In order to deal with AND/OR-parallelism in the SUNY dataflow machine, AND- and OR-dataflow nodes are created dynamically. Figure 3 shows how *and-* and *or-nodes* are created. These nodes are stored in the node table of the PU that processed the node that generated them. The process of a query in the dataflow machine is shown in Figure 4. The nodes or-list and unify are generated dynamically; when the query fires the top node in the figure the bottom node is generated.

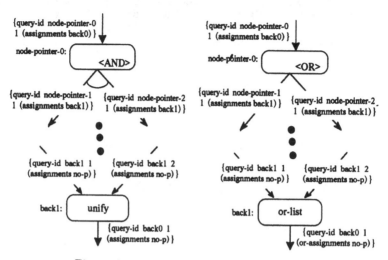

Figure 3. And- and or-node dynamic generation.

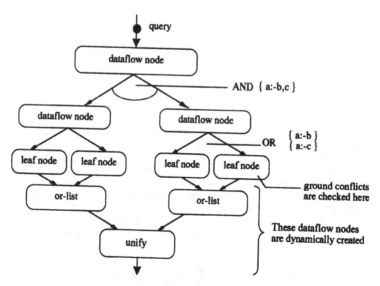

Figure 4. A query execution in the dataflow machine.

In this approach, information always flows on a single way. Thus, nodes are release once they generate new tokens. This scheme yields several advantages:
- *Dataflow nodes are side-effect free.* In parallel processing, side-effect might be costly since synchronization is required. It can be disastrous when the processes are out of synchro-nizations.
- *Dataflow nodes are history insensitive.* The output of each dataflow node depends only of its inputs and the context.
- *Dataflow nodes are always ready.* Once a dataflow node execution is completed, this node will be ready to receive new tokens.
- *Dataflow nodes are self-content.* Each node can be tested independently; if the program of each node is written in a functional style, program proofs might be accomplished (Henderson 1980).

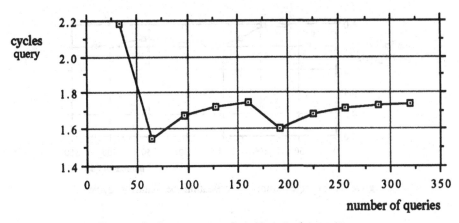

Figure 5. Average query throughput in the machine

PERFORMANCE EVALUATION

In order to evaluate the proposed architecture a software simulator was implemented. A family tree application was studied. This application includes rules such as *grandparent (x y):- parent (x z), parent (z y)*. For this rule, for example, an AND dataflow node is generated. The number of rules that were implemented is 288. Queries are sent in a form of tokens to the dataflow machine. The number of queries that were sent to the machine had a wide range. Each query required a minimum of three unifications.

As the number of queries that are sent to the dataflow machine increases the ratio of cycles per query improves as shown in Figure 5. When few queries are processed, the machine will have some idle processors. As the machine reaches its maximum execution throughput, the cycles per query ratio tends to be constant.

Figure 6 shows the number of dataflow cycles that are required as the number of queries increases. It seems to have a linear relation; however it is expected that this relation may change as the machine reaches its saturation. Memory, queues, and communication bandwidth are going to be the determining factors in the saturation of the machine. The average number of unifications per cycle is shown in Figure 7. It shows that the unification throughput is quite high and remains constant above 80% for varying number of queries.

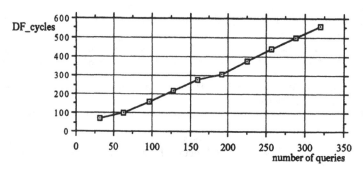

Figure 6. Number of dataflow cycles vs queries graph

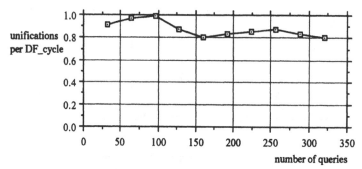

Figure 7. Average number of unifications per dataflow cycle

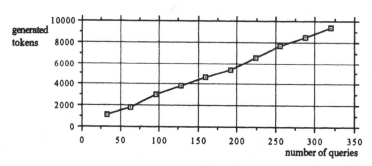

Figure 8. Number of tokens generated vs number of queries graph

Figures 8 and 9 show the amount of task generated. The number of tokens that were generated in the machine is shown in the Figure 8. This large amount of tokens can be handled by the machine, since tokens tend to have a short life span. Dynamic node creation (shown in Figure 9) is not as high as the token generation; however, these nodes have to reside in memory for some time till they find their partner tokens.

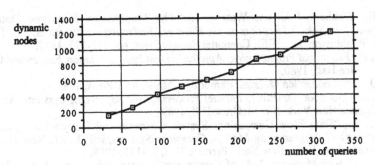

Figure 9. Number of nodes dynamically generated.

CONCLUDING REMARKS

A dataflow machine for AI processing would improve performance by providing decentralized parallelism, concurrent multi-task execution, and simple inter-processor communication. For the application studied in this paper, it has been observed that by creating new nodes at run time the dataflow nodes are always ready for a new set of tokens. Although mixing AND- and OR-parallelism adds some code to the PU's program, the number of applications for this approach is expected to be much higher. Simulations have shown that with a modest amount of memory and small queues this machine is able to handle a large number of queries, tokens, and dynamic dataflow nodes. Other AI applications for this machine are being studied; these applications include neural network processing and semantic networks.

REFERENCES

Arvind and Culler, D. E. "Dataflow Architectures," in *Selected Reprints on Dataflow and Reduction Architectures,* S. S. Thaker, Washington, DC: IEEE Computer Society Press, pp. 79-101, 1987.

Bohm, A. P. W. and Gurd, J. R., "Iterative Instructions in the Manchester Dataflow Computer," *IEEE Trans. Parallel and Distributed Systems,* vol. 1, no. 2, pp. 129-139, April 1990.

Buehrer, R. and Ekanadhm, K. "Incorporating Data Flow Ideas into von Neumann Processors for Parallel Execution," *IEEE Trans. on Computers,* vol. C-36, no. 12, pp. 1515-1522, December 1987.

Ciepielewski, A. and Haridi, S., "Execution of Bagof on the OR-Parallel Token Machine," *Proc. Int. Conference on Fifth Generation Computer Systems,* pp. 551-560, 1984

DeGroot, D., "Restricted AND-Parallelism and Side Effects in Logic Programming," in *Parallel Processing for Supercomputers and Artificial Intelligence,* K. Hwang and D. DeGroot (Eds.), New York: McGraw-Hill, pp. 487-522, 1989.

Delgado-Frias, J. G. and Moore, W. R. (Eds.), *VLSI for Artificial Intelligence.* Boston, MA: Kluwer Academic Publishers, 1989.

Dennis, J. B., "Dataflow Supercomputers," in *Selected Reprints on Dataflow and Reduction Architectures,* S.S. Thaker (Ed.), Washington, DC: IEEE Computer Society Press, pp. 102-110, 1987.

Dennis, J. B., "Models of Data Flow Computation," in *Control Flow and Data Flow: Concepts of Distributed Programming,* Manfred Broy (Ed.), Berlin, Germany: Springer-Verlag, pp. 346-381, 1985.

Gurd, J. R., Kirkham, C.C. and Watson, I., "The Manchester Prototype Dataflow Computer," in *Selected Reprints on Dataflow and Reduction Architectures,* S.S. Thaker (Ed.), Washington, DC: IEEE Computer Society Press, pp. 111-129, 1987.

Henderson, P., *Functional Programming: Application and Implementation.* Englewood Cliffs, NJ: Prentice-Hall, 1980.

Hillis, W.D., *The Connection Machine.* Cambridge, Mass.: MIT Press, 1985.

Hwang, K. and DeGroot, D. (Eds.), *Parallel Processing for Supercomputers and Artificial Intelligence.* New York, NY: McGraw-Hill, 1989.

McGraw, J. R., "Data Flow Computing: System Concepts and Design Strategies," in *Designing and Programming Modern Computer Systems,* vol. 3, S.P. Kartashev and S.I. Kkartashev (Eds), New York: Prentice Hall, 73-125, 1989.

Smith, A. J., "Cache Memories," *ACM Computing Surveys,* vol. 14, no. 3, pp. 474-530, 1982.

Uhr, L., *Multi-Computer Architectures for Artificial Intelligence: Towards Fast, Robust, Parallel Systems.* New York: John Wiley & Sons, Inc, 1987.

Veen, A. H., "Dataflow Machine Architecture," *ACM Computing Surveys,* vol. 18, no. 4, pp. 365-396, December 1986.

Wah, B. and Li, G-J, *Computers for Artificial Intelligence Applications.* Washington, DC: IEEE Computer Society Press, 1986.

Watson, I. and Gurd, J., "A Practical Data Flow Computer," *IEEE Computer,* vol. 15, no. 2, pp. 51-57, February 1982.

1.4 Incremental Garbage Collection Scheme in KL1 and Its Architectural Support of PIM

Yasunori Kimura
AI Lab.
Fujitsu Laboratories Ltd.

Takashi Chikayama
Research Dept.
ICOT

Tsuyoshi Shinogi
AI Lab.
Fujitsu Laboratories Ltd.

Atsuhiro Goto
Research Dept.
ICOT

Abstract

This paper describes an incremental garbage collection (GC) scheme for the parallel logic programming language KL1 that uses one extra bit of information attached to pointers to data objects rather than the data objects themselves.

This bit is called 'multiple reference bit (MRB)', and signals whether or not an object is single referenced. This MRB-GC scheme is considered a kind of reference counting GC where information is contained in pointers. This facilitates implementation on multiprocessors since reference updating can be done without reading data objects.

Software simulation by a single processor implementation of this scheme shows that compared to a non MRB-GC implementation, only about half the heap area is needed to run most KL1 programs. The lifetimes of garbage collected cells are quite short, so the cache hit ratio will increase, and the number of stop-and-collect GCs decrease. The larger the percentage of active cells, the more effective this scheme will be.

A special hardware and instructions to implement this scheme on PIM/p is described. A small quantity of hardware is required to do this, and enables efficient implementation of MRB-GC on PIM/p.

INTRODUCTION

Research on a Parallel Inference Machine (PIM) has been going on at ICOT as a part of Japan's Fifth Generation Computer Systems Project[Uchida 1988]. The language on PIM is the concurrent logic programming language called KL1 which is based on GHC[Ueda 1986] and has various features to support the PIM Operating System (PIMOS) [Chikayama et al 1988].

This paper presents an incremental garbage collection (GC) scheme of KL1 along with some software simulation results and its architectural support of PIM/p (the 'p' stands for

VLSI for Artificial Intelligence and Neural Networks, Edited by J.G. Delgado-Frias and
W.R. Moore, Plenum Press, New York, 1991

33

```
filter(P, [X|Xs0], Ys0) :- X mod P =:= 0 | filter(P, Xs0, Ys0).     (1)
filter(P, [X|Xs0], Ys0) :- X mod P =\= 0 | Ys0 = [X|Ys1],
                                            filter(P, Xs0, Ys1).     (2)
filter(P, [],      Ys0) :- true | Ys0 = [].                         (3)
```

Figure 1. KL1 program of 'filter'

'prototype') [Shinogi et al 1988], one of the PIM models proposed by ICOT and Fujitsu researchers.

Since KL1 is a side-effect free language, programming and debugging on parallel machines is expected to be easy. However, a naive implementation of KL1 uses a large amount of memory during execution, and invokes garbage collection frequently. General garbage collection on parallel machines is much more difficult and time-consuming than for a single processor. Therefore, to run KL1 programs efficiently on PIM/p, general garbage collection must be avoided as much as possible.

We therefore proposed an incremental garbage collection scheme called MRB-GC [Chikayama and Kimura 1987]. MRB-GC uses one extra bit of information attached to pointers to data objects rather than the data objects themselves. This bit is called a 'multiple reference bit (MRB)', and signals whether or not an object is single referenced. This MRB-GC scheme is a reference counting GC where one bit of information is contained in pointers. This facilitates implementation on multiprocessors since reference updating can be done without reading data objects.

OVERVIEW OF KL1

Syntax

KL1, a concurrent logic programming language based on flat GHC, is one of the committed choice languages[Ueda 1986]. A KL1 program is a finite set of guarded Horn clauses in the following form:

$$H : -G_1, \cdots, G_m | B_1, \cdots, B_n. \ (m \geq 0, n \geq 0)$$

where H is called the head, G_i the guard goals, and B_i the body goals. '|' is called the commitment operator. The part of a clause preceding '|' is called the passive part, and that following it is called the active part or the body.

Figure 1 shows a program which filters a specific number (passed by 'P') and its integer multiples from the list of integers passed as the second argument. When a goal 'filter(2, [2,3,4,5,6], Res)' is given for example, 'Res' will be bound to '[3,5]' after execution.

Garbage Collection for KL1

Like other symbol processing languages such as Lisp and Prolog, KL1 consumes a large amount of memory quickly. In Lisp, however, programmers can keep the workspace size small by using functions with side effects such as 'rplaca' and 'rplacd'. In Prolog, memory areas reclaimed by backtracking are implicitly re-used by the language processor.

KL1 has neither side effects nor a backtrack mechanism. Some other scheme must thus be considered to avoid invoking general garbage collection. One solution is to introduce an incremental garbage collection mechanism. Incremental garbage collection reclaims garbage cells during execution and these areas can be reused in later execution.

MRB SCHEME
MRB

As mentioned above, MRB requires one extra bit of information attached to pointers and basically signals whether or not an object is single referenced. This scheme has the following advantages when compared with conventional reference counting schemes.

1. Only a small amount of memory (1 bit for each pointer) is needed to maintain the reference count.

2. Updating the reference count can be carried out without accessing the data object itself.

In this scheme, when a data object is created with a reference count of '1' and if the reference count doesn't change, the data object can be reclaimed after being consumed by a goal. 'Consume' means to read the content of the data object; the data object itself is never used by any goals.

The updating of the reference count is examined by the compiler. If the number of references to an object increases, the compiler generates an instruction to turn the MRB on. If an object can be reclaimed, an instruction to reclaim the object is generated.

Note that once an MRB is turned on, the data object is never reclaimed by MRB-GC. Therefore, reclamation by this scheme is not perfect. However, according to our preliminary experiment, most data in KL1 is single referenced. This scheme is thus expected to be sufficient to run most KL1 programs.

Definition of MRB

An informal description of MRB is provided in this section. For more details, see reference [Chikayama and Kimura 1987].

When a data object is referenced from a KL1 program, the data object is usually referenced through some indirect cells (reference cells). We call this pointer chain a *reference path*. The reference path is classified into two kinds. One is SRP (Single Reference Path) whose chain doesn't have any pointers with their MRBs on, and the other is MRP (Multiple Reference Path) whose chain may have pointers with their MRBs on.

SRP and MRP are expressed by ○('off') and ●('on') as follows:

○: Reference path to the data object is itself only (single referenced).

●: There may be other reference paths to the data object (multiple referenced).

This is shown in Figure 2.

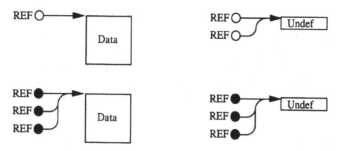

Figure 2. Definition of MRB

The treatment of MRB for pointers to uninstantiated variables is a little bit different from this definition. In KL1 or other logic programming languages, uninstantiated variables basically are pointed to from two reference paths. One is to instantiate the variables, and the other is to read the contents of the variables. We define the meaning of MRBs for the pointers to the uninstantiated variables as follows:

O: There is another SRP, or there may be several MRPs to the uninstantiated variable.

●: There may be several MRPs or an SRP to the uninstantiated variable.

Maintenance of MRB

During KL1 execution, MRB should be maintained so that the conditions mentioned in the above section are satisfied. MRB is maintained both during compilation and at runtime.

Maintenance by compiler

The compiler reads each KL1 clause and examines the occurrence of variables. It then generates instructions to turn MRBs of variables on, when needed. This is done based on the following rules.

1. If a variable doesn't occur in the passive part but the variable occurs more than two times in the body,

   then the MRB of the variable in the body should be on,

   otherwise the MRB should be off.

2. If a variable occurs in the passive part and the variable appears more than one time in the body,

   then the MRB of the variable should be turned to on in the body,

   otherwise the MRB of the variable doesn't change.

```
p :- true | q(X), r(X, [car|cdr]).        (1)
p :- true | q(X), r(X, [car|cdr]), s(X). (2)

p(X) :- true | q(X).                      (3)
p(X) :- true | q(X), r(X).                (4)
```

Figure 3. Maintenance by compiler

Figure 3 shows an example of maintenance by the compiler. In the figure, the variable 'X' in clauses (2), (4) are 'on' in the body, while the ones in clauses (1), (3) are not changed.

Maintenance at runtime

To maintain MRB at runtime, the following two cases should be considered. One is when a variable is dereferenced, and the other is when a variable is instantiated.

During dereferencing a reference path, the MRBs of the indirect cells are accumulated, and after dereferencing, the value accumulated becomes the MRB of this path. If any cell with its MRB on appears in the chain, the result MRB is also on. If and only if there are no cells with their MRB on, the MRB of this path is off.

When a variable is instantiated with some value, the MRB of the instantiated variable is determined based on the following rule:

If the reference paths to both the variable and the value are SRPs, the MRB of the instantiated variable is off. Otherwise, the MRB is set to on.

GARBAGE COLLECTION BY MRB

Certain memory areas can be reclaimed without using general garbage collection mechanisms when data in KL1 is maintained by MRB. That is, a memory area may be reclaimed when the last reference path to the area is *consumed*. A reference path to a data object is known to be the last path when it is an SRP. A reference path to an already instantiated variable cell is known to be the last path when it is an SRP and the MRB of the data is off. Reference paths are consumed in the following ways.

Dereference : While dereferencing a variable, an indirect cell can be reclaimed if the MRB of the reference to the cell is off and the MRB of the cell is also off. In Figure 4, after dereferencing, the two indirect cells can be reclaimed. One is pointed to by variable 'X' and the other points to the cons cell.

Structure unification : If a goal is reduced after one of its arguments is unified with a structure in the passive part, the reference path to the structure given as an argument is consumed in the unification. For example, in

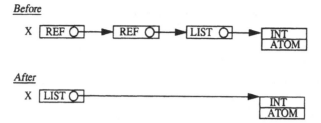

Figure 4. Reclamation of indirect cells

```
p([X|Y]) :- true | b(X), c(Y).
```

the reference path to the list cell unified with [X|Y] will never be used after unification. The reference path is thus SRP, of which the list cell can be reclaimed.

Unification with a void : When an argument is unified with a void variable, the reference path passed as the argument is consumed. So if the path is SRP, the contents of the variable can be reclaimed. Here, a void variable means that the variable appears in the passive part, but not in the body.

```
p(Void) :- true | true.
```

'Structure unification' and 'unification with a void' can be checked by the compiler, so instructions for trying to reclaim the data are generated. These are called 'collect-list'(if structure is a vector, 'collect-vector'), and 'collect-value'. However, reclamation during dereferencing is done at runtime because the compiler doesn't know the structure of an indirect cells chain in general.

EXPERIMENTS

Software simulation

We did some software simulation to confirm the effectiveness of MRB-GC. We implemented a KL1 emulator which emulates the behaviour of a single processing element of PIM/p, on a UNIX machine and ran some benchmark programs (Table 1) [Tick 1988]. 'Reduction' is the number of goal reductions done to perform a benchmark program, and roughly indicates how big the program is.

The benchmark programs are first compiled to KL1-B code [Kimura and Chikayama 1987] which is an abstract instruction set for KL1, and is similar to WAM [Warren 1983] in Prolog. Then programs are executed by the emulator interpreting KL1-B instructions one by one.

The behaviour of MRB-GC on a multi-processor system, especially the relationship between MRB-GC and the locally coherent cache mechanism, is discussed in [Nishida et al 1990].

Table 1. The amount of heap areas used

program	reductions	MRB-GC		ratio
		none(A)	used(B)	(B/A)
prime	5,786	10,848	1,503	0.14
queen	38,878	817,070	459,919	0.56
bup	34,857	66,655	20,076	0.30
kl1cmp	14,919	34,969	17,873	0.51
espascal	335,115	471,760	50,284	0.11
etsmall	918,520	3,174,541	671,354	0.21
tri	666,325	1,209,532	1,209,529	1.00
semi	292,309	493,383	101,265	0.21
pax	17,530	24,298	12,784	0.53

Results

Table 1 lists the amount of heap required to execute benchmark programs for the conditions when MRB-GC is used and when it is not used. 'Heap' means memory area that is used for variable cells, cons cells and vector areas. From this table, execution with MRB-GC requires less heap than that without MRB-GC. This also indicates that most of the data in KL1 is single referenced. This verifies our assumption.

Figure 5 shows the lifetimes of cells which are reclaimed by MRB-GC. Here, the lifetime is defined as the number of reductions between when the cell is allocated and when it is reclaimed. The horizontal axis is the number of reductions during which the garbage-collected cells were alive, and the vertical axis is the ratio of the garbage-collected cells at a specified number of reductions to the total number of garbage-collected cells. This figure shows that most of the garbage collected cells have relatively short lifetimes. This means that a small portion of memory is used over and over again. We can thus expect that the cache hit ratio will increase by using MRB-GC.

In MRB-GC, once data is multiple referenced, it is never reclaimed. Another general GC mechanism is thus needed. We used a traditional copying GC scheme for this purpose in the experiments. Table 2 lists the number of times copying GC was invoked to execute benchmark programs. This figure indicates that by using MRB-GC, the number of times copying GC needs to be done can be reduced. This is one of our initial goals to reduce the number of times general garbage collection is invoked.

Figure 6 shows the relationship between the ratio of the active cells to the whole memory size and the ratio of the execution times between when MRB-GC is used and not used. The horizontal axis is the active cells ratio to the whole memory size. This was measured by counting the active cells when copying GC was invoked in various sizes of memory. The vertical axis is the time ratio, i.e. '(execution time when MRB-GC is used)/(execution time when MRB-GC is not used)'. If the time ratio is more than 1.0, execution time when MRB-GC is used is slower than when MRB-GC is used at a specified active cells ratio. From this figure, if the active cells ratio exceeds 40 ~ 50 %, execution time when MRB-GC is used is faster than when MRB-GC is not used.

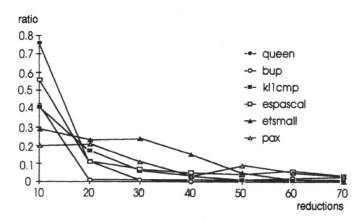

Figure 5. The lifetimes of garbage collected cells

Table 2. The number of times copying GC is invoked

program	memory (Kwords)	MRB-GC none	MRB-GC used	program	memory (Kwords)	MRB-GC none	MRB-GC used
prime	50	52	0	etsmall	50	72	30
queen	20	58	27	tri	100	10	10
bup	20	8	1	semi	100	19	2
kl1cmp	10	5	2	pax	30	1	0
espascal	20	34	2				

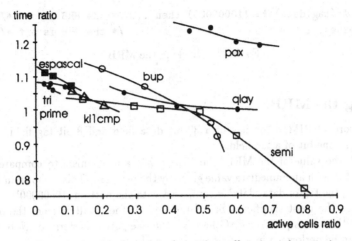

Figure 6. The relationship between the active cell ratio and execution time

These statistics are all taken from the software emulator. While KL1 instructions and MRB maintenance are emulated by software, the copying GC routine is written directly in the C language. Therefore, if MRB-GC is implemented on PIM with some hardware support, we can expect MRB-GC to be much faster than non MRB-GC.

ARCHITECTURAL SUPPORT OF MRB

We have been designing a parallel inference machine PIM/p using VLSI technology. The PIM/p executes RISC-like instructions with a four-stage pipeline mechanism. It also has a 'Macro-call' and 'indirect registers' mechanism which enables good subroutine performance. Details of these features are discussed in [Shinogi et al 1988].

To implement MRB-GC efficiently on PIM/p, the following points should be considered.

- Checking whether the MRB is on or off at runtime should be fast.

- During dereferencing, the values of MRB's are accumulated. Dereferencing is quite often called in KL1. This operation should also be quite fast.

- We cannot presume when a cell is reclaimed by MRB-GC; memory areas need to be maintained by free lists rather than stacks. Free list maintenance should thus be fast.

To meet these requirements, the PIM/p has been designed to have the following special hardware facilities.

```
if (tag(data) && !10000000) then ... /* the MRB is on  */
else ...                             /* the MRB is off */
```

Figure 7. Checking the MRB

Checking the MRB

The data word of PIM/p consists of a 32-bit data field and 8-bit tag field. MRB is represented as one bit of a tag field.

To check the value of the MRB, the PIM/p has a mechanism to compare any bit pattern of a tag with an immediate value given by the program. This is shown in Figure 7. In this figure, the tag of data 'data' is compared with the pattern '10000000'. The MRB is assigned to the most significant bit of the tag. If the result is true, the operation when the MRB is on is performed. Otherwise, the else part is performed. Note that this operation can be performed in a single machine cycle.

Dereference

While dereferencing a variable, the MRB's of indirect cells have to be accumulated. To do this efficiently, the PIM/p can read data from memory or transfer data between registers. At the same time, the MRB of source data is logical-or'ed with that of another data item in a register. Figure 8 shows the operation to read the memory pointed to by register 'R2' to register 'R1'. After the operation, R1 holds the pointer in memory 'A', and R2 holds the pointer in the memory location which is also pointed to by 'A'. Note that the MRB of R2 is set to the result of logical-or'ing T1 and T2. This is expressed as

DEREF < R1 >, < offset > < R2 >

in the program.

Free list maintenance

In MRB-GC, the speed of getting a new cell from a free list and returning the reclaimed cell to the list greatly influences runtime efficiency. We thus have the PIM/p mechanism do these operations in a single machine cycle. Figure 9 shows the operation to get a cell from free list. Register 'R2' points to the top of the free list. After the operation, register 'R1' holds the pointer to the cell gotten, and R2 points to the next top. In this case, the tag value given by the instruction is entered in register R1. The instruction 'Pop with Tag'

POPT < R1 >, < offset > < R2 >, < im >

is used for this purpose. 'Im' specifies the tag of the cell gotten from the free list by this instruction. When the new tag doesn't need to be specified, the instruction 'POPW(Pop Word)' can be used. In POPW, the tag of R1 doesn't change by the execution of this instruction.

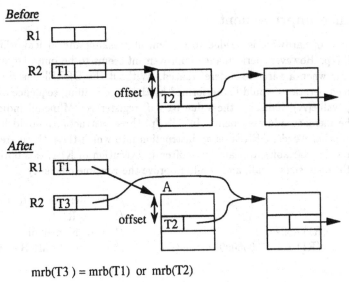

$$mrb(T3) = mrb(T1) \text{ or } mrb(T2)$$

Figure 8. MRB in dereferencing

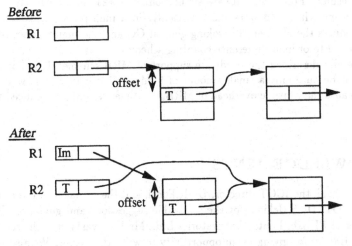

Figure 9. Free list maintenance

To return reclaimed cells to the free list, the instructions 'PUSHT(Push with Tag)' and 'PUSHW(Push Word)' are prepared.

Performance improvement

A small amount of hardware is needed to implement masking and logical-or'ing of tag values on PIM/p. However, performance improvement seems to be quite large. For example, consider when a variable is dereferenced. Without the DEREF instruction, the following three operations would be performed by the correponding sequence of instructions. Here, 'value(A)' indicates the value part of register A, 'M[mem]' indicates the content of the memory address 'mem'. In PIM/p, three instructions would be needed to do this. In other words, DEREF is an instruction into which these three are merged. Since dereferencing variables appears quite often in execution of KL1, this optimization would keep the code sizes small, and would improve the runtime efficiency.

```
R1 ← R2;                               /* transfer the content of */
                                       /* R2 to R1 */
R2 ← M[value(R1)+offset];              /* read the memory */
tag(R2) ← (tag(R1) && !10000000) or tag(R2);   /* update the MRB of R2 */
```

CONCLUSION

We have presented an incremental garbage collection scheme called MRB-GC and its simulation results. From the software simulation, it works very efficiently in a single processor system. It would work more efficiently in a multiprocessor system because MRB-GC reduces the number of invoking general GC and the maintenance of MRB is easier compared to ordinary reference counting schemes.

We have also described the hardware support of MRB scheme. It is not only easy to implement because only a small amount of hardware is required, but would also be effective because the runtime overhead of MRB maintenance could be reduced to almost zero.

ACKNOWLEDGEMENTS

The authors thank the ICOT director, Dr. K.Fuchi, and the manager of the research department, ICOT, Dr. S.Uchida, for their valuable suggestions and guidance. We thank the Manager of AI Lab, Fujitsu Laboratories Ltd., Mr. H.Hayashi, and the section manager, Mr. A.Hattori for giving us an opportunity to write this paper. We also thank our colleagues, Messrs T.Ozawa and A.Hosoi for their valuable comments on the earlier draft of this paper.

References

[Chikayama and Kimura 1987] Chikayama,T., Kimura,Y.: Multiple Reference Management in Flat GHC. Proc. *Int. Conf. on Logic Prog. '87*, pp.276–293, 1987.

[Chikayama et al 1988] Chikayama,T., Sato,H., Miyazaki,T.: Overview of the Parallel Inference Machine Operating System (PIMOS). Proc. *Int. Conf. on FGCS '88*, pp.230–251, 1988.

[Kimura and Chikayama 1987] Kimura,Y., Chikayama,T.: An Abstract KL1 Machine and its Instruction Set. Proc. *Symp. on Logic Prog. '87*, pp.468–477, 1987.

[Nishida et al 1990] Nishida,K.,Kimura,Y.,Matsumoto,A.,Goto,A.: Evaluation of MRB Garbage Collection on Parallel Logic Programming Architectures. Proc. *Int. Conf. on Logic Prog.'90*, 1990

[Shinogi et al 1988] Shinogi,T., et. al: Macro-call Instruction for the Efficient KL1 Implementation on PIM. Proc. *Int. Conf. on FGCS '88*, pp.953–961, 1988.

[Tick 1988] Tick,E.: Performance of Parallel Logic Programming Architectures. TR-421, ICOT, 1988.

[Uchida 1988] Uchida,S., et al: Research and Development of the Parallel Inference System in the Intermediate Stage of the FGCS Project. Proc. *Int. Conf. on FGCS '88*, pp.16–36, 1988.

[Ueda 1986] Ueda,K.: Guarded Horn Clauses : A parallel logic programming language with the concept of a guard. TR-208, ICOT, 1986.

[Warren 1983] Warren,D.H.D. : An Abstract Prolog Instruction Set. Technical Note 309, SRI International, 1983.

1.5 COLIBRI: A Coprocessor for LISP based on RISC

Christian Hafer, Josef Plankl and Franz Josef Schmitt

Siemens AG, Corporate R&D, ZFE IS SYS 1
Otto-Hahn-Ring 6, D-8000 Munich 83

Abstract

Traditional LISP machines are based on processors with complex microcoded instruction sets. Those processors require enormous efforts in both hardware and software design to achieve high LISP performance.

In our approach the power of RISC is used to speed up the AI language LISP by designing a dedicated VLSI LISP processor used in a coprocessor board for standard UNIX® workstations. The RISC approach leads to a significant reduction in system design complexity. The base of our development is a RISC processor tuned to the key features of LISP. The system yields the performance of todays specialized microcoded LISP machines. The performance goal is achieved by using an appropriate instruction set including mechanisms for garbage collection, list operations and fast function calls.

INTRODUCTION

LISP is one of the first high level programming languages. Its concepts are different from those that underlie languages like FORTRAN. First implementations using standard HW built for FORTRAN like languages tended to be slow. An analysis revealed that a few key features of LISP determine execution time of programs. These features include function calls, dynamic type checking and dynamic memory management.

LISP machines were built to get a combination of advantages from LISP and special HW: flexibility from LISP and high performance from the HW.

First LISP machines were built in 1970 - 1975 at the MIT. The CONS and the CADR (Knight *et al* 1980) were microcoded machines with complex CPUs. Most of today's LISP machines, like Symbolics (Moon 1985) or TI's Explorer are its direct descendants. These machines typically are stack based architectures, having a

VLSI for Artificial Intelligence and Neural Networks, Edited by J.G. Delgado-Frias and
W.R. Moore, Plenum Press, New York, 1991

large micro coded instruction set (Pleszkun and Thazhuthaveetil 1987) and a complex CPU.

The idea of using RISC (Reduced Instruction Set Computer) came up in the early 80's. It was shown that fulfilling some simple constraints (load/store architecture, non complex addressing modes, no complex operations) the design effort could be kept small, resulting in chips with high performance.

Since all measurements were made with programs written in C the question arose: will RISC work for LISP as well (Ponder 1983)? Projects at Stanford and the UCB were started to evaluate LISP on a RISC. SPUR (Larus et al 1986), built at Berkeley, was specifically tuned to the requirements of LISP. At Stanford a dialect of LISP (PSL) was ported to the MIPS-X Processor (Steenkiste and Hennessy 1987, Steenkiste and Hennessy 1988, Steenkiste and Hennessy 1989). Both implementations suggested that LISP will run on a RISC with sufficient speed.

COLIBRI was influenced by both processors, SPUR and MIPS-X. In contrast to SPUR and MIPS-X, COLIBRI was designed to be a coprocessor within a UNIX® system. The goal was to build a high-performance system using integrated HW/SW design. Based on the COLIBRI CPU in Harvard architecture we implemented a system environment including optimizing compiler and LISP runtime system.

Our results show that the chosen approach leads to a system architecture combining the flexibility of LISP with the efficient features of a RISC design.

HW Architecture

COLIBRI has been designed as a coprocessor board for UNIX® workstations. This approach reduces system design complexity since COLIBRI uses the I/O-devices provided by the host. The coprocessor board is composed of the components shown in Figure 1:

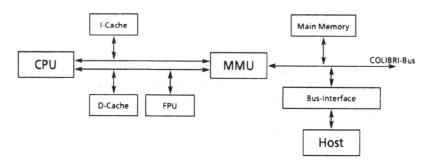

Figure 1 HW-Architecture

All components except for CPU and MMU are standard parts. CPU and MMU are designed to work in a tight cooperation. The bus interface is configurable, so an adaption to different buses is supported.

COLIBRI is a load/store architecture with single cycle operations only. To ensure an uninterrupted instruction flow, COLIBRI implements the Harvard architecture with separate instruction and data caches of 64 KB each. Each cache is connected to the CPU via its own address and data bus.

COLIBRI has a reduced instruction set. The instructions are coded in a simple and regular format. Since COLIBRI is a LISP coprocessor the CPU supports the performance relevant LISP features.

Function calls are supported using a large register file of 250 registers. The register file is divided into 42 global and 208 local registers. The local registers are partitioned into 13 overlapping register windows of size 22 registers. Each window has 6 input, 10 local and 6 output registers (Figure 2). The output registers of

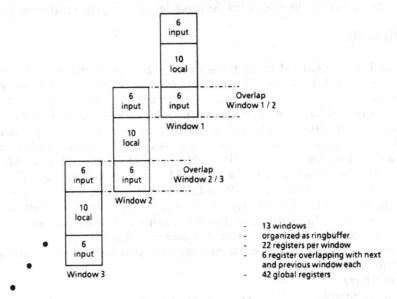

Figure 2 Registerfile

window i overlap the input register of window i+1. At any time one window designated by a hardware pointer is selected. The registers addressed by COLIBRI instructions are either global or local to the selected window. Windows are automatically switched at CALL operations.

Dynamic typing is supported by a tagged architecture combined with special instructions. The 32 bit words are divided into a 5 bit tag field and a 27 bit data/address field. This simplifies type checking at runtime. Type checks and dynamic memory management are further supported by a specialized trap concept.

Typical LISP applications are requiring a large address space. COLIBRI uses word addressing and disjoint address spaces for data and instructions. Thus the virtual address space is 128 MWords for instructions and data each. The different address spaces are accessed by specialized load and store instructions.

REPRESENTING LISP FEATURES IN HW

RISC designs are based on a few empiric rules. Two of the most important ones are the following:
- Additional instructions are implemented only if they result in a remarkable overall performance gain.
- Use only single word instructions and a small number of instruction formats.

These rules differ dramatically from the rules used to build earlier LISP machines. The following chapters will show how the RISC requirements can be fulfilled when building a RISC LISP processor. In doing so we identify the most heavily used LISP features and describe their implementation in COLIBRI. We will demonstrate that the given LISP features determine system performance.

Function calls

Common LISP consists of three types of language constructs, namely special forms, macros and functions. Whereas the compiler is supposed to have deeper knowledge about special forms, macros and functions are implemented in a different way. Macros are used to implement data and control abstractions. They are expanded into function calls and special forms. Given this kind of language it is important to speed up function calls. Therefore COLIBRI uses sophisticated call mechanisms. Function calls in LISP can be classified in different ways. We will give the classifications and show how COLIBRI deals with the different calls.

The first classification is into calls to LISP primitives and calls to user defined functions. The primitives themselves (more than 1000 in Common LISP) are split into two kinds of functions. The basic functions are characterized by short runtime, use of only a few registers and the absence of function calls.
Calls to user defined functions and more complex system functions are members of one of two subclasses:
- recursive
- nonrecursive.

Each of these can be divided into either calls being the last action inside a function at runtime or calls where the caller has to do some more computations after returning from the callee.

The actions required for each of these calls differ dramatically. COLIBRI supports the different types of function calls by providing three call instructions, CALL, CALL-NW and CALL-REG. We will explain their semantics in detail.

Typical LISP programs consist of a lot of small functions. Thus function calls are more important in LISP than in programming languages like PASCAL.

Calls to user defined LISP functions are supported by the COLIBRI instruction CALL. This instruction switches to a new register window. An old window is pushed onto a special stack if necessary. Since COLIBRI provides 13 overlapping windows, most of the calls can be handled by simply switching the window. This leads to a reduced call overhead, faster function calls and reduced memory traffic.

An analysis on the kind of function calls showed, that more than 50% of all calls are to predefined system functions (Steenkiste and Hennessy 1987). Up to

60% of these calls are to leaf functions, i.e. functions which don't call any other function. Since most of these leaf functions are small and need only a small number of registers, they can be evaluated using the same register window as the caller. COLIBRI uses the instruction CALL-NW to support this kind of calls. Using this instruction leads to a significant reduction of window switches, which in turn results in a reduced number of window pushes and thus reduces the memory traffic.

The COLIBRI system is characterized by a tight integration of SW and HW. This can be demonstrated by using function calls which are supported by both the processor and the compiler.

The compiler tries to minimize the number of CALL instructions to achieve high performance. It identifies several kinds of function calls and optimizes the calling sequences.

- Calls to very short system functions (function code only a few instructions) are automatically expanded inline.
- Functions being too large for inline coding and on the other hand being too small for reserving a window are compiled using the CALL-NW instruction.
- The CALL instruction is reserved for calling complex functions.

System primitives are highly optimized by choosing the appropriate calling sequence as well as effectively utilizing the pipeline.

Furthermore the compiler detects calls which are the last action inside a function. This case is divided in tail recursion (the function calls itself) and tail transfer (another function is called). In both cases the compiler converts the calls into jumps. Thus tail recursive functions are automatically converted to iterations which can be processed faster than function calls.

COLIBRI supports function calls by both HW and SW mechanisms. These are:
- Tail recursive calls   are compiled to jumps to the start address of the function.
- Linear recursive calls   are either compiled into a CALL-REG instruction.
- Non recursive calls   are treated in different ways:
  - Very small primitives are expanded inline
  - Small primitives which include no more function calls are compiled using the CALL-NW instruction and run in the context of the caller.
  - Function calls which are the dynamically last action inside a function are compiled using JUMP-REG.
  - Calls where the callee's result is used in further computations in the callers context are compiled using the CALL-REG instructions.

Generic arithmetic

LISP uses generic arithmetic, i.e. each operation works an all types of numbers. If necessary, automatic conversions between the types of numbers are performed. Measurements have shown, that in most cases the numbers are of type integer.

COLIBRI supports this scheme. The compiler assumes the operands to be of type integer and generates simple instructions for integer operations. Additions and subtractions are done by single cycle COLIBRI operations. When running the program, the processor checks the types of both operands by comparing their tag fields in parallel with the arithmetic operation. If both operands are of type integer, the operation continues without interrupt.

If the infrequent case happens (i.e. one or both operands are not of type integer) COLIBRI starts a datatype exception. This routine checks both parameters, converts them to a common format and does the computation using the FPU. After finishing the FPU operation the routine returns to the program where the interrupt was triggered and resumes computation.

List operations and type checks

Lists are the fundamental data type of LISP. Basically each list is build of cells. Each cell consists of a first element (the car of a list) and the rest (the cdr, a pointer to the next list cell). In COLIBRI car and cdr of a cell are stored in two contiguous memory cells which constitute a cons cell. A special instruction called cxr is used to access both car and cdr. Using cxr with an offset 0 yields the car, using cxr with offset 1 yields the cdr of a list. The instruction cxr starts from a given pointer in one of the registers. The processor HW uses the tag of the pointer to check whether the access is to a cons cell. This check is done in parallel during the data access. If the datatype is valid (cons or nil), the operation performs without interrupt. Otherwise a trap is used to start the debugger.

Common LISP consists of a lot of type predicates which are used frequently. In addition many operations (like arithmetic) need to check the type of their operands. COLIBRI supports fast type checks by a special single cycle type check operation. This is done by directly accessing the tag field inside one word.

Dynamic garbage collection

Due to the language definition LISP requires dynamic memory management. Lots of data are generated and stored at runtime. This data cannot be stored in a simple stack fashion. A complex memory allocation and management scheme is required. Most of the data is used only temporarily and can be deleted a short time after its creation. Since memory allocation is done implicitly, memory consumption is transparent to the user.

A garbage collector searches the memory in regular intervals and looks for memory cells being allocated without being referenced. It collects those cells and declares them as free to reuse. Since in a LISP system GC is frequently done, the choice and implementation of a GC Scheme is an important task when designing a LISP system (Steele 1975).

The requirements for the COLIBRI garbage collector are:
- complete collection, including cyclic structures.
- memory compaction. The GC should return the free memory as one big block, not as a list of small pieces.
- short interrupts. The GC should be transparent to the user, i.e. the runtime overhead for GC should be kept as low as possible.

Generation Scavenging, first described and implemented in the SOAR project (Ungar 1986), was chosen as a basis for our GC. That algorithm is based on a lifetime analysis of objects in LISP systems. This analysis has shown that most objects are deleted a short time after creation. The probability for an object to survive a certain time grows with the object's age. Thus the generation scavenging GC does frequent collections on young objects (which are allocated in a small memory region only) and few collections on older objects.

Implementations of this GC scheme are usually supported by HW features:
- Each object has to be marked with its age, i.e. the number of GC runs it has already survived. The SOAR implementation uses four generations of objects and needs two bits from each memory word to store the generation tag.
- Old and new objects are stored in different memory regions. The border between these regions has to be supervised to catch pointers from old objects to new objects. These references are collected and stored in a separate memory region for performance considerations.

COLIBRI uses a 32 bit architecture to allow the use of standard memory boards. The 32 bit words are divided into a 27 bit data/address field and a 5 bit tag field. This conflicts with the GC requirement of having two age bits. COLIBRI restrictions concerning the GC are the following:
- The GC has to run inside the register file. Register window over/underflow during a GC run is not allowed.
- The memory is 32 bit wide. Given data/address and tag part there is no space left for generation bits.

Our implementation utilizes a modified generation scavenging algorithm. Age information is not explicitly coded. A specific memory layout is used, so that an object's age can be derived from its memory location. A new data type to be used during GC and an adapted copy algorithm are the basis for the GC. Using this modifications our GC runs inside the register file without overflows, regardless of the nesting depth of the data structures to be collected.

Old objects pointing to young objects are stored in a separate list of references. To avoid the necessity of checking pointer values in software before storing them COLIBRI uses a special register in combination with a special store operation. The register contains a memory address. The special store instruction does an automatic runtime check using the content of the special register. If the check results in a border violation, an interrupt routine is started to insert the violating pointer into the list of references.

EFFECT OF THE COLIBRI ARCHITECTURE ON LISP PERFORMANCE

In the following section we discuss the characteristics of the COLIBRI architecture and their effects on LISP performance. Figure 3 (Steenkiste and Hennessy 1988) shows the quantitative effects of the LISP features and their contribution to runtime behaviour. These statistics are a result of analyzing 11 LISP programs implemented in PSL (Portable Standard LISP) on an early RISC processor. Among those programs were a simple interpreter of a LISP subset, an information retrieval system, a function evaluator with rational numbers, parts of the PSL LISP Compiler and benchmarks from the Gabriel benchmark set.

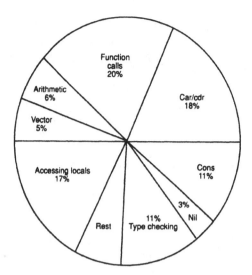

Figure 3 Runtime distribution

Function calls

20% of the measured LISP program runtime are spent for function calls. There are three kinds of calls. In the programs being considered about 62% of the calls are directed to the LISP runtime system. Those functions are usually simple. Furthermore the remaining user defined functions can be divided into two classes of different complexity. In COLIBRI we use coupled HW/SW features for optimal support of function calls.

LISP primitives: car, cdr, cons

According to Figure 3 about 29% of the LISP operations in total refer to the functions car, cdr and cons. Evaluating the Gabriel bechmarks Boyer, Browse and Polynomial Manipulation those functions make up to 54% of the operations. The effect of an efficient realization of these primitives can be observed looking at table 1 (measured using PSL implemented for a RISC processor).

The COLIBRI compiler uses inline coding for these functions. According to the COLIBRI instruction set the routine for cons needs two instructions, the code for car and cdr needs one instruction word each. The compactness und runtime efficiency of that code results from four reasons:
- Type checking is done simultaneously to the intrinsic function, avoiding runtime overhead.
- Due to fast memory accesses the result of a load operation can be used in the next but one cycle.
- The tagged architecture with separate data and type fields in a 32-bit word avoids extra code for data extraction.
- Checking of the memory bounds (cons) is an integrated part of the memory manager and is realized as a part of the MMU.

Table 1 Runtime in cycles and percentage of total runtime

	PSL[1)]	PSL[2)]	COLIBRI[3)]
cons	19 (11%)	5 (3%)	2
car		2 - 3 (10%)	1 - 2
cdr		2 - 3 (8%)	1 - 2

1) Portable Standard Lisp in original implementation

2) Optimized Portable Standard Lisp, without type checking

3) COLIBRI with typechecking

Type checking

Several LISP functions necessitate on the fly type checking. That is for example:
- Arithmetic operations (about 6%),
- type checking for LISP predicates (about 11%) and
- comparison against nil (LISP function *null*) (about 3%).

In total these operations are consuming about 20% of the runtime (Figure 3). In addition there are checks concerning the appropriate number of parameters involved in function calls. COLIBRI supports the LISP processing by a tagged architecture as well as parallel type checking of the operands during the execution of the instructions (generic arithmetic).

Type checking is supported by the tagged architecture and additionally by special test instructions. Those test instructions extract and check data types in one machine cycle. The complete implementation of LISP predicates like consp including generation of the boolean result therefore needs a runtime of three machine cycles.

The case that just one type is acceptable is handled by an instruction with a filter property. This instruction checks in a single machine cycle whether the operand is permissible. If it is not, an error handling routine is entered.

Accessing variables

17% of the operations in the LISP programs under consideration refer to variable accesses (Figure 3). Accessing is supported in COLIBRI by
- single cycle memory operations and
- a register window of appropriate size.

Therefore local variables and intermediate variables generated by the compiler can be allocated in a register and can be accessed at once by subsequent operations (all arithmetic and logical COLIBRI instructions are operating on registers). If data have to be transferred to or from main memory a delay of just one machine cycle is introduced.

CONCLUSION

HW and SW components of COLIBRI have been developed simultaneously and adapted to the LISP application requirements. Based on the LISP specific features an architecture for a single board LISP system is presented giving the performance of today's commercially available LISP machines. COLIBRI's high performance stems from an integrated hardware and software design from beginning.

Essential parts of COLIBRI are fast function calls and dynamic storage management. Function calls are supported on the base of special RISC instructions assisted by optimizing compiler techniques. Dynamic storage management is sped up by specialized trapping and a garbage collector adapted to the COLIBRI architecture.

REFERENCES

Gabriel, R.P., "Performance and Evaluation of LISP Systems", *The MIT Press*, 1985

Johnson, D.,"Trap Architectures for LISP Systems", *UCB-Report No. UCB/CSD 88/470*, Univ. of California, Berkeley, 1988

Knight, T.F., Moon, D.A., Hollway, J. and Steele, G.L., "CADR", *AI Memo 523*, MIT AI Laboratory, September 1980

Larus, J.R., Hilfinger, P.N., Patterson, D.A., Taylor, G.S. and Zorn, B.G., "Evaluation of the SPUR LISP Architecture", *The 13tn Annual International Symposium on Computer Architecture*, Tokyo, 1986, pp. 444 - 452

Mohnberg, A., "Garbage Collection für COLIBRI: Anforderungen, Konzepte und Implementierung", *Diploma thesis*, Christian-Albrechts-Universität zu Kiel, 1989

Moon, D.A., "Architecture of the Symbolics 3600", *Proceedings of the 12th Annual International Symposium on Computer Architecture*", 1985, pp. 76 - 83

Patterson, D.A., "Reduced Instruction Set Computers", *CACM*, Volume 28, No. 1, Januar 1985

Pleszkun, A.R. and Thazhuthaveetil, M.J., "The Architecture of LISP Machines", *Computer (1987)*, März 1987, pp. 35 - 44

Ponder, C., "... but will RISC run LISP??, (a feasabilty study)"*Report No. UCB/CSD 83/122*, EECS, Univ. of California, Berkely, 1983

Steenkiste, P. and Hennessy, J., "LISP on a Reduced-Instruction-Set Processor: Characterization and Optimization", *Technical Report CSL-TR-87-324*, Stanford University, März 1987

Steenkiste, P. and Hennessy, J.,"LISP on a Reduced-Instruction-Set Processor: Characterization and Optimization", *Computer (1988)*, Juli 1988, pp. 34 - 45

Steenkiste, P. and Hennessy, J., "A Simple Interprocedural Register Allocation Algorithm and its Effectiveness for LISP", *ACM Transactions on Programming Languages and Systems*, Vol.11, No.1, Januar 1989, pp. 1- 32

Steele, G.L. Jr., "Multiprocessing Compactifying Garbage Collector", *CACM*, Vol. 18, No. 9, November 1975, pp. 495-508

Ungar, D., "The Design and Evaluation of a High Performance Smalltalk System", *The MIT Press*, 1986

1.6 A CAM Based Architecture for Production System Matching

Pratibha and P. Dasiewicz

Department of Electrical Engineering
University of Waterloo, Waterloo, N2L 3G1, Ontario, Canada

Abstract

This paper presents a high performance architecture to support the execution of the match phase in OPS-like production system languages. The use of specialized CAM memories together with a non-state saving matching algorithm provides a significant performance increase. This architectural approach has eliminated the problems inherent in many other approaches, namely interprocess(or) communications, memory contention, load balancing and sychronization. Initial simulations with sample OPS5 programs indicate speedup in the order of 1000 with respect to a VAX 11/785 implementation.

INTRODUCTION

Expert knowledge consists of problem understanding and heuristic problem solving rules for a domain specific task. The most widely used paradigm for developing expert systems is the production system model. A Production System consists of the following components: a collection of rules, a collection of facts and an inference engine to match the facts to the rules. Each production rule has a condition part, indicated by the keyword IF. The conditions specify the working memory instances to which the rule applies. The rule also has an action part indicated by THEN. The action provides instructions to change the current working memory state if the rule conditions are true. An example of an OPS5 rule is shown in Figure 1. The inference engine is a finite state machine which cycles through the three phases of the production system execution cycle:

1) Match: An attempt is made to match the LHS of the rules to the knowledge base (Working Memory). The successful rule instantiations form the conflict set for that cycle.

2) Select: The conflict set is examined and a single rule selected for firing in some predefined manner.

VLSI for Artificial Intelligence and Neural Networks, Edited by J.G. Delgado-Frias and
W.R. Moore, Plenum Press, New York, 1991

57

3)   Act: Rule firing occurs which leads to either addition of new facts or deletion of existing facts. These changes may in turn cause more rules to be instantiated and the process continues until no further rules are applicable or the desired goal is achieved.

```
(p p1
(INV ^inp <X> ^out <Y>);              If gate is an INV, with input X
                                      and out_net Y

(INV ^inp <Y> ^out 3);                and input of INV is Y and
                                      out_net 3

(AND ^inp1 1 ^inp2 2 ^out <X>);       and inputs of AND gate
                                      are 1 and 2 and out_net is X
-->
(make AND ^inp1 1 ^inp2 2 ^out 3);    make AND gate with
                                      inputs 1 and 2 and out_net 3
```

Figure 1 Example OPS5 Rule

Production system execution tends to be very computationally intensive, the major bottleneck being the match phase. The match phase can consume 80% or more of a program's execution time. For the efficient execution of programs of any significant size this bottleneck must be overcome.

Many architectures have been proposed ranging from uniprocessors to multiprocessors with shared and distributed memory organizations eg., Lehr's PSM [Lehr 1988], CMU PSM [Forgy 1986], DADO [Stolfo 1984], MAPPS [Oshisanwo 1987], PESA-1 [Ramanarayan 1986], CUPID [Kelly 1987] and FAIM [Davis 1985]. In the multiprocessor architectures load balancing, synchronization and communication overheads are complex and often overbearing. The shared memory approach, in addition, suffers from memory contention problems.

The RETE [Forgy 1982], a widely used algorithm to perform the match phase execution, obtains it's efficiency by saving as much state information between cycles as possible to avoid recomputation. This algorithm stores all partial matches that occur. When executing programs of any significant size, the partial matches generated often become combinatorially explosive. This leads to serious memory requirement problems. Another approach is the TREAT [Miranker 1987] algorithm (used in DADO), which limits the state information stored.

The CAM based Matching unit for Production Systems (CAMPS) presented in this paper is a co-processor designed to speed up the match phase of the production system execution cycle. A highly intelligent Content Addressable Memory forms the processing unit as well as the storage unit. It enables massive parallelism to be exploited during the search for matches as the entire memory is searched in one cycle. The use of an intelligent memory enables the comparisons to be performed in the memory itself. This overcomes the Von Neumann bottleneck of extensive data movement and address calculations during comparisons. The CAMPS algorithm is defined for sequential execution of OPS5 programs. No intermediate state information is saved since the cost of recomputation of this information is comparatively negligible.

THE CAMPS MATCHING ALGORITHM

The algorithm compiles the left hand side of the rules into a data-dependency network. The compiling process starts with processing each condition element in the rule. The tests that try to satisfy each condition element in the rule individually are called *intra-condition* tests. For the rule to be instantiated it is necessary to satisfy the conditions across the condition elements within the rule. These tests are called *inter-condition* element tests.

The nodes that perform the intra-condition tests are called the *constant-test* nodes. The attribute value against which they are to be compared is known at compile time. After the intra-condition tests have been exhausted, the inter-condition test nodes are formed to check for the inter-CE consistency of the variable bindings. These nodes are called the *two-input* nodes. The two-input nodes can further be classified as *and* nodes and *not* nodes. If the condition element is positive, (ie. for the rule to be satisfied the presence of a WME is necessary), the node is an *and* node. On the other hand, if the CE is negated, (ie. the absence of a matching WME is essential), then the node is a *not* node.

The algorithm takes advantage of the similarity of condition elements between rules by performing the common tests once. According to Gupta's statistics, the reduction in the number of nodes in the network obtained due to sharing of nodes is two to three times the number of non-shared network nodes. The other advantage is avoiding replication of the node information in the memories. Since the CAMs are relatively expensive, one of the primary concerns is to minimize the amount of information stored in the memory.

Figure 2 depicts a CAMPS network for the rule shown in Figure 1. Every node is identified by its node number and its parent node number. The parent node is the immediately preceding node connected to the node by the data-flow path, (eg. node number 7 is the parent of node number 8L). The two-input nodes in addition have a level number associated with them. The level number refers to the depth of the two-input node in the network. Associated with each two-input node is the level required by the node. The level required gives the level number and the node side ie. left or right, from which the attribute is required, (eg. node number 8L requires attribute entering from level 0 right hand side). Each node has a comparison descriptor which specifies the boolean operation to be performed when searching the node.

The CAMPS algorithm does not maintain any intermediate match information. Since the time to perform a search of the entire CAM is in the order of nano seconds, a non-state saving approach is preferable. The overhead of recalculating the partial match information is much less compared to the overhead of saving the intermediate state information generated, which may be combinatorially explosive in size.

Arrival of a Token from the Host

The incoming token enters the network at the root node. After satisfying the constant-test nodes in the network, the token can arrive at a two-input node in such a way as to create three different network configurations.

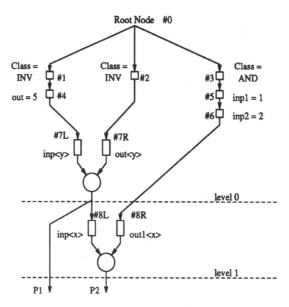

Figure 2 CAMPS Network

Case 1: The token traverses the network such that it enters a two-input node at level 0. A two-input node at level 0 indicates that it is the first node to perform variable bindings between condition elements. The path traversed by the token is shown in Figure 3(a).

Case 2: When the working memory change token arrives at a two-input node, not the terminal node, at a level other than 0, the path followed by the token is shown in Figure 3(b).

Token entry to a two-input node at a level other than 0 indicates that the matched token entry satisfying this node has succeeded all the node tests preceding the node of entry. Therefore, after satisfying the node of entry, the preceding nodes are evaluated until the node at level 0 has been matched. The control flow then backtracks to the node of entry and searches the succeeding nodes.

Case 3: If the token traverses the network in such a way that the two-input node it enters is not at level 0 and is a terminal node, then the path followed by the token is shown in the Figure 3(c). The entry at a terminal node implies that once the node at level 0 has been searched, all the inter condition tests have been performed. Hence, the node at level 0 acts as a terminal node.

The CAMPS algorithm selects the first matched token and traverses the network to determine the rule instantiation. It then backtracks to the last node which generated multiple matches, selects the next matched token and repeats the node tests to determine the instantia-

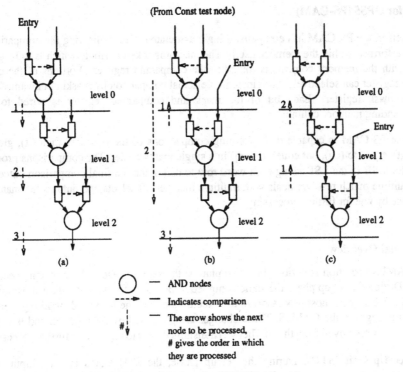

Figure 3 Control Flow in CAMPS Algorithm

tion of the rule. This process is continued until all possible instantiations of the rule have been searched.

A node may have more than one child node. In this case, one path is initially selected. All possible node activations in that path are evaluated. Then the algorithm backtracks to the node that was shared by more than one node. The other path is then processed in the same way.

THE CAMPS ARCHITECTURE

The CAMPS architecture provides hardware support for sequential execution of the match phase of OPS5 programs. It acts as a high performance matching co-processor for a host processor. The other two phase of the program executions, ie. the conflict resolution and the act phases, are executed by the host processor. The unit requires the host to send changes made to the working memory. The rule instantiations found are reported back to the host which is then responsible for the execution of the rest of the cycle.

CAM for OPS5 (PS-CAM)

Each cell in the PS-CAM has comparison logic associated with it allowing the comparisons to be performed within the memory itself. The incoming token attribute which is to be compared with the memory contents is routed to the comparand register. Portions of the comparand register can selectively participate in the actual comparison by masking unwanted bits by the mask register. Each bit of the mask and comparand register is wired to the corresponding memory column.

The PS-CAM is capable of performing comparisons of the type less than (lt), greater than (gt), equal to (eq), not equal to (neq) in a single match cycle. The comparisons proceed from the MSB to the LSB along each word row to determine the final comparison outcome. The multiple match resolver deals with multiple matches. It selects and outputs the matched rows one by one for further processing.

Functional Overview

The CAMPS operation is divided into two phases: the set up phase and the match execution phase. During the set up phase the static compiled information for the network is downloaded to the CAMPS by the host processor. In the execution phase, the host sends working memory element changes to the CAMPS. These changes are processed by the CAMPS and the result (rules added or removed from the conflict set) transmitted back to the host for further processing.

Set Up Unit (STU): During the set up phase, the STU stores the two-input node numbers and their respective node descriptors required by the CAMPS algorithm for searching the nodes for matches. This information is stored as:

{parent node #, node #, lev #, lev reqd, comparison type, attr #}

The STU consists of a memory with a 16 bit wide content addressable memory and a 20 bit wide RAM. The comparison circuitry is required to perform only equality comparisons.

During the execution phase, the STU is accessed to extract the node descriptors corresponding to the two-input node to be evaluated.

CAM Matching Unit (CAMU): The CAMU is the main functional unit in the architecture. It provides storage for the working memory elements and support for node evaluation. It consists of two matching units, MU-L and MU-R, that relate to the left hand side and the right hand side of the nodes. This subdivision allows comparisons and store operations, on the incoming working memory element attributes to be performed in parallel. Each MU consists of a 56 bit wide PS-CAM unit and a 3 bit wide RAM.

During the set up phase, the information related to the constant-test nodes is stored in the CAMU. The right hand side of each constant-test node is fixed and known at compile time. Therefore, the information for a constant-test node is loaded directly into the CAMU. The fields stored at each CAMU word are:

{node #, parent node #, attr val, token #, comparison type}

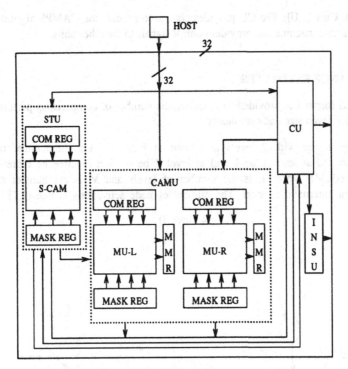

Figure 4 CAMPS Architecture

During the execution phase, the CAMU evaluates the active nodes in the network. The constant-test nodes have their RHS previously stored during the set up phase, so the WME attributes are stored in the LHS and compared with the RHS. When the token from the host arrives, the attributes are loaded into the comparand registers of both subunits. The MU-R performs the comparison while the MU-L unit performs the storage. The matched information is then used to determine the next node to be activated.

The incoming token can have a positive or a negative tag. If the token tag is positive, the side from which it enters initiates a write in the corresponding MU. The other unit performs a search cycle. If the token tag is negative, then the side it enters from and the other side both initiate a search cycle. All the matched entries in the PS-CAM side it enters from are marked deleted. The comparison results obtained from the other side of the PS-CAM determine outcome of the nodes.

Instantiation Unit (INSU): The INSU is designed to record rule instantiations corresponding to one rule at a time. Once all the condition elements of a rule are satisfied by a set of working memory elements, the INSU sends the stored join information to the host processor for further processing. It is then ready to store the next set of instantiations.

Control Unit (CU): The CU provides control to execute the CAMPS algorithm. It is designed as a state machine and provides control signals to the other units.

PERFORMANCE ESTIMATES

A generalized formula is provided to calculate the number of comparisons performed in a network of any given size and complexity.

Consider a tree with 2 levels as shown in Figure 5. Let the number of partial matches generated at level 1 be 1 and at level 2 be m_1. Let the tree be represented by the tuple tree(L,M), where L is the number of levels and M is the number of partial matches at the intermediate level. The number of node activations in tree (2,1) is:

$$2 + (m_1 - 1) \tag{1}$$

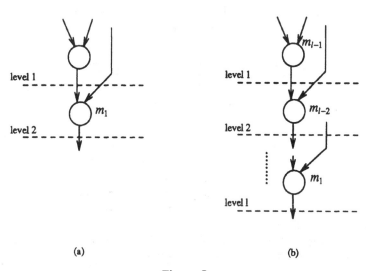

(a)   (b)

Figure 5

If the number of partial matches at level 1 are m_2, then the tree (2,1) has to be traversed m_2 times to find all the matched token pairs. Equation 1 becomes:

$$(2 + (m_1 - 1))(m_2 - 1) \tag{2}$$

From the above results the number of node activations generated in a tree with l levels is

$$[(((l,1) + (j,1)*(m_j - 1)) + (((j+1,1) + (j,1)*(m_{j-1}))*(m_{j+1}-1)) \ldots$$

$$+ (((l-1,1) + (j,1)*(m_j - 1))*(m_{l-1} - 1))] (m_l - 1) \tag{3}$$

where j = 2.

From the formula above, it is concluded that the number of node activations is a function of the partial matches generated at each level. Each node activation is independent of the size of the memory the incoming token must be compared against to find a successful match. If the incoming WME is required by more than one rule, then the number of node activations is equal to the sum of the activations in the individual paths corresponding to the two rules.

Simulations of the architecture have been performed at the register transfer level. The test program analysed consists of two rules. The CAMPS network consists of 5 *constant-test* nodes and 2 *and* nodes. The problem size varies with the number of initial working memory elements. The test program was analyzed by varying the working memory size and the number of partial matches generated. Table 1 shows the simulation results obtained by executing the test program on CAMPS and a VAX 11/785. The entries in column 1 show the execution speeds with variable working memory size and constant partial matches generated. These figures are indicative of the time spent in loading the working memory contents in the CAMPS. Column 2 shows the execution timings with varying partial matches generated. Speed ups of the order of 10^3 are obtained.

Table 1 Program Execution Characteristics

Characteristics	Partial Match(10)		WM size(40)	
	WM Size		Partial Matches	
	17	40	10	23
CAMPS Time(us)	20.8	46.4	46.4	48.8
VAX time(ms)	50	60	60	70
Speed Up	$2.4*10^3$	$1.3*10^3$	$1.3*10^3$	$1.2*10^3$

CONCLUSIONS

The CAMPS architecture is designed as a coprocessor attached to a conventional host and executes the match phase of the production system execution. A non-state saving algorithm called the CAMPS matching algorithm is defined for sequential execution of the match phase on the CAMPS architecture.

The gain in performance obtained is in the order of 10^3 times over the VAX 11/785. The time taken to perform a single search cycle is independent of the working memory size. As the size of the Working Memory becomes significantly large and the potential partial matches generated increase, conventional architectures severely degrade in performance as can be seen by the examples illustrated above. The match time is 80% or more of the total execution time. If the number of comparisons to be performed is large, the percentage time spent in the match phase can be as large as 99% or higher. This has an adverse affect on the performance of the conventional architectures. The CAMPS architecture on the other hand maintains a consistent performance over a wide range of program size.

In this approach some of the problems currently encountered by conventional architectures have been overcome. Since the incoming tokens are being processed sequentially, no synchronization mechanism is required. Problems such as load balancing, memory contention and communication overheads are completely eliminated. The communication involved between the host and CAMPS is minimal. An intermediate host will however be required to avoid the bottleneck between the host and CAMPS. The hardware complexity of CAMPS is small as compared to VAX or existing high performance production system architectures.

REFERENCES

Davis, A.L. and Robinson, S.V., "The Architecture of the FAIM Symbolic Multiprocessing System", *Proc. of IJCAI*, pp. 32-38, 1985.

Forgy, C.L., *OPS5 Users Manual*, Technical Report CMU-CS-81-135, Carnegie-Mellon University 1981.

Forgy, C.L. and Gupta, A., "Preliminary Architecture of the CMU Production System Machine", *Proc. of the 19th Annual Hawaii International Conference on System Sciences*, pp.194-200, 1986.

Forgy, C.L., "RETE: A Fast Algorithm for the Many Pattern/Many Object Pattern Match Problem", *Artificial Intelligence 19*, pp.17-37, September 1982.

Kelly, M.A. and Seviora, R.E., "A Multiprocessor Architecture for Production System Matching", *Proc. of AAAI*, pp. 36-41, 1987.

Lehr, T.F., "The Implementation of a Production System Machine", *Proc. of the 19th Annual Hawaii International Conference on System Sciences*, pp.177-186, 1988.

Miranker, D.P., "TREAT:A Better Match for AI Production Systems", *Proc. of AAAI*, pp.42-47, 1987.

Oshisanwo, A.O. and Dasiewicz, P., "A Parallel Model and Architecture for Production Systems", *Proc. of 1987 International Conference of Parallel Processing*, pp.147-153, August 1987.

Ramnarayan, R., "PESA-1:A Parallel Architecture for OPS5 Production Systems", *Proc. of the 19th Annual International Conference of System Sciences*, pp.201-205, 1986.

Stolfo, S.J. and Miranker, D.P., "DADO:A Parallel Processor for Expert Systems", *Proc. of IEEE*, pp.74-81, 1984.

Stormon, C.D. and Oldfield, J.V., "An Architecture Based on Content-Addressable memory for the Rapid Execution of Prolog" *Proc. of the Fifth International Conf. and Symposium on Logic Programming*, pp.1448-1473, 1988.

1.7 SIMD Parallelism for Symbol Mapping

Chang Jun Wang and Simon H. Lavington

Department of Computer Science
University of Essex
Colchester CO4 3SQ

Abstract

Variable-length character strings and other symbolic objects form the major data items in Artificial Intelligence and related applications. The rapid manipulation of such symbols is greatly facilitated if they are first mapped into a simple internal identifier space. We describe SIMD-parallel associative hardware which achieves this mapping. Our hardware unit, known as the lexical token converter, is part of a novel architecture for knowledge-based systems. This architecture uses the concept of active memory to achieve high-speed manipulation of symbolic structures. We describe this concept and, in particular, its conventions for information representation.

INTRODUCTION

Symbol manipulation lies at the heart of knowledge-based systems. The generic operations of AI programs, such as pattern-directed searching, variable binding, set intersection and transitive closure, all take place on symbolic data. More particularly, all such operations involve associative matching of variable-length lexical strings. Since the matching, or comparison, of symbolic data is so fundamental to information systems in general, it is natural to consider ways in which this activity could be speeded up by some form of associative hardware. The variable length of symbolic objects, and the potential overlap between the internal representation of strings, numerals, pointers, etc makes the design of general-purpose hardware support very difficult. Hence, the representation of variable-length character strings, generically known as lexemes, is of crucial importance. The design and implementation of parallel hardware to handle lexemes is the central theme of this paper. This theme is set in a consistent architectural framework in which the associative matching of symbolic data is an underlying principle rather than an awkward afterthought.

Before describing the parallel hardware, it is important to justify the choice of architectural framework within which it is implemented. In the next two sections we therefore introduce some primitive operations on symbolic data and set them in the context of a novel associative memory system. The system is known as **active memory**. We then present a scheme for low-level information representation within the active memory, focussing on the encoding of lexemes. It is shown that this encoding calls for a special associative sub-unit called the **lexical token converter**.

VLSI for Artificial Intelligence and Neural Networks, Edited by J.G. Delgado-Frias and
W.R. Moore, Plenum Press, New York, 1991

We describe the operational requirements for this unit, its implementation using SIMD techniques, and its performance. Finally, we outline an improved implementation using transputers to control the various sub-sections of the active memory.

ARCHITECTURAL FRAMEWORK

Operations on symbolic data structures such as sets, graphs and relations, may be classified into a limited number of primitives. From a user's view, these primitives can effectively define an architectural interface between software and hardware. After analysing many information systems, expressed in a variety of knowledge representations, we offer the following list of primitives as an operational interface:

(i) **relational and set primitives:** insert, delete, member, select, project, intersect, difference, union, join, duplicate removal.

(ii) **set aggregate primitives:** cardinality, maximum, minimum, average.

(iii) **recursive query primitives:** transitive closure of a relation, reachable node set, n^{th} wave of tuples, 'is there a path between two specified nodes?', return the path between two specified nodes, composition of relations.

(iv) **graph aggregate primitives:** shortest path, longest path, arc average, node average.

(v) **special primitives:** (yet to be decided, but possibly including: sort, modify, range search, fuzzy search, Euclidean distance, Hamming distance).

The operations in groups (i) and (ii) will be familiar to relational database practitioners. Group (iii) operations support the evaluation of linear recursive rules in deductive/logic databases (Robinson and Lavington 1990); the term 'wave' refers to a primitive of the delta Wavefront algorithm which is used for evaluating transitive closure. Lest these operations appear too biassed towards the deductive database paradigm, it should be noted that relational operations also seem to be at the heart of other popular AI paradigms. For example in production systems, a set of rules is applied to a set of facts by attempting to match the condition-part of a rule with fact patterns. Each of the conditions of a rule is a tuple whose terms may be values (ground term) or variables. A condition may be regarded as defining a relation, which is instantiated by a subset of zero or more facts in the factbase, a fact being a tuple of ground terms. Pattern matching can thus be defined as finding the join of the relations associated with all of the conditions of each rule. A rule is satisfied if its join is non-null. Further comments of the relevance of sets and relations to Constraint Satisfaction and Truth Maintenance systems are given in Lavington and Waite 1989.

The above commands operate on data structures such as sets, relations, graphs and networks. Conventionally, these structures would be held in RAM, together with any new structures created as a result of primitive diadic relational operations. More generally, Figure 1(a) shows a conventional hierarchy of memory devices, M1 (typically faster, volatile) and M2 (slower, non volatile). In Figure 1(a) data processing can only take place if the data to be processed is within the CPU's addressing range (here M1). Thus, persistent data structures are in general moved from M2 to M1, whereupon the CPU takes (reads) fine-grain elements of the data structure in order to operate upon them. There are three points to note about the conventional computing environment represented by Figure 1(a):

(i) A physical address-mapping is necessary between M_1 and M_2; this physical mapping does not normally reflect the logical structure of the data. Hence memory management ('paging and protection') has to be carried out with reference to coarse physical address boundaries.

(ii)   The bandwidths of both interconnecting highways has to be high, if high overall performance is to be maintained.

(iii)   All responsibility for the exploitation of parallelism resides within the CPU.

Point (i), with its dependence on physical addressing, represents a serious impediment to the ideal of a large associative memory system. Furthermore, point (ii) arises because of the inability of M1 and M2 to select information by value. Ideally, we need to replace M1 and M2 in Figure 1(a) by associative (ie content-addressable) memory. We also need to use an associative memory's innate ability to compare data values, in order to **process** information in situ. In other words, the value-comparisons inherent in operations such as intersection should take place within associative memory units which are thought of as **active** (rather than passive). If the active memory can process structured data autonomously, then some of the responsibility for exploiting parallelism may be transferred away from a conventional CPU and its software.

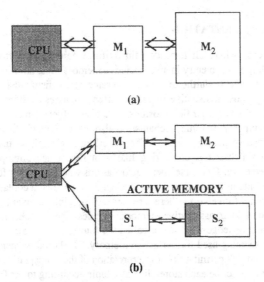

(a)

(b)

Figure 1 Adding active memory to a conventional computer

THE ACTIVE MEMORY CONCEPT

In Figure 1(b) the computing system has been augmented by the addition of an autonomous unit labelled Active Memory. This may also contain a hierarchy of devices, S1 (faster, volatile) and S2 (slower, non-volatile), but this internal arrangement is invisible to the CPU. Both S1 and S2 have limited (i.e. special-purpose) computational ability in addition to their ability to store information. Apart from explicit insert and delete commands, data is persistent within the Active Memory. This property of persistence is extended to any new data structures created as a result of operations involving existing data structures. Such action has implications for data consistency, naming conventions and version control. These are issues which are the subject of current research.

As was mentioned earlier, the Active Memory is associative. That is to say, the CPU refers to a data object held within the Active Memory by a unique name, instead of by a conventional address. The term 'name' is taken to include 'descriptor', 'interrogand', or 'pattern', so that variables and wild cards are accommodated. A consequence of this is that named objects can have varying granularity. The hidden memory management within the Active Memory should also be of variable granularity, being based on logical descriptors rather than on physical addresses - (see Lavington et al, 1987). The data-manipulation commands built into the Active Memory reflect the common operations on frequently-used data structures, as given earlier. Such operations exhibit much scope for parallelism. Note that the Active Memory is primarily intended for structured data arising from a finite, but useful, sub-set of users' abstract data type declarations. Other (possibly un-structured) data may be held as usual in M1 and M2 in Figure 1(b). For further comments on handling persistent objects, see Lavington and Davies, 1990.

A prototype hardware implementation of the active memory's relational algebraic commands has been described elsewhere (Lavington, Robinson and Mok, 1988). We now focus on the low-level representation of symbolic data within the active memory, and in particular the scheme for representing lexical objects. We begin with a general discussion of associative memory principles.

INFORMATION REPRESENTATION

Except in the trivial case where all lines contain uniform objects, eg virtual addresses in a translation look-aside buffer, each entry in an associative memory must have a certain field that is invariant for that class of object. Furthermore, the accessing mechanism must take account of the fact that, in a general-purpose associative memory, different classes of stored object may have differing field formats. If a particular field-position for a given object can contain alternatives, as for example with union types, then some mechanism is also required which distinguishes primitive types during the associative match process. The underlying principle is that the comparison hardware must be certain that it is comparing like with like, when attempting to match an interrogand with a stored entry. Of course, there are occasions when a match is forced, for example when the stored entry contains a named variable or when the interrogand contains a wild card.

Within the foregoing framework, there are several possible conventions for low-level information representation in an associative memory. We describe the scheme we have used for the last few years for a knowledge-base server called the Intelligent File Store, IFS/1 (Lavington 1988);this scheme is also being used for our active memory. It should be mentioned that we are working on a revision that will permit a richer interpretation of the concept of type. In the existing IFS/ 1, it is convenient to describe each stored line as a tuple according to the following format:

        $<L><TF><T1><T2> \dots <Tm><M1><M2> \dots <Mn>$

where:

    $<L>$ is an optional label (eg gödelisation)
    $<TF>$ is an invariant term for a particular tuple format
    $<T1><T2> \dots$ are terms in a wff
    $<M1><M2> \dots$ are optional modifiers for the $<L>$ and $<T>$ fields

The <terms> may be lexemes (eg character strings), integers, labels (eg gödel numbers), abstract nodes, named variables, etc. The <terms> are all mapped into fixed-length internal indentifiers (IDs). Thus, IDs are used to represent all primitive objects. To distinguish primitive types, each ID has the format:

    <tag><unique sub_code>

<tag> is usually four bits. The total length of an ID is a system-configuration constant, set by software in the range two to eight bytes. For the rest of this paper we shall assume a typical ID length of four bytes.

From a system viewpoint, the existence of a typed ID space raises two implementation issues:

how to map rapidly into and out of the ID space; how to manage the ID space so as to ensure uniqueness of encryption within any one <type> of object, in a multi-user environment. These issues are most acute in the case of lexical tokens, and justify the provision of hardware assistance. The task of a unit called a Lexical Token Converter (LTC) is therefore twofold: firstly, to translate from the lexemes (e.g. character strings) used in an AI program into and out of the ID space; secondly, to allocate and deallocate lexical IDs in a consistent manner, keeping a dictionary of all lexemes known to the system so far. The LTC is thus two-way associative memory with additional ID allocation/deallocation features. There are other desirable properties of the LTC such as the ability to perform fuzzy searches. These will be discussed in the next section, when the LTC's performance targets are described.

OPERATIONAL REQUIREMENTS FOR THE LTC

In order to implement the two-way associative memory outlined above for the LTC, it is necessary to be more precise about the size of lexical objects, the total number of such objects in a knowledge base, and the desired speed of associative search. The commonest example of a lexical token is a word in a natural language. A random sample of 2063 English words indicates that the maximum length and average length of English words is 20 and 7.24 characters respectively. Information systems, unlike most natural languages, may also choose to treat compound words and related groups of words as single entities. An extreme example is a postal address, which might be up to 80 characters in length. Although there is really no upper limit to the number of characters that *could* be treated as an entity, it should always be possible, as in the case of postal addresses, to decompose very long strings into more manageable sub-units. It may be noted that the size of a typical object in Object-Oriented systems is commonly stated to be about 50 bytes. Human Computer Interface considerations suggest the width of a lineprinter page (say 120 characters) as a sensible upper bound to lexemes in the LTC.

The total number of unique lexemes in a knowledge base might be expected to bear a statistical relation to the total size of the knowledge base. We have examined statistics from 66 small database systems in an attempt to deduce some natural connection between database size and number of lexemes (Wang 1987). As a working approximation, we assumed a combinatorial function connecting number of entities to number of relationship instances. Using the best fitted curve, it is predicted that a database of overall size 16Mbytes would be expected to have 100,000 lexemes and a database of 400 Mbytes would have 200,000 lexemes. These figures roughly accord with the observation that the European Law Commission's EUROLEX database, when of size 50 Mbytes, contained about 120,000 distinct lexemes. Assuming an Internal Identifier length of 4 bytes and an average lexeme length of 8 characters, a Lexical Token Converter of between one and ten Mbytes total capacity should suffice for practical knowledge bases. Modular extensibility without loss of search speed would be a distinct advantage.

As far as speed of search is concerned, it is naturally desirable that the LTC should be faster than conventional software table look-up. As is shown later, a dedicated single-board computer may be hand-coded to carry out simple searches in say two hundred microseconds. Fuzzy searches, i.e. those in which some of the interrogand characters are wild cards, take up to three seconds on the same single-board computer. Another perspective on desirable search speed comes from the IFS architecture described in Lavington et al 1987. Within the IFS, the LTC operates in support of a 4Mbyte associative cache which has a typical search time of 250 microseconds (Lavington 1988). Bearing in mind the total IFS problem-solving activity, it is unlikely to be cost-effective to make the LTC more than say ten times faster than the main associative cache. Finally, it may be assumed that, if successful, a knowledge-base query usually produces more output (i.e. result lexemes) than the number of lexemes appearing in the input query. Therefore, if technical compromises have to be made, it is better that the translation <ID> to <lexeme> be faster than the reverse translation.

IMPLEMENTATION AND PERFORMANCE

The size requirement for the Lexical Token Converter (up to 10 Mbytes) is clearly beyond the range of cost-effective implementation using CAM chips. Fortunately, the search times required (a few tens of microseconds) allow the effect of CAMs to be achieved indirectly via other means. There are several existing designs for 'dictionary machines', ie machines which offer functions such as SEARCH (for a key), INSERT (a key) and DELETE (a key). An early example is Lieserson's Systolic Priority Queues (Leiserson 1979), which can be modified to perform dictionary functions. This machine stores key-record pairs in sorted order over a linear chain of processors which are connected as leaf nodes of a binary tree. The performance of Lieserson's machine is of time O(log N). Other designs based on tree structures have been proposed, eg Ottmann et al 1982, Fisher 1984, Atallah and Kosaraju 1985, Somani and Agarwal 1985, and Goyal and Narayanan 1988. The emphasis has been to maintain a performance of time O(log N) whilst reducing the pipeline steps, avoiding excessive hardware complexity at each node, and avoiding excessive inter-node connectivity. The designs of Ottoman et al and Atallah et al can only achieve the O(log N) performance when the actual number of stored elements is less than the square root of the number of processors.

The designs for dictionary machines mentioned above are all subject to trade- offs concerning processing node complexity, structural complexity, achieving optimal performance of O(log N), etc. Most machines assume that the dictionary data is relatively static, and many assume that it has been pre-sorted. Although most existing designs can be made to perform two-way search, none seems to be able to accommodate both variable-length items and fuzzy searching. The lack of modularity (ie extensibility) of many of the designs is also seen as a disadvantage.

Design

For the reasons given above, and in order to meet the 10 Mbyte capacity requirement derived earlier, a simpler approach has been taken for the design of the LTC. The philosophy is to store each string and its accompanying ID as a variable-length record in RAM, at an address partly determined by an 8-bit hash key derived from the string. The total RAM is divided into many modules, each equipped with a search engine. During an associative look-up, all modules commence searching in parallel in a SIMD fashion, but the detailed operation of each search engine then becomes quasi- asynchronous due to the varying lengths of records. Each module of RAM, its search engine and other logic, is known as a flexible associative memory (FAM) module. Since each FAM contains both memory and search capability, a modularly extensible architecture results in which search speed remains constant as capacity is increased.

Several FAM modules are driven by a central LTC controller, which is itself flexible enough to accommodate several types of stored record. When used for lexemes, each cell in FAM has the following format:

<header><ID><lexical string>

The l.s. 7 bits of the one-byte header give the size of the cell as a byte count (excluding the header itself). The m.s. bit of the header is a deletion marker, used when an LTC entry is deleted (see below). Character strings of length 1 - 120 bytes are catered for. The ID, whose length is system-configured, has the format:

<type><unique sub-code>

The l.s. 8 bits of the sub-code are a hash address, defining one of 256 hash bins. The remaining sub-code bits form a count for a particular bin, derived from 256 up-counters maintained by the LTC controller. The l.s. 2 bits of each count are used to partition a hash bin into four divisions, so that an LTC search with ID known is on average four times faster than a search with string known. This speed differential reflects the observation that the translation ID $\rightarrow$ lexeme is required more frequently than the translation lexeme $\rightarrow$ ID. The LTC naturally provides the basic operations of insert, search, and delete.

Implementation

We now describe the first implementation of the Lexical Token Converter, completed in 1986, since this is the version on which we have done the most performance measurements. This version is incorporated in the IFS/1 knowledge-base server. A new implementation for our active memory is discussed later.

An overall diagram of the Lexical Token Converter is shown in Figure 2. The Controller, which is connected to other IFS units and/or a host computer via a VME bus, sequences the correct searching activity in n FAM modules which are attached to a sub-system bus. The Controller has memory-mapped command, status and responder registers, by means of which other VME units may initiate the following commands:

INSERT	<header><ID><lexical string>	
SEARCH	either:	<?><ID><?>
	or:	<header><?><lexical string>
	or:	<?><?><lexical string with wild cards>
DELETE	<?><ID><?>	

The fuzzy search facility includes bit-masking facilities - (useful for causing the ASCII case bit to be ignored)-and the facility to handle an unknown number of trailing wild-card characters. Fuzzy searching may of course result in multiple responders; these are placed by the LTC Controller in a FIFO, to be read out by the calling process.

The Controller in Figure 2 consists of a microprogrammed control unit (MCU), supervising the action of 12 finite state machines implemented in TTL-compatible programmable array logic. It occupies two 6-layer double Euro cards. The LTC's sub-system bus consists of two 8-bit data highways, a 10-bit address highway and 8 control lines. Each FAM module presently contains 256K of type 8263 DRAM accessed in page mode - (the design was first implemented in 1986; jumpers are provided so that denser DRAM chips can be used in a future upgrade). A FAM's memory is organised for addressing purposes as four banks of 64K bytes, each bank being divided into 256 physical rows corresponding to quarters of 256 logical hashing bins. The hashing bins are denoted as H0 - H255 in Figure 2. All these physical addressing details are of course hidden from the user, who simply treats the LTC as a large, elastic, associative memory.

Variable-length cells, or records, are stored consecutively within a FAM row, empty spaces being indicated by a nil header. The search engine in the FAM module consists of addressing logic and matching logic. The former includes an adder, which gives the ability to skip forwards or backwards as required by the variable-length entries. The latter comprises two byte-wide comparators and associated masking logic which provides the following search functions:

equivalence match
don't care
range search using two arguments and the operators =,<,>,<=,>=
masked search using a bit-wise boolean AND operation.

Each FAM occupies a double Euro card. FAMs are arranged in card cages holding up to 18 FAM

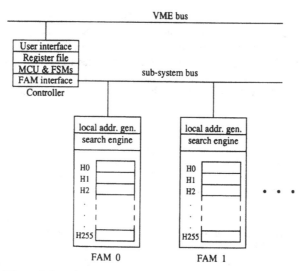

Figure 2 Overall block diagram of the Lexical Token Converter

cards plus driver/terminator. The number of FAM modules in a given system can be extended without reducing the search performance significantly. Physical memory utilisation is of course dependent upon the distribution of hashed values. In practice, we have observed utilisation ratios of 75 percent or better. The statistics given earlier therefore indicate that a modest 8-module LTC can be expected to hold at least 128K distinct lexemes, and that this would cater for a knowledge base of at least 50 megabytes of raw data.

Performance

The search speed of the LTC varies according to the comparand, amount of data currently being stored, and the chance distribution of short and long strings. When the LTC is filled to capacity with pseudo-randomly generated strings whose length lies in the range 1 to 32 characters, the following average times are measured:

    INSERT: 30.2 microseconds
    SEARCH with ID known: 37.9 microseconds
    SEARCH with string known: 334.2 microseconds
    DELETE: 42.4 microseconds.

It is interesting to compare these figures with equivalent software times. In order to place the software at an advantage, we took a dedicated M68020-based single-board computer with dual-ported RAM running at 20 MHz. This was hand- coded for an efficient search algorithm based on hashing, with the size of each hashing bin arranged to be identical to that of a single FAM module. Using the same randomly-generated data as above, the equivalent hand-coded software times were: 80 microseconds, 60 microseconds, 210 microseconds, and 110 microseconds. The hardware LTC thus performs rather better than the 'best' hand-coded software, with the advantage that the hardware is modularly extensible and not tuned to a particular static dictionary. When fuzzy searches are carried out, the hardware LTC out-performs the software by about two orders of magnitude. With regard to cost, the LTC Controller is comparable in price to a single-board computer. Each FAM module is slightly more expensive than a simple DRAM board of the same capacity: the extra logic on a FAM board increases the chip count by 12 percent. For comparison, the cost per bit of FAM pseudo-CAM is about two orders of magnitude cheaper than would have been the case if the associative memory had been based on true CAM chips such as the Am99C10.

AN IMPROVED IMPLEMENTATION

In evolving from the VME-based IFS/1 architecture to the new concept of active memory, the emphasis has been to allow both storage and processing of symbolic data to be carried out relatively independently of the host computer. The active memory, as shown in Figure 1(b), thus acts rather like a co-processor. Because of the requirement for increased functionality, and because of changes in technology since 1986, our new implementation scheme replaces the microprogrammed control unit and MSI/PAL finite state machines by transputers. In brief, we now employ MIMD distributed control of upgraded versions of the previous SIMD search modules. This is cheaper and easier to implement, gives greater operational flexibility, but carries a slight performance penalty.

Figure 3 shows an overall diagram of the active memory system. At its heart are several modules labelled Transputerised CAM+RAP. These are based on upgraded versions of the IFS/1's SIMD search modules - (see for example Lavington, Robinson and Mok 1988) - and implement the repertoire of relational, set and graph primitives presented earlier. In the initial implementation, each Transputerised CAM+RAP box in Figure 3 will contain 4 Mbytes of associative memory. Further details are outside the scope of this paper. Modules labelled Tram in Figure 3 are conventional T425 transputers plus 1 Mbyte DRAM; they act as intermediate nodes for internal communication and minor processing within the active memory. The box labelled Transputerised LTC is the root node whose principal task is to convert between external lexical representations used by the host computer and Internal Identifiers. The whole active memory system is modularly extensible. The (CAM+RAP) semiconductor storage and the disc storage of Figure 4 will be integrated into a one-level associative memory by a scheme known as semantic caching (Lavington et al, 1987).

The Transputerised LTC is shown in more detail in Figure 4. It follows the general philosophy of Figure 2. However, the new transputer technology not only enhances the functionality but also reduces the total cost significantly. The controller implemented using MSI and PAL consists of two 6-layer double Euro-cards with about 120 chips, while the implementation using transputers will have only about 30 chips which can be easily accommodated on a single Euro-card. This means that the cost of the transputerized controller is only about one third of that of the former MSI and PAL implementation. However, it should be pointed out that the performance of the transputerized controller is slightly slower than the micro-programmed implementation, because the signals issued by the transputer are in terms of T-cycles while those by the micro-programmed controller are in terms of clock cycles. Experiments indicate that an average degradation of 20 to 50% should be expected. However, this degradation is not significant compared with the overall flexibility we have gained.

So far, we have deliberately avoided committing ourselves to VLSI design. However, it is interesting to note that there are opportunities within the LTC for reducing the chip count. In particular, the local search engine in each FAM is an ideal functional unit to implement as an ASIC device. It is currently implemented with two PAL16A4, three PAL12L8, one 8 bit register and two comparator devices. These eight MSI components could be reduced to a 30 pin functional comparator and a 24 pin local address generator, hence reducing the chip count by a factor of 4.

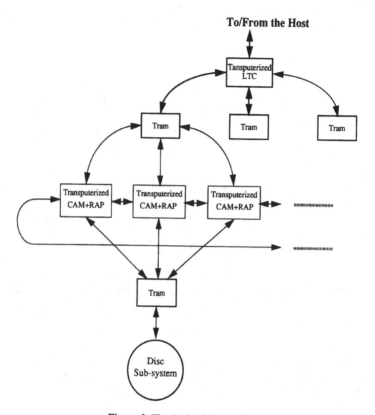

Figure 3 The Active Memory System

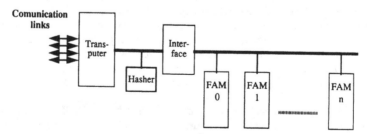

Figure 4 Details of the Transputerized LTC

CONCLUSION

The Lexical Token Converter is a flexible form of dictionary machine that can handle large quantities of symbolic data. It employs a SIMD-parallel, modularly- extensible design that significantly out-performs functionally-equivalent software. The cost of an LTC system is much the same as a single-board computer having a similar RAM capacity. The LTC uses off-the-shelf components and it may be attached to a variety of commercially-available computers, in support of AI-related applications. Since the LTC's Controller is microprogrammed/transputerised, the precise format of stored data can be varied to suit architectures which differ from the one described in this paper.

The prototype LTC system was completed in 1986. It has been evaluated as a sub- unit in a VMEbus-compatible knowledge-base server known as the Intelligent File Store. The IFS contains a large associative (ie content-addressable) memory, comprising an associatively-accessed disc front-ended by a 4Mbyte associative cache. Entries in this one-level associative memory are formed from concatenations of typed Internal Identifiers. When an ID is of type lexeme, the LTC is responsible within the IFS system for mapping strings into and out of the ID space and for ensuring the uniqueness of individual mappings. The manipulation of knowledge within the IFS, for example through operations on sets and graphs, is carried out in terms of fixed-length ID comparisons. The presence of the LTC thus helps to reduce the necessity to operate directly on objects which are represented in the real world as variable-length strings. By employing a large (2^{64}) typed ID space, a variety of primitive objects in addition to strings can be handled associatively without fear of encryption clashes.

Three production versions of the IFS and its LTC have been built. The first production system was delivered to the Artificial Intelligence Applications Institute at Edinburgh University in December 1987 where it has been used, amongst other things, as a clause retrieval unit for Prolog. The speed-up for ground clause retrieval depends upon the strategy employed to integrate the IFS's associative memory with the Prolog host computer's RAM. Since Prolog systems usually only index on first argument, the relative speed-up factor also depends upon the number and position of wild cards in a query. For a simple database of 19,604 ground clauses we have measured speed-up factors of between 2 and 2000 times, when comparing the IFS with Quintus Prolog running on a Sun 3 (Lavington, 1988). The presence of the LTC helps to keep the size of the clause base compact in the IFS's associative cache. The 19,604 tuples occupied 705,744 bytes of associative cache and a further 31,320 bytes in the LTC. For comparison, the same database occupied 1,293,480 bytes within Quintus Prolog.

ACKNOWLEDGEMENTS

The research described in this paper was supported by the Science and Engineering Research Council, the Alvey Directorate, and International Computers Ltd. Construction of a production IFS/1 was made possible by a contract from the UK Department of Trade and Industry. The IFS is very much a team effort, and the contribution of all members of the team is acknowledged.

REFERENCES

Atallah M J and Kosaraju, S R, "A Generalized Dictionary Machine for VLSI". *IEEE Transactions on Computers*, vol c-34, no 2, Feb 1985, pp 151 - 155.

Fisher, A L "Dictionary Machines with a small Number of Processors". *Proc 11 Annual Int Symp Architecture Univ Michigan*, Ann Arbor, 1984, pp 151 - 156.

Goyal, P and Narayanan, T S "Dictionary Machine with Improved Performance". *The Computer Journal*, vol 31, no 6, 1988, pp 490 - 495.

Lavington, S H, Standring, M, Jiang, Y J, Wang, C J and Waite, M E, "Hardware Memory Management for Large Knowledge Bases". *Proc of the Conference on Parallel Architectures and Languages Europe*, Eindhoven, June 1987, pp 226-241. (Published by Springer-Verlag as Lecture Notes in Computer Science, Nos. 258 & 259).

Lavington, S H, "Technical Overview of the Intelligent File Store". *Knowledge-Based Systems*, Vol.1, No.3, June 1988, pages 166 - 172.

Lavington, S H, Robinson, J and Mok, K Y, " A High Performance Relational Algebraic Processor for Large Knowledge Bases". In: *VLSI for Artificial Intelligence*, Delgado-Frias and Moore (Eds), Kluwer Academic Press, pages 133-143, 1989.

Lavington, S H and Waite,M E, "Handling AI Structures Declaratively". *Proc SERC/IED Workshop on Handling Large Knowledge Bases Declaratively*, Sept 1989. (Available from the Systems Architecture Directorate, DTI, 66-74 Victoria Street, London SW1E 6SW.

Lavington, S H and Davies,R A J, "Active memory for managing persistent objects". Presented at the *International Workshop on Computer Architectures to support security and persistence*, Bremen, FRG, May 1990. Proceedings to be published by Springer-Verlag.

Leiserson, C E, "Systolic Priority Queues", *Technical Report CMU-CS-79-115*, Carnegie-Mellon Univ, Pittsburgh, PA 1979.

Ottmann, T A, Rosenberg, A L and Stockmeyer, L J, "A Dictionary Machine for VLSI". *IEEE Transactions on Computers*, vol c-30, no 9, Sept 1982, pp 892 - 897.

Robinson, J and Lavington, S H," A Transitive Closure and Magic Functions Machine". *Proc 2nd Int Symposium on Databases in Parallel and Distributed Systems*, Dublin, July 1990, pages 44-54.

Somani, A K and Agarwal, V K "An Efficient Unsorted VLSI Dictionary Machine". *IEEE Transactions on Computers*, vol c-34, no 9, Sept 1985, pp 841 - 851.

Wang, C J, "The Lexical Token Converter - Hardware Support for Large Knowledge Based Systems". PhD thesis, University of Manchester, May 1987.

1.8 Logic Flow in Active Data

Peter S. Sapaty

V. M. Glushkov Institute of Cybernetics
Ukrainian Academy of Sciences
252207 Kiev, USSR

Abstract

A new model for highly parallel and distributed processing in huge amounts of complexly structured data has been presented. The model, called Logic Flow in Active Data, consists of the two integral parts: Active Knowledge Network keeping distributed information in an intelligent and self-organising form, and the WAVE language, spatially interpreted by the Active Knowledge Network in a fully distributed, logic-flow, asynchronous, and wavefront mode. The proposed model offers a possible universal solution for the advanced high-performance Artificial Intelligence computers and systems comprising unlimited numbers of processing elements and working efficiently without any centralised algorithmic, control, or communication facilities.

INTRODUCTION

Advanced knowledge base and Artificial Intelligence systems will comprise huge amounts of complexly structured and diverse data which may be efficiently handled and processed only when distributed among great numbers of processing elements having distributed memory and control. This task cannot be solved efficiently within the conventional algorithmic philosophy where data items are cut out from some store and processed by a separated thread of control (or by a number of them), or propagate as independent values or messages between active local procedures. *The data themselves, with complex relations between them, are becoming intelligent and active systems, they cannot be partitioned and processed by some separated facilities without losing their integrity.*

In the present paper, we describe a new, universal and integral model, based on our previous works (Sapaty 1974 - 1989), called *Logic Flow in Active Data*, for highly parallel and distributed computing in a network-structured and active data continuum where the task solving is based on a spatial activation of distributed intelligencies associated with the data. This activation process is governed on the topmost semantic level by the universal *spatial* control, wave, logic, propagating in parallel in the space and colonising the active data in an

VLSI for Artificial Intelligence and Neural Networks, Edited by J.G. Delgado-Frias and
W.R. Moore, Plenum Press, New York, 1991

79

asynchronous wavefront mode, thereby making arbitrary parallel and distributed data processing as well as creation and transformation of the very data continuum.

LOGIC FLOW IN ACTIVE DATA (LFAD) MODEL

The LFAD model (Figure 1) consists of the two integral parts: *Active Knowledge Network* (AKN), keeping arbitrary distributed data in an active self-organising form, and the *spatial WAVE language* being directly and spatially processed by the AKN in a fully distributed, logic-flow mode (the former being considered as a spatial universal computer of the latter).

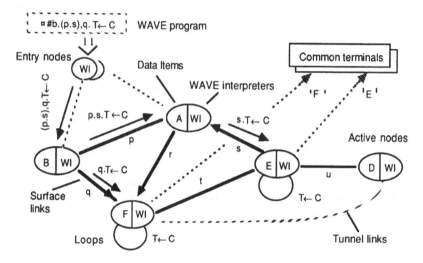

(a) Active Knowledge Network

```
wave    ::= zone {. zone}
zone    ::= sector {,sector}
sector  ::= move | action | (wave)
```

(b) The WAVE language recursive structure

Figure 1 Logic Flow in Activa Data model

AKN (shown in Figure 1a) consists of nodes and different kinds of links connecting them. The nodes keep arbitrary data items: values, properties, procedures, etc. (left part of nodes), as well as local copies of the WAVE language interpreter WI with local memories (right part of nodes), the latter making local processing or activation (if procedures) of data items, communication with other nodes as well as interpreting the WAVE programs (or their fragments) propagating in AKN space through these nodes in an asynchronous, logic-flow, wavefront mode, spreading the tails of the programs to other nodes. The links being of the three types: *surface,* reflecting semantic relations between data items (oriented or unoriented) and behaving as bi-directional channels, *tunnel,* permitting direct jumps between (remote) nodes, directly using their addresses, and *loops,* symbolising local actions in nodes with wavefronts remaining in them.

A special *entry node* (or a number of them, for multiuser applications), is added to AKN, having the same copy of the WI, through which (using only tunnel links, possibly in a broadcasting, content-addressable mode) the initial activation of AKN takes place. Nodes of AKN have unique abstract addresses in the physical continuum (the entry node has a zero address in space). A *common terminal* (or a number of them) is added to AKN for collection of the results issued autonomously by distributed and self-organising data.

The WAVE program enters AKN through the entry node, as shown in Figure 1a where the depicted concrete task is:

> starting from a node (or nodes) with a content *b,* find all nodes in AKN which are reachable from *b* using independently *p* followed by *s,* or *q* types of links, the reached nodes should issue their contents (*C*) to a common terminal (*T*).

The gradual propagation (with transformations in nodes) of this program is shown in Figure 1a, the final nodes (E and F), being active, send their contents to the terminal. The solution has been excusively by the distributed data activities spatially processing the WAVE language.

The main idea of the WAVE language is shown in Figure 1b. The WAVE program (wave program, wave formula, wave logic, or merely a *wave*) represents a sequence of some constructs called *zones,* initally applied to the entry node of AKN, and causing, zone after a zone, a wavefront propagation in space, carrying the tail of the formula. Each new zone being applied to a set of nodes of AKN, outlined by a previous zone, thus making data items and multiple dynamic control locations of wave algorithms to be *the same points* in active data space. Each zone consists of *sectors* describing peculiarities of the WAVE logic propagation in different directions from the same source (thus activating diverse processes in different parts of AKN). Sectors may describe elementary *moves* in space, local *actions* on data in nodes of AKN, or again, be arbitrary waves in brackets, thus setting a recursive defintion of a wave program, supplying it with an unlimited power of colonising and processing the distributed data space. The nested-bracketted wave structure, unlike traditional interpretation of a bracketted formula (algebraic expressions, functional languages, graph reduction, etc.) oriented on a gradual substitution of its parts by results of data processing (i.e. reduction, or *folding*), describes, quite opposite, navigational, or *unfolding* process when the wave formula covers the distributed data, being split and replicated, with losing utilised parts. *The data do not substitute the results of operations, but diverse operations themselves are covering and activating the data space as a system.*

The LFAD model, comprising AKN with the recursively defined WAVE language, spatially governing it on the topmost semantic level, offers the universal solution for advanced highly parallel computers for knowledge processing, not burdened by any centralised (algorithmic, control, or communication) resources. The wave algorithms *are not networks of cooperating processes,* as in other approaches for distributed processing (neural networks, networks of cooperating sequential processes, object-oriented programming, etc.), they represent the next, higher level of abstraction. They *are* processed, or interpreted, by data networks with some universal activities in nodes (not specific functions, as usual). Being the top level creative models, they *dynamically develop (infer) certain networks of cooperating processes* in some universal, highly intelligent but originally amorphous data space.

AKN, where each data item is associated with the WI, is only a convenient abstraction for a user, considering all the data space to be intelligent and active. For the sake of efficiency, however, a large AKN may be arbitrarily mapped onto any multiprocessor architecture, or a distributed computer network, each processor having only one copy of the WI, serving a corresponding subnetwork in its memory, and spreading the wave logic to other processors only when the data relations penetrate beyond its borders (as shown in Figure 2). No centralised resources are needed to govern the systems.

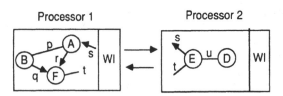

Figure 2 Partitioning of a large knowledge network

ECHO - EXTENTION OF THE WAVE LANGUAGE

General description

A syntax of the new version of the WAVE language is shown in Figure 3 where "::=" is used for a definition of syntactic categories (words in lower case letters), square brackets identify optional constructs, curly brackets embrace constructs that may be repeated zero or more times, and the vertical bar is a delimiter of alternatives. Words in capitals, and other characters, are the language symbols.

wave	::=	zone { . zone }
zone	::=	[control :] sector { , sector }
sector	::=	move | action | (wave) | ?unit [(varlist)]
control	::=	SQ | OS | OP | AS | AP | RP | WT | ET | CN | DN | DA
move	::=	[sign] unit [# [unit]] | empty
action	::=	unit operator [unit] | ⊥ | ! | ↑
unit	::=	integer | string | variable | ¤ | [echo] (wave)
operator	::=	= | ≠ | < | ≤ | ∈ | ∉ | + | − | * | / | ⊕ | ⊖ | ⊘ | & | ←
variable	::=	N { aldig } | F { aldig } | C | A | P | L | S | O | T
echo	::=	SUM | MIN | MAX | ONE | NMB | SRT | LGC

Figure 3 The WAVE language

At the top level a program in the WAVE language (a *wave*) represents a sequence $z_1.z_2. \dots .z_m$ of constructs z_i called *zones*, separated by a dot. Zones describe successive steps of the wavefront propagation through AKN, each zone producing a set of (local) goal nodes, or *Goal Set* (GS) in AKN, to which the next zone is applied (separately to each node of the GS). GS is usually a fringe set covered by a zone, whereas all nodes covered by it represent a (local) set of passed nodes, or *Passed Set* (PS) where PS⊃GS. Due to loops in the AKN model, PS_i and GS_i may include nodes, correspondingly, from PS_{i-1} and GS_{i-1}. The first zone, z_1, is applied to the entry node of AKN, producing PS_1 and GS_1.

A zone generally consists of a one or more *sectors* $s_1, s_2, \dots, s_n$ (separated by a comma), describing peculiarities of the parallel or sequential wavefront propagation from the same source in different directions through links in AKN (surface, tunnel or loops). A zone may be prefixed by a *control* construct (with a colon as a delimiter) giving it an additional interpretation while colonising the AKN space. Sectors may be simple or compound. Simple sectors may be either elementary *moves*, activating a one-link-depth wavefront propagation in AKN (parallel, if there is more than one link from a node with the same content), or elementary *actions*, describing local data processing in AKN nodes, with a wavefront looping in them. Compound sectors may be *arbitrary waves* in brackets, thus providing a nested-bracketted, recursive general definition of the wave, which permits us to express within the WAVE syntax arbitrary complex navigation and data processing procedures over the distributed AKN space. A compound sector may be also represented by a *call* construct (prefixed by "?"), causing an injection into the main wave of new subwaves at the points of its distributed interpretation in AKN (equivalent to procedure calls in conventional languages). Moves, actions, and calls are defined over *units* being either direct informational *objects* (*integers*, *strings* as arbitrary sequences of characters in quotation marks or identifiers starting from lower case letters, *variables*, or a special character "¤" used only in moves), or *accessors*. A variable content may be either a *scalar* (integer or string) or a *vector* (a sequence of scalars, which may be created only by vector operators).

The accessors (possibly prefixed by *echo*-functions) correspond to arbitrary waves in brackets and name contents of the GS produced by these waves, starting at the current node of AKN, where the wavefront currently resides. These contents (regarded together as vectors) may be processed as data in current nodes or changed by an assignment. Accessors represent a simple but powerful extension of the WAVE kernel (Sapaty 1989). Being arbitrary waves themselves, they may describe arbitrary complex addressing schemes, permitting to directly work in any node of AKN with arbitrary remote data.

The first unit in a move establishes link types which are to be passed, using a *sign*, if needed: "+" for forward, and "−" for backward propagation of oriented links. The sign does not affect unoriented links, whereas its absence permits oriented links to be passed in both directions. The "¤" is used (depending on the context) to identify either tunnel links in AKN or broadcasting from a node to all neighbouring nodes through surface links (using sign for orientation, if needed). The second unit in a move, if present (with "#" as a delimiter), sets the node contents (as strings) or their addresses in AKN (as integers) that the links must lead to. An empty move means simply the looping of a wavefront in a current node.

Actions activate an *operator* on the two units and may be either *filters* or *assignments* having the simplest syntactic representation. A filter sets some condition to be true to pass a loop, using operators "=" (equal to), "≠" (not equal to), "<" (less than), "≤" (less than or equal to), "∈" (belonging to), or "∉" (not belonging to). The latter two operate on vectors, considering them as sets. An assignment stores the result obtained from the two units into the first unit (represented as a variable or an accessor). It uses tradtional arithmetic operators on scalars ("+","−","*","/") as well as the three simple operators on vectors: "⊕" - appending a vector (or a scalar) to another one forming a new vector, "⊖" - deleting an element with a given content from a vector, and "Φ" - separation of a vector (the second unit) into its first element, or head (put into the first unit), and a tail (put into the second unit). Both units ought to be variables or accessors. The "&" is used for string concatenation, and "←" merely assigns a content of the second unit to the first one (as a variable or an accessor). The second unit may be omitted when undefined, the absent value is interpreted as a zero number or an empty string, depending on the type of operation. Assignment by the "←" of an absent value to a variable causes the deletion of this variable from AKN. There are no special data types definitions, the data types being dynamically determined and changed during operations on them.

The three special halts ("⊥", "!", "↑") are used for premature termination of the wave processes. The "⊥" and "!" block spreading of the wave from the current node ("!" additionally deleting a track of the wave propagation terminating at this node). The "↑" activates an urgent abortion of the distributed multiple wave processes which have reached the current node, deleting the whole track tree (or its subtree, headed by the *WT* control construct or produced by an accessor). In the call construct, the unit (a variable or an accessor) establishes the source from which a text of a subwave for injection into the main wave is to be taken, with setting actual parameters (if any) by a list of variables separated by a comma (*varlist*).

Spatial variables

Unlike conventional languages which presume that variables are kept together in some store, the WAVE language deals with the variables dynamically scattered throughout the AKN space during distributed asynchronous processes in it. It has three types of spatial variables: nodal, frontal, and environmental, having quite different forms of usage. The *nodal variables* appear in nodes of AKN while wavefronts reside in them, and may be subsequently shared by other wavefronts passing these nodes. They remain in nodes until the complete disappearance of all tracks associated with the nodes (i.e. until termination of all wave processes affecting these nodes). The nodal variables have dual semantics: on the one hand, they behave as usual variables naming some contents, and on the other hand, they may be regarded as temporary nodes of AKN with contents as variable meanings, these nodes being connected to the permanent nodes of AKN by temporary links having names of the variables. A wavefront may formally pass these temporary links and enter the temporary nodes, putting the latter into some GS (the possibility mainly used in accessors). The variable names, when used for naming the corresponding temporary links, must be put into quotation marks.

The *frontal variables* (if created) belong exclusively to the wavefront tokens moving in AKN, and cannot be shared (being replicated and individualised for each sector). Their life cycle terminates with an expiration of the wavefront, and they are not transferred from the main wave into accessors, although the latter, as full-scale waves on definition, may use their own frontal variables. Nodal and frontal variables may be represented by arbitrary identifiers composed from alphabetical or digital characters (*aldig*) beginning, correspondingly, with *N* or *F*.

The *environmental variables* permit a local access from the spreading wave program to different elements of AKN while wavefronts reside in nodes (some of them being read or write only). They are specified by one-letter identifiers and have the following meanings: C - a content of a current node, A - an address of a current node (read only), P - a predecessor node address (read only), L, S - correspondingly, a content and a sign of the link through which the wavefront came into the node, O - an order of the link through which the wavefront came (read only), T - a common terminal (the only non-local common resource).

Spatial control constructs and echo-functions

The control constructs supply a zone, spreading through AKN, with a variety of different control and service features. Five constructs: SQ *(Sequence)*, OS *(Or Sequential)*, OP *(Or Parallel)*, AS *(And Sequential)*, AP *(And Parallel)* split the zone into separate branches and provide their co-ordinated sequential or parallel propagation in AKN. The splitting rule is the following. If a zone explicitly consists of a number of sectors then the latter directly correspond to branches. Otherwise the zone is interpreted as an arbitrary wave and the branches are trying to be formed by splitting its head zone, with replication and attaching the common tail to each branch. If this head zone cannot be explicitly split into sectors (say, being a move or, again, an arbitrary wave), then not the current node of AKN, but nodes of the GS produced by the head zone, become sources of the branches (each one for a new branch), and all the branches are represented by the same common tail. A single branch may result if the splitting process fails. The success or failure of a branch deployment in AKN, influencing the invoking of other branches, depends on whether the GS on this branch is not empty. The resultant GS on the controlled zone is amalgamated from the GS on different branches, in accordance with the type of a control construct used (GS of only one of branches for OS and OP, union of GS on all branches for SQ, and either union of all GS or empty for AS and AP).

The other control constructs act as follows. RP *(Replicate)* repeats a successive deployment of the zone in the AKN space while it produces a non-empty GS (the same RP construct, followed by the tail of the wave, begins to deploy from each new GS), otherwise the tail is deployed from the current node. WT *(Waiting Total)* suspends the deployment of the next zone until after the termination of all processes caused by the current zone, i.e. provides a (distant) synchronisation of the distributed wave processes. ET *(Emit Total)* makes all nodes, successfully covered by the zone (the PS), to correspond to its GS (not only the fringe nodes). CN *(Create Network)*, DN *(Delete Network)*, and DA *(Delete Arcs)* supply the corresponding zone with an ability to make arbitrary changes to AKN, including the creation of arbitrary initial networks in an empty space.

The main distinguishing feature of the WAVE language is that its constructs (unlike, say, Lisp), *do not return values* to be used by other functions, the operations themselves are being spread throughout the distributed data and making data processing *directly in an active data space*. Only accessors, established in the present version of the language, permit to return (possibly remote) GS as a result to be subsequently processed in the nodes of AKN which activated the accessors. This process is based on an extended semantics of the echo-messages, used previously exclusively for the distributed control of an execution of the spatial control wave logic. The echo-functions used with accessors establish different forms of collecting information about GS, produced by the accessor. They work in parallel on the corresponding track trees, and permit to simplify the WAVE programming in many cases, as well as to decrease the overhead cased by the additional track trees when programming in the WAVE kernel. The main echo-functions are: SUM (returns the sum of all contents of a GS), MIN, MAX, ONE (return, correspondingly, minimum, maximum, or arbitrary one element of a

GS), *NMB* (returns a number of elements in a GS), *SRT* (returns a sorted list of the GS contents), *LGC* (returns a logical result: "1" if the GS is not empty, and "0" otherwise). An accessor with an echo-function omitted returns merely an unordered list of all contents of a GS.

THE TRACK SYSTEM

The syntax and semantics of the WAVE language describing a parallel colonisation of the data space permit *its direct parallel and distributed interpretation in an active data* by the data activities, in practically any kind of distributed multiprocessor environment, because no centralised algorithmic, control or communication facilities are needed. The parallel interpretation of the language, made by local copies of the wave interpreter associated with the distributed data, is based on leaving *tracks* in the distributed data space which serve both as *parse trees* of the language strings (being matched with, and formed by the active data), and as the dynamically created in space *control* and *data channels* used for distributed unwrapping of the nested wave programs, remote control of execution of the spatial control logic of the language, and accumulation of the remote data for local processing in different nodes of AKN. The track system, being generally (due to the possibility of a multisource initial search of AKN) a forest-like and spatially-linked list, distributed in the data space, permits to pass through it different kinds of *forward* and *echo messages*. The forward messages, replicated in the track nodes, include suspended tails of waves to be sent to the GS outlined by the previous constructs, values to be assigned as contents of the remote data nodes, abortion messages (for garbage deletion from AKN, or forcible termination of the wave processes), etc.

There are a number of special control echo-messages which propagate backwards through the track system, being merged in nodes. The merge rule is simple: *the resultant message from merging of any two messages is the one with the higher priority* (or the same, if the messages are identical). The main control echo-messages (listed in a sequence according to their priorities, starting with the highest one) are: "$\uparrow$" (an emergency abortion signal deleting the tracks when the corresponding halt has been reached by the wave interpreters in nodes of AKN, also causing propagation of forward abortion signals in all subordinate track trees), "$\varnothing$" (O.K. signal, indicating normal termination of the wave in this direction), "$\perp$" (O.K. signal, indicating planned forcible termination by the corresponding halt), "!" (O.K. signal, indicating planned termination by the corresponding halt with deleting tracks which are not needed more), "*" (non-O.K. signal, indicating a failure of the wave process in this direction, caused either by a negative result of the wave algorithm or by the program failure, say, due to a syntactic fault, with deletion of tracks).

The resultant echo-message leaves a track node and propagates to a parent node (also marking the link) only when messages from all descendant nodes are merged (except "$\uparrow$", immediately aborting all tracks). In the present version of the language with the accessors, a new kind of an echo-message, a *value* (*v*), is used. The values, meeting each other in nodes of the track forest during the echo processes, are merged into the resultant value in accordance with the type of an echo-function used. Information about the latter is being attached to all nodes of the tracks during forward interpretation process. Merging values with the control echo signals is based on the priority scheme described above, and the extended priority list, including values, is: $\uparrow$, v, $\varnothing$, $\perp$, !, *. Only the resultant O.K. echo-message (v, $\varnothing$, $\perp$, or !), received by a node of AKN, indicates a success of the wave deployment in the corresponding direction in a data space. After an accessor completes its function, the tracks in the data space, created by the corresponding wave, are immediately deleted. Tracks caused by the main wave are deleted only when the whole wave process terminates, or when the wave processes in certain directions fail or are forcibly halted by "!" or "↑" constructs.

THE WAVE PROGRAMMING

The wave programs describe a navigational process in the abstract data space, usually without reference to any physical resources. However, if needed, details about allocation of the data in space may be inferred from traversing their contents and relations, and subsequently used (as unique node addresses), say, in establishing priorities in parallel competitive processes, or for tunnel jumps in AKN. Two simple examples of wave programs are shown below.

Finding connected components: The task is to find in AKN, shown in Figure 4a, all q-connected components. A modification of the parallel field algorithm (Sapaty 1984b) is used where each node with an individual color (corresponding to its content) tries to colonise the whole q-component it belongs to (Figure 4b). The colonisation process fails (as for node 4)

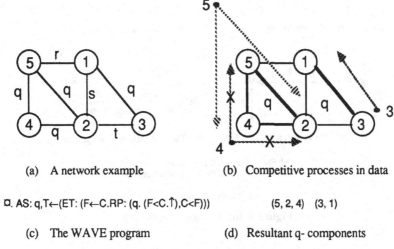

(a) A network example   (b) Competitive processes in data

◻. AS: q,T←(ET: (F←C.RP: (q. (F<C.↑),C<F)))   (5, 2, 4)   (3, 1)

(c) The WAVE program   (d) Resultant q- components

Figure 4 Finding connected components

when a node having a stronger content (node 5) has been met. Only the strongest nodes are the winners (5, and 3), raking together all nodes in their components into the resultant lists. The corresponding WAVE program is shown in Figure 4c, the result being depicted in Figure 4d. The wave program starts in each node having q-type arcs (using ◻ and *AS* constructs) with subsequent activating the accessor (the bracketted wave) whose GS should be sent to the terminal (*T*). In accessor, *ET* sets all PS to be its GS, frontal variable *F* holds the wave color, assigned to it as the starting node content (*C*), and the cyclic (*RP*) construct spreads in parallel through all *q* links, being successively repeated when the color is stronger than the node contents (*C*<*F*), aborting all the accessor if *F*<*C*, and stopping the wave otherwise. If arbitrary (non-unique) node contents are likely, then the waves must be colored by the node addresses.

Information-control task: This may be an exemplary task for distributed control of complex processes with parallel inference of the situation occured. Let the knowledge base be represented by AKN shown in Figure 5a where nodes may correspond both to passive data items and to local control procedures. The situation to be responded by the control system is

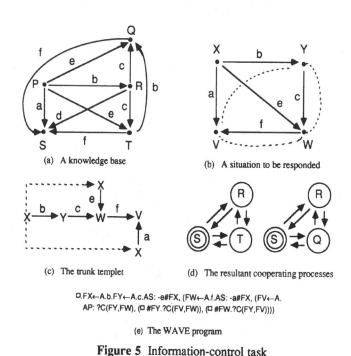

(a) A knowledge base

(b) A situation to be responded

(c) The trunk templet

(d) The resultant cooperating processes

□.FX←A.b.FY←A.c.AS: -e#FX, (FW←A.f.AS: -a#FX, (FV←A.
AP: ?C(FY,FW), (□ #FY.?C(FV,FW)), (□ #FW.?C(FY,FV))))

(e) The WAVE program

Figure 5 Information-control task

represented by an arbitrary network pattern (shown in Figure 5b), all nodes of which are free variables, links reflect relations between them. The task is to find all inclusions of the whole pattern into the AKN, and activate in parallel all the 3-cliques of processes corresponding to Y, V, and W variables (shown by dotted lines in Figure 5b). In Figure 5c the pattern is represented by a special *trunk templet* which may be directly coded in the WAVE syntax (reflecting a minimum path through all variable nodes). This templet, initially injected into all nodes of AKN, is trying to be successively matched with the distributed data (from the left to the right), with the same content of X repeatedly used, finding in parallel two complete inclusions into the AKN in Figure 5a, and producing the two resultant cliques of processes shown in Figure 5d. The corresponding wave program is shown in Figure 5e where frontal variables *FX, FY, FW, FV* successively accumulate addresses of nodes of the AKN which are successfully matched together by the templet. *AS* is used twice for conditional prolongation of the templet matching if branches *e* and *a*, leading to the earlier determined content of X (*FX* variable is used), succeed. When the last node V of the templet succeeds (indicating a success of the whole templet), it activates in parallel (*AP* construct) its local procedure, as well as procedures in nodes matched by Y and W variables, as their contents (tunnel jumps in AKN are used, by addresses in *FY* and *FW*), with exchange of their addresses for subsequent direct communication of the procedures (the latter may be represented in the WAVE or in any other language, say, OCCAM). As the result of this program, the two independent 3-cliques of cooperating processes are activated, with the node S as their supervisor (in both cases).

The WAVE language has been successfully used for highly parallel and distributed programming of the most different classes of problems on complexly structured data, including classical tasks of the graph and network theory, optimisation and computations on networks, parallel inference on semantic networks, complex information acquisition and retrieval in advanced knowledge base systems. As the main routines of the distributed data processing are imbedded into the self-organisation of data within the LFAD model, the WAVE programs are extremely compact, issuing at the same time a maximally possible parallelism in distributed computing. Some (simplified) basic network search mechanisms, often used for a distributed logic-flow programming, are shown in Table 1, where the wave processes are initially activated in some node *a* of AKN (or *a* and *b*, for a multisource search).

Table 1 Main network distributed search mechanisms

Kind of search	WAVE program
asynchronous	□#a.RP:(N=.N←1.□)
selective	□#a.RP:(N=.N←1.p,q,-r)
evolvent	□#a.RP:(F⊕A.□.A∉F)
multisource	□#a,□#b.RP:(N=.N←1.□)
synchronous	□#a.WT:((WT:□).□).□
depth-sequential	□#a.F←'(N=.N←1.SQ:(□.?F))'.?F
pipeline	□#a.N←'(F+1.(RP:(□.N1<F.N1←F)),?N)'.?N

In the *asynchronous* search, the spanning tree of AKN is formed by the cyclic (*RP*) construct propagating through all kinds of links between nodes (□ construct), marking nodes (using the nodal *N* variable) for blocking the cycling.

The *selective* asynchronous search differs from the previous one by using certain types of links, possibly setting orientation (say, *p,q,* or *-r* in Table 1).

The *evolvent* search finds in parallel all simple paths in AKN (without repetition of nodes) thus receiving the spanning tree with possible overlapping of different branches in AKN space. The *F* variable is used to accumulate the passed paths.

The *multisource* search permits to start the wave processes simultaneously in different nodes of AKN. One of its varieties is the *associative* search, starting in parallel in all nodes.

The *synchronous* search makes the spanning tree of AKN to be formed synchronously and in parallel, step by step, starting from a certain node. There is a variety of possibilities to do so in the WAVE language. In Table 1 only the simplest local solution is represented, with the three steps using the nested *WT* construct.

The *depth-sequential* search creates exclusively sequentially all the depth spanning tree of AKN, using the recursively unfolding in space call construct (prefixed by "?"), and attaching to all nodes of the tree the *SQ* construct causing sequential deployment of branches. The frontal *F* variable holds a subwave body (as a string) to be recursively injected into the main wave.

The *pipeline* search permits to organise the pipeline supervision of AKN, regularly erupting the wave strings (following one after the other in space in a pipelined fashion), each making an individual asynchronous search of AKN, with a stronger color than the previous ones (the *F* variable is used for colors, and the *N1* variable for current marking the nodes). The subwave to be recursively injected is represented by the nodal *N* variable.

A great deal of other distributed network search mechanisms, as well as their combinations, are used for parallel soving of complex problems on graphs and networks. All of them work in AKN without any centralisation, in a fully distributed manner.

Although the wave programs, describing parallel data processing directly in terms of data contents and relations between them, are often much simpler than in conventional languages, a translation into the WAVE lanugage (designed as a machine language for direct implementation in a distributed hardware) from other user-oriented formalisms may be welcome. For example, the AKN in figure 5a, written as a set of facts: $a(p,s). e(p,q). b(p,r). e(p,t). d(r,s). c(r,t). c(r,q). b(t,q). f(q,s). f(t,s)$, and the network pattern in Figure 5b as a goal clause with free variables: $?- b(X,Y), c(Y,W), e(X,W), f(W,V), a(X,V)$, can be easily converted into the network forms by mere interpreting binary predicates as arcs connecting (constant or variable) unique nodes, with subsequent direct coding in the WAVE syntax.

CONCLUSIONS

We have presented a new and universal model for highly parallel and distributed processing in very large knowledge base and Artificial Intelligence systems, comprising the Active Knowledge Network, AKN, keeping arbitrary data in a self-organising form, and the spatial WAVE language, directly interpreted by the AKN in a logic-flow mode. The WAVE language is *the only language* through which an access to AKN can be made. It can create in parallel arbitrary AKN in an empty space, make arbitrary changes in it, or solve on it arbitrary computational or logical problems in parallel. The overall spatial governing of AKN in the WAVE language may range from the top level activation and coordination of the procedures associated with distributed data, to the tiny details of parallel processing in passive information.

The LFAD model allows us to build highly parallel computers for AI applications with the intelligence imbedded into the deepest levels of their architectures, thus permitting their functioning in a fully distributed and self-organising mode. Such computers, comprising large numbers of processing elements, may consist of the two integral parts: *an interpretation network (IN)*, and *an access network (AN)*, the former keeping a large AKN in a distributed form and spatially interpreting the WAVE language, and the latter making a distributed multiuser access to the IN, collecting results flowing out of the IN, as well as handling external memory devices (Sapaty 1988, 1989). No centralised algorithmic, control, or communication facilities are needed for efficient functioning of such computers within the LFAD model.

ACKNOWLEDGEMENTS

This work has been carried out within the Alexander von Humboldt Fellowship programme, FRG. Many thanks to my sponsor in Germany, Prof. Dr. R. Vollmar, to Dr. W.R. Moore, Oxford University, and to Dr. José G. Delgado-Frias, SUNY at Binghamton, for the support and fruitful discussions of the presented ideas, to Henning Fernau and Peter Borst, Karlsruhe University, for cooperation in formalising and implementing the WAVE language interpreter on a SUN network, as well to Doris Neuerer for help in preparing this paper.

REFERENCES

Sapaty, P.S., "On possibilities of organising the intercomputer dialogue in ANALITIC and FORTRAN languages", *Preprint 74-29, Inst. Cybernetics Press*, Kiev, 1974 (in Russian).

Sapaty, P.S., "On efficient structural realisation of operations on semantic networks", *Proc.USSR Academy of Sciences, Technical Cybernetics*, no. 5, 1983 (in Russian).

Sapaty, P.S., "A WAVE approach to the languages for semantic networks processing", *Proc. Int. Conf. on Knowledge Representation: Artificial Intelligence*, Kiev, 1984 (in Russian).

Sapaty, P.S., "Active informational field as a model of structural solving tasks on graphs and networks", *Proc. USSR Academy of Sciences, Tech. Cyber.*, no. 5, 1984 (in Russian).

Sapaty, P.S., "A WAVE language for parallel processing of semantic networks", *Computers and Artificial Intelligence*, vol. 5, no. 4, 1986, Bratislava.

Sapaty, P.S., "The WAVE-0 language as a framework of the navigation structures for knowledge bases using semantic networks", *Proc. USSR Academy of Sciences, Technical Cybernetics*, no. 5, 1986 (in Russian).

Sapaty, P.S., "Parallel processing for knowledge representation", in *Infotech State of the Art Report on Parallel Processing*, Pergamon Press, England, 1987.

Sapaty, P.S., "WAVE-1: a new ideology of parallel processing on graphs and networks", *Future Generations Computer Systems*, vol. 4, North-Holland 1988.

Sapaty, P.S., "The WAVE model for advanced knowledge processing", *Report no. OUEL 1803/89*, University of Oxford 1989.

1.9 Parallel Analogue Computation for Real-Time Path Planning

Lionel Tarassenko   Gillian Marshall‡   Felipe Gomez–Castaneda†
Alan Murray†

Department of Engineering Science
Oxford University, Oxford, OX1 3PJ, UK

†Department of Electrical Engineering
Edinburgh University, EH9 3JL, UK

‡Also: RSRE, St. Andrews Road, Great Malvern
Worcester, WR14 3PS

Abstract

This paper introduces the concept of a resistive grid for solving the path planning problem for a mobile robot in real time. The robot's environment is mapped onto a grid of hexagonal or rectangular cells of uniform resistance except that obstacles are represented by regions of infinite resistance. If current is injected at the nodes corresponding to the robot's present position and its goal, the path of maximum current will give a guaranteed path to the goal. The method is particularly amenable to implementation in VLSI. A test chip using novel amorphous silicon technology has been fabricated.

INTRODUCTION

The use of resistive grids for parallel analogue computation was first suggested by Horn (1974) in the mid-seventies to find the inverse of a discrete approximation to the Laplacian. Since then, the resistive grid idea has been exploited by Mead, for example in his silicon retina (Mead 1988) or for computing optical flow (Hutchinson *et al* 1988). Although these resistive grids cannot be said to be neural networks in the conventional sense, they also perform parallel *analogue* computation and they have the same advantages, in terms of speed and fault–tolerance, as any hardware realisation of neural networks.

The resistive grid path planner described in this paper is one of the modules at the heart of a VLSI neural network system which we are developing for real–time robot navi-

VLSI for Artificial Intelligence and Neural Networks, Edited by J.G. Delgado-Frias and
W.R. Moore, Plenum Press, New York, 1991

93

gation. The problem of path planning in this context is the computation of a collision–free route in a structured indoor environment from the robot's initial (or present) position to a goal. As the robot's working environment may change rapidly, for example as people or other vehicles move in the workspace, a *real time* solution to the path planning problem is required. In our navigation system, the obstacles are detected by another neural network module (not described in this paper) which associates certain motor behaviours with different types of sensory input data, for example the taking of evasive action when a moving object is approaching the robot at speed (*path refinement*). Information about obstacles is fed to the resistive grid path planner approximately once every second and this allows the path to be *reconfigured* if required.

PATH PLANNING WITH RESISTIVE GRIDS

In our approach, the robot's environment is mapped onto a resistive grid of hexagonal or rectangular cells. Each resistor in the grid can only have one of two values: R_∞ if it is part of a region corresponding to an obstacle, R_0 otherwise. Current is injected at the node which corresponds to the robot's present position (P) and it leaves at the node corresponding to its goal (G). Since obstacles are represented by regions of infinite resistance, the current flowing between P and G is forced to flow around them.

The method is best understood (Tarassenko and Blake, 1990) by considering the continuous equivalent of the resistive grid (for example, a sheet of material of uniform conductivity in which holes have been cut to represent the obstacles). All the current streamlines from P to G will skirt around the obstacles; thus the tracking of a streamline will produce a guaranteed collision–free path from source to goal. For simple cases such as circularly symmetric conductivity distributions in 2D, Laplace's equation can be solved in order to calculate the value of the potential ϕ at every point within the workspace. Following a current streamline is then simply a matter of performing gradient descent in ϕ.

It is not possible, however, to solve Laplace's equation analytically for realistic environments. With the resistive grid, the problem is discretised and mapped onto a hardware representation which can be implemented in VLSI. As soon as a constant current source is connected to the grid, the resistive network settles into the state of least power dissipation and the node voltages can be read out (hardware solution of Kirchoff's equations instead of Laplace's equations for the continuous case). The path from P to G can then be tracked from *local* voltage measurements: for each node, the next move is identified by measuring the voltage drop ΔV between that node and its nearest neighbours (6 measurements for a hexagonal grid) and selecting the node which corresponds to the *maximum* value of ΔV.

Our results so far indicate that this approach produces paths which are often close to being optimal (in terms of the length of the path). Although the method relies only on *local* measurement of voltages, it is not affected by the problem of local minima (and hence trapping of the mobile robot) as with other path planning techniques. This is shown in Figure 1, for example, where the robot is initially placed at the centre of a maze (P) and a path has to be found to the goal (G). The dotted line shows the (optimal) path computed as the robot moves towards the goal: at every succesive node, the current source is re–

applied and ΔV_{max} is identified locally by measuring the voltage drop between that node and its 6 nearest neighbours. The solid line is the result given by the same method but from a *single application* of the current source at P and G.

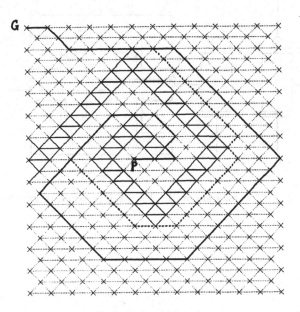

Figure 1. Path from middle of maze

VLSI IMPLEMENTATION

The VLSI implementation of the resistive grid method will allow us to solve the path planning for complex environments *in real time*. MOS switches are ideal implementations of the binary resistors in the grid. Each transistor can be programmed to be either open (R_∞) or closed (R_0) from a RAM cell connected to its gate. A static RAM cell is shown in Figure 2, but a dynamic RAM would do equally well if suitable refresh circuitry was also included.

Applying the voltage

Any point on the grid could represent the robot's goal, and so it should be possible to connect any node to ground. Similarly, any point could represent the robot's present position, and it should therefore also be possible to connect any node to the positive power rail, V_{DD}. If each node is given a unique (x, y) address, then a suitable subcircuit is shown in Figure 3.

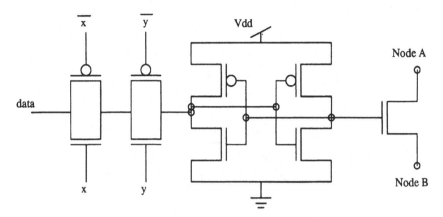

Figure 2. Circuit diagram of SRAM switch attached to gate of transistor

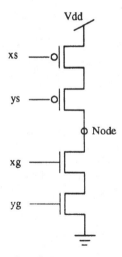

Figure 3. pull-up and pull-down transistors at each node

PMOS transistors are used as pull-ups, since these pass 5V better than NMOS. Conversely, NMOS transistors are used as pull-downs, since they pass 0V better. This means that the voltage difference between source and goal is maximised. The y-pull-up and pull-down transistors can be shared between nodes with the same y-addresses, which reduces the number of transistors to two *per node*.

Reading out the path

A preliminary study has been carried out to investigate the feasibility of computing the robot's path entirely in hardware, ie. sensing the six voltages nearest to the source node and finding ΔV_{max} with a set of comparators. The node voltages need to be buffered before they can be read out, using for example a source-follower (Figure 4). This circuit couples input to output through the gate of a transistor and hence draws no current. The source-follower has a gain of less than one and is not linear over all its operating range, but it does have a monotonic transfer function and so is adequate for our purposes. Moreover, it only requires two transistors per node. A more ideal voltage buffer (e.g. an op-amp) would contain many more transistors and require too much silicon area per node.

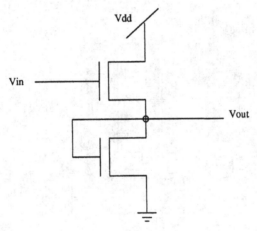

Figure 4. Source-follower buffer

The intelligence needed to determine the path of maximum current from P to G can be supplied off-chip, in which case the VLSI resistive grid is simply used as a hardware solution of Kirchoff's equations. The buffered node voltages are demultiplexed on-chip and fed to a 10-bit A/D converter which is then read by an off-chip microprocessor. Since a new path only needs to be computed approximately every second, interpolation schemes can be incorporated in the software to generate smooth paths from the discrete grid.

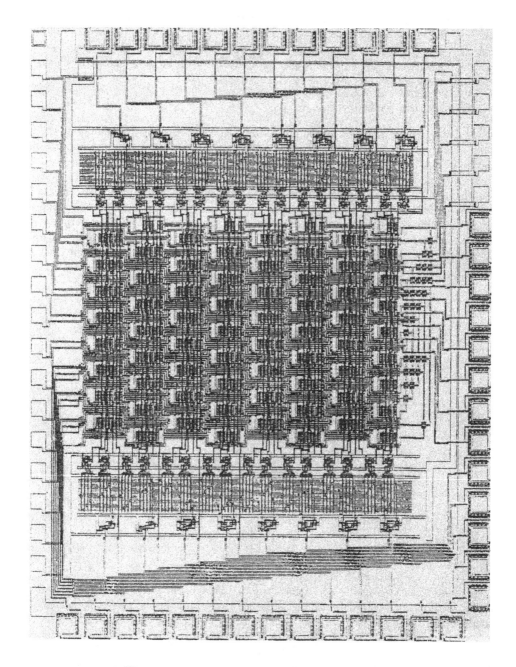

Figure 5. Layout of the amorphous silicon chip

Amorphous silicon

An alternative approach to implementing the resistive grid path planner in VLSI is to use the novel amorphous silicon (α-Si) technology being developed at Edinburgh and Dundee Universities (Rose *et al*, 1990). Recent work has led to a two–terminal α-Si device that acts as an *analogue* resistor, with values electronically programmable (*and re–programmable*) between 1KΩ and 5MΩ. With programmable analogue resistors, it is possible to devise a feedback scheme whereby the path of maximum current is enhanced to the detriment of other sub–optimal paths. After initial application of the potential between P and G, the node voltages are read out and the resistors (other than obstacles) are re–programmed so that their *conductance* is increased in proportion to the voltage drop across them. If the procedure is repeated several times, more and more current will gradually flow through the desired path, thereby making its identification much easier.

For the moment, however, we have been concentrating on developing a test chip without implementing the feedback scheme (ie. the resistors are programmed to be either 1KΩ or 5MΩ). The chip layout is shown in Figure 5. Neighbouring α-Si resistors are connected to each other and to the rest of the hexagonal array by pass transistors. A second network is used to apply programming pulses to the terminal nodes of individual resistors and to read the node voltages out once the potential has been applied between P and G. One of the problems still to be overcome is that the amorphous silicon devices require that a 12–13V "forming" pulse be applied before they can be used. Small-geometry CMOS processes are not normally robust against such potentials, and the test chip of Figure 5 is therefore implemented in 5μ NMOS technology.

CONCLUSION

We have shown that the computationally–intensive task of path planning for a mobile robot can be solved in real time with a resistive grid method. False solutions, in the form of local minima, do not occur. Most importantly, perhaps, is the ease with which the path planner can be implemented in VLSI. The architecture is regular, the "unit cell" tiny, and the resultant integration densities high. It is easy to envisage chips with tens of thousands of grid points providing an accurate representation of a robot's environment, while demanding little space or power in the robot frame.

REFERENCES

Horn, B.K.P. "Determining lightness from an image" *Computational Graphics & Image Processing*, **3**, 277–299, 1974.

Hutchinson, J., Koch, C., Luo, J. and Mead, C.A. "Computing motion using analog and binary resistive networks" *IEEE Computers*, **21**, 52–63, 1988.

Mead, C.A. and Mahowald, M.A. "A silicon model of early visual processing" *Neural Networks*, **1**, 91–97, 1988.

Rose, M.J., Hajto, J., LeComber, P.G., Gage, S.M., Choi, W.K., Snell, A.J., Owen, A.E. "Amorphous Silicon Analogue Memory Devices" *J Non–Cryst. Sol.*, **115**, 168–170, 1989.

Tarassenko, L. and Blake, A. "Analogue computation of collision–free paths" *OUEL Report 1858/90*, Oxford University Engineering Department, 1990.

2.1 An Extended Prolog Instruction Set for RISC Processors

Andreas Krall

Technische Universität Wien
Argentinierstraße 8
A-1040 Wien

Abstract

Conventional microprocessors and RISC processors do not adequately support the implementaton of logic programming languages. This paper presents extensions of a RISC processors's instruction set to enable a simplified and more efficient implementation of Prolog. The extensions are very general so that they can be used for most processors.

The first part of the paper gives a short introduction to Prolog implementation techniques. The most common abstract machines are the Warren Abstract Machine and the Vienna Abstract Machine. Both can be implemented using interpretative and compiling techniques. To enable efficient implementation the instruction set of RISC processors should be enhanced by instructions for sequential memory access, instructions for tag handling and some special instructions. Those instructions can easily be added to existing processors without increasing the cycle time or the cycle count. The extensions are compared to existing microprocessors and special purpose hardware.

INTRODUCTION

For six years the main research of our group at the Technical University of Vienna has been the implementation of logic programming languages. Following the Warren Abstract Machine (Warren 1983) we developed the Vienna Abstract Machine (Krall 1987, Krall and Neumerkel 1990). All of our implementations are done in software on standard processors. In order to speed up the execution we designed a special purpose Prolog processor and developed an assembler, a C compiler and a software emulator for this processor. We estimated the development cost and execution speed gain of such a processor implemented in VLSI and recognized that a compiled Prolog would be faster on a standard processor with current technology than a special purpose Prolog processor with a year-old technology.

VLSI for Artificial Intelligence and Neural Networks, Edited by J.G. Delgado-Frias and
W.R. Moore, Plenum Press, New York, 1991

101

So we decided to extend the instruction set of a standard RISC processor by instructions which enable a faster execution of compiled and interpreted Prolog programs or can reduce the size of a compiled Prolog program. The instructions have been extracted from the macro processor versions of our Prolog interpreters and compilers. This macro processor version has been designed to develop a Prolog system for a new processor by changing only about 200 lines of assembler code. The instructions are grouped into memory access, tag handling and special instructions. New instructions are introduced only if they can be executed in one cycle. If an instruction requires two cycles, it is split into two. Our instruction set extensions are oriented towards the MIPS R2000 (Kane 1987) and Motorola 88000 (Motorola 1988) instruction sets.

PROLOG IMPLEMENTATION TECHNIQUES

There are two ways to implement programming languages: the compiler approach and the interpreter approach. Both approaches can be applied to the different abstract machines, i.e. the WAM (Warren Abstract Machine) and the VAM (Vienna Abstract Machine).

The WAM corresponds to the implementation model of conventional procedural languages. A set of Prolog clauses is treated in the same way as a procedure of a conventional programming language. For each procedure call a stack frame is created containing the local variables and control information. Parameters are passed through a register interface. The caller copies its arguments into the argument registers. The callee unifies the variables in its stack frame with the values contained in the argument registers. The WAM can be implemented with interpreter techniques as well as compiler techniques.

Our approach is the VAM. The VAM does not separate unification into parameter passing and parameter unifying. To achieve this, the VAM uses two instruction pointers (program counters), one pointing to the code of the caller, the other pointing to the code of the callee. The caller´s instructions and operands are fetched using the caller´s instruction pointer, and the callee´s instructions and operands are fetched using the callee´s instruction pointer. The instruction fetch, instruction decoding and the unification of the operands can be done in parallel. The VAM is well suited for interpretation but compilation is also applicable combining instructions at compile time and reducing the two instruction pointers to one.

Interpreters

Because of the high semantic gap between the Prolog programming language and the hardware, interpreters are usually used for its implementation. An interpreter keeps the internal representation of Prolog programs small. Furthermore, Prolog programs can be distributed in internal representation for different hardware architectures, if the interpreters use the same internal representation. Optimizations are restricted to a single clause to enable dynamic database updates and fast translation of clauses into their internal representation. A disadvantage is that the instructions cannot be very specialized while keeping the size of the interpreter small.

In general an interpreted program runs about four times slower than a compiled program. This is because instruction and operand fetch and decode uses software, whereas in a compiled program this is done by hardware. For instruction and operand fetch the memory is accessed sequentially. Instructions are fetched via a pointer and the pointer is incremented. Decoding is usually implemented using the switch statement of the C programming language. A C compiler translates the switch statement into a boundary check and a jump to an address fetched from a jump address table.

A faster instruction fetch and decoding can be done using assembler and direct threaded code (see Bell 1973). In a direct threaded code interpreter the instruction serves as the jump address. Therefore direct threaded code eliminates the boundary check and a memory access (the fetch of the jump address via the table). There remains only the instruction fetch, the jump and the increment of the pointer.

Compilers

Compilers translate Prolog programs to machine code. Compilers have better possibilites for optimizations. They generally assume that programs are static and perform type inference, partial evaluation, abstract interpretation and eliminate superfluous instructions. They produce very fast, but also very large code (about five to ten times the size of interpreted code). If the code becomes too big subroutine calls must be generated instead of expanded code. Sequential access of structures is similar to that of interpreters, only instruction/operand fetch and decoding are eliminated.

Resolution and unification

Prolog programs execute unifications most of the time. Unification compares two terms. If both terms are constants, the unification succeeds if the constants are equal. If one term is an unbound variable and the second term is a constant, the constant is assigned the variable. If both terms are unbound variables, the variables are bound together. If both terms are structures, the unification succeeds if the unification of all subterms of the structure succeeds. Therefore, the unification is implemented as a comparison of values contained in variables combined with an assignment.

In about half the cases unification is reduced to a single assignment (at the first occurence of a variable). If one term is a constant, the variable must be tested against the unbound, reference or value tag. First the value contained in the variable is compared with the constant. If they are not equal, tests for unbound or reference tags are done. If both unification partners are variables, the full unification algorithm is executed. The tags of variables must be checked against unbound, reference, list, structure or constant. If they are lists or structures, the unification routine is called recursively for all structure arguments.

If the unification fails, the execution is reset to a so called choicepoint. A choicepoint contains the registers to be reset and a pointer to the trail stack. The trail stack contains the address of variables to be reset.

THE EXTENDED INSTRUCTION SET

We have ported our Prolog interpreters to different hardware architectures and evaluated the different architectures. For the development of a Prolog RISC processor the same design principles (as descibed by Patterson 1985) are applied as for general purpose RISC processors. A Prolog RISC processor is based on a load/store architecture and should have 32 registers. Due to the recursive nature of Prolog register windows (like used in the SPARC processor, Sun 1987) are not practical. Two source operands and one destination operand should be supported by arithmetic and logical operations. Loading of values from memory and conditional and computed branches are more frequent than in conventional languages. Therefore, there should only be one delay slot after a load. Branches have one delay slot, but branch prediction should be used if possible. Instructions for sequential accessing memory and for manipulating tags need to be added.

Memory access instructions

Prolog accesses data structures sequentially. Furthermore, Prolog interpreters access the intermediate code sequentially. An autoincrement indirect addressing mode for the first source operand fullfills the requirements for a sequential memory access perfectly. In general an autoincrement addressing mode increases the number of cycles for the instruction while waiting for the data to become valid. A solution is to introduce one or two more pipeline stages for address calculation and memory access (like in the Motorola 68040, Edenfild et al. 1990). The penalty is the increase of delay slots for branch instructions, which is worse for Prolog than for procedural programming languages.

Our solution is to combine the autoincrement indirect addressing mode with prefetching of the next memory cell. Each general purpose register in the processor is coupled with a prefetch register and a valid tag. The prefetch register holds the value of the memory location the general purpose register points to. The valid tag indicates, if the values in the prefetch register the general purpose register corresponds. In a processor which uses register scoreboarding, this prefetching is implicit and hidden from the programmer. Every time an autoincrement indirect addressing mode is used, a value is prefetched from memory. So only the first instruction in a sequential memory accessing instruction sequence is delayed and the other instructions are executed in one cycle.

In a processor without scoreboarding, like the MIPS processor, the prefetch is made explicit to the programmer. A prefetch instruction is introduced. A prefetch instruction is an add instruction (address calculation instruction), which stores the result of the address calculation in the general purpose register and loads the prefetch register from memory. After one cycle the value becomes valid in the prefetch register. Now the memory can be accessed sequentially by instructions using autoincrement indirect addressing modes. If a prefetch accesses an invalid memory location, an exception is raised only, if the value in the prefetch register is to be used later on. Because the value of the computation and the incremented register must be written back to the register file, the register file must have two write ports. To ease the implementation of the numerous Prolog stacks, the store instruction should additionally support an autodecrement indirect addressing mode.

For implementing intermediate code interpreters the autoincrement indirect addressing mode must be available for control instructions too (direct threaded code). Two instructions are needed: jmp (Rn)+ and jmp (Rn)+, Rm. The first instruction is only a special case of the the the second instruction using regiser zero for Rm and is used for absolute direct threaded code. The second instruction uses the sum of register Rm and the value register Rn points to as a jump address. The second form of the jump instruction is needed for relative direct threaded code. The register Rm then contains the base address of the interpreter. This instruction is also needed for the implementation of the VAM. The VAM has two instruction pointers. The instruction fetch and decode can be implemented using an add and a jmp instruction: add help,(instrptr1)+,baseaddress; jmp (instrptr2)+,help.

Another possibility to support relative direct threaded code is an autoincrement indirect branch instruction (program counter relative). But this would require two additions for branch address calculation (add offset, program counter and autoincrement indirect value) and one additional instruction for a two pointer direct threaded code. All autoincrement instructions are not only useful for implementing Prolog, they are necessary for all interpretative languages, for string manipulation and for numerical applications using arrays and vectors.

Tag manipulation instructions

The most important instructions for speeding up Prolog implementations are instructions for tag decoding. Although unbound variables, references to variables, lists, structures and constants (integers, atoms, nil) are the commonly used types in Prolog, the types can not be restricted to this set because of extensions like floating point numbers, big numbers or constraints. Therefore the design of tag and value field should be left to the language designer. Fixed sized, variable sized or split tag fields are possible at any position in a machine word.

The branch instruction must be able to compare two registers. It is not sufficient for a branch to compare a register to zero. The most common comparison is between two values. Furthermore, unbound variables are commonly represented by self referencing pointers. The test for unbound needs comparison of registers. The compare and branch instruction must support autoincrement indirect addressing mode, due to the comparison of intermediate code operands and string comparisons needed for the string database.

Two jump instructions are introduced for fixed sized tag fields. The instruction switchtag Rs,tagstart,tagsize assumes that a table with 16 bit offsets directly follows the instruction. Tagsize bits are extracted from register Rs at bit position tagstart; the extracted bits are shifted 1 bit left, and added to the program counter. The offset at the computed address is fetched from memory, shifted 2 bits left and added to the program counter. This branch has two delay slots due to the memory access. This instruction is also used to implement the C switch statement. The jmptag Rs,tagstart,tagsize,shiftfactor instruction has only one delay slot. It shifts the extracted bits shiftfactor bits left and adds them to the program counter.

Variable sized and split tags can be supported by a three and four way branch. The three way branch instruction distinguishes between less than, equal to or greater than zero. It can be used for a fast decoding of value, reference or unbound, if unbound variables are represented as zero. The four way branch b00/01/10/11 Rs,tagstart,offset01,offset10,offset11 distinguishes depending on the two bits at position tagstart using one of the three offsets. The disadvantage of this instruction is that only five or six bits can be used for the branch offsets. All branches have one delay slot.

Special instructions

The following instructions are more specific to Prolog and are used mainly for an efficient control flow. Double word load, store and move instructions are often needed. The frame pointer and progam counter are always stored and loaded as a pair. Choicepoint creation and backtracking store and load at least six registers. A WAM additionally stores the argument registers, and a VAM stores the local variable registers. Therefore double register load/stores nearly double the memory throughput. The efficiency of shallow backtracking can be increased, if the creation of a choicepoint can be delayed by an instruction which copies selected registers of one half of the register file to the other half.

The min and max instructions are useful for stack adjustments. The min (max) instruction sets the destination register to the minimum (maximum) of the two source registers. The check instruction simpifies the check, if a variable needs to be stored on the trail stack. It checks, if the destination register lies between two registers or is greater than a third register. This instruction can also be used for general bound checks, using zero for some source registers.

Summary

The following table summarizes the above presented instructions. If not especially noted the size is a 32 bit word. The extension .b specifies a byte memory operand, the extension .h specifies a half word memory operand and the extension .d specifies a double word operand. Byte and halfword operands are sign extended to word size.

arith/log.bh	Rd,(Rs1)+,Rs2	postincrement indirect addressing
fetch.bh	Rd,address	load Rd with adress and prefetch word
store.bh	Rd,-(Rs)	predecrement store
jmp.bh	(Rs1)+,Rs2	direct threaded jmp
beq/ne	Rs1,Rs2,offset16	branch with register comparison
beq/ne.bh	(Rs1)+,Rs2,offset16	branch with memory comparison
switchtag	Rs,start5,size5	table jump
jmptag	Rs,start5,size5,shift5	computed program counter relative jump
bnz/np/zp	Rs,offsset11,offset11	three way branch
b00/01/10/11	Rs,t5,o5,o5,o6	four way branch dependent on two bits
load/ store.d	Rd,address	register pair load/store
movedreg	Rd,Rs	register pair move
copylow/high	mask16	move register file half
min/max	Rd,Rs1,Rs2	minimum/maximum function
check	Rd,Rs1,Rs2,Rs3	(Rd>Rs3)|((Rd<Rs2)&(Rd>Rs1))
b(no)check	offset16	branch if check flag is (not) set

Our estimates have shown that these extensions speed up interpreters between 50 and 100% and compilers between 30 and 50%. The higher speed up of interpreters is due to the more efficient instruction fetch and decode using the direct threaded jump instruction. Using the extended instruction set a high optimized inner loop of the deterministic append predicate can be executed in 6 cycles per logical inference.

COMPARISON WITH DEDICATED PROLOG HARDWARE

There are different approaches building dedicated hardware for Prolog. One approach is to build special processors in discrete logic or VLSI like the PSI (Nakashima and Nakajima 1987), the PLM (Dobry et al 1984), the Warren processor (Tick and Warren 1984), the CHI (Konagaya et al. 1989), the IPP (Abe et al. 1987) and the HPM (Nakazaki et al. 1985), another approach is to microprogram an existing processor like the VAX 8600 (Gee et al. 1987) or compile Prolog to microcode (Fagin et al. 1985). Yet other related approaches are to build an unification coprocessor (Woo 1985), to build a very specialized RISC processor (Mills 1989), to use the SPUR, an existing general purpose Lisp oriented RISC processor (Borriello et al. 1987), to use a standartd microprocessor (Mulder and Tick 1987) or just to define an intermediate language (Van Roy 1989).

The special purpose Prolog processors all have a similar architecture. They are micropro-grammed processors oriented to the WAM. The macro instructions are the instructions of the WAM. Small differences are in memory architecture, tag handling and micro instructions. They have the same advantages and disadvantages as interpreters fully implemented in software. The object code size of compiled programms is very small, but the instructions are fixed. An optimizing Prolog compiler generating code for a general purpose processor outperforms a Prolog processor due to instruction elimination and more efficient use of the instruction set.

A unification coprocessor performs very fast the general unification, but there is an overhead communicating with the host processor. Usually the unification can be reduced to an assignment or a comparison. The general unification can be performed between 5 and 10 cycles and contribute to only 5% of the dynamic executed WAM instructions (see Touati and Despain 1987).

The approach of the Low RISC is similar to our's. The main difference is that the Low RISC has only seven instructions and is no general purpose processor. There as an overhead communicating with a host processor. The tag usage is predefined. Furthermore the Low RISC does not support interpreters.

Although designed for LISP the SPUR has an similar instruction set. Missing are the sequential memory access instructions and the multiway branches. Fast tag testing is supported but wasting memory.

CONCLUSION

An extended RISC processor supports interpreters, compilers and mixed systems. The inner loop of the deteministic append can be executed in six cycles. Considering the technology gap of special purpose Prolog processors and the hardware and software costs more attention should be payed to extended instruction sets for all purpose processors.

REFERENCES

Abe, S., Bandoh, T., Yamaguchi S., Kurosawa, K. and Kiriyama, K., "High Performance Integrated Prolog Processor IPP", *14th Annual International Symposium on Computer Architecture*, pp.100-107, 1987

Bell. J.R., "Threaded Code", *Communincations of the ACM*, vol. 16(6), pp. 370-372, 1973

Borriello, G., Cherenson, A., Danzig, P. and Nelson, M., "RISCS vs. CISCS for Prolog: A Case Study", *Architectural Support for Programming Languages and Operating Systems*, SIGPLAN 22(10), pp.136-145, 1987

Dobry, T.P., Patt, Y.N. and Despain, A.M., "Design Decisions Influencing the Microarchitecture for a Prolog Machine", *17th Annual Microprogramming Workshop*, New Orleans, pp.217-231, 1984

Edenfild, R., Gallup, M.G., Ledbetter, W.G., McGarity, R.C., Quintana, E.E. and Reininger, R.A., "The 86040 Processor", *IEEE Micro*, pp.66-78, February 1990

Fagin, B., Patt, Y., Srini V. and Despain Alvin, "Compiling Prolog Into Microcode: A Case Study Using the NCR/32-000", *18th Annual Workshop on Microprogramming*, Pacific Grove, pp.79-88, 1985

Gee, J., Melvin, S.W. and Patt, Y.N., "Advantages of Implementing PROLOG by Microprogramming a Host General Purpose Computer", *Logic Programming 87*, Melbourne, pp.1-20, 1987

Kane, G., *MIPS R2000 RISC Architecture*, Englewood Cliffs, Prentice Hall,1987

Krall, A., "Implementation of a High-Speed Prolog Interpreter", *SIGPLAN '87 Symposium on Interpreters and Interpretative Techniques*, St. Paul, pp.125-131, 1987

Krall, A. and Neumerkel, U., "The Vienna Abstract Machine", *Programming Language Implementation and Logic Programming*, Linköping, pp.121-135, 1990

Konagaya, A., Habata, S., Atarashi, A. and Yokota, M., "Performance Evaluation of a Sequential Inference Machine CHI", *Logic Programming 89*, Cleveland, pp.1148-1164, 1989

Mills, J.W., "A High-Performance Low RISC Machine for Logic Programming", *Journal of Logic Programming*, vol. 4, pp.179-212, 1989

Motorola, *MC88100 User's Manual*, Motorola, 1988

Mulder, H. and Tick, E., "A Performance Comparison between PLM and a M68020 PROLOG Processor", *Logic Programming 87*, Melbourne, pp.59-73, 1987

Nakashima, H. and Nakajima, K., "Hardware Architecture of the Sequential Inference Machine: PSI-II", *1987 International Symposiium on Logic Programming*, pp.104-113, 1987

Nakazaki, R. et al., "Design of a High-Speed Prolog Machine (HPM)", *12th Annual International Symposium on Computer Architecture*, pp.191-197, 1985

Patterson, D., "Reduced Instruction Set Computers", *Communications of the ACM*, vol. 28(1), pp.8-21, 1985

Sun, *The SPARC Architecture Manual*, Sun, 1987

Tick, E. and Warren, D.H.D., "Towards a Pipelined Prolog Processor", *New Generation Computing*, vol. 2, pp.323-345, 1984

Touati, H. and Despain, A., "An Empirical Study of the Warren Abstract Machine", *1987 International Symposiium on Logic Programming*, pp.114-124, 1987

Van Roy, P., "An Intermediate Language to Support Prolog's Unification", *Logic Programming 89*, Cleveland, pp.1148-1164, 1989

Warren, D.H.D., "An Abstract Prolog Instruction Set", *TR. 309*, SRI International, 1983

Woo, N.S, "A Hardware Unification Unit: Design and Analysis", *12th Annual International Symposium on Computer Architecture*, pp.198-205, 1985

2.2 A VLSI Engine for Structured Logic Programming

Pierluigi Civera[†], Evelina Lamma[‡], Paola Mello[‡], Antonio Natali[‡],
Gianluca Piccinini[†] and Maurizio Zamboni[†]

[†] Politecnico di Torino, Dipartimento di Elettronica
Corso Duca degli Abruzzi 24, 10129 Torino, Italy

[‡] DEIS - Università di Bologna
Viale Risorgimento 2, 40136 Bologna, Italy

Abstract

Extending logic programming towards structuring concepts such as modules, blocks, taxonomy of logic theories, viewpoints leads, from the implementation point of view, to the development of more complex, specialized execution models to achieve acceptable efficiency. In this work we address the effective implementation of a general framework, subsuming standard Prolog, where different languages for structuring logic programs can be efficiently supported and integrated. The implementation is based on an extension of the abstract machine developed by D.H.D. Warren (WAM), and is obtained by adding a specialized processor, based on a microprogrammed VLSI architecture, to a standard CPU.

INTRODUCTION

A crucial research topic of logic programming is how to introduce structuring concepts in it. Some proposals extend logic programming with concepts very similar to those of procedural languages such as modules and blocks (Giordano et al. 1988), (Giordano et al. 1989), (Logicware 1985). Other proposals, integrating logic and object-oriented programming, introduce inheritance between separate logic theories (see (Fukunaga and Hirose 1986), (Kauffman et al. 1986), (Gallaire 1986), (Zaniolo 1984)). Moreover, dynamic composition of logic programming theories, instead, has been proposed for building viewpoints and performing hypothetical reasoning ((Gabbay and Reyle 1984), (McCarty 1988)). It should be therefore of great interest to defining a general framework on the basis of which some different proposals of structuring logic programs can be well-described, integrated and efficiently implemented. A first step in this direction can be found in (Broggi et al. 1989) and (Mello et al. 1989), where a general

VLSI for Artificial Intelligence and Neural Networks, Edited by J.G. Delgado-Frias and
W.R. Moore, Plenum Press, New York, 1991

109

framework that subsumes and integrates some of the most well-known proposals for structuring logic programs is designed and its declarative and operational semantics is formalized. In this paper we focus more deeply on implementation issues. We show that this general framework can be efficiently implemented by easily extending well-known techniques used for standard logic programming. The general framework, in fact, is implemented on the basis of an extended Warren Abstract Machine (Warren 1983) (hereinafter called S- WAM) supporting different structured logic programming languages. While in (Lamma et al. 1989) the focus is on the S-WAM design, in this paper we describe the real, efficient implementation of the general framework in a compilation-based environment. Since executing Prolog and logic languages on general-purpose systems quickly overloads the machine and limits performances, recently some research projects (see (Dobry 1984), (Nakajima et al. 1987) and (Civera et al. 1989a)) propose fully dedicated Prolog machines. Following this approach, the implementation here described is based on a special-purpose VLSI microcoded architecture dedicated to the execution of S-WAM instructions. This dedicated architecture (hereinfater called S-PROXIMA) is obtained as a rather natural extension of the PROXIMA Prolog machine (Civera et al. 1989b). Block-, module-, inheritance-based logic programs, together with systems for hypothetical reasoning, can be implemented and integrated on this efficient architecture.

A GENERAL FRAMEWORK FOR STRUCTURING LOGIC PROGRAMS

In this section, we briefly present a general framework for structuring logic programs, suitable for implementing block-, module-, inheritance-based systems and hypothetical reasoning representation. A deeper discussion together with a declarative characterization can be found in (Mello et al 1989) and (Broggi et al. 1989). Here only a sketch is given in order to well understand the implementation. The basic idea originates from Contextual Logic Programming (Monteiro et al. 1989). A structured logic program can be conceived as a collection of independent modules, called units. A unit consists of a set of clauses and is denoted by a unique atomic name. Units can be (possibly dynamically) connected into hierarchies (called contexts) which, in turn, provide the set of definitions for query evaluations. As a matter of fact, contexts are represented as ordered lists of units of kind $[u_N,..,u_i,..,u_1]$ and denote the union of the sets of clauses of the composing units.

Different policies for composing units into contexts can be adopted and, accordingly, different classes of structuring mechanisms can be identified, as discussed in (Mello et al. 1989) and (Broggi et al. 1989). In figure 1, some proposals for structuring logic programs are classified in terms of the policies of unit compositions introduced in the following. For the sake of simplicity predicate extension/overriding is not taken into account.

Extension and overriding for predicate definitions

In logic programming non-determinism is present since each procedure p/n may correspond to different clauses. In this setting two forms of non-determinism are provided.

A procedure, in fact, may have multiple definitions not only in the same unit (*intra-unit non-determinism*), but also in different units of the same context (*inter-unit non determinism*). Two different policies can be adopted with reference to predicate definitions in the context:

1. The most recent predicate definition **overrides** the previous ones for the same predicate. Only intra-unit non-determinism may be present.
2. The most recent predicate definition **extends** the previous ones for the same predicate. Both intra- and inter-unit non- determinism may be present.

In the general framework, the default policy is predicate overriding. To obtain the predicate extension policy for predicate p/n, the following declaration must be inserted: $extends(p/n). If this declaration is present in a unit U, not only the definition of p/n in U, but also those in units before U in the current context will be taken into account. Moreover, to support information hiding, a predicate definition p/n is exported from a unit U (i.e. visible outside it) only if the declaration: $visible(p/n) is present in U.

	Dynamically Configured	Statically Configured
Evolving Binding	Multi-Prolog N-Prolog Clausal Intuitionistic Logic Modules	SPOOL Class Template Language (*)
Conservative Binding	Contextual Logic Programming Prolog/KR	Meta-Prolog SPOOL Class Template Language Block and Modules Prolog/KR

(*) when using the label self

Figure 1 Embedding different proposals in the general framework

Conservative and Evolving Policies for Binding Predicate Calls

In order to evaluate a predicate call in a context we have to find, in that context, the appropriate set of definitions, i.e. the binding for predicate calls. Two different policies of binding - referred to as conservative and evolving (see (Broggi et al. 1989)) - can be adopted. Let us suppose that $C=[u_N,..,u_i,..,u_1]$ is the current context. If an evolving policy is adopted, the predicate definition for a call p occurring in unit u_i, is given by the clauses of the whole context C. We will refer to C as the global context (GC). If a conservative policy is adopted, the predicate definition for a call p occurring in unit u_i, is given by the clauses of the sub-context $[u_i,..,u_1]$. We will refer to this sub-context as the partial context (PC). Structured logic programming systems adopting a conservative policy are more static, efficient and safe.

The general framework here considered supports both policies and adopts the conservative one as default. Evolving predicate calls are prefixed by the symbol #. In order to support both the policies, two different contexts (i.e. the global and the partial one) have to be maintained by the run-time support of the language.

Building the Context

A context can be built by using the context extension operator (firstly introduced in (Monteiro et al. 1989)). If $C=[u_N,..,u_1]$ is the current context, the evaluation of the extension formula $u>>G$ causes the proof of G to be performed in the new context $[u,u_N,..,u_1]$, obtained by adding the unit u on top of the previous context C.

Since in our framework two contexts are taken into account, two different extension operators ($>>$ / $>>>$ referred to as cactus/linear) are provided. The goal $u>>g$ extends the current partial context with unit u, and then makes GC equal to PC. By converse, the goal $u>>>g$ extends the current global context with unit u, and then makes PC equal to GC.

Static and Dynamic Scope

In our framework, a context represents a sort of binding environment for predicate calls. By analogy with traditional procedural languages, we can have a static policy of scope if a fixed context (hereinafter called closure) is statically associated with a unit. Whenever a static unit u (i.e. a unit with a static policy of scope) is asked for the proof of a goal g (e.g. by invoking the goal $u>>>g$) the proof of g takes place in closure of u, whatever the current context is. A dynamic policy of scope, on the other side, provides a more flexible framework. In this case no context is statically associated with the unit. Whenever a dynamic unit u (i.e. a unit with a dynamic policy of scope) is asked for the proof of a goal g (e.g. by invoking the goal $u>>g$) the proof of g takes place in the current, dynamic context of the computation. Static policies of scope are more efficient than dynamic ones, since in them a greater number of predicate calls can be completely solved at compilation time. Our framework supports and integrates both policies by allowing us to define dynamic and static units (i.e. units for which a context is explicitly specified).

IMPLEMENTATION ON A DEDICATED COPROCESSOR

In this section, we present the implementation of the general framework discussed before. The implementation is based on an extended Warren Abstract Machine (referred to as S-WAM in the following). In the S-WAM a new stack, representing the current global and partial contexts, has been added to WAM, along with new instructions to expand/contract it. Moreover, the structure of both the choice point and the environment of the WAM have been expanded to consistently handle new registers and some optimizations have been also considered, for limiting the overhead in the case of execution of standard Prolog programs. The different languages of figure 1 can be effectively implemented on this S-WAM-based architecture, after a suitable compilation phase. An emulation environment has been used to develop the model, select and evaluate different architectural solutions, and produce the microcode of the dedicated coprocessor.

P. Civera, E. Lamma, P. Mello, A. Natali, G. Piccinini and M. Zamboni

The most important features to be optimized are the memory structure usage and the internal microparallelism achievable. The data obtained let the designer to tune the model optimally. The Architectural Prolog Evaluator (APE), written in Prolog, analyzes the emulation traces to perform architectural comparisons of different hardware solutions. The tool analyzes the traces comparing each operation with an input data base representing the target architecture. After generating the microcode (Civera et al. 1988), a microcode machine emulator is finally used to test the microarchitecture and to optimize the microcode. The optimization mainly concerns jump prediction and microroutine efficiency.

The Run-time Structure

The compiler has been obtained by extending a standard Prolog compiler (VanRoy 1984), written in Prolog, which translates Prolog programs into WAM instructions. The extensions of the compiler deal with units, context extension operators, bindings for predicate calls with respect to the global or partial context, and inter-unit non-determinism. The compiler classifies predicate calls occurring in a unit U as:

1. **local** if a local predicate definition for it exists in U;
2. **eager** if no local predicate definition for it exists in U;
3. **lazy** if it is prefixed by the # operator.

A new memory area, called the context stack, is added to the WAM to support units and their combination into contexts. This stack represents the binding environment for conservative and evolving binding policies. The context stack grows whenever an extension $U>>G$ (or $U>>>G$) occurs and shrinks when G is deterministically solved or definitely fails. Three new registers refer to this stack: PC, representing the partial context, GC the global one, and IE_top the top of the context stack. Each object on the context stack is an instance environment associated with a unit U and allocated on the context stack whenever U is involved in a context extension. An instance environment for U consists of a number of cells, where the bindings for eager predicate calls occurring in U are recorded. These bindings depend on the context on which U is allocated and are actually solved the first time the call is performed for dynamic units. Since each unit U can be allocated several times in the context (i.e. several instances of U exist in the context), we can say that instance environments are for units what environments are for clauses in the case of standard logic programming implementation (Bruynooghe 1982). In particular, each instance of a unit U, shares the same code and has a private set of references for eager goals in U. For a comparison with alternative solutions see (Lamma et al. 1989). A similar area is not provided for lazy calls, since they are to be solved newly each time the call occurs (so the name lazy), while bindings for local calls are directly determined by the compilation process.

The architecture

The computational requirements of new programming paradigms can be satisfied designing physical architectures based on specific VLSI (Very Large Scale Integration) devices. For this reason, the implementation of structured logic programming here presented is based on a dedicated microcoded coprocessor (called S-PROXIMA, i.e. Structured PROlog eXecutIon MAchine) which directly implements the S-WAM. S-PROXIMA has been derived from PROXIMA architecture, which directly implements the basic WAM in hardware, by enhancing its instruction set for contexts handling. The main problem that arises when language primitives are executed by a dedicated architecture, is related to the definition of the abstraction level of the target code. In S-PROXIMA the S-WAM instruction set has been identified as the most effective level of target code also considering the code memory bandwidth required for each logical inference executed. In such a way, S-PROXIMA is a direct VLSI interpreter of the S-WAM instruction set and this influences the overall processor architecture. In fact, the complexity of S-WAM instructions imposes the use of microprogramming techniques for the control unit of the executor. The overall processor architecture is shown in figure 2.

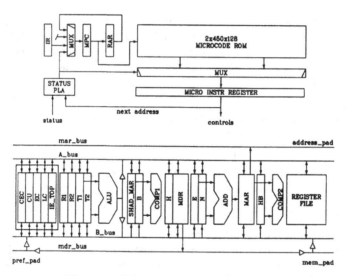

Figure 2 S-PROXIMA block diagram

Three main functional units can be identified in S-PROXIMA:
-code fetching and decoding unit;
-control unit;
-execution unit.
The instruction set has been coded to optimize the bandwidth and the code memory space requirements in a variable length format. A functional block fetches instructions directly solving indexing operations. Each decoded and aligned instruction is stored in a queue where it is read and executed by accessing the proper microroutine in the microcode ROM (MR). The translation of the S-WAM instructions in microcode has been carried out to obtain the highest concurrency on the operations of the execution unit. The use of the horizontal microprogramming techniques and the definition of a fully specific execution unit allow a high throughput to be reached. The resulting microcode is 128 bits wide and 900 lines long. Of course, S-PROXIMA microcode is

larger than PROXIMA one, to deal with units and contexts. About 30% of the overall microcode of S-PROXIMA is dedicated to the new S-WAM instructions. The design of the execution unit has been conceived to allow the most microconcurrency to be achieved. The execution unit is organized on two 32 bits internal busses exploiting a Harvard architecture. The architecture is oriented and optimized to the specific Prolog tags operations (i.e. generation, alteration and testing). Since tag testing is often used in Prolog execution, S-PROXIMA architecture direcly supports these operations by using dedicated hardware structures (multibranching technique). In the execution unit, S-WAM registers are divided in two main classes. The first class deals with all the registers that often require logical/arithmetical operations. To reduce execution overheads they are individually implemented with local computation capabilities. This is the case, among others, of the new S-WAM registers. The second class concerns the registers that can be stored in a register file without any loss of microconcurrency. A sophisticated addressing mechanism for the register file has been designed to permit up to four different sources and three operations concurrently. Many local connections are used together with the two main internal busses to increase the microconcurrency.

The S-PROXIMA processor has been designed by using silicon compilation techniques. The silicon compiler $Genesil^{TM}$ produces the physical layout from the structural description of the architecture with a parametric definition of the target technology. The whole system has been partitioned in two chips to get technologically feasible dimensions:

- An IPU (Instruction Processing Unit), devoted to the code prefetching and decoding;
- A DPU (Data Processing devoted to the data processing.

The two integrated circuits have been implemented with submicron CMOS technology; their dimensions are $6.9 \times 6.9mm^2$ and $8.1 \times 8.9mm^2$ for IPU and DPU respectively.

IPU   DPU

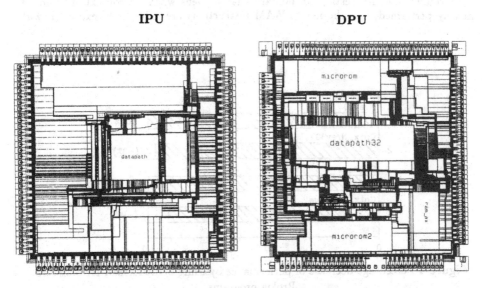

Figure 3 S-PROXIMA IPU and DPU floorplan and routing

The operating fequency is extimated about 20 MHz with average performance for pure Prolog execution of 500 KLips. The floorplan and routing of the two devices are shown in figure 3.

PERFORMANCE RESULTS

The design of S-PROXIMA has been supported by a set of measurements performed on different benchmarks to detect the best allocation of the new registers required by the context instructions, without deep modification of the basic structure of PROX-IMA. This, in fact, guarantees that the execution of standard Prolog programs on S-PROXIMA will not be heavily penalized. For this reason, the measurements have been carried out on the basis of a comparison between the execution of Prolog programs on PROXIMA, and the execution of the same programs, written in a single unit, on S-PROXIMA. The Prolog programs considered are reported in (Sterling and Shapiro 1986). As it is shown in figure 4, the decrease of performance is limited but significant (3-9%).Since this overhead could be unacceptable, S-PROXIMA can be configured in two modes: Pure Prolog execution and Context Extended mode. In the first case no overhead is paid. It is interesting to analyze the causes of the computational overhead introduced by handling contexts with respect to the standard Prolog execution. These comparisons are useful, from the architectural point of view, to identify the contributions related to the internal operations and the memory accesses. Figure 5 shows how memory accesses do not influence the overall performance. This is a good result from the architectural point of view, since the memory bandwidth is unaffected. This result is even more important, since memory requirements represent a bottleneck of Prolog execution. Therefore the major overhead of Prolog programs on S-PROXIMA is due to internal activities (register transfers, increments, decrements, tests, etc.) and could be reduced by architectural optimizations.

It could also be interesting to compare what happens when the context handling is heavily performed, i.e. the new S-WAM instructions are extensively executed, with

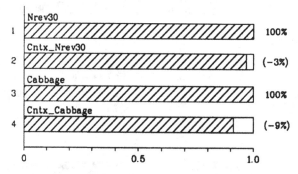

Figure 4 Percentage decrease of performance by using S-PROXIMA for standard Prolog programs

respect to standard Prolog execution. The results are reported in figure 6 and have been obtained by considering different sets of benchmarks involving standard Prolog programs (rows 1, 3, 5, 7) and structured logic programs (rows 2, 4, 6, 8). In particular, only dynamically scoped units have been taken into account, since in this case the greater overhead due to contexts is payed.

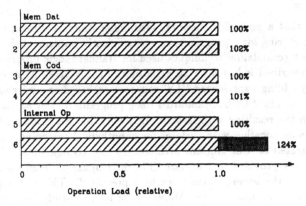

Figure 5 Memory accesses and internal operations for standard Prolog programs on S-PROXIMA normalized wrt PROXIMA

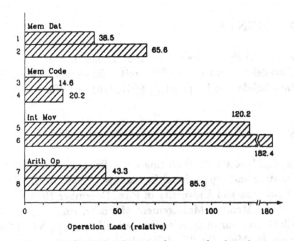

Figure 6 Operations per logical inference for standard and structured program execution in S-PROXIMA

A significative increase of memory accesses is present when dealing with contexts. The number of the internal transfers increases about 50% because of the new registers used in the context handling. This is partially due to the non complete optimization of the S-PROXIMA architecture for the new S-WAM instructions. Similarly, the number of the arithmetic operations doubles, pointing out the weight of the context stack management and the unit descriptor accesses. The increase of memory accesses, occurring when dealing with contexts, is mainly due to the management of the new memory structures where the accesses to each S-WAM memory area are reported. In fact, the Trail and the Heap are unaffected while the local (Environment) and the Context stacks together with the Unit Table are more intensively used.

CONCLUSIONS

This work shows that a general framework, subsuming standard Prolog and different languages for structuring logic programs, can be efficiently implemented by easily extending well-known compilation techniques used for standard logic programming. The implementation described is based on an extension of the Warren Abstract Machine, and is obtained by adding a specialized VLSI coprocessor, based on a microprogrammed architecture, to a standard CPU. Standard Prolog programs do not pay any overhead when executed on the resulting architecture. In theory, block-, module-, inheritance-based logic programs, together with systems for hypothetical reasoning, can be implemented and integrated on this efficient architecture (see (Broggi et al. 1989)). But up to now no tool is provided to translate different languages based on these structuring concepts into the general framework here presented. This is a topic that we plan to investigate in the near future. Moreover we plan to study how to implement "generic" modules such as the ones introduced in (Monteiro et al. 1989), (Miller 1986) and (Giordano et al. 1988) in the S-WAM.

ACKNOWLEDGEMENTS

This work has been partially supported by the "Progetto Finalizzato Sistemi Informatici e Calcolo Parallelo" , and by the "Progetto Finalizzato Materiali e Dispositivi Elettronici allo Stato Solido" under grant n. 890154761 of CNR.

REFERENCES

Brogi,A., Lamma,E., Mello,P.: "Structuring Logic Programs: A Unifying Framework and its Declarative and Operational Semantics",*DEIS and DI Technical Report*, University of Bologna and University of Pisa, December 1989.

Bruynooghe,M.: "The Memory Management of Prolog Implementation",*Logic Programming*, Clark and Tarnlund eds., Academic Press, pp. 83-98, 1982.

Bugliesi,M., Lamma,E., Mello,P.: "Fold/Unfold Transformation for Structured Logic Programming", *Proceedings 5th Italian Conference on Logic Programming*, Padova, June 1990.

Civera,P.L., Piccinini, G., Zamboni,M.: "Using Prolog as a Computer Architecture Description and Synthesis Language", *IFIP Conference*, Pisa (I), September 1988.

Civera,P.L., Piccinini, G., Zamboni,M.: "Implementation Studies for a VLSI Prolog Coprocessor", *IEEE MICRO*, February 1989.

Dobry,T.P. , Despain,A.M. , Patt,Y.N. : "Decisions Influencing the Microarchitecture for a Prolog Machine", *Proc. 17th Annual Workshop on Microprogramming*, Vol. 17, CS Press, October 1984, pp. 217-231.

Fukunaga,K., Hirose,S.: "An experience with a Prolog-based Object-Oriented Language", *OOPSLA-86*, Portland, Oregon, September 1986.

Gabbay,D.M., Reyle,N.: "N-Prolog: An Extension of Prolog with Hypothetical Implications",*Journal of Logic Programming*, n. 4, 1984, 319-355.

Gallaire,H.: "Merging Objects and Logic Programming: Relational Semantics", *AAAI '86*, August 1986.

Giordano,L., Martelli,A., Rossi,G.F.: "Local Definitions with Static Scope Rules in Logic Languages", *Proceedings of the FGCS Int. Conf.*, Tokyo, 1988.

Giordano,L., Martelli,A., Rossi,G.F.: "Extending Horn Clause Logic with Module Constructs", *University of Torino Technical Report*, Torino, 1989.

Kauffman,H. , Grumbach,A.: "MULTILOG: MULTIple worlds in LOGic Programming", *Proc. ECAI-86*, Brighton (UK), North- Holland, 1986.

Komorowski,H.J.: "A specification of an abstract Prolog machine and its application to Partial Evaluation", *Linkoping University*, Dissertation, 1981.

Lamma,E. , Mello,P., Natali,A.: "The Design of an Abstract Machine for Efficient Implementation of Contexts in Logic Programming", *Proc. 6th ICLP*, Lisbon (P), The MIT Press, 1989.

Lloyd,J.W., Shepherdson,J.C.: "Partial Evaluation in Logic Programming", *Technical Report CS-87-09*, University of Bristol, Dicembre 1987.

McCarty,L.T.: "Clausal Intuitionistic Logic. 1. Fixed- Point semantics", *Journal of Logic Programming*, no. 5, 1988, 1-31.

Mello,P., Natali, A., Ruggieri,C.: "Logic Programming in a Software Engineering Perspective", *North American Conference on Logic Programming*, October 1989, MIT Press.

Miller,D.: "A Theory of Modules for Logic Programming", in *Proc. 1986 Symp. on Logic Programming*, Salt Lake City (USA), September 1986.

Monteiro,L., Porto,A., "Contextual Logic Programming", in *Proc. 6th ICLP*, Lisbon (P), The MIT Press, 1989.

"MProlog Language Reference Manual", LOGICWARE Inc., Toronto (C), 1985.

Nakashima,K.: "Knowledge Representation in Prolog/KR", in *Proc. of Int.l Symp. on Logic Programming*, Atlantic City, February 1984.

Nakashima,H., Nakajima,K.: "Hardware Architecture of Sequential Inference Machine PSI-II", *Technical Report TR-265, ICOT*, June 1987.

Sterling,L. , Shapiro,E.: "The Art of Prolog", *The MIT Press*, 1986.

Van Roy,P.: "A Prolog Compiler for the PLM", *Report No. UCB/CSD 84/203*, Computer Science Division, University of California, Berkeley, 1984.

Warren,D.H.D.: "An Abstract Prolog Instruction Set", SRI *Technical Note 309*, SRI International, October 1983.

Zaniolo,C. : "Object-oriented Programming in Prolog", *Proc. International Symposium on Logic Programming, IEEE*, Atlantic City, February 1984.

2.3 Performance Evaluation of a VLSI Associative Unifier in a WAM Based Environment

P.L. Civera, G. Masera, G.L. Piccinini, M. Ruo Roch and M. Zamboni

Politecnico di Torino, Dipartimento di Elettronica
Corso Duca degli Abruzzi 24, 10129 Torino, Italy

Abstract

The unification task is one of the most complex and time-consuming activities in the execution of Prolog programs. The solutions currently implemented in Prolog machines are based on the sequential execution of Robinson's based algorithms using some architectural supports to data tags testing and manipulation and to the intrinsic recursivity of the algorithm. In this work the application of associative techniques is evaluated inside a WAM environment and a detailed comparison is done with respect to the sequential solution. The structure of an incremental VLSI unifier, able to work properly with an existing Prolog processor, is derived from the analysis of experimental data.

INTRODUCTION

The first Prolog execution models, based on the interpretation of the clauses, could not give any support to unification task, since the whole process can be solved only at run-time. More than 4.7 unifications per logical inference are typically executed on a set of benchmark programs. With use of compilation techniques, introduced by D.H.D.Warren (Warren 1983), the number of unifications to be solved at runtime drops to 2.7 per logical inference, as a consequence of the great number of simple terms and variables to be unified in current Prolog programs. However, dynamically built complex terms, such as structures and lists, although less frequent, require the unification to be carried out at runtime. Among the investigated techniques to achieve consistent speed-up for unifications, one of the most promising approaches is the application of associative techniques to the term matching and variable binding.

An associative method for an existing WAM machine environment (Civera et al. 1989b) has been investigated and designed. The original unification algorithm, based on a microcoded implementation of a modified Robinson's algorithm, has been replaced

VLSI for Artificial Intelligence and Neural Networks, Edited by J.G. Delgado-Frias and
W.R. Moore, Plenum Press, New York, 1991

by a new module that simulates the associative techniques and permits performance analysis (Passatore 1990). The computational effort required by the new solution has been carefully analyzed and studied with the purpose of a specific VLSI implementation. The target of the work is to integrate an associative modular VLSI unit in a conventional Prolog processor. Some architectural design decisions derived from the analysis of the associative method have been discussed in the second part of the paper.

UNIFICATION ALGORITHM

The unification is the keypoint for all the applications of first order predicate calculus such as theorem proving and logic programming. The Robinson's resolution principle (Robinson 1965) was the first attempt to mechanize the logical derivation process. Kowalski applied this basic principle to logic programming in 1974. Subsequent work was centered on the definition of an efficient unification algorithm for the Prolog language. In this direction researchers tried to optimize the basic Robinson's algorithm and to define new algorithms; the most important works in this area are due to Paterson and Wegman (1978), Corbin and Bidoit (1987), Martelli and Montanari (1982).

All these algorithms refer to sequential execution with different orders of complexity. The version used inside the VLSI Prolog processor PROXIMA - a machine designed by the authors (Civera et al. 1989b) - is a revised version of the Robinson's algorithm, microcoded in the control store of the processor. The limit of this approach can be identified in the strict sequentiality of the operations, bounding the performance to the speed of the sequential processor. Associative techniques and systolic approaches have been investigated by (Ng et al. 1989), (Robinson 1986), (Shobatake and Aiso 1986), (Nakamura 1984), (Oldfield 1986), (Oldfield 1987a), (Oldfield et al. 1987) to exploit the potential parallelism of the unification task.

The associative technique is able to speed-up the matching part of the algorithm, as it allows the concurrent management of the subterms involved in the unification. The algorithm kernel is the partial unification of elementary subterms through an array of pattern matching units. Each unit is able to signal the mismatch of two subterms to the following units and a complete match occurs when all the units have signalled a partial match. In the same time each matching unit must build the substitution vector for the unified subterms.

The associative algorithm was developed starting with the following assumptions:

- the PROXIMA machine has been selected as the working system;
- the associative unification algorithm has to be fitted into a working system, not considering stand-alone environment possible optimizations;
- the sequential unification algorithm already implemented in the PROXIMA processor is assumed as the reference model for performance comparison.

From these assumptions it is possible to derive a consistent set of measurements that lead to the architectural definition of the VLSI unifier.

The complexity evaluation of the unification process has been one of the most studied parameters to compare different algorithms. The basic concept is to determine how the computation grows as the number of symbols p in the terms to be unified increases. The complexity of the Robinson's algorithm has been considered, for a long time, $M \cdot p^2$

in the worst case. By a suitable representation of the terms, the complexity becomes linear. Also the Martelli's algorithm is showed to be linear, but in the application field, like a Prolog machine, this criterion does not appear so effective as in the theory. The main problem is that the frequency of terms with a high value of p is quite low; therefore, in order to grant high performance, it is basic to keep the multiplication factor M (instead of the complexity growth of the unification algorithm) as low as possible. This policy requires to simplify the basic unification algorithm. In such a way the *occur check* function that does not influence the complexity degree of the algorithm, is not implemented in practical unifications. The architectural solutions in Prolog machines have been thought to keep the basic unification process cost as low as possible. On the other hand, an implementation of a linear algorithm (as Martelli's one) shows unacceptable basic unification costs with current technology. In this direction the aim of reducing the unification overhead in a practical system using associative techniques does not basically influence the complexity of the process, but lowers the latency of elementary unifications. The algorithm we have implemented in VLSI on the base of the Robinson's work (Robinson 1989) shows clearly an exponential complexity, but our whole analysis is empirically based on the experimental data obtained measuring a real system, instead of theoretical evaluations.

PERFORMANCE EVALUATION

As noted above, the Robinson algorithm has an exponential complexity. In other words, the computational weight C can be written, in the worst case, as:

$$C \sim M \cdot p^2 \tag{1}$$

$$p = \min(p_1, p_2) \tag{2}$$

where p_1 and p_2 are the numbers of symbols contained in the two terms to be unified, respectively, and M is an architecture dependent parameter. Actually, expression (1) is not a practical one, as quite often the terms to be unified include several constants. Then a more detailed expression, derived from the splitting of p in its possible parts, could be:

$$C \sim M_{vv} \cdot p_{vv}^2 + M_{cv} \cdot p_{cv}^2 + M_{vc} \cdot p_{vc}^2 + M_{cc} \cdot p_{cc}^2 \tag{3}$$

$$\sim M_{vv} \cdot p_{vv}^2 + 2 \cdot M_{cv} \cdot p_{cv}^2 + M_{cc} \cdot p_{cc}^2 \tag{4}$$

where the symbols have the following meanings:

M_{vv}	:	weight of a variable to variable unification
p_{vv}	:	number of variables to be matched with variables in the terms
M_{cv}	:	weight of a constant to variable unification
p_{cv}	:	number of constants to be matched with variables in the terms
M_{vc}	:	weight of a variable to constant unification
p_{vc}	:	number of variables to be matched with constants in the terms
M_{cc}	:	weight of a constant to constant unification
p_{cc}	:	number of constants to be matched with constants in the terms

Of course, the associative approach to unification is not able to change the overall order of complexity of the algorithm, but it can strongly reduce the M coefficients in equation (4). First of all, all constant to constant unifications can be performed concurrently, leading to a strong reduction of the last term in the cited equation. Moreover, recursion can be avoided when two constant terms of arbitrary complexity are recognized by the associative unifier, so reducing the exponent of this term to exactly one. The first two terms in equation (4) could become dominant, because of the high number of variables contained in the elements to be unified. In this case, as recursion proceeds, the number of constants increases, in spite of the number of unbound variables. Therefore a certain decrease in the exponent of the other terms in the equation is indirectly obtained.

Table 1 Benchmark programs

name	reference	lines	Logical Inference
cabbage	Art of Prolog	47	1793
color	UCB-PLM	18	596
jugs	Art of Prolog	44	342
map2	Art of Prolog	33	5131
mu3	UCB-PLM	22	298
qsort	WARREN-SRI	10	424
queen4	UCB-PLM	9	152
sieve	UCB-PLM	18	563
cmos	POLITO	24	50
genx1	UCB-PLM	55	98
lispwam	POLITO	194	850
mob	UCB-PLM	22	110
nrev	WARREN-SRI	7	496
roadmap	CLOKSIN	61	2201
PLM-comp	UCB-PLM	2365	26433

The working system is a 32 bit Prolog machine developed by the authors and consists of two VLSI integrated circuits, the IPU (Instruction Processing Unit) and the DPU (Data Processing Unit), able to execute Prolog programs compiled into the Warren instruction set (Civera et al. 1989a). A set of benchmark programs, shown in table 1, has been selected and executed on a chip set simulator including the associative *unify* routine. Table 2 reports the most significant data for the unify task.

The first parameter to be studied is the number of *unify* calls per logical inference: as between 2 and 7 unifications are required to perform a Logical Inference, an average of 5 millions of unifications per second is required to achieve a computational power of 1 MLips. Moreover each unification requires from 8 to 20 microoperations, and the computational weight in the execution algorithm reaches 20% with an average value of about 12%. These values refer only to complex unification calls and it can be expected to increase in future applications, due to higher complexity of the terms to be unified.

The percentage of failed unifications is also representative: assuming no special optimization of the compiler, a significant number of *unify* calls, ranging from 10 % to 50 %, report a failure condition. The introduction of a parallel associative matching of terms will anticipate the failure condition, increasing performances.

The measurement reports a reduced number of memory accesses (1.2 average) and a small number of machine microoperations per *unify* call (12.8 average): this means that the unification task involved are too simple to exploit the potentiality of the associative method.

Table 2 Unifications in WAM based environment

name	n/LI	microop/UNI	max. recur.	% failed
cabbage	1.63	21.54	22	33.4
cmos	3.46	9.51	1	32.4
color	2.20	7.83	1	53.88
genx1	2.33	11.61	1	0.87
jugs	2.44	26.89	10	27.78
lispwam3	1.92	11.24	1	27.58
map2	0.92	9.62	1	42.36
mob	3.65	9.32	1	21.48
mu3	3.15	18.73	13	25.82
nrev	1.79	12.94	1	0.00
qsort	3.00	3.00	1	0.00
queen4	2.77	11.10	1	8.55
roadmap	7.11	12.69	1	31.90
sieve	3.16	12.79	1	18.81
plm	0.60	15.31	10	6.49
average	2.68	13.75	-	-

The need to compare the associative unifier with respect to the microcoded version also varying some architectural parameters requires to define some simple and basic relations that have been trimmed by accurate simulations.

The formula (5) simply states that the gain introduced by the associative unifier ASS_{gain} with respect to the microcoded execution in a WAM based environment, is:

$$ASS_{gain} = \frac{U_{li} \cdot (N_{uni}^s - N_{uni}^a)}{N_{li}^s} \tag{5}$$

where the following symbols have been used :

N_{li}^s : number of cycles per *Logical Inference*
N_{uni}^s : number of cycles per *Sequential Unification*
U_{li} : number of unifications per *Logical Inference*
N_{uni}^a : number of cycles per *Associative Unification*

Equation (5) has to be modified in the evaluation of the number of sequential cycles required to execute a logical inference or a unification by introducing the microconcurrency factor K that identify a microprogrammed machine. K can be seen as:

$$K = f(\mathcal{M}, \mathcal{A}) \tag{6}$$

that indicates the dependency of K both on the memory, $\mathcal{M}$, and on the processor architecture $\mathcal{A}$. In our specific case it is possible to write the following equations:

$$N_{li}^s = \frac{N_{opli}^s}{K_{li}} \tag{7}$$

$$N_{uni}^s = \frac{N_{opuni}^s}{K_{uni}} \tag{8}$$

where the following additional symbols have been used :

N^s_{opli} : number of operations per *Logical Inference*
N^s_{opuni} : number of operations per *Sequential Unification*
K_{li} : number of operations per cycle in *Sequential Execution*
K_{uni} : number of operations per cycle in *Sequential Unification*

From the results of this brief analysis, the gain offered by the associative execution of the unification depends on the sequential algorithm (N^s_{opuni}, N^s_{opli}), the processor architecture (K_{uni}, K_{li}) and, of course, the associative unification algorithm (N^s_{uni}). The distinction done between K_{li} and K_{uni} has not any important effect on the evaluation of equation (5), since the same architecture is used to perform both normal computation and unification. As a consequence, the theoretical upper limit of ASS_{gain} is indipendent of the actual value of K, being equal to the relative weight of unification on the overall program execution. On the other hand an important refinement that has to be considered in the previous equations is related to the different weights to be assigned to failed versus successfully terminated unifications. Some new symbols have to be defined:

U^S_{li} : number of succeeded unifications per *Logical Inference*
U^F_{li} : number of failed unifications per *Logical Inference*
N^{sS}_{opuni} : number of sequential cycles per succeeded *Unification*
N^{sF}_{opuni} : number of sequential cycles per failed *Unification*
N^{aS}_{uni} : number of cycles per succeeded *Associative Unification*
N^{aF}_{uni} : number of cycles per failed *Associative Unification*

The total number of unifications can be expressed as:

$$U_{li} = U^S_{li} + U^F_{li} \qquad (9)$$

The complete formula to estimate the gain by using an associative unifier in a microcoded WAM based system is:

$$ASS_{gain} = \frac{U^S_{li} \cdot \left[\left(N^{sS}_{opuni}/K_{uni}\right) - N^{aS}_{uni}\right] + U^F_{li} \cdot \left[\left(N^{sF}_{opuni}/K_{uni}\right) - N^{aF}_{uni}\right]}{N^s_{opli}/K_{li}} \qquad (10)$$

All the benchmark programs have been simulated and their performances in terms of processor microcycles and the ASS_{gain} parameter have been reported into the table 3.

The improvement achievable with associative techniques is rather low, ranging from 10 to 15 %. Furthermore, the need to exchange data between the sequential machine and the associative one increases the computational weight of this solution. The low value of ASS_{gain} is a direct consequence of the compile-time solved unifications, which hide a great fraction of the unifications actually performed by a program. Moreover, the hidden fraction is mainly composed of unifications between terms with a lot of constants, on which the parallelism of associative unifications could be better exploited. As a consequence, the use of a tailored compiler would increase the ASS_{gain}, raising the pipelining between the processor and the associative unifier.

Table 3 ASS_{gain} values for the benchmark set

name	N_{li}^t	ASS_{gain}				
		$N_{uni}^a = 0$	$N_{uni}^a = 1$	$N_{uni}^a = 2$	$N_{uni}^a = 3$	$N_{uni}^a = 4$
cabbage	93.44	13.00	11.26	9.52	7.78	6.04
cmos	124.24	9.66	6.88	4.09	1.31	-1.48
color	90.55	7.01	4.58	2.14	-0.29	-2.73
genx1	122.80	8.34	6.45	4.56	2.66	0.77
jugs	131.70	17.57	15.72	13.87	12.01	10.16
lispwam3	81.46	9.97	7.61	5.24	2.88	0.52
map2	67.54	4.64	3.28	1.92	0.55	-0.81
mob	103.98	9.33	5.82	2.31	-1.19	-4.70
mu3	128.53	17.52	15.08	12.63	10.18	7.73
nrev	48.00	20.06	16.34	12.62	8.90	5.17
qsort	109.44	14.76	12.02	9.27	6.53	3.78
queen4	107.53	8.77	6.20	3.62	1.05	-1.53
roadmap	302.59	11.31	8.96	6.62	4.27	1.92
sieve	138.03	11.17	8.88	6.59	4.31	2.02
plm	63.87	4.25	3.30	2.35	1.41	0.46
average	114.25	11.16	8.82	6.49	4.16	1.82

ARCHITECTURE

The design has been considered to outline the hardware requirements, its complexity in terms of circuitry and silicon area.

A full associative memory, containing all the terms of a program and possibly the program itself, is not feasible with up to date silicon technology, so that the target solution is limited to an associative unifier, holding the two terms under unification. A proper up-load mechanism interfaces the unifier with the processor memory. The sequential interface is a limiting factor of the design.

The unifier is based on a set of cells, each of them able to match simple Prolog terms. The cells are arranged in a uni-dimensional array (vector) and the vector holds the two terms under unification. The access to the terms during up-loading is managed in stack mode. Dereferenced terms, in words of 32 bits, are pushed into the unifier and the resulting status (fail/succeed) is tested by the processor; when the unification succeeds, the *mgu* is available on top of the stack.

An internal sequencer executes the steps required by the algorithm, which is based on three main control steps: Loading, Matching and Binding.

The loading step does not consist only in the terms up-loading, but it involves also their correct distribution among the cells of the unifier. Before starting the matching phase, a correct position of all the symbols (32 bit words representing constants and variables) must be reached along the stack. An auto-numbering mechanism has been provided to achieve a positional order; each word of the terms receives an ordering number (index), which identifies the argument and the nesting level. The auto-numbering process depends on the data type (tag) and the car/cdr bit. Each cell must carry two elements with the same index number; if one cell contains elements with different indexes, it has to pass along the highest index element to the next one. The loading of two terms is represented in figure 1a. The load and shift process ends when in the two stacks all the elements are paired with the same index. This step can signal a failure when terms having different structures are being combined (shifted).

The second step (matching) is merely associative: all the elements are associated with the corresponding ones concurrently. The matching mechanism considers data type (tag) as constants; free variables need different matching criteria. The status of matching process ripples through the cells of the unifier and a status signal (fail/succeed) is generated. The output does not concern the definitive output status of the unifier, unless it is signalling a failure; a positive matching starts the next phase (binding).

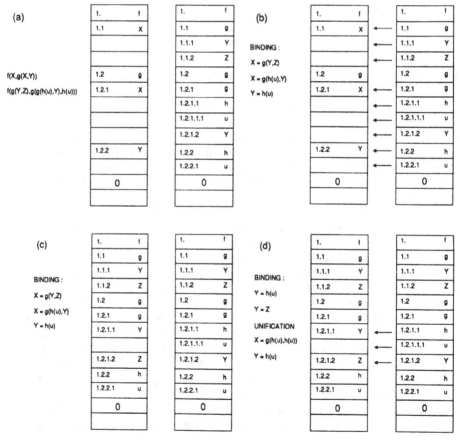

Figure 1 Loading (a) and binding (b,c,d) phases of the associative unification of the terms $f(X,g(X,Y))$ and $f(g(Y,Z),g(g(h(u),Y),h(u)))$

The third step refers to the variable binding: free variables during the match step could be bound to constants, lists or structures. The binding process records the occurred bindings, that need to be reported (as elements of the substitution vector) in the *mgu*. Sometime the binding of variables to complex structures needs further processing, because these structures can contain other variables to be bound. A flag in this phase is held to take note of further processing or completion.

If further processing is required, the terms must be re-arranged (shift down) to allow room for the new bindings.

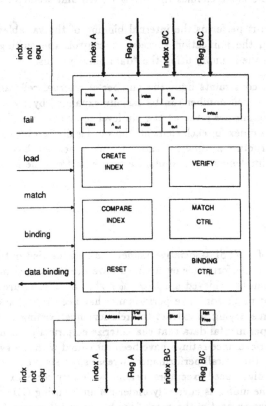

Figure 2 Block diagram of the basic associative unifier cell

The completion flag causes a valid status output (succeed) and the terms in the two stacks are identical and represent two copies of *mgu*. The several iterations for a unification example are depicted in figure 1b,1c,1d. The VLSI unifier architecture is represented in figure 2; it is composed of several combinatorial blocks under the control of a sequential part based on ordinary PLAs.

Six main blocks can be identified in the basic cell.

- *CREATE INDEX*: it creates the level index for the symbol stored in the cell, during the loading. It is enabled by the LOAD signal.

- *COMPARE INDEX*: this block compares the indexes of the symbols stored in the cell. The equality of the level of the indexes is evaluated. The INDX_NOT_EQU signal, in chaining connection, enables the following cell.
- *VERIFY*: the unit verifies the unifiability of the terms stored in the cell. The kernel of this unit is a CAM array for the arguments matching.
- *RESET*: it is used before the loading of a new couple of terms to initialize the internal structure.
- *MATCH_CTRL*: it is a PLA that manages all the operations related to the matching phase. The block enables the BIND_CTRL unit when variable bindings are required.
- *BIND_CTRL*: it performs the internal binding of the variables and the shift of terms. When the unification succeeds it controls the writing of the bounded variables into the memory using the "data binding" bus.

Implementation constraints limit the number of internal cells and the number of the index parts. The cell number can be easibily expanded by cascading two or more unifiers. Internal signals are given at the pin level to allow a chaining. A 32 bit word has been selected as index for each element; the word is divided into 8 by 4 bit fields; so up to 8 levels of structure nesting are allowed, where each can have a maximum of 16 arguments. These implementation limits are rather far from the normal programming levels.

CONCLUSIONS

The design study of a VLSI associative unifier has been carried out in a WAM based environment and the performance evaluations have been analyzed in this paper. The performance that can be achieved are 10-20 % higher than in a pure sequential execution on a dedicated processor. The performance has been rated on a set of standard benchmark programs, trying to extract the relationships existing among architectural parameters and experimental data that characterize empirically the unification in Prolog. Even if the performance ratings have been measured within a system introducing several restrictions, the overall performance increase suggests the use of VLSI hardware unificators only in high speed executors, dealing with very complex terms.

The design of the unifier is currently under definition using GDT^{TM} module generator tool for the development of the specialized blocks in 1.2 micron CMOS technology.

REFERENCES

Civera, P., et al., "A 32 bit processor for Compiled Prolog", *VLSI for Artificial Intelligence*, Kluwer Academic Publishers, pp.13-26 1989.

Civera, P., Piccinini, G., Zamboni,M., "Implementation Studies for a VLSI PROLOG Co-Processor", *IEEE MICRO*, February 1989 Vol.9 No. 1.

Corbin, J., Bidoit, M., "A Rehabilitation of Robinson's Unification Algorithm", *Information Processing 83*, REA Mason (ed), Elsevier Science Publishers B.V., pp. 909-914, 1983.

130

Martelli, A., Montanari, U., "An Efficient Unification Algorithm", *ACM Transactions on Programming Languages and Systems*, Vol. 4, No. 2, pp. 258-282, 1982.

Nakamura, K., "Associative concurrent evaluation of Logic Programs", *Journ. of Logic Programming*, Elsevier Science Publishers, pp. 109-118, 1989.

Ng, Y., Glover, R., Chng, C.L., "Unify with active memory", *VSLI for Artificial Intelligence*, Kluwer Academic Publishers, pp. 109-118, 1989.

Oldfield, J., "Logic Programs and Experimental Architecture for their Execution", *Proceedings IEE*, 133, Pt.E, No.3,May 1986, pp.163-167.

Oldfield, J., "Accelerating Programming System with the Aid of VLSI Components", *Tech. Rep. Computer Laboratory*, University of Cambridge, 1987.

Oldfield, J., Stormon, C.D., Brule, M., "The Application of VLSI Content-Addressable Memories to the Acceleration of Logic Programming System", *COMPEURO 87* pp.27-30, 1987.

Paterson, M.S., Wegman, M.N., "Linear Unification", *Journal of Computer and Systems Sciences*, pp.158-167, 1978.

Passatore, S., "Studio e valutazione di architetture associative per l'esecuzione di Prolog", *Graduation Thesis*, Politecnico di Torino (I), 1990

Robinson, J.A., "A machine-oriented logic based on the resolution principle", *Journ. Ass. Comput. Mach.*, pp. 23-41, 1965.

Robinson, I., "A Prolog Processor based on a Pattern Matching Memory Device", *3rd International Conference on Logic Programming*, Springer-Verlag, pp. 172-179,1986.

Robinson, I., "The Pattern Addressable Memory: Hardware for Associative Processing", *VLSI for Artificial Intelligence*, Kluwer Academic Publishers, pp.119-129 1989.

Shobatake, Y., Aiso H., "A Unification processor based on uniformly structured cellular hardware", *IEEE Proceeding on Computer Architecture*, pp. 140-148, 1986.

Warren, D.H.D, "An abstract Prolog Instruction Set", *Technical Note 309, SRI*, Menlo Park, CA 1983.

2.4 A Parallel Incremental Architecture for Prolog Program Execution

Alessandro De Gloria, Paolo Faraboschi, Elio Guidetti

Department of Biophysical and Electronic Engineering
University of Genoa
Via Opera Pia 11A - 16145 - Genoa - Italy

Abstract

Logic programming is nowadays a subject of large attention, as many researchers believe that it can map AI problems into machine code more easily than traditional high- level languages. Besides, the demand of increasing computation power for symbolic processing and the availability of VLSI products with low fabrication cost is giving a strong impulse to the development of integrated circuits dedicated to the execution of symbolic languages, instead of the adaptation of general purpose processors as in recent past.

SYMBOL represents an experiment in applying RISC design philosophy and compiling techniques derived from scientific computation to the exploitation of fine-grain parallelism in Prolog compiled programs.

Gate-level simulations of a three-processors architecture realized with a 2 micron standard cell technology and operating at 30 MHz exhibits 600 KLips average performance on standard Prolog benchmarks and 1.2 Mlips peak.

INTRODUCTION

SYMBOL is a parallel incremental architecture designed to support Prolog intensive applications, and intended to work as a Hardware Accelerator attached to a host workstation.

The architecture is based on a RISC VLSI processor supporting simple arithmetic, logic and control operations, with no interpretation level between instruction and hardware. Pipeline techniques have been intensively adopted, both for ALU and memory access organization. Moreover, as the architecture is completely exposed to the compiler, no hardware interlock has been introduced to avoid data stalls, but every conflict is statically solved at compilation time.

The design of the instruction set and of the architecture of Symbol has been based upon an extensive statistical analysis of standard Prolog benchmarks.

The adopted Prolog execution model is derived from the Warren Abstract Machine (WAM) introduced by Warren (1983).

VLSI for Artificial Intelligence and Neural Networks, Edited by J.G. Delgado-Frias and
W.R. Moore, Plenum Press, New York, 1991

133

Following RISC philosophy, most functions have been moved from hardware to software (compiler), in order to save silicon resources for the implementation of those hardware structures which could give best enhancement in performance.

According to the required cost/performance ratio, the architecture can be composed of an arbitrary number of processors, whose synchronization is statically realized at compilation time.

In the paper, after the description of the design philosophy of the project, the architecture of Symbol will be presented together with the microarchitecture of the RISC processor. Finally, results obtained on some standard Prolog benchmarks will be shown.

DESIGN PHILOSOPHY

The Risc Approach

As RISC machines have demonstrated (Gimarc 1988), an approach that privileges simplicity and regularity in the architecture design can bring to a significant speed-up in performance, because machine cycle can be shortened with respect to microprogrammed solutions. So, only those resources (operations) which are justified by their frequency of use and which can be successfully exploited by a compiler have been introduced in the instruction set of Symbol.

Any interpretation level between instructions and hardware have been avoided in order to minimize the complexity of the control unit. Saving hardware resources by avoiding complex control structures allows to focus one's effort on the study of the data path by designing specialized structures for data manipulation and for the exploitation of the parallelism intrinsic in the application. Some of the most significant features implemented to reduce the semantic distance between WAM and machine code deal with the Datapath structure, the Memory management and the Conditional Jumps organization, and are described below.

1 - As the WAM supports four tagged data types (variables, lists, constants, structures), the data path of Symbol is conceived with the capability to manage tagged data, and registers are organized into three independent data fields (Value, Tag, Cdr). The Instruction Set is register-oriented, with only direct and immediate addressing modes, and the only instructions which can access memory are explicit load and store operations.

2 - Memory in the WAM is organized into a code segment and a data segment, furtherly sub-divided into five stacks (environment, choice point, heap, trail and push-down list); so, the adoption of the Harvard memory organization (separate data and instruction memory buses) provides to avoid data and code access conflicts. Moreover, a particular attention has been focused on the optimization of memory accesses, and, by using accurate pipeline techniques, a cache load or store operation can be issued at each machine cycle.

3 - As confirmed by previous studies (Tick 1987), we have found that (Fig. 1) Prolog programs are characterized by a high frequency of conditional jumps operations (around 30%), which often test a condition on the tag fields of data. In order to reduce the overhead of redundant compare operations, the control structure has been provided with the capability of branching directly on the tag fields. Also, delayed branches, overlapping and multi-way jumps optimization techniques have been implemented both in hardware

and in software, so that the pipeline cycles after a control operation (usually wasted) could be well exploited by the compiler.

Fine Grain Parallelism In Prolog

Even if the WAM, traditionally used in microprogrammed machines (PLM), has been adopted as the reference execution model, SYMBOL applies the RISC design philosophy and extends it to meet synchronous parallel architecture features. In fact, its architecture can be composed of an arbitrary number of processors in order to exploit fine-grain parallelism.

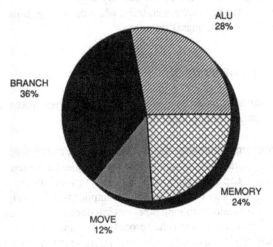

Figure 1 Percentage of instructions executed in the considered benchmarks.

The greatest problem in finding parallelism in Prolog code comes from the high percentage of conditional jumps operations which make difficult to find reasonable degrees of instruction concurrency inside each basic block. To overcome this difficulty, an in-house arrangement of the "Trace Scheduling" technique has been chosen for the compiler, thus allowing to exploit parallelism among basic blocks with a global compaction algorithm, based on statistical information upon execution frequency of instructions.

The parallel RISC approach in Prolog machine design shows other important features, mainly about the execution of applicative programs where the development stage has been completed and the programs have to be used in real applications. In fact, in these cases, the compiler allows to tune the machine code to exploit features specific of the program to speed up the execution.

The fine grain parallelism supported by the architecture, together with the Trace Scheduling compilation algorithm allows to overcome the Branch problem present in Prolog. In fact, in applicative programs, large pieces of code can be identified where the managed data structure are of fixed type or may very seldom change, so it is rather easy to predict (via, for in stance, a preliminary execution) which branches will be most probably taken. So, priority for compaction is given to the most frequently executed "traces" of instructions, and higher possibilities of code motion are given to the compiler in order to keep the data path fully operative. This optimization is not possible with microprogrammed machines implementing the WAM because branches operations are not exposed to the compiler and therefore only general optimization on single basic blocks of the microprogram can be applied.

Disadvantages of a larger code size due to the introduction of compensation copies, are overcome by the advantage of a faster execution of the most frequently executed parts. Moreover, taking into account a hierarchical memory organization, only a small frequently executed code will be kept in fast cache memories, while other large parts of program will be stored (and compacted) in slower (mass) storages.

THE ARCHITECTURE OF SYMBOL

The Prolog execution model is based on a refinement to the Warren Abstract Machine, and the compilation of a program is accom plished in three steps:

1 - The Prolog Program is compiled into WAM mnemonic instructions.
2 - WAM instructions are macro-expanded into the assembler mnemonic intermediate code for Symbol. In this step some early optimization, like variable renaming, is performed.
3 - The code is processed by the Parallelizing Compiler which arranges instructions into parallel machine operations, solving pipelines interlocks and register allocations.

Symbol is intended to work as an attached processor to a host workstation. This means that all communications with the "outer world", including interrupts, I/O or floating point processing, is demanded of the host, whose duty is to solve all those situations that may occur at run-time and which are not forecast by the compiler. For instance whenever cache misses occur, the processor is halted until the host has terminated the appropriate actions. This is done also because all operations must require a known and fixed amount of time to be executed for the compiler algorithm.

The system architecture can be composed of an arbitrary number of processors, depending on the required cost/performance ratio. In multi-processsor configurations, an instruction of Symbol is composed of the instructions of all the processors which are issued at the same cycle with a unique control flow (Fig. 2).

Simulations with infinite resources models have shown that a number of three processors guarantees about 90% of the maximum performance achievable by the adopted model.

When more processors are used, synchronization among them is achieved by means of an external logic network. In fact, as more branch instructions can be issued at the same cycle (multi-way jump), some strategy has to be used to solve conflicts when more than one condition is true. So the compiler includes some bits in the intructions to specify the priority of the branch operation. The external controller decides which processor Program Counter will be enabled in the next cycle. Moreover, as only absolute jumps are allowed, it is not necessary to update the Program counters of all the processors every time a jump is taken.

THE RISC PROCESSOR

Instruction Set

The instruction set is defined at Programmer and Hardware level.

The Programmer Level is composed by simple mnemonic instructions which do not contain any information about machine structures.(e.g. operations duration, registers) and have been conceived to express elementary functionalities directly executable by hardware units.

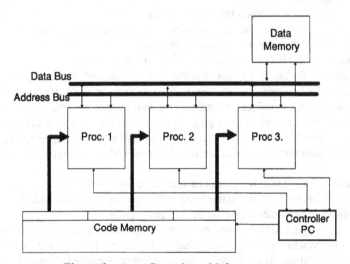

Figure 2   A configuration with 3 processors.

Programmer level instructions are translated into the hardware level code by the optimizing compiler, which takes into account the structure of the machine, including pipeline organization and instructions formats.

Hardware Level instructions are 64 bits wide and are organized into two formats, one for direct and one for immediate addressing. In the direct addressing format a memory access, an ALU operation and a register move are possible in a single cycle for each processor, while in

137

immediate addressing mode only a control operation and a memory access. The organization in formats has been determined by the need to shorten the instruction bit length, due to pin limitation of the chip package. Anyway, benchmarks simulations results show a low performance decaying (about 10%) with respect to a full parallel version.

Instructions controlling pipeline operations specify source operands and operation in the first cycle, while destinations of results are specified at the last cycle of the operation. Pipeline registers are always transparent to the compiler and are re-written at each machine cycle.

Microarchitecture

The operative part of Symbol (Fig. 3) is composed of:
- a multi-port register bank of 15 registers,
- an Arithmetic-Logic Unit,
- a Sequencing unit,
- a data memory interface.

The Register bank is composed of 16 32-bits registers organized into three separate and independently addressable fields:
- value (28 bits), used to store addresses or constants
- tag (3 bits), used to store data specifications (list, structure, atom, variables) as well as arithmetic flags deriving from compare operations
- cdr (1 bit), used for list concatenation and for some status flags.

Unlike common Prolog processors, Symbol has no reserved registers (apart from the Program Counter) for environment variables, so that the compiler could freely decide where to store a variable, in order to reduce the traffic on the buses connecting the processors. In fact, when data have to be transferred among processors the memory buses have to be used, and so memory accesses are disabled. The correctness of the parameters passing between procedures is guaranteed by constraints imposed to the compiler on variable allocation on procedure entries and exits.

Independent paths connect the other units with the register bank.

The processor has no dedicated status word, and flags resulting from ALU operations can be stored (only when necessary) in the tag field of any register.

The Arithmetic-Logic Unit is based on a carry-select adder with a single stage pipeline structure. The introduction of the pipeline, despite of an increase in the number of cycles to execute a programs (about 10 %), improves the overall permormance for the shortening of the machine cycle (30 % reduction).

As in other RISC machines, the sequencer has a reduced complexity, because of the simple control instructions supported that actually are only branch-on-condition and jump (direct and indirect). A little hardware support has been added for pipelined jumps management, as when one jump is executed in any processor, sequencers of all processors must be disabled in the following two cycles, in order to preserve program flow correctness (Ellis 1985).

Data Memory is interfaced through non-multiplexed data and address buses, which are also used for processor-to-processor register movements. Addresses and the different fields of data can come from different processors with no constraints. Memory operations are organized in a three-stages pipeline, with the assumption of an external memory (or cache) with a single cycle access time. MAR and MDR registers are external to the processor, and transparent to the compiler.

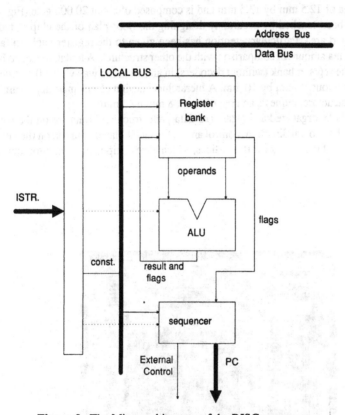

Figure 3 The Microarchitecture of the RISC processor.

The control part of Symbol is just composed of decoders for the instructions fields, which are fixed for each format and directly control functional units and bank ports of the architecture. Code Memory access is organized in a three-cycle pipeline, also considering the decoding phase (which is very simple indeed). An external Program Counter and Instruction Register are included for the pipeline.

VLSI Implementation

The RISC processor has been designed by using a hierarchical standard cell envinronment. The chip has an area of 12.5 mm by 13.5 mm and is composed of about 20.000 gate (Fig. 4).

The layout has been reached by accurately designing the floor-plan of the chip to reduce connection length and area. Particular attention has been given to the register bank, in fact it requests the larger area amount in comparison with the other structures. A tentative step to build the layout of only the register bank (without decoders) in an automatic way with a flat structure results in an area of about 10 mm by 10 mm. A hierarchical design of this module, taking into account its regular structure, requests an area of about 8 mm by 4 mm.

The layout has been organized as in standard data-path structures. Data are on the metal1 layer and run on the horizontal direction, control are on the metal2 layer and run on the vertical one. The components of the chip are vertical slices, which have equipotential input/output ports

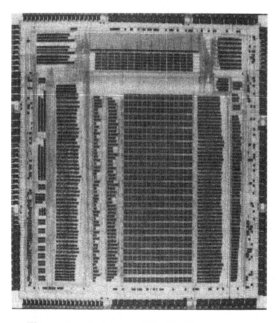

Figure 4   The layout of the RISC processor.

both on the left and right side. The position of the data ports of a component corresponds to the position of the ports of the other component, so that the slices can be connected by abuting.

The hierarchical standard cell approach allows to arrange the layout as in the full-custom methodology and the designer can completely drive the layout. Moreover this approach avoids some time consuming activities as the layout design of the base cell, and can be used also by non-specialist layout-designer.

RESULTS

We have simulated the Symbol architecture by using a behavioural simulator with an accurate timing which has been extracted from the gate level simulation of the RISC processor. All the escape functions contained in the considered benchmarks (except I/O functions)have been completely executed by the architecture. Sometimes results for Prolog benchmarks are expressed in logical inference per second (LIPS), where a logical inference in warren code is concluded after the execution of a CALL. EXECUTE or escape function. As in general this quantity is ambiguous and can be well defined only for a few benchmarks (e.g. Naive Reverse), we preferred to show the execution time.

Table 1 A comparison of performance between 5 Prolog machines and Symbol.

Bench-mark	Quintus	VLSI-PLM	KCM	BAM-1	BAM-2	Symbol-1	Symbol-2
log10	0.468	0.137	0.039	0.0149	0.0263	0.0382	0.0096
times10	1.05	0.247	0.082	0.0267	0.0403	0.0853	0.0241
nrev30	4.87	2.10	0.65	0.135	0.308	0.673	0.2376
qsort50	16.9	4.24	1.32	0.196	0.371	1.482	0.8810
conc30	-	0.137	0.059	-	-	0.0376	0.0170

The considered benchmarks are the following:
- **CONC30**: Concatenate a list of 30 elements.
- **NREV30**: Reverses a list of 30 elements.
- **QSORT50**: Sorts a list of 50 integers by using the quicksort algorithm.
- **LOG10**: Operates symbolic differentiation on a 10 times nested logarithmic functions.
- **TIME10**: Operates symbolic differentiation on a 10 factor product.

Table 1 shows a comparison of the Symbol architecture (using three processors, 33 ns clock cycle and a 3 cycle pipelined memory access time) with the VLSI-PLM (Dobry 1987) (using a 1 cycle memory access time and 100 ns clock cycle), the KCM (Benker et al. 1989) (using a 80 ns clock cycle), the BAM (Holmer et al. 1990) with auto modes (BAM1) and no modes (BAM2) (using a 33 ns clock cycle and 128 KB instruction and data cache) and the Quintus-Prolog (running on a Sun 3/60). Times are expressed in milliseconds.

Two different sets of results are given for the Symbol Architecture:
1- Symbol-1 shows results of benchmarks for standard WAM model, which means with no a-priori assumption on the type of data the procedures have to deal with.
2 - Symbol-2 shows performance of the architecture on a post-processed code of benchmarks. The post processor is user-assisted and works on the basis of warren code semantic

in the particular context, taking into account a fixed structure of input data. So, large parts of redundant code are eliminated, as well as time consuming operations such as tag testing, general unification, environment and choice point trimming for backtracking.

CONCLUSIONS

In this paper we have presented an architecture for the exploitation of fine-grain parallelism in Prolog. The approach can be characterized by two main features:

1 - The use of global code optimization techiniques derived from scientific computation

2 - The adoption of a simple RISC architecture with no-interpretation levels between instructions and hardware.

The architecture shows good performance if we consider its simplicity, and it can be enhanced by adding more processors, without any intervention on the hardware or on the compiler.

Future work regards the implementation of an enhanced fully automatic post-processor allowing to generate only the code actually needed for the computation.

REFERENCES

Benker, H., Beacco, J., Bescos, S., Dorochevsky M., Jeffre Th., Pohimann, A., Noye, J., Poterie, B., Sexton, A., Syre, J., Thibault, O., Watzlawik, G., " KCM: A Knowledge Crunching Machine", *16th International Symposium on Computer Architecture*, pp. 186-194, 1989.

Borriello, G., Cherenson, A., Danzig, P., Nelson, M., "Special or General-Purpose Hardware for Prolog: A Comparison", *Technical report*, University of California at Berkeley, 1986

Dobry, T., "A High Performance Architecture for Prolog", PhD Thesis, University of California at Berkeley, 1987.

Ellis, J., *Bulldog: A Compiler for VLIW architectures*, The MIT Press, Boston Mass., 1985.

Fisher J., "Trace Scheduling techniques for global microcode compaction", *IEEE Trans. on Computer*, vol. C-30, pp. 478-490, 1981.

Fisher J., "Very Long Instruction Word Computers and the ELI-52", Micro-16, pp. 140-150, 1983.

Gee, J., Melvin, S., Patt, Y., "The implementation of Prolog via VAX8600 Microcode", *MICRO19*, ACM, 1986.

Gimarc, C. and Milutinovic, V., "RISC Principles, architectures and design", in *High-Level-Language Computer Architectures*, Computer Science Press, 1988.

Hennessy, J., "VLSI Processor Architecture", *IEEE Trans. on Computer*, pp. 1221-1246, 1983.

Holmer, B., Sano, B., Carlton, M., Van Roy, P., Haygood, R., Bush, W., Despain, A., Pendleton, J., Dobry, T., "Fast Prolog with an Extended General Purpose Architecture", *17th International Symposium on Computer Architecture*, pp. 282-291, 1990.

Srini, V., Tam, J., Nguyen, T., Chen, C., Wei, A. Testa J., Patt, Y.,Despain, A., "VLSI Implementation of a Prolog Processor", Proceedings of *VLSI Conference,* Stanford, 1987.

Tick, E., "Studies in Prolog Architectures", *Technical Report*, Stanford University, 1987.

Warren, D., *An Abstract Prolog Instruction Set*, Artificial Intelligence Center, SRI International, 1983.

2.5 An Architectural Characterization of Prolog Execution

Mark A. Friedman and Gurindar S. Sohi +

Department of Engineering and Computer Science, Trinity College
Hartford, CT 06106

+ Computer Science Department, University of Wisconsin-Madison
Madison, WI 53706

Abstract

We present an instruction-level profile and a higher-level operation profile obtained from simulations on a set of mid-sized Prolog programs for a load-store architecture we have developed. Our architecture serves as a platform to effectively emulate the functionality of the Warren Abstract Machine (WAM) using an enhanced, but more traditional instruction set. We compare our instruction profile to similar research on Pascal and Lisp to find that Prolog has a higher frequency of use of bit and shift instructions and branch and jump instructions and makes less use of loads and stores. The higher-level profile shows tag operations to be one of the costliest operations. We present and evaluate architectural enhancements to support tag operations obtaining a twenty percent performance improvement. We then look at the potential performance improvements and limitations of a pipelined implementation of our architecture. We find that the high frequency of branches and jumps and data dependencies resulting from emulating WAM operations combine to limit the benefits of a pipelined implementation.

INTRODUCTION

Our research centers on discovering implementation improvements and optimizations which lead to more efficient processing of programs written in the Prolog programming language. Our work to date has been in two directions. First, we have performed a detailed study of the static and dynamic characteristics of Prolog by exploring the frequency and costs of different operations by compiling a set of mid-sized benchmark programs to our own instruction set and then simulating their executions. Second, we have looked at some specific implementation alternatives and measured the costs and savings of these alternatives as they occur when

VLSI for Artificial Intelligence and Neural Networks, Edited by J.G. Delgado-Frias and
W.R. Moore, Plenum Press, New York, 1991

applied within our system. In this paper, we present a small portion of our results from these two areas. Specifically, we present a dynamic instruction profile grouped by opcode and a higher-level operation profile. We then show dynamic performance improvements which result from enhancing our base architecture with support for tag operations. The last portion of this paper examines potential benefits and limitations of a pipelined implementation of our architecture.

METHODOLOGY

The SIMPLE Prolog System

We have developed the SIMPLE (Simple Instruction Set Machine for Prolog Execution) Prolog System to drive our study. The SIMPLE system consists of a compiler and a simulator. The front end of the compiler translates Prolog code into operations representative of the Warren Abstract Machine (WAM) model (Warren1983). It uses a portion of the PLM compiler developed by Van Roy at Berkeley (Roy1984). The back end expands this intermediate form into SIMPLE instructions. The simulation program executes SIMPLE code and generates an extensive set of static and dynamic information, and instruction and memory reference traces. The SIMPLE architecture utilizes a load-store instruction set. SIMPLE contains seven major categories of operations. These are: moves between registers, load and store operations, arithmetic operations (that is, integer addition and subtraction), bit and shift operations, unconditional and conditional branches (which generate a target address specified by an offset from the current instruction address), and jumps (which specify their target addresses directly). Our architecture is similar in philosophy to that of modern RISC machines (Patterson1985, Hennessy1985). It contains a limited-sized instruction set of basic and frequently used operations which are suitable for implementation in a single machine cycle. Thus, the SIMPLE architecture serves as our base platform to effectively emulate the functionality of the Warren Abstract Machine model.

Our Prolog Benchmark Suite

Eleven benchmarks were used to derive our profiling measurements. The benchmarks cover a wide range of applications representing the more popular uses of Prolog. Each was chosen and developed carefully to insure good Prolog programming style. The benchmarks include incremental generate and test search programs (*cannibals, cryptoarithmetic, queens*), a planning problem (*routes*), an Algol-like compiler (*compiler*), a natural language parser (*grammar*), some applications more mathematical in nature (*hexconversion, primes, rowreduce*), a database application (*statistics*), and a text processing example (*characters*). We chose to develop our own benchmark suite because the benchmarks predominantly referenced in the literature (Warren1977, Dobry1985) are small-sized examples of Prolog code that do not necessarily exhibit the traits of larger applications. Our benchmarks are of a medium size. Table 1 shows their static and dynamic SIMPLE instruction counts and the corresponding counts of Warren operations that are represented by the SIMPLE code. The mean values of these statistics show a static size of 15,000 instructions and a dynamic size of 4,700,000 instructions. Our benchmarks are statically larger than each of the standard benchmarks

Table 1   Benchmark Characteristics

Benchmark	Static Instruction Counts		Dynamic Instruction Counts	
	Warren Operations	SIMPLE Instructions	Warren Operations	SIMPLE Instructions
cannibals	807	22988	264582	10660841
characters	348	8959	189192	4136390
compiler	1471	38778	124438	3329389
cryptoarithmetic	458	12761	364398	10331487
grammar	993	33067	95298	3149615
hexconversion	329	6606	180291	5622912
primes	172	4754	111170	2064403
queens	201	5471	267578	7000636
routes	1161	26392	154631	5501016
rowreduce	980	20584	164292	4247533
statistics	1429	30179	94553	2534097
geometric mean	598	15126	166832	4669031

chosen by Warren and by the Programmed Logic Machine (PLM) research group. Dynamically, our benchmarks are one to two orders of magnitude larger than these other benchmarks. This group of benchmarks have been used by nearly all other researchers as well, including the LOW RISC group (Mills1989), the implementors of Prolog on SPUR (Borriello1987), and the developers of the PSI machine (Taki1984). Our benchmarks are also comparable to the six additional benchmarks introduced in the recent Berkeley Abstract Machine (BAM) work (Holmer1990). With the exception of one of these newer benchmarks, our benchmarks are of comparable size or larger.

CHARACTERIZATION OF PROLOG

A Dynamic Instruction Profile

We display the dynamic instruction profile for our set of programs grouping instructions into their seven major operation categories in figure 1. We compare our data with similar measurements for Pascal and Lisp as reported by Steenkiste and Hennessy (Steenkiste1986). This figure shows that instruction frequencies for Prolog further extend the instruction frequency deviations in the direction in which Lisp deviates from Pascal. All three languages use the same percentages of computational instructions (move, arithmetic, bit, and shift). The most striking difference between the three is how their use differs between arithmetic and bit and shift operations. The high use of bit and shift instructions in Prolog is caused by the tagged representation of objects in the WAM model. Bit and shift operations are used for tag and value field extraction, tag and value field combining, and sign extensions for the value fields. The low use of arithmetic instructions occurs because of Prolog's preference towards symbolic processing. Most of the activity within its model of execution and within the

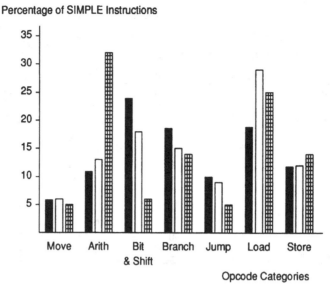

Figure 1 Dynamic Frequencies for Prolog (black), Lisp (white), and Pascal (checked)

applications most suited for its use is not heavily computational. In addition, when performing computations, Prolog represents arithmetic expressions in exactly the same way in which it represents other objects. Thus, even a computationally intensive application will spend time creating and manipulating data structures which represent arithmetic expressions. In fact, the large majority of arithmetic instructions (nearly ninety percent) are used for addressing computations to reference the different stack areas and not for source-level arithmetic operations.

Our instruction profile shows higher frequencies for both branch and jump instructions in Prolog than in Lisp and Pascal. Branch instructions are used to make comparisons between the tag of a value within a register and an immediate tag value, comparisons between two value fields or two addresses, and to branch unconditionally around code within a procedure. Jump instructions are used to also compare tags, values, and addresses. Additionally, they allow procedure calls and procedure returns through unconditional jumps. The high frequency of jump instructions occurs because of the high frequency of recursive calls in Prolog. All iteration is effectively accomplished through recursion. The high frequency of branch instructions is due to unification operations. That is, there is a frequent need to compare and match the corresponding fields of different objects and then act accordingly.

The operations in which Prolog has lower frequencies of use than Pascal and Lisp are loads and stores. Although, one may think that this decreased percentage of memory references will reduce the concern of slow memory access time, these concerns are not lessened. Because Prolog's data representation (more specifically, the heavy use of pointers) reduces the locality of memory references, efficient memory design is very important to an efficient Prolog system (Tick1985).

A Higher-Level Operation Dynamic Profile

We next look at the dynamic frequencies of higher-level operations. Figure 2 shows the number of dynamic instructions used for tag operations, memory accesses, memory addressing, and procedure call and returns. The most costly of these four groups are the tag operations which accounts for forty percent of the dynamic instructions. Tag operations include the checking of tag fields for specific immediate values, the extraction of the entire tag field or a portion of a tag field, the extraction of the value or address field of an object, and the combining of a tag and value field into a single object. Twenty-five percent of the instructions executed are used to reference memory. Figure 2 shows how these instructions divide into the different memory areas (as is determined by their addressing mode). Addressing calculations to enable memory references account for fifteen percent of the dynamic instructions. Eight percent of the dynamic instructions are used to implement procedure call and return operations.

SUPPORT FOR TAG OPERATIONS

The high cost of tag operation execution makes it a suitable target for architectural enhancement. Tag operations are expensive because our base architecture treats each object as a sin-

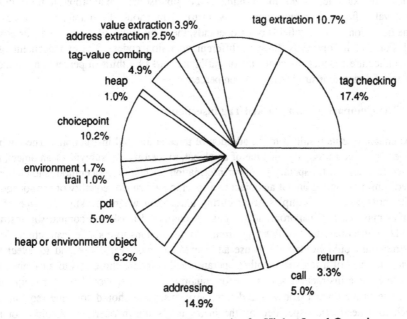

Figure 2 Dynamic Instruction Frequencies for Higher-Level Operations

gle entity. Examining or manipulating either of the tag or value fields requires extracting that field. Creation of new objects requires a combining operation after the tag and value fields are created independently. The architectural characteristic of single-entity objects contrasts with the WAM's data representation of independent tag and value fields and results in the large frequency of bit and shift operations which we saw previously. Many of these instructions will be eliminated through the enhancements we now discuss.

Table 2 displays the benefits of our tag operation enhancements. It shows the reduction in dynamic instruction use for each enhancement as a percentage of the SIMPLE instructions of our base architecture. Overall, our results show that the combined effects of the tag operation enhancements we will discuss can lead to a twenty-three percent reduction in static code size and a twenty percent improvement in performance.

A Tagged Architecture

Our first architectural enhancement to assist in tag operations is to allow the architecture to recognize that each data object consists of a tag field and a value field and to treat each field appropriately for different operations in our instruction set. As an example, an add instruction should only add the value fields of its two source operands and store the result of its operation in the value field of its destination operand. A second example would be in the use of a register as a base register. Here once again, only the value field of the register should take part in computing an effective memory address. Both of these examples enhance execution by eliminating the need to extract a field from an object (through a bitwise AND instruction or a shift left followed by a shift right) prior to operating on the field's value. Certain operations, (for example, moves, bit masking, and comparisons), are appropriate for both tag fields and value fields. For these operations, instructions should be redefined for cases to apply the operation to the tag fields of its operands, the value fields of its operands, or possibly both fields of its operands, through different operation codes. The enhancement of a tagged architecture reduces the code size of our benchmarks by thirteen percent and reduces the number of dynamic instructions by seven percent.

Masked Tag Comparison and Masked Tag Insertion

The next enhancements result from the addition of three additional instructions. The tag bits of an object are used to identify the type of an object, to identify the subtype of an object, for garbage collection, and for specifying other information. A common operation is to compare a selected subset of the tag bits of an object to a specific pattern (for equality or for nonequality). The most common examples occur during unification when checking the type of an object after masking out inappropriate tag bits. A combined mask and comparison instruction would reduce operations of this type from two instructions to a single instruction. Two new instructions could be defined to use an immediate mask value operand to select the appropriate tag bits of a register (another operand) and compare those bits to an immediate pattern value. One instruction would test for equality. The other would test for inequality. The outcome of the comparison would determine if execution should continue sequentially or branch to a destination specified by the instruction's fourth operand. Addition of the

Table 2 Performance Improvements with Support for Tag Operations

Benchmark	Percentage of SIMPLE Instructions				
	A Tagged Architecture	Masked Tag Comparison	Masked Tag Insertion	Overlapped Tag Operations	Total
cannibals	6.7	12.5	0.5	2.1	21.8
characters	4.1	12.8	0.3	1.4	18.6
compiler	7.7	9.8	0.7	2.0	20.2
cryptoarithmetic	6.7	9.6	0.8	2.1	19.2
grammar	9.2	10.3	1.0	3.0	23.5
hexconversion	8.4	8.2	1.1	2.7	20.4
primes	5.5	10.2	0.6	2.0	18.3
queens	7.1	9.8	1.1	2.9	20.9
routes	7.0	9.5	0.8	2.2	19.5
rowreduce	7.0	10.0	1.0	2.6	20.6
statistics	4.2	11.7	0.4	1.8	18.1
arithmetic mean	6.7	10.4	0.8	2.3	20.1

masked tag comparison instruction reduces the number of static instructions by nine percent and the number of dynamic instructions by ten percent.

A third additional instruction would be useful which performed a combined mask and move operation. This instruction would assist in operations with a need to insert a pattern of tag bits into a subset of the bit positions of an object. The new instruction could be defined to use an immediate mask value to select the appropriate tag bits to alter within a register and set those bits to an immediate pattern. The addition of the masked tag insertion leads to a small performance gain of two percent static improvement and one percent dynamic improvement.

Overlapped Tag Operations

A final tag operation enhancement would be to allow operations on the tag fields and operations on the value fields to proceed in parallel since these two types of objects are distinct and will have no data dependencies between them. The overlapping of tag operations would not reduce the static size of programs. They would reduce the dynamic number of instructions but by only two percent.

INSTRUCTION LEVEL PARALLELISM

Pipelining is an effective technique to increase parallelism at the instruction level (Kogge1981). Theoretically, pipelining offers a speedup equal to the number of pipeline stages which are used during implementation. In practice, instruction dependencies, involving both control and data information, limit performance because they reduce the amount of potential parallelism that is actually realized (Kunkel1986). A control dependency occurs in the case of a conditional branch or jump where the execution of an instruction following the branch is dependent on the branch or jump outcome. A data dependency occurs when one instruction establishes a result that is used as input by another instruction. Data dependencies may arise through computational instructions or through load instructions. Both control and data dependencies result in a stall of the pipelined execution until all needed information becomes available for the instruction to be executed.

Pipelined Performance Improvements

Performance improvements obtained through pipelining are shown in figure 3. We computed the execution time for our benchmarks for various pipeline depths for two architectural models. Using the execution time of the non-pipelined variation of each model, we calculated the speedups obtained for each model for each pipeline depth. We averaged these values across our benchmarks to obtain the results in figure 3.

A basic block is a sequence of instructions following a branch or jump instruction up to and including the very next branch instruction. The division of a program into basic blocks identifies and separates the control dependencies of a program. To obtain the execution time for each benchmark, we scheduled the instructions within its basic blocks taking into account pipeline stalls caused by data dependencies and determined the number of pipeline stages needed to execute each basic block. The number of stages needed to execute a benchmark is calculated by summing the products of the frequency of a basic block by the number of

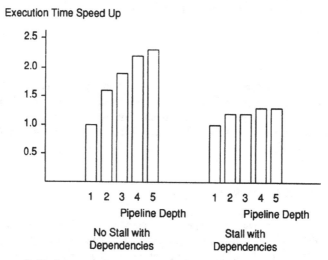

Figure 3 Performance Improvements with Pipelined Architecture

stages it needs to execute. By making the assumption that the cycle times of a model are independent of the number of pipeline stages in a cycle, (that is, we assume that a single stage of a pipeline of depth N will take 1/N the time of the cycle time of a non-pipelined machine), we can compute a relative execution time for each pipeline depth. The two architectural models we use differ in the length of dependency pipeline stalls. In both models, we assume that a branch or jump instruction will stall the pipeline a single cycle (N stages). In the first model, we do not stall at all for data dependencies. The first model gives the ideal maximum speedups taking into account only control dependencies. In the second model, we assume that the result of a computational operation takes a single cycle (N stages) before it is available for use in a subsequent instruction and that it takes two cycles (2N stages) before the value of a load instruction is available in its destination register.

In figure 4, we see that the speedups obtained are less than ideal for both models. For the model which ignores data dependencies, pipelines of depth 2, 3, and 4, give speedups of only 1.6, 1.9, and 2.2. After three stages, the speedups for this model level off. Thus, the frequencies of branch and jump instructions alone are significant limitations to pipelined speedups. For the model which includes pipeline stalls for data dependencies, speedups are still lower and leveling off occurs almost immediately. Both pipelines of depth 2 and 3 give speedups of only 1.2.

SUMMARY

In this paper, we presented a dynamic, high-level operation distribution and found that the most costly operations during Prolog execution are tag operations, followed by memory accesses, and then followed by memory addressing. We showed how to enhance the performance of tag operations which resulted in a reduction of code size of twenty-three percent and a performance improvement of twenty percent for our benchmarks. We also showed an instruction level profile and saw that the percentage of bit and shift instructions and branch and jump instructions were higher than corresponding percentages of other languages while the percentage of arithmetic instructions and loads and stores were lower than in Pascal and Lisp. Our tag operation enhancements greatly reduces the number of bit and shift instructions. We looked at performance improvements which could be obtained from a pipelined implementation of our architecture. Because of the high frequency of branch and jump instructions speedups from pipelining were less than ideal. Further limitations due to data dependencies result nearly eliminate the benefits of a pipelined implementation.

ACKNOWLEDGMENTS

We are grateful to the Aquarius project at UC Berkeley and would especially like to thank Peter Van Roy, Barry Fagan, and other members of the PLM group for providing the PLM compiler and simulation tools.

This work was supported in part by NSF Grant CCR-8706722 and a grant from the University of Wisconsin Graduate Research Committee.

References

Borriello, G., Cherenson, A. R., Danzig, P. B., and Nelson, M. N., "RISCS vs. CISCS for Prolog: A Case Study," in *Proceedings of the Second International Conference on Architectural Support for Programming Languages and Operating Systems*. Palo Alto, California, October 1987.

Dobry, T. P., Despain, A. M., and Patt, Y. N., "Performance Studies of a Prolog Machine Architecture," in *Proceedings of the 12th Annual International Symposium on Computer Architecture*. pp. 180 - 190, December 1985.

Hennessy, J., "VLSI RISC Processors," *VLSI Systems Design,* vol. 1, pp. 22 - 32, October 1985.

Holmer, B. K., Sano, B., Carlton, M., Roy, P. Van, Haygood, R., Bush, W. R., Despain, A. M., Pendleton, J. M., and Dobry, T., "Fast Prolog with an Extended General Purpose Architecture," in *Proceedings of the 17th International Symposium on Computer Architecture*. Seattle, Washington, May 1990.

Kogge, P. M., *The Architecture of Pipelined Computers*. New York: McGraw-Hill, 1981.

Kunkel, S. R. and Smith, J. E., "Optimal Pipelining in Supercomputers," in *Proceedings of the 13th Annual International Symposium on Computer Architecture*. pp. 404 - 411, June 1986.

Mills, J. W., "A High Performance LOW RISC Machine for Logic Programming," *Journal of Logic Programming,* vol. 6, pp. 179 - 212, 1989.

Patterson, D. A., "Reduced Instruction Set Computers," *Communications of the ACM,* vol. 28, pp. 8 - 21, January 1985.

Roy, P. Van, "A Prolog Compiler for the PLM," Report No. UCB/CSD 84/203, University of California, Berkeley, California, November 1984, Master's Thesis.

Steenkiste, P. and Hennessy, J., "Lisp on a Reduced-Instruction-Set Processor," *Proceedings of the 1986 Conference on Lisp and Functional Programming,* pp. 192 - 201, August 1986.

Taki, K., Yokota, M., Yamamoto, A., Nishikawa, H., Uchida, S., Nakashima, H., and Mitsuishi, A., "Hardware Design and Implementation of the Personal Sequential Inference Machine (PSI)," in *Proceedings of the International Conference on Fifth Generation Computer Systems*. 1984.

Tick, E., "Prolog Memory-Referencing Behavior," Technical Report No. 85-281, Standford University, Stanford, California, September 1985.

Warren, D. H., "Applied Logic -- Its Use and Implementation as a Programming Tool," University of Edinburgh, 1977, PhD Dissertation.

Warren, D. H., "An Abstract Prolog Instruction Set," Technical Note 309, Artificial Intelligence Center, SRI International, Menlo Park, California, October 1983.

2.6 A Prolog Abstract Machine for Content-Addressable Memory

Hamid Bacha

International Computer Services
2-212 Center for Science and Technology
Syracuse, New York 13244-4100

Abstract

This paper presents a Prolog Abstract Machine that takes advantage of the parallelism inherent in Content-Addressable Memory. It is conceived along the same lines as the Warren Abstract Machine (WAM) which is by now the most famous model for fast execution of compiled Prolog code. Content-Addressable memory is used for the management of the global stack. A special representation for Prolog terms is introduced. An instruction set built around this representation is then presented and shown to lead to a high-speed abstract machine model that is superior to the WAM. The numerous advantages of this model over the WAM model are then discussed.

INTRODUCTION

The Warren Abstract Machine (WAM) (Warren 1983) is by now the most famous model for fast execution of compiled Prolog code. Most of the successful commercial Prolog systems are based on this model. The secret behind its efficiency is its faithfulness in capturing the essence of the Prolog inference mechanism. For this reason, the WAM is thought to be the optimal model for Prolog compilation under a conventional computer architecture. To get any speed up beyond what the WAM has to offer, one has to start thinking about different architectures. One area where some researchers have focussed their attention is that of Content-Addressable Memory (CAM) (Naganuma et al 1988, Oldfield 1986, Stormon et al 1988). Unfortunately, all the models known to the author are built around interpreted Prolog where the CAM is used primarily to speed up the unification operation. The speed attained is not expected to be much higher than that achievable by the WAM. In this paper, we present the first abstract machine for compiled Prolog that utilizes content-addressable memory. In this model, content-addressable memory is used for the management of the global stack. We first introduce a representation for Prolog terms that results in very compact storage and leads to a model that is visibly superior to the WAM. We then show how these terms are stored in the CAM and discuss the set of instructions that manipulate them. After that, we exhibit a short program that uses most of these instructions and show how it is executed by our abstract machine. Finally, we discuss the advantages of our model over the WAM model.

VLSI for Artificial Intelligence and Neural Networks, Edited by J.G. Delgado-Frias and
W.R. Moore, Plenum Press, New York, 1991

153

CONTENT-ADDRESSABLE MEMORY

A content-addressable memory is an advanced memory device made up of an array of memory words and is capable of performing a pattern matching operation between the content of each word and a specified bit pattern. This operation is carried out in parallel for all the words, and is present in addition to the usual read and write operations. A CAM word has generally a much larger number of bits than a word in conventional random access memory (RAM). For the prototype CAM developed here at Syracuse University, a CAM row (or word) is made up of a multiple of 32 bits obtained through a horizontal cascading of 32 bit-wide CAM words. A commercial version of this chip is now being marketed by Coherent Research, Inc. A bit can be set to zero, one, or don't care. For our purpose, it suffices to know that a CAM is an array of memory words. The CAM is presented with a bit pattern. This bit pattern can be written to a specific word, a group of selected words, or all the words. It can also be compared to all the words simultaneously. If there is one or more matches, some operation may be requested on the matching words. We may, for example, read them (one at the time) or override them with another bit pattern in one parallel operation.

SOURCE OF INEFFICIENCY IN THE WAM

While the WAM architecture is suitable for a very fast Prolog machine, it nevertheless has some shortcomings associated with the use of random access memory (RAM) for managing the global stack. Specifically, each time a new variable is encountered (put_var, some unify_var), a location has to be reserved for it right away and tagged as unbound. That variable may never be used again (as a result of a subsequent failure and backtracking for example). When it is used, by the time it needs to be instantiated one or more choice points may have been created. For this reason a test has to be made to determine whether the variable needs to be trailed. If we could just delay the creation of unbound variables until they need to be instantiated, we would not have any need for the trail. The variables would always be created on top of the heap. A recent paper in the Journal of Logic Programming (Beer 1988) touched on this issue by focusing on a subset of variables that need not be created until ready to be instantiated. The requirement for these variables is that they occur no more than once in any given goal. The author used the tag "new unbound" to identify these variables. A location for these variables is however reserved and there is some overhead associated with avoiding dangling references. The method we propose applies to all unbound variables regardless of how many times they occur anywhere, does not require a location to be reserved for them, has no overhead, and still enjoys all the advantages of (Beer 1988), namely:

-no creation of unbound variables
-no dereferencing of argument registers for these variables
-no trail check
-no trailing of any variable

The key idea here is that we do not need locations for new variables. Instead, a name is associated with each new variable (actually a number known as the node descriptor as will be discussed later on). In the WAM model, when a variable occurs several times in a goal, a memory location is assigned to it and a pointer to that location is loaded into several argument registers. In our model, a name is associated with the variable and that name is loaded into the appropriate argument registers. Instead of random access memory, content-addressable memory is used for the management of the global stack. Whenever the value of a variable is needed, the variable name is presented to the CAM and the corresponding value is retrieved. If no value exists in CAM, the variable is still unbound. Whenever a variable needs to be instantiated, its name and value are recorded in CAM. This is equivalent to always having the variable that is about to be bound reside on top of the heap. Thus there is never any need to check for trailing or to have a trail present. Notice that we not only avoid the creation of unbound variables, we do not even reserve a location for them. The use of content-addressable memory eliminates the address-dependency of variables which was identified earlier as a source of inefficiency in the WAM. To exploit this feature of the CAM, we need to introduce a special representation for Prolog terms that enables us to identify the arguments of structures independently of their memory locations.

TERM REPRESENTATION

Every Prolog term can be depicted graphically as a tree structure in a natural way. Variables and constants have only a root node. For a structure, the main functor is the root node and its arguments the direct descendants of this root node. Each argument is in turn the root of a subtree, and so on until all the leaf nodes are only variables and constants. Figure 1.a shows the tree representation for the structure f(a, g(a,b), X).

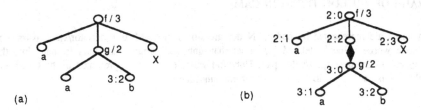

(a)   (b)

Figure 1 Representation of Prolog Terms

For our purpose, we associate with every node a **descriptor** and a **value**. The descriptor uniquely identifies each node and has the form NN:AN where NN is the node number and AN is a argument number. The descriptor of the root node of any structure has the form N:0 where N is a unique number for every new term. The arguments of this structure will have descriptors of the form N:1 through N:n where N:i is the descriptor of the ith argument. We need to make one small change to the tree representation. If the ith argument is a constant or a variable, the value of the node whose descriptor is N:i is the constant itself or is undefined, respectively. But if the ith argument is a structure, the value of the node whose descriptor is N:i is a new node descriptor M:0. M:0 is in turn the descriptor of the root node of the substructure which is the ith argument of the top structure. This process can be repeated for nested structures to any arbitrary depth. The value of a root node with descriptor NN:0 is the functor represented by that node. Figure 1.b shows the structure f(a, g(a,b), X) using the new representation. In this example, the functor f/3 is the value of the root node with descriptor 2:0. The three arguments are represented by nodes with descriptors 2:1, 2:2, 2:3 and values 'a', 3:0, and X (or 'undef'), respectively. Since the value of node 2:2 is 3:0, we say that node 2:2 references node 3:0 which is the root of the subtree representing the term g(a,b). (The symbol "<--->" between two nodes N and M means that node N references node M, i.e. the value of node N is M.) Throughout this presentation, we usually say node N:i to mean the node whose descriptor is N:i. Also, for the sake of clarity, we call the nodes of the form N:0 root nodes, and the nodes of the form N:i, with i > 0, leaf nodes.

The representation of lists is a bit tricky. The simplest way to represent a list is as a structure '.'/2 where the first argument of '.' is the head and its second argument is either NIL or a reference to another list. This representation is shown in Figure 2.a for the list [a,b,c]. The problem with this representation is that we are wasting a node for every element in the list because many nodes have the redundant value '.'/2. A more compact representation is to store the tail as the value of the root node. If T:0 is a node representing a list, then the value of T:0 is the tail node and the value of T:1 is the head node. Figure 2.b shows the same list [a,b,c] using the compact representation.

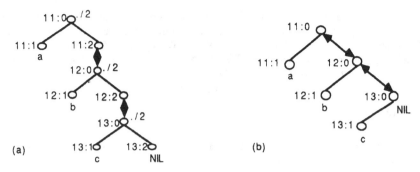

Figure 2 Two Different Representations for Lists

STORAGE OF PROLOG TERMS IN CAM

Prolog terms are represented by nodes. Nodes are stored in CAM as descriptor/value pairs. For every node whose value is defined (i.e. other than unbound variable) an entry is made into the CAM to record the descriptor/value pair. Unbound variables are not represented in the CAM and their absence is used as an indication of their unboundedness.

Call #	NODE		
	Descriptor	Value	
	ND#:ARG#	TAG	TERM
	2:0	STR	f/3
	2:1	CST	a
	2:2	REF	3:0
	3:0	STR	g/2
	3:1	CST	a
	3:2	CST	b
	11:0	LST	12:0
	11:1	CST	a
	12:0	LST	13:0
	12:1	CST	b
	13:0	LST	NIL
	13:1	CST	c
	21:0	STR	k/5
	21:5	REF	21:1

Figure 3 Term Representation in the CAM

Figure 3 shows the entries in the CAM for the terms f(a, g(a,b), X) and [a,b,c] from the previous examples, as well as the term k(A,B,C,D,A). For the last term, only the fifth argument represented by 21:5, is present in CAM. It references node 21:1, thus making the first argument and the fifth argument identical. Since the root node descriptor for k/5 is 21:0, we know that the node descriptors for its arguments are 21:1 through 21:5. Since the CAM is accessed by content instead of by address, we can retrieve the value of these nodes when needed just by knowing their node descriptors. For this reason, the arguments of a structure do not have to be stored in contiguous locations following the functor. In fact, they do not have to be stored at all if they are unbound variables. By contrast, the complete structure has to be created on the heap when dealing with the WAM model. Moreover, all the unbound variables have to be initialized. This is the first major improvement of our abstract machine over the WAM.

Our node descriptors are the equivalent of references in the WAM. A descriptor can be considered as a tagged Prolog object. It can be stored, for example, in a 32 bit argument register using the first 2 bits for a tag, the next 6 bits for the argument number, and the last 24 bits for the term number. This gives us a maximum of 64 arguments per structure, and over 16 million different terms (2^{24}) to play with. This should be more than satisfactory for any large scale Prolog program since the term numbers are recycled on backtracking and, if need be, during garbage collection.

THE CAM PROLOG ABSTRACT MACHINE

The architecture of our abstract machine differs from that of the WAM in many respects. First, the data areas of our model consist of the code area and the local stack only. There is no trail in our model because there is never any need to trail any variable. No time is wasted checking whether a variable should be trailed, and no time is spent managing the trail. Since content-addressable memory is used for managing the heap, there is no need for the top of the heap (H) register or heap backtrack (HB) register. The S register is also eliminated because there is no read or write mode when dealing with lists and structures. The local stack is organized as in the WAM and holds the choice points and the environments. The procedural instructions (CALL, EXEC, PROCEED) are a carry over from the WAM. The major changes involve the instructions responsible for matching head arguments, loading argument registers, and creating terms on the heap. The GET, PUT, and UNIFY class of instructions are replaced by a new set of more compact and more efficient instructions suitable for dealing with the CAM. The points raised in this section will be explained in more detail in the following sections.

Two global variables are needed, one to hold the next node or term number (call it TN) and the other to hold the next call number (call it CN). TN is incremented by one whenever a new node is created. CN serves as a time stamp to be associated with each CAM entry. It is incremented by one unit after each procedure call. It is saved in the choice point and reset to a previous value on backtracking. Upon failure, all CAM entries with a call number higher than or equal to that stored in the top most choice point are reset to unused, i.e. returned to the pool of free CAM words. Backtracking is carried out in parallel for all CAM entries concerned in few associative operations without any special hardware. It is equivalent to resetting register H to HB in the WAM. However, there is no resetting of any variables to "undef" because no variable was ever trailed.

THE INSTRUCTION SET

In this section, we introduce the STORE, LOAD, and MATCH class of instructions. The STORE instructions are used with terms that cause some nodes to be stored in the CAM. The LOAD instructions either load new node descriptors into registers or transfer data between registers. These instructions have no effect on the CAM. The MATCH instructions match a given clause head against incoming argument registers. They may cause some entries into the CAM. Before we describe these instructions in detail, we would like to provide a quick overview of the representation we use for Prolog terms. As we said earlier, Prolog terms are represented as tree structures. Each node within a tree has a descriptor and a value. The value has a tag identifying the type of term represented. Only the descriptor part of the node is stored in the argument registers (Ai registers), the temporary registers (Ti registers) and the permanent variables (Pi variables). The value of a node is stored in the CAM, with the node descriptor serving as a reference for accessing it. We will use the symbol TRM to stand for a structure, a constant, or a node descriptor. What it does not stand for is a variable or a list. Ai:N (with N >= 1) means the Nth argument of the term whose root node descriptor is Ai or Ai:0 (Ai and Ai:0 will be used interchangeably).

The STORE Instructions

The STORE class of instructions store nodes representing terms in the CAM and load the node descriptors into the appropriate registers. It consists of the following instructions:

```
store_term        Ai, TRM
store_new_list    Ai, Tj
store_new_plist   Ai, Pj
store_tail_list   Ai, Tj
store_tail_plist  Ai, Pj
store_nil         Ai
```

Only the first instruction deals with non-list terms, while the rest of the instructions deal with lists. The store_term instruction gets the next term number available and makes an entry into the CAM using this term number as a descriptor of a node whose value is TRM. The node descriptor is then loaded into Ai. The next example shows the use of this instruction. The variables X and Y do not take up any storage in CAM since they are unbound.

```
p :- q(a, f(X, b, Y)).

store_term   A1, a
store_term   A2, f/3
store_term   A2:2, b
exec         q/2
```

To store a list in the CAM, we need to differentiate between the initial creation of the list (first node) and the subsequent creation of the lists making up its tail, the tail of its tail, etc. The store_new_list instruction makes an entry in the CAM for a new list and loads the node descriptor for this list in register Ai. It also loads the descriptor for the tail of this list in register Tj. The instruction store_tail_list is then used to construct the rest of the list. It takes a descriptor of a list whose tail is still an unbound variable, and turns this variable into a new list. A descriptor for the new list is loaded into register Tj. The difference between store_new_list and store_tail_list is that the first instruction sets both of its operands while the second instruction sets only its second operand. The difference between the XX_list and XX_plist is that the latter uses a permanent variable for its second operand while the former uses an argument register. The last instruction, store_nil, installs NIL as the tail of the node list in its operand. The following example illustrates the use of these instructions. The table to the right shows the entries in the CAM made by the instructions on the same line.

```
p :- q([a, b, c], [s | X]), r(X).
```

		DESC	TAG	TERM
allocate	1			
store_new_list	A1, T2	11:0	LST	12:0
store_term	A1:1, a	11:1	CST	a
store_tail_list	T2, T3	12:0	LST	13:0
store_term	T2:1, b	12:1	CST	b
store_nil	T3	13:0	LST	NIL
store_term	T3:1, c	13:1	CST	c
store_new_plist	A2, P1	14:0	LST	15:0
store_term	A2:1, s	14:1	CST	s
call	q/2, 1			
load_pterm1	A1, P1			
dealloc_exec	r/1			

The load_pterm1 instruction merely transfers the content of the permanent variable P1 to argument register A1. The LOAD class of instructions is explained next.

The LOAD Instructions

The LOAD class of instructions merely loads new node descriptors into registers or transfers data between registers or between registers and permanent variables. It makes no entries into the CAM. It consists of the following instructions:

```
load_new_var     Ai
load_new_pvar    Ai, Pj
load_term        Ai, Tj
load_pterm1      Ai, Pj
load_pterm2      Pi, Tj
```

The load_new_var instruction gets a new term number N and loads the node descriptor N:0 into register Ai. The load_new_pvar does the same thing but also saves a copy of the descriptor in the permanent variable Pj. The load_term and load_pterm1 instructions load argument register Ai from either register Tj or permanent variable Pj respectively. The load_pterm2 instruction saves argument register Tj in permanent variable Pi. Again, we will provide an example to show these instructions in use.

p(X) :- q(X, Y, Z), r(X, Y).

```
allocate         2
load_pterm2      P1, A1    % save A1 in P1
load_new_pvar    A2, P2    % load new node descriptor in both A2 and P2
load_new_var     A3        % load new node descriptor in A3
call             q/3, 2
load_pterm1      A1, P1    % load A1 from P1
load_pterm1      A2, P2    % load A2 from P2
dealloc_exec     r/2
```

The MATCH Instructions

The MATCH class of instructions is used to match the head of a given clause against the incoming argument registers. It consists of the following instructions:

```
match_term       Ai, TRM
match_list       Ai, Tj, Tk
match_plist      Ai, Tj, Pk
match_nil        Ai
```

Notice that the last three instructions deal with lists while the first instruction deals with any other term. We do not have to distinguish between constants and structures. The main reason the WAM uses separate instructions for constants and structures is that in the case of a structure, the machine is set to a read or write mode. In read mode, the S register is made to point to the next argument of the structure. We do not have any read or write mode. Once a root node descriptor T:0 (corresponding to a functor) is known, the arguments are addressed as T:1 through T:N and can be stored anywhere in the CAM. The following example illustrates the situation for the clause p(f(X,Y,a), b).

```
match_term       A1, f/3
match_term       A1:3, a
match_term       A2, b
```

The incoming argument registers A1 and A2 contain node descriptors. These node descriptors may have values associated with them or represent unbound variables (no descriptor/value pair stored in CAM). If A1 is the descriptor of a bound variable, its value should be the functor f/3 or the unification fails. If A1 is the descriptor of an unbound variable, it is bound to f/3 and a descriptor/value pair is entered in the CAM to record this unification. When the unification succeeds, A1 contains the descriptor of a root node for the structure f/3. Therefore, the arguments of this structure are A1:1, A1:2, and A1:3 respectively. The next instruction matches the third argument of f/3 against the constant 'a'. Again, if it is an unbound variable, a new entry is made into the CAM. The variables X and Y are simply ignored. In the WAM, these two variables would have to be installed on the heap when in write mode.

To handle lists efficiently, we make use of three instructions. The match_list instruction uses three registers (Ai, Tj, and Tk), and expects a list or an unbound variable in its first argument. Otherwise, it fails. If the first argument is an unbound variable, it is unified with a list node and this binding is recorded in CAM. The descriptor for that list node is loaded in Tj and the descriptor for the tail of the list is loaded in Tk. On the other hand, if the first argument was already bound to a list, no new list is created but again the descriptor for that list is loaded in Tj while the descriptor for the tail of the list is loaded in Tk. The instruction match_plist is the same as match_list, except that the tail of the list is returned in a permanent variable Pk. The match_nil instruction expects a list whose tail is NIL (a one element list) or a list with an unbound variable as tail. In the latter case, it sets the tail to NIL. The following example illustrates the use of these instructions for the clause append([H | T], L, [H | Z]) :- append(T, L, Z).

```
match_list      A1, T4, A1
match_list      A3, T5, A3
match_term      T4:1, T5:1
execute         append/3.
```

To cover both the case of bound and unbound variables in this above example, let's consider the goal append([b,c], L1, L2) shown in Figure 4. In this case, A1 is bound to a list and A3 is an unbound variable.

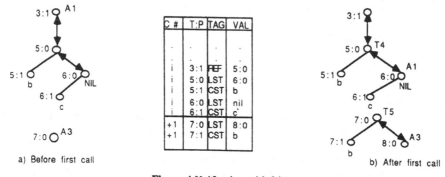

a) Before first call

b) After first call

Figure 4 Unification with Lists

Register A1 contains either the descriptor of a list node, or a reference (to a reference, to a reference, to ...) to the descriptor of a list node. The first match_list sets T4 to the descriptor of the list node (5:0), then sets A1 to the tail of the list, which in this case is the descriptor 6:0. The head of the list can now be accessed as T4:1 or descriptor 5:1. A3 is an unbound variable, so the second match_list makes an entry into the CAM for a list node using the descriptor found in A3 (possibly after dereferencing A3). At this point A3 can be overwritten, so it is set to the descriptor of the tail of the newly created list, which is 8:0. T5 is set to the descriptor of the new list which is 7:0. The head of this list is now accessed as T5:1 or descriptor 7:1. The match_term instruction ensures that the heads of the first and third lists (5:1 and 7:1) are identical by setting 7:1 to constant b.

EXAMPLE

Consider the following program which uses most of the instructions covered. It has been specifically constructed to include constants, structures, lists, and of course unbound variables. We made sure to cover the cases where the matching is between structures, between an unbound variable and a structure, and between an unbound variable and a list.

```
p([H | T], f(a, X, Y), b) :- q(H, X, Z), r(Z, T).
q(1, g(s, U), []).
r([], [2,3]).
```

The goal ':- p(X, f(a, Y, Z), W)' is to be solved relative to the above program. We are going to present the instructions for our abstract machine corresponding to the above program and goal. The table to the right of the instructions shows the entries made into the CAM by some of these instructions. To make it easy to follow the instructions, we included in parentheses the descriptors left in the registers after each instruction completes. Initially, CN is set to 0 and TN is set to 1. We start the execution by loading the arguments of the goal, then making a call to p/3.

				Call #	DESC	TAG	TERM
load_new_var	A1	(1:0)					
store_term	A2, f/3	(2:0)		0	2:0	STR	f/3
store_term	A2:1, a			0	2:1	CST	a
load_new_var	A3	(3:0)					
call	p/3.						
*************	*********						
p/3:							
allocate	2						
match_plist	A1, T1, P1	(1:0,1:0,4:0)		1	1:0	LST	4:0
load_term	A1, T1:1	(1:1)					
match_term	A2, f/3	(2:0)					
match_term	A2:1, a	(2:1)					
load_term	A2, A2:2	(2:2)					
match_term	A3, b	(3:0)		1	3:0	CST	b
load_new_pvar	A3, P2	(5:0,5:0)					
call	q/3, 2						
load_pterm1	A1, P2	(5:0)					
load_pterm1	A2, P1	(4:0)					
dealloc_exec	r/2						
q/3:							
match_term	A1, 1	(1:1)		2	1:1	CST	1
match_term	A2, g/2	(6:6)		2	2:2	REF	6:0
				2	6:0	STR	g/2
match_term	A2:1, s	(6:0)		2	6:1	CST	s
match_term	A3, nil	(5:0)		2	5:0	CST	nil
proceed							
r/2:							
match_term	A1, nil	(5:0)					
match_list	A2, T1, T2	(4:0, 4:0, 7:0)		3	4:0	LST	7:0
match_term	T1:1, 2	(4:0)		3	4:1	CST	2
match_nil	T2	(7:0)		3	7:0	L	NIL
match_term	T2:1, 3	(7:0)		3	7:1	CST	3
proceed							

Having successfully executed the program, we can know read the answer substitutions for X, Y, Z, and W. The variable X was loaded in argument one as the descriptor 1:0. Checking entry 1:0 in the CAM, we see that it is a list whose head 1:1 is the constant '1' and whose tail is 4:0. Again, checking entry 4:0 in the CAM, we see that it is a list whose head 4:1 is the constant '2' and whose tail is 7:0. Finally entry 7:0 shows a list whose head 7:1 is the constant '3' and whose tail is NIL. This gives us the list [1,2,3] as the substitution for X. A similar reading of the CAM shows that the values for Y, Z, and W are g(s, V1), V2, and b respectively.

As a second example, let's use the clause 'p :- q([X, g(A, B, C), Y])' and see how the instructions generated for our abstract machine compare to those for the WAM. Notice that we used a lot of variables to emphasize that our model treats variables implicitly while the WAM has to explicitly initialize them. The WAM instructions are presented first, with comments on the right hand side.

```
put_structure    g/3, A2     % p :- q(REG2 = g(
unify_void       1           % A,
unify_void       1           % B,
unify_void       1           % C)
put_list         A3          % REG3 = [
unify_void       1           % Y |
unify_nil                    % []]
put_list         A4          % REG4 = [
unify_value      2           % REG2 |
unify_value      3           % REG3]
put_list         A1          % [
unify_void       1           % X |
unify_value      4           % REG4])
execute          q/1         % .
```

Next, we present the instructions for our abstract machine. The entries made into the CAM by each instruction are shown to the right of the instruction.

		Call #	DESC	TAG	VALUE
store_new_list	A1,T2		1:0	LST	2:0
store_tail_list	T2,T3		2:0	LST	3:0
store_term	T2:1,g/3		2:1	REF	4:0
			4:0	STR	g/3
store_nil	T3		3:0	L	NIL
execute	q/1				

Only 5 instructions are needed compared to WAM's 14 (actually 12, since the three consecutive 'unify_void 1' should be combined into 'unify_void 3').

INDEXING

We did not mention the indexing instructions till now because they are independent of our model. The indexing instructions from the WAM, for example, are very adequate with our approach. Many methods have also been suggested for using the CAM for clause indexing (Colomb and Jayasooriah 1986, Stormon et al 1988, Wise and Powers 1984). These methods usually rely on multiple argument indexing. They provide better clause selection then that of the WAM, but they also have a higher overhead. We feel the best approach is a mixture of both. The WAM indexing can be used with procedures having a small number of clauses. The CAM indexing can be reserved to procedures with a large number of clauses. A more detailed discussion of this subject is beyond the scope of this paper.

ADVANTAGES OVER THE WAM

Following is a brief list of the advantages that the abstract machine model presented in this paper enjoys over the Warren Abstract Machine:

- When binding a variable, there is no need to check whether it should be trailed.
- No trailing means no resetting of variables on failure, and no trail to manage.
- No need to check for unsafe variables because there are none.
- No read or write mode when dealing with lists and structures. This eliminates the S register.
- Using CAM to manage the heap eliminates the H and HB registers.
- No need to initialize unbound variables when a structure is built. Arguments of structures are accessed by position and their absence from the CAM indicates that they are unbound.
- Fewer number of instructions means a less complex compiler and a smaller emulator. The 26 GET, PUT and UNIFY instructions from the WAM are replaced by 15 new instructions that are no more complex than their WAM counterparts.
- More efficient performance of the "occur check"
- Fast garbage collection.

Lack of space prevents us from discussing in detail why the occur check can be done very efficiently. The delay for the creation of unbound variables provides one half of the story and is explained in (Beer 1988). The other half of the story has to do with the fact that the "occur check" has to be performed only if the variable to be unified already occurs in a certain structure. This condition can easily be verified in CAM by checking (in parallel) whether there is any node in the CAM whose value is the descriptor of the variable in question. This should eliminate most occur checks. Moreover, when an occur check needs to be performed, only the branch from the given variable to the root of the structure needs to be checked. Clearly, the occur check does not depend on the complexity of the structure, but rather on the length of the branch along which the variable in question occurs.

As far as garbage collection is concerned, it is carried out in parallel. This feature has nothing to do with our approach, but is rather an inherent feature of the CAM. Once the marking phase identifies all the cells in use (which is done sequentially), a single operation is used to collect the garbage in parallel by setting all unmarked cells to garbage. Also, the term numbers and call numbers can be recycled during this operation. Large gaps will exist between useful term numbers, i.e. term numbers associated with nodes that are still active. The same is true for the call numbers. Using 32 bits for call numbers, the only way we run out of call numbers is if there are at least 2^{32} active nodes. This is not very likely for most applications.

Using 3 CAM words for each node stored seems excessive compared to the WAM. However, the fact that unbound variables are not stored and no memory is reserved for the trail compensates to a certain extent for this shortcoming. With some modification to the CAM, it should be possible to do away with storing the call numbers all together.

When we talk about advantages, we should certainly look at the disadvantages as well. One problem with using the CAM is the difficulty of utilizing virtual memory. The advantages of the CAM are lost if part of the heap is on disk. Another problem is that content-addressable memory is not that readily available yet. A prototype of a sophisticated CAM was developed at Syracuse University. The company Coherent Research, Inc. here in Syracuse has developed a newer version of that prototype which is now commercially available. We hope that the price of CAM chips will go down considerably in the near future and get closer to that of regular RAM. Advanced Micro Devices already has CAM chips (256x48bits) selling for $42 a piece.

The implementation of an interactive incremental Prolog compiler based on the work outlined in this paper has been completed. It has been interfaced to a CAM simulator. Real time benchmarks will be conducted once a VME board with CAM chips is completed in the near future. From our initial simulations, the results seem to indicate that in the worst case, our approach is as good as an equivalent WAM-based compiler.

AKNOWLEDGEMENT

This work was supported by the New York State Center for Advanced Technology in Computer Applications and Software Engineering at Syracuse University and Coherent Research, Inc. (CRi).

REFERENCES

Beer, Joachim (1988), "The Occur-Check Problem Revisited", Journal of Logic Programming. 1988 Vol. 5, pp. 243-261

Bowen, K.A., Buettner, K.A., Cicekli, I., Turk, A. (1986), "A Fast Incremental Portable Prolog Compiler", in proc. of 3rd International Conference on Logic Programming, London 1986.

Brule, M.R., "The Use of Content-Addressable Memory in Executing Logic Programs", Master's degree thesis, Syracuse University, August 1988.

Colomb, R.M., "Use of Superimposed Code Words for Partial Match Data Retrieval", The Australian Computer Journal, Vol. 17, No. 4, Nov. 1985.

Colomb, R.M., Jayasooriah, "A Clause Indexing System for Prolog Based on Superimposed Coding", The Australian Computer Journal, Vol. 18, No. 1, Feb. 1986.

Gabriel, J., Lindholm, T., Lusk, E.L., and Overbeek, R.A., "A Tutorial on the Warren Abstract Machine", Argonne National Laboratory report ANL-84-84, June 1985.

Nakamura, D., "Associative Concurrent Evaluation of Logic Programs", Journal of Logic Programming, Vol. 1, No. 4, Dec. 1984.

Naganuma, J., et al., "High-Speed CAM-Based Architecture for a Prolog Machine (ASCA)", IEEE Transactions on Computers. Vol. 37, No. 11, Nov. 1988.

Oldfield, J.V., "Logic Programs and an Experimental Architecture for their Execution", in proceedings of IEE, Vo. 133, Pt. E, No.3, pp163-167, May 1986.

Stormon, C.D. et al., "An architecture Based on Content-Addressable Memory for the Rapid Execution of Prolog", in proceedings of 5th International Conference on Logic Programming, Seattle, Wa. 1988.

Warren, D.H.D., (1983), "An Abstract Prolog Instruction Set", Technical Note 309, Artificial Intelligence Center, SRI International, 1983.

Wise, M.J., Powers, D.M.W., "Indexing Prolog Clauses via Superimposed Code Words and Field Encoded Words", in proceedings of International Symposium on Logic Programming, Atlantic City, NJ, Feb. 1984. IEEE Computer Society Press.

Warren, D.S., "Efficient Prolog Memory Management for Flexible Control Strategies", in proceedings of International Symposium on Logic Programming, Atlantic City, NJ, Feb. 1984. IEEE Computer Society Press.

Kacsuk, P. and Bale, A., "DAP: A Set Oriented Approach to Prolog", The Computer Journal, Vol. 30, No. 5, 1987.

2.7 A Multi-Transputer Architecture for a Parallel Logic Machine

Mario Cannataro, Giandomenico Spezzano and Domenico Talia

CRAI

Località S. Stefano, Rende (CS), Italy

Abstract

This paper describes the design and the implementation of a logic programming language on a massively parallel VLSI architecture in an efficient and scalable way. This implementation is based on the AND/OR Process Model which allows the exploitation of both AND and OR parallelism in logic programs. A distributed memory model is used, and a decentralized control mechanism has been designed. The parallel architecture, which the system is implemented on, consists of a network of Inmos Transputers, the AND/OR processes are implemented as Occam processes mapped onto the Transputer nodes.

INTRODUCTION

The availability of a logic programming environment on a parallel VLSI architecture makes possible to reduce the software design overhead and to achieve high performance (Treleaven *et al* 1987). Furthermore, the implementation of these tools will allow the exploitation of the VLSI technology by supplying a high-level language that will be used to implement complex applications achieving high performance.

The parallelism in the execution of a logic program derives mainly from the nondeterminism of its resolution procedure. The two major forms of parallelism are *AND parallelism* and *OR parallelism*. AND parallelism is obtained by parallel resolution of the subgoals in the body of a clause. OR parallelism is obtained by solving in parallel the clauses whose heads unify with the goal. The implementation of both OR and AND parallelism is expected to cope with problems like: multiple binding management, combinatorial explosion of the number of processes because of the OR parallelism, and

VLSI for Artificial Intelligence and Neural Networks, Edited by J.G. Delgado-Frias and
W.R. Moore, Plenum Press, New York, 1991

165

binding conflicts for variables shared among the literals of a body in the AND parallelism.

The purpose of this paper is to describe the design and development of a parallel implementation, on a VLSI multicomputer with distributed memory, of a *Horn clause* based language. The selected parallel model is the AND/OR Process Model.

The AND/OR Process Model (Conery and Kibler 1981, Conery and Kibler 1983) is an abstract model for the parallel execution of logic programs based on the use of concurrent processes cooperating by message passing. The goal of this model is the exploitation of AND and OR parallelism. According to the model, a logic program is solved by a network of concurrent processes. In the AND/OR Process Model, there are two kinds of processes: *AND process* and *OR process*. An AND process is created to solve a goal statement which consists of a conjunction of literals (subgoals). An OR process is created by an AND process to solve one of those literals.

The remainder of the paper is organized as follows. In the first section we describe the basic features of the parallel logic system and the main architectural choices. The second section gives the details of the parallel architecture and in particular of the parallel run-time support. The next section discusses the techniques used for the implementation of the distributed memory management. Finally, in the last section the main novel features are summarized and the future work plans are outlined.

BASIC CHOICES

The major aim of our implementation of a parallel logic machine is to study the development of the logic programming paradigm in the context of a distributed architecture without shared memory, composed of a large number of processing elements (Cannataro *et al* 1989).

The semantics of the model is based on "pure logic programming", i.e., the Horn clauses, instead of Prolog, that has many characteristics of the Von Neumann architectural model. According to the AND/OR Process Model, the parallel execution of the logic programs will be exploited by the run-time support and does not require annotations by the programmer (Conery 1987).

The architecture which fulfills the system requirements is a cellular one, composed of a large number of homogeneous nodes (processor + memory) and connected by an intercommunication network. The network is of the near-neighbor kind with point-to-point communications. A message is sent from the sender to the addressee without using switch elements for the routing (*direct network*) (Seitz 1984). The message is sent to the neighbor that will take care of routing it towards the next node and so on until the destination is reached.

On this architecture, a source logic program is translated into a network of cooperating processes written in the concurrent "target" language Occam 2 (Inmos 1988), then these processes are mapped onto the machine's processors. The parallel machine on which the system will be implemented is a distributed memory MIMD machine and consists of a network of T800 Inmos Transputers (Inmos 1989).

The parallel programming on Transputer-based systems is simplified by the use of the Occam concurrent programming language. The combination of the Transputer and Occam constitutes a *process-oriented* system to support an efficient implementation of distributed memory parallel applications, such as the AND/OR Process Model.

According to the requirements of the AND/OR Process Model, our research goal, and the Transputer characteristics, the main features of the parallel logic machine are :

❑ It consists of a very large number of virtual processors (processes) located anywhere in the parallel machine. All the processes are created statically and activated dynamically. A distributed load balancing algorithm is provided for the activation of processes.

❑ It is highly distributed, so there are no shared resources. Each virtual processor manages its own data structures and cooperates with the others by message passing.

❑ No centralized scheduling is necessary. The global scheduling is achieved using the local information of each virtual processor.

❑ The variable binding management uses the *closed environment* technique that is based on copying and fits the distributed memory organization.

SYSTEM ARCHITECTURE

This section describes the architecture of the parallel machine, in particular after a general overview of system organization, the parallel run-time system is discussed.

Overview

The architecture of the parallel logic machine consists of the following components: **Shell, Precompiler, Loader,** and **Run-time system.** The Shell, the Precompiler, and a part of the Loader run on the PC-hosted Transputer, whereas the other components are mapped onto the Transputers of the toroidal mesh (figure 1).

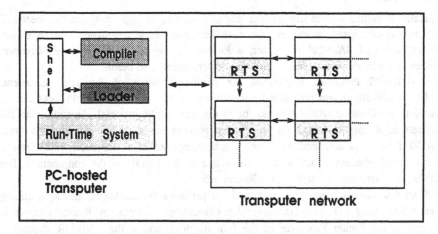

Figure 1 The architecture

The Shell is an interpreter that makes available to the user a set of commands to interface the parallel logic machine, and in particular its static tools, i.e. editor, precompiler, and loader.

Using the Shell commands, a user can define the logic programs, load the program clauses on the Transputer network, enter the logic query and receive the program results. For these purposes the Shell interacts with the Precompiler, the Loader and the Run-time system running on the PC-hosted Transputer.

The Precompiler performs the translation of the clauses of a logic program into an internal format that can be used by the processes of the Run-time system. It is composed of a parser and a code generator that transform a logic program into an internal representation suitable for the AND/OR processes. The output of the Precompiler is the input for the Loader.

The Loader is composed of a process running on the PC-hosted Transputer which manages the clause partitioning, and one process on each Transputer that implements the loading of the partitions of the clause database on the parallel machine. After the loading of all the clauses of a program, the processes of the Loader reach a wait status until a new loading request is done.

The Run-time system is the heart of the parallel logic machine. It consists of a set of cooperating virtual machines mapped onto the Transputer nodes. On each node, the virtual machine is implemented by a set of processes. The Run-time system is highly decentralized: no master nodes are provided on the toroidal mesh, and no central scheduler is implemented. The global scheduling of the parallel execution of a logic program is implemented by the cooperation of the processes of Run-time system.

Three functional layers can be identified into the Run-time system of the parallel logic machine: the *Communication Layer*, the *Control Layer*, and the *Resolution Layer*. Each layer is implemented by means a set of concurrent Occam processes mapped onto the Transputer nodes.

Run-time System

The parallel Run-time system implements the execution of a logic program by means of a collection of concurrent processes. On each Transputer node are mapped the following processes: a set of *AND/OR Processes*, a *Router*, a *Loader,* and a *Clause Manager*. These processes implement the three functional layers mentioned before.

The AND/OR Processes implement the parallel solution of the goal statement, according to the algorithms provided by the abstract model. An AND/OR Process can be executed in AND mode (AND Process) or in OR mode (OR process), depending on the parameters of a start message that the parent process sends it at the activation time. An AND Process is activated to solve a goal composed of a conjunction of literals, whereas an OR Process is activated to solve one of the literals of the conjunction. The AND/OR Processes are connected to the Router process.

A Router process is running on each node. It performs the routing of messages among the processes using the four Transputer links avoiding deadlock. A Router process is connected to the Router Processes of the four neighbor nodes, the AND/OR Processes, the Loader, and the Clause Manager.

The Loader process implements the loading of the partitions of the logic clauses on the various nodes of the parallel machine. The Loader communicates the clause partition to the local Clause Manager and returns in a wait state until it will receive a new request of loading.

The Clause Manager process performs the management of the local partition of the clause database. Furthermore, it performs the unification of a literal with a clause of its partition. Notice that either all the clauses which compose a procedure or none of them are located in a partition. The set of all the Clause Manager processes compose a *decentralized manager* of the data base of logic clauses distributed on the Transputer network.

DISTRIBUTED MEMORY MANAGEMENT

This section presents the distributed memory organization and the data management in the Run-time system. The basic principle is that each AND/OR Process uses its local data to solve a subgoal, and processes cooperate by message passing. Starting from the representation of the basic data types of a logic language (constants, variables, complex terms) we construct more complex data structures to represent the components of a logic language. Finally we define the data structures and the basic operations used either in the AND/OR Processes and in the Clauses Manager.

Literals, clauses and bindings environments

In the sequential implementations of logic languages the data types are represented by a TAG that identifies the type, and an ADDRESS, usually a pointer to the real data object. In a distributed memory implementation, where each process only refers its own local memory, it is convenient to use a memory model that does not use absolute addresses. In our implementation a segmented memory model is used (Conery 1988). The ADDRESS field is split into a frame address and an offset in it. Figure 2 shows the complete cell

C = cdr-bit, F = frame/heap-bit I sign-bit

Figure 2 Elementary data cell

TAG indicates the data types of the logic language, C is used in the list implementation, F is used in the address de-referencing, FRAME/HEAP ADDRESS is the address (i.e. the name) of a frame/heap and OFFSET is the offset of the referred object into the frame/heap.

Literals. A literal is represented using three data structures: the Literal Descriptor, the Term Descriptor (heap) and the Binding Descriptor (frame). The Literal and Term Descriptors are the skeleton of the literal; regarding also the Binding Descriptor we obtain an instance of the literal.

❑ the **Literal Descriptor** for the literal **f (t1,...,tn)** is a set of n+1 cells where the first one contains the functor name and the arity, the remaining n are constants, variables (references to the frame) or terms (references to the heap),

❑ the **Binding Descriptor (frame)** is a set of variable cells, they can be unbound or bound either to terms on the heap and variables on the same frame (after the unification),

❑ the **Term Descriptor (heap)** is a set of functor or list cells whose components can be functor, list, constant and variable (references to the frame) cells.

The binding environment contains the literal's variables. The variable cells on the heap and on the literal descriptor are references to the binding environment. After unification only the binding and term descriptors can be affected.

Clauses: The clause **A :- B1,...,Bn** is a set of **n+1** literal descriptors, **n+1** binding descriptors and a term descriptor. Each literal of the clause (head, body) is described by a literal descriptor, while there is only a term descriptor for the clause. The binding environment for the clause is composed of a global environment (global variables in the head) and a local environment (local variables in the body). The first binding descriptor is associated to the clause's head and contains the global environment; the local environment is split into n binding descriptors associated to the body literals.

To guarantee the single assignment property is necessary that, for each variable, there is a single instance cell. A global variable into the literal **Bi** is a reference from the binding descriptor **i** to the binding descriptor **0**. A local variable into the literal **Bi** is a reference from the binding descriptor **i** to the binding descriptor **j** where the variable was firstly named ($j \leq i$). This clause representation organizes the binding environment in a set of sub-environments. Because of each literal refers only its own environment, this organization is suitable for a distributed memory implementation.

Data structures and memory organization

The defined data structures are rather general to allow the representation of: a literal with multiple bindings (literal to be solved by an OR Process), a goal statement with multiple bindings (conjunction of literals to be solved by an AND Process), a set of clauses (data base partition into the Clause Manager). The following data structures contain a set of literal, binding and term descriptors:

Literal.Descriptor, Binding.Descriptor, and *Heap.Descriptor.*

To improve the memory utilization (the language Occam does not permit dynamic allocation) the Binding.Descriptor and Heap.Descriptor are implemented by a single data structure, named Frame.Descriptor. From a logical point of view the Frame.Descriptor is divided into two parts, the former contains the binding descriptors, the latter the term descriptors. These two logical structures are managed using a LIFO strategy: the allocation of a new frame is made from the top to the bottom, the allocation of a new heap from the bottom to the top. Therefore the middle part of the Frame.Descriptor can be used by both structures, optimizing the memory utilization. Furthermore the LIFO strategy avoids *garbage collection*. To identify literals, conjunctions, clauses on those structures the following data structures are provided:

Literal.Descriptor.Index, Frame.Descriptor.Index, and *Heap.Descriptor.Index.*

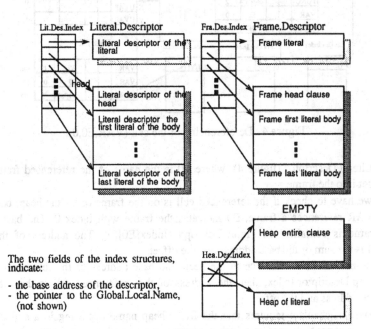

Figure 3 Memory organization when a literal and a clause are stored.

The element **i** of these structures contains the base address for the **ith** literal/frame/heap and a pointer to another structure, Global.Local.name, whose use will be explained later.

To locate the clause **A :- B1,...,Bn** are sufficient:

- **n+1** indexes (**L0,L1,...,Ln**) of the Literal.Descriptor.Index to identify the literal descriptors;

- **n+1** indexes (**E0,E1,...,En**) of the Binding.Descriptor.Index to identify the binding descriptors;

- **1** index **H** of the Heap.Descriptor.Index to identify the term descriptor.

To locate the conjunction **B1,...,Bn** the same indexes are sufficient, without the index to identify the head literal. To locate the literal **Bj** three indexes, identifying its literal, frame and heap descriptor, are sufficient. Figure 3 shows the memory organization when a literal and a clause are stored.

Dereferencing mechanism

All the operations involving accesses to memory require a mechanism to de-refer an address in a value. For the sake of clarity we will show the basic mechanism, then a problem raised by this basic approach, and our final solution.

Basic mechanism. Let be (L0=0, E0=0, H0=0) the set of indexes that identify the literal f(X,p(X,Y)). Suppose that we have to dereference the cell (VAR,E0,0) at the subscript 2

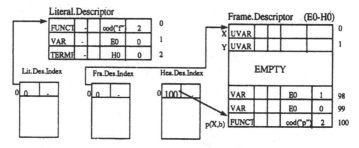

Figure 4 Dereferencing of the cell (VAR,E0,0).

into the Literal.Descriptor (figure 4), where E0 is the name of the referenced frame and 0 is the offset into the frame.

First, we have to check if the referenced cell is on the frame or on the heap, because of the cell VAR references a frame, E0 indicates the frame with index 0. The base address of the frame is contained in Frame.Descriptor.Index[E0][0]. The address of the referenced cell is the sum of the base address and the offset.

If the initial cell is a reference to the heap, the base address of the referenced heap is on the Heap.Descriptor.Index, then the address of the referenced cell is the subtraction of this base address and the offset.

This basic mechanism requires that the frame/heap name occurring in a cell is unique into the environment. A case in which a name is duplicated occurs when a literal has to be copied to allow some operations on the copy. As we will see the copy occurs very frequently.

Let be (L0, E0, H0) the literal to be duplicated, and (L1, E1, H1) the first names suitable into the xxx.Descriptor.Index, then to maintain the same basic mechanism is necessary to rename, for every cell into the copied literal, the old names E0, H0 with E1, H1. The disadvantage of this approach is that the renaming operation has cost linear with the size of the structures to be copied.

Proposed mechanism: The proposed mechanism does not require the renaming operation also if it adds some little overhead respect to the basic mechanism. Let consider a literal whose cells refer the frame and heap with the names E, H. These **global names** are generated by the precompiler and will be not changed during the execution. When a literal is used in a process, it will   assume some **local names** depending on the free locations on the xxx.Descriptor.Index. These local names are used by the process to identify the literal. To each literal are then associated the global names defined by the precompiler and local names used by the process. The structure containing these informations is the Global.Local.Name   and   it   is   bound   to   the   literal   by   the   second   field   into   the xxx.Descriptor.Index. Notice that is not necessary to store the name of the literal descriptor because it is never referenced. The dereferencing of a cell consist of two steps:

      □ it needs to determine the local name of the referenced frame/heap, this is found
          into the location of the Global.Local.Name pointed by the second field of the

xxx.Descriptor.Index; then this local name is used to determine the base address of the referenced frame;

❑ to access the referenced cell the basic mechanism is then used.

Regard to a conjunction or a clause, the same mechanism is used. The global and local names are sufficient to dereference a cell if the referred environment is closed (Conery 1988). An environment composed of a literal, a frame E and a heap H is closed if does not exist a cell that refers a frame/heap different by E and H. If the environment is not closed two sub-environments can be identified.

Let be ENV0 and ENV1 the global names of the two environments, and GL0 and GL1 the corresponding entries on the Global.Local.Name. To derefer a cell is necessary determine in which environment the referenced frame/heap must be de-referenced, that is if the local names have to be taken from GL0 or GL1, next the basic mechanism is used. Because of it can happen that the global names of two environments are equals, the flag F specify if a cell has to be dereferenced in an environment or in another one.

CONCLUSION AND FUTURE WORK

This work has described how a parallel logic machine can be implemented in an efficient and scalable way on a massively parallel VLSI architecture, using the abstract AND/OR Process Model.

According to the AND/OR Process Model, a logic program is transformed to a network of concurrent processes that exploit both AND and OR parallelism. These processes are the heart of the Run-time system of the parallel logic machine. The Run-time system has been designed to obtain an efficient execution of non-annotated logic programs on a distributed memory MIMD architecture. It has been implemented in a completely decentralized way, using a distributed memory management model based on copying. This model avoids that a process must access a global memory space or a memory location of another process during its running. Each process holds all the data are necessary to perform its task. The processes scheduling is obtained through the cooperation of the processes of the Run-time system mapped onto the Transputer nodes.

The tools composing the programming environment and the Run-time system processes are implemented on a network of 40 Transputers connected to a Transputer hosted on a PC. The source language used is the Occam language. Due to the lack in the language of mechanisms for the dynamic memory allocation, the data structures has been implemented using arrays, and some special techniques have been designed to achieve a good management. At the moment, only the OR parallelism has been implemented. The source code of the Router process is about 1800 lines, whereas an AND/OR Process consists of 2440 code lines. The code of the Clause Manager is about 2200 lines and the code of the Loader process in the current version is about 250 lines.

We are testing and evaluating the system using some classical logic programs. The first results are interesting, in fact they show a good scalability of the parallel logic machine. Although the current implementation of the system is based on interpretation, the final goal of our research work is the implementation of a compiled version of the AND/OR Process Model. In fact a compiler can execute more controls and optimizations, and it can generate code which takes advantage of this knowledge, providing better performance.

A compilation model can be based on the association of an AND process with the body of a clause, and an OR process can be associate with the heads of the clauses of a procedure. This solution should simplify the system architecture because it eliminates the Clause Manager process.

In the future work, in particular for the AND parallelism implementation, will be take into account the interesting proposal of *Restricted AND-Parallelism* by DeGroot (1984). This method tries to simplify the AND parallelism evaluation strategy by transferring to compile-time decisions about clause execution ordering.

ACKNOWLEDGEMENTS

This work has been partially supported by "Progetto Finalizzato Sistemi Informatici e Calcolo Parallelo" of CNR. We would like to thank Prof. Marco Vanneschi for many constructive comments and suggestions in the design of the parallel architecture.

REFERENCES

Cannataro M., G. Spezzano, and D. Talia," A Highly Decentralized Architecture for the Parallel Execution of Logic Programs", *Proc. of the IFIP Working Conference on Decentralized Systems,* Lyon, pp. 127-143, 1989.

Conery J.S., *Parallel Execution of Logic Programs*, Kluwer Academic Publisher, 1987.

Conery J.S. and D.F. Kibler, "Parallel Interpretation of Logic Programs", *Proc. Conf. on Functional Progr. Lang. and Computer Arch.*, ACM Press, pp. 163-170, 1981.

Conery J.S. and D.F. Kibler, "And Parallelism in Logic Programs", *Proc. Int. Joint Conf. on Artificial Intelligence*, Germany, pp. 539-543, 1983.

Conery J.S., "Bindings Environments for Parallel Logic Programs in Non-Shared Memory Multiprocessor", *Internal Report,* Univ. of Oregon, 1988.

DeGroot D., "Restricted AND-Parallelism", *Proc. Int. Conf. on Fifth Generation Computer Systems 1984*, pp. 471-478, ICOT, Tokyo, 1984.

Gallizzi E., Cannataro M., Spezzano G., and Talia D., "A Deadlock-Free Communication System for a Transputer Network", *Proceedings of 12th OUG*, IOS Press, pp. 11-21, 1990.

Inmos, *Occam 2 Reference Manual*, Prentice Hall, England, 1988.

Inmos , *Transputer Databook*, Inmos Ltd., England, 1989.

Seitz C., "Concurrent VLSI Architectures", *IEEE Trans. on Computers,* vol. c-33, pp. 1247-1265, 1984.

Treleaven P., *et al*, "Computer Architectures for Artificial Intelligence", *Lecture Notes in Computer Science*, vol. 272, pp. 416-492, Springer-Verlag, 1987.

3.1 Computational Capabilities of Biologically-Realistic Analog Processing Elements

Chris Fields, *Mark DeYong, and *Randall Findley

Computing Research Laboratory and
*Department of Electrical and Computer Engineering
New Mexico State University, Las Cruces, NM 88003-0001, USA

Abstract

The processing elements employed in conventional artificial neural networks are highly abstract models of biological neurons. We are taking an alternative approach of designing a processing element that directly models signal processing in biological neurons, in order to investigate the computational capabilities of such models. The processing elements can be used to develop systems that exhibit a variety of computational capabilities, and are amenable to fabrication in dense arrays.

INTRODUCTION

The processing elements (PEs) employed in conventional artificial neural networks (ANNs) are highly abstract models of biological neurons. The most common PE, in which incoming signals are summed, and then convolved with a sigmoidal transfer function, embodies two basic assumptions. First, it is assumed that communication between neurons can be approximated by a slowly-varying scalar signal, which is typically interpreted as the frequency of action potentials (APs). Second, it is assumed that computation within neurons occurs instantaneously - i.e. that there is no delay between the arrival of an incoming signal and its effect on the output. While these assumptions are biologically unrealistic (Selverston 1988), they are generally viewed as providing an adequate approximation, that is relatively straightforward to implement, with which to carry out high-level computational studies (Sejnowski *et al* 1988, Durbin 1989).

We are taking the alternative approach of designing a PE that directly models signal processing in biological neurons, in order to investigate the computational capabilities of such models. An initial design has been developed based on standard CMOS and bipolar device

VLSI for Artificial Intelligence and Neural Networks, Edited by J.G. Delgado-Frias and
W.R. Moore, Plenum Press, New York, 1991

technologies, and shown to support a variety of computational capabilities, including the generation of complex rhythmic patterns, standard logic functions, and winner-take-all mechanisms (DeYong *et al* 1990, Findley *et al* 1990). This paper outlines our strategy, reviews the results obtained with our initial design, and describes our current PE design, which addresses several shortcomings of the initial PE.

STRATEGY

Our hypothesis is that useful computational capabilities may be discovered by modelling both the signal processing that takes place within neurons, and the characteristics of the pulse streams exchanged between neurons, in some detail. The appropriate level of description is that of electrophysiological measurements, at which the shapes and relative timing of both APs and postsynaptic potentials (PSPs) are the observables. This level of description is well below that of either abstract mathematical models of ANNs (reviewed by Grossberg 1988) or conventional analog VLSI models (reviewed by Card and Moore 1989, Foo *et al* 1990), and corresponds roughly to that of mathematical simulation models based on the membrane equations (Wilson and Bower 1989, Miall 1990). It is illustrated schematically in Figure 1.

Thus far, we have focussed on modelling a generic spiking neuron with either excitatory or inhibitory (or both) chemical synapses, although the current PE design (see below) allows electrical and graded-release synapses to be modelled also. Such neurons are common both in

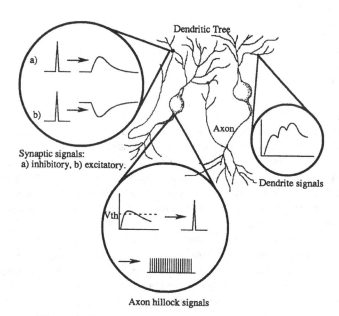

Figure 1 Signal processing in a generic spiking neuron.

invertebrates, and in the vertebrate cortex and motor system. They can be viewed as hybrid devices, which employ relatively slow analog signal convolution to compute an output from a set of positive or negative inputs, but use a relatively fast, digital encoding - the AP - for communication. This focus on spiking neurons can be contrasted with that of, e.g. Mead and Mohowald (1988), who have used resistive arrays to model graded-release neurons in the early visual system.

Our PEs, which are described in detail below, directly model six functional components of the spiking neuron: the postsynaptic region, the dendritic tree, the cell body or soma, the action potential initiation zone or axon hillock, the axon, and the presynaptic region. The PEs generate waveforms that model both excitatory and inhibitory PSPs, and APs. The shapes and timing characteristics of these waveforms can be adjusted as parameters of the model. We can, therefore, model streams of APs that have no well-defined frequency, and can examine the effects of interactions between multiple PSPs in a dendritic tree in detail. Such investigations are not possible with PEs that operate only on scalar levels.

Spiking neurons operate in a voltage range of roughly -80 mV, the approximate Nernst potential for K^+ ions, to roughly 50 mV, the approximate Nernst potential for Na^+ ions, with a typical resting potential of approximately -60 mV (Kandel and Schwartz 1985, Ch. 6). We have scaled this operating range linearly to the 0 - 5 V range; we have also scaled the few ms temporal operating range typical of spiking neurons to the few ns range. This scaling allows us to model synapses and the axon hillock with small numbers of CMOS devices, which may be operated above the threshold voltage. Operating above threshold avoids the noise sensitivity and fan-out problems of subthreshold devices such as used by Mead (1989). Transistor-level design, as opposed to the more common op-amp level designs (several examples appear in Card and Moore 1989), also allows a considerably greater flexibility in modeling waveforms, and in combining analog and digital characteristics in a single device. Designing at this level allows for minimal device count, which in turn yields more dense VLSI layouts.

BEHAVIOR OF INITIAL PE DESIGN

Chemical synapses respond to action potentials by producing time varying signals similar to those shown in Figure 1. The signal may be either positive or negative with respect to the resting potential for excitatory or inhibitory synapses, respectively. The dendrite has two functions. First, all incoming synaptic signals are temporally summed in each branch of the dendrite. The combined signal is then attenuated and delayed as it travels along the dendrites to the soma. Once the soma potential exceeds a threshold value, an action potential is produced by the axon hillock. If the soma potential remains above the threshold for a sufficient period of time the hillock will produce a stream of action potentials.

The initial PE design comprises circuits that model the behavior of excitatory and inhibitory chemical synapses, the dendritic tree, the soma, and the axon hillock. These components are shown schematically in Figure 2. The axon and presynaptic regions are modeled by metal wires.

The model synapses respond to pulses at their input terminals by generating PSPs that are qualitatively indistinguishable from the alpha functions described by Wilson and Bower (1989). Example PSPs, together with APs, are shown in Figure 3.

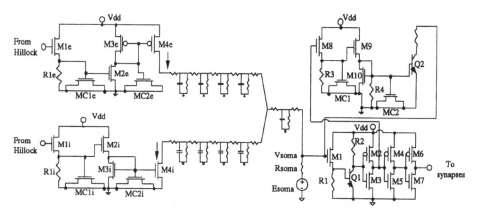

Figure 2 Schematic diagram of the initial PE. Excitatory (upper) and inhibitory (lower) synapses appear on the left; the RC network models the dendritic tree.

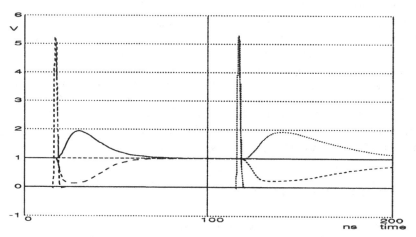

Figure 3 Model APs and PSPs generated by the initial design.

The synapse models are current sources with parasitics intentionally added in. The transistor M1 (with subscript e for the excitatory synapse and i for the inhibitory synapse) determines how much charge will be stored in capacitor MC1. The input to the synapses is an impulse-like action potential. Thus, a sufficient amount of charge must be stored on the capacitor in order to allow a slow exponential decay in the output current (see Figure 3). The fall time of the synaptic currents supplied to the dendritic tree is determined by the time constant of the RC network R1, MC1.

Transistor M2 is operated in the saturation region and therefore is the simplest type of current source (inhibitory) or current sink (excitatory). The current source/sink feeds a current mirror made up of transistors M3 and M4. Capacitor MC2 is supplied to control the rise time of the current. The amplitude of the current can be varied through a reasonably wide range by varying the ratio of gains of the two transistors, where the gain (β) is defined by $\beta = Kn' (W/L)$. In this equation, Kn' is a process dependent parameter called the trans-conductance parameter, W is the user defined width of the transistor (in the direction perpendicular to current flow) and L is the length (in the direction of current flow).

This design gives the designer a high degree of control over the shape of the output current waveform. Rise time, fall time, and amplitude have all been simulated over a relatively wide range of values with little distortion. Only two versions of each type of synapse have been used in our system simulations. This is for two reasons: 1) This reduces the amount of SPICE code required for simulation purposes, 2) This adheres to the building block structure we are trying to create.

The axon hillock is the action potential initiation zone. Figure 3 shows a typical action potential created by the circuit shown in Figure 2. The input to the circuit is the voltage that accumulates at the base of the dendritic tree due to the currents supplied by the synapses. M1 and R1 are adjusted so that the voltage at the base of Q1 is equal to the diode voltage (vd) of the base - emitter junction when the voltage at the gate of M1 is equal to the desired threshold voltage. R2 is a large resistor which gives Q1 a large gain. Thus as the voltage at the base of Q1 crosses vd, the voltage into the first inverter (M2, M3) will switch quickly from +5 V to 0 V. The output is then staged up through two more inverters in order to increase the drive capabilities. Since BJTs are typically much faster than MOSFETs, the rise of the AP will be limited to the slew rate of the output inverter. It is apparent that the rest of the circuit is a modified version of the inhibitory synapse. Thus, when the output reaches the switching point of transistor M8, the input (Vsoma) is forced near 0 V. This causes transistor Q1 to turn off and resets the AP. The parameters of the inhibitory circuitry are set so as to simulate the refractory period of a biological axon hillock (i.e. the minimum time between action potentials found when Vsoma remains above the threshold voltage). This refractory period is roughly 5 times the width of an AP.

MODELS

A variety of computational systems based on this initial PE design have been simulated. One set of systems mimics the complex rhythmic patterns produced by central pattern generators (CPGs) found in invertebrate motor systems. Additionally, a set of standard logic devices has been produced, which implement the OR, XOR, and Inversion functions. Both sets of systems are described in DeYong et al (1990) and Findley et al (1990).

Winner-take-all (WTA) networks are traditional neural network structures used in the selection of a single winner from a group of competitors (Feldman and Ballard 1982, Lippmann 1987). Figure 4 shows a system that has the capability of performing two types of WTA. Selection can be based upon the frequency of incoming APs (MAX frequency NET or MAXfNET) or upon the relative timing of the arriving signals (temporal WTA or TWTA). The structure is a traditional single-layer, mutual-inhibition network. Which of the two WTA mechanisms the circuit performs is determined by the relationship between the timing constants of the inhibitory synapses and the periods of the incoming AP streams. This bifunctional WTA thus illustrates the central role played by pulse shape and relative timing in neural computation.

An action potential received by the inhibitory synapses will set up a period of inhibition in the rest of the network. If this period of inhibition is less than the period of any incoming AP stream, the circuit will function as the MAXfNET. This is due to the existence of gaps between

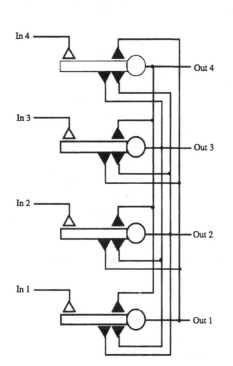

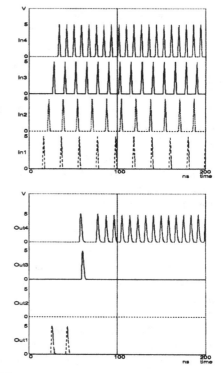

Figure 4 This network serves as the TWTA and the MAXfNET depending upon the timing of the network and the AP streams.

Figure 5a (top) & 5b (bottom) represent the MAXfNET input and output respectively.

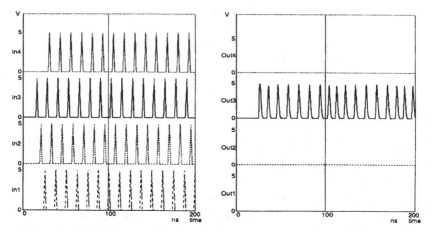

Figure 6a (left) & 6b (right) represent the TWTA input and output respectively.

the periods of inhibition. The probability of a higher frequency line receiving an AP during one of these gaps is much higher than that of a lower frequency line. Additionally, when a higher frequency line is selected, the gaps will become smaller and the probability of selecting another line becomes less. This type of network is purely probablistic, and convergence is not guaranteed. This nondeterminism is typical of WTA structures. Figure 5 shows a simulation of the MAXfNET. The selection is made in approximately 50 ns under the worst-case condition, in which the highest frequency AP stream arrives last, approximately 15 ns after the first arriving AP stream. If the period of inhibition is greater than the period of all incoming AP streams, the circuit will function as a TWTA network. Once any PE receives an AP and induces a period of inhibition on all other PEs, the second period of inhibition will be set up before the first has ended. Thus the periods of inhibition will overlap and no later arriving AP streams can be selected. This overlap is sufficient to assure convergence. Figure 6 shows that selection is made almost instantaneously, even though there is only a small difference in arrival times.

AN IMPROVED PE

The desire for an even more biologically accurate model neuron, and for a less process-dependent implementation led to the design of a second generation PE. While the previous model is more biologically realistic than any other VLSI model of which we are aware, there are several additional features of neurons that contribute to their computational capabilities. These include the propagation of slow signals down the axon, the existence of electrical and graded-release synapses, and various mechanisms for adaptation and modulation. Our current PE design addresses some of these issues. It moreover employs more compact circuits, which may be fabricated at considerably higher densities than was possible with the initial design.

Figure 7 shows the schematic representation of the new processing element. The synapse and dendrite models have been combined in such a manner as to provide a method for the adaptation of synaptic efficacy and a reduction in the actual VLSI layout area. Varying the gate

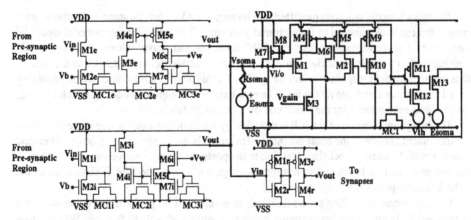

Figure 7 Schematic diagram of the second generation PE. Excitatory (upper) and inhibitory (lower) synapses appear on the left. The axon hillock (upper) and presynaptic region (lower) appear on the right.

voltage Vw (see Figure 7) causes the synaptic signal to change both amplitude and timing characteristics. Vw has a 2 volt dynamic range, from 2 to 4 volts, in which the synaptic waveform changes smoothly. Outside of this range, no effect is noticed on the waveform. Figure 8 shows SPICE simulations of the excitatory synapse through its dynamic range. The weighting capability and the reduction in layout are due to the lumped model of the RC network that models the dendritic tree.

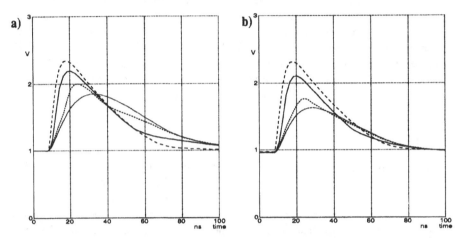

Figure 8 SPICE simulations of the redesigned excitatory synapse model. The waveform has its highest amplitude when Vw is at or below 2 volts. The waveform is then attenuated and spread out as Vw is increased. Additional waveforms are shown for increasing attenuation for Vw equal to 2.5, 3, and 4 volts. The attenuation difference between a) and b) is due to a higher value of resistance (M7e) in a).

The hillock model has been modified to reference the APs from the soma potential when it crosses the threshold, instead of from ground potential. This will allow us to model electrical interactions between adjacent cells through RC networks, and graded-release synapses. A cell with high activity can, in particular, cause the resting potentials of coupled neighbors to increase, thus modulating their responses to incoming APs. The hillock model now also has the capability for adaptation via a variable threshold. The new design is completely CMOS, which removes the previous requirement for the more complex BiCMOS fabrication process.

The presynaptic region of the cell is modeled by a pair of inverters which serve to remove the modulated portion of the soma potential. This models the presynaptic region of a chemical synapse, which has no direct electrical link to the postsynaptic region; communication across the synaptic junction is via neurotransmitters. Figure 9 shows the SPICE simulation of the hillock and the presynaptic region.

Current system modelling shows that little or no changes in performance occur when the redesigned PE is substituted into systems previously simulated with the first PE. With the new electrical coupling available between PEs, we can model systems in which there is a concept of a functional neighborhood, with the activity of a PE dependent not only upon its synaptic inputs, but also to a lesser degree, on those of its neighbors.

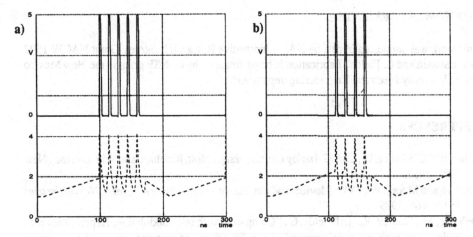

Figure 9 SPICE simulations of the redesigned hillock and presynaptic region models. The bottom trace shows the output of the hillock and how the APs are produced on top of the soma potential. The top trace shows the output of the presynaptic region. The difference between a) and b) is due to an increase in threshold voltage (2.0 to 2.4 volts).

FABRICATION

The layout of all devices has been completed for a 2 micron, n-well process. Nearly half of the layout area of the synapses is made up of capacitors. The synapses may be arrayed end to end without additional layout, but N^2 bussing requirements for N hillocks will prevent a uniform method of providing a two-dimensional array. The layout of the hillock has been designed to allow for an increase in the size of all circuit elements by approximately fifty percent without changing the size of the layout. The hillock also has the capability of being arrayed end to end.

A fully interconnected structure is being designed with both inhibitory and excitatory synapses. The structure will consist of arrays of hillocks and excitatory and inhibitory synapses. Initial estimates indicate that an array of 10 hillocks and 200 synapses (100 excitatory and 100 inhibitory) will fit on the TINYCHIP package provided by the Metal Oxide Semiconductor Implementation System (MOSIS), which has a total work area of 1800 x 1830 microns.

CONCLUSION

We have shown that analog VLSI methods can be used to design processing elements that are substantially more realistic models of neurons than have been achieved previously. These PEs can be used to develop systems that exhibit a variety of computational capabilities, and are amenable to fabrication in dense arrays. They provide a basis for investigating the types of computation that can be performed efficiently by biological nervous systems, as well as an alternative to traditional ANNs for fast signal-processing applications.

ACKNOWLEDGEMENTS

This work was supported in part by NASA Innovative Research Program Grant NAGW 1592 to J. Barnden and C. Fields. Fabrication is being financed by an NSF grant to the New Mexico State University Electrical Engineering department.

REFERENCES

Allen, P. and Holberg, D., *CMOS Analog Circuit Design*, Holt, Rinehart, and Winston, Inc., New York, 1987.

Card, H. and Moore, W., "VLSI devices and circuits for neural networks", *Int. J. Neural Systems* 1: 149-165, 1989

DeYong, M., Findley. R., and Fields, C., "Computing with fast modulation: Experiments with biologically-realistic model neurons", *Proc. Fifth Rocky Mountain Conf. on AI*, Las Cruces, NM. pp. 111-116, 1990.

Durbin, R., "On the correspondence between network models and the nervous system", In: R. Durbin, C. Miall, and G. Hutchinson (Eds) *The Computing Neuron*, Wokingham, U.K., Addison-Wesley. pp. 1-10, 1989.

Feldmann, J. and Ballard, D., "Connectionist models and their properties", *Cognitive Science*, 6: 205-254, 1982.

Findley, R., DeYong, M. and Fields, C., "High speed analog computation via VLSI implementable neural networks", *Proc. 3rd Microelectronic Education Conference and Exposition*, San Jose, CA. pp. 113-123, 1990.

Foo, S., Anderson, L., and Takefuji, Y., "Analog components for the VLSI of neural networks." *IEEE Circuits and Devices*, vol. 6, no. 4, pp. 18-26, 1990.

Grossberg, S., "Nonlinear neural networks: Principles, mechanisms, and architectures", *Neural Networks*, 1: 17-61, 1988.

Kandel, E. and Schwartz, J., *Principles of Neural Science*, New York, Elsevier, 1985.

Lippmann, R., "An introduction to computing with neural nets", *IEEE ASSP*, vol. 3, no. 4, pp. 4-12, 1987.

Masaki, A., Hirai, Y., and Yamada, M., "Neural networks in CMOS: A case study", *IEEE Circuits and Devices*, vol. 6, no. 4, pp. 18-26, 1990.

Mead, C., *Analog VLSI and Neural Systems*, Reading, MA, Addison-Wesley, 1989.

Mead, C. and Mahowald, M., "A silicon model of early visual processing", *Neural Networks*, 1: 91-97, 1988.

Miall, C., "The diversity of neuronal properties", In: R. Durbin, C. Miall, and G. Hutchinson (Eds) *The Computing Neuron*, Wokingham, U.K., Addison-Wesley. pp. 11-34, 1989.

Sejnowski, T., Koch, C., and Churchland. P. , "Computational neuroscience", *Science*, 241: 1299-1306, 1988.

Selverston, A., "A consideration of invertebrate central pattern generators as computational databases", *Neural Networks*, 1: 109-117, 1988.

Weste, N. and Eshraghian, K., *Principles of CMOS VLSI Design: A system perspective*, Reading, MA, Addison-Wesley, 1985.

Wilson, M. and Bower, J., "The simulation of large-scale neural networks", In. C. Koch and I. Segev (Eds) *Methods in Neuronal Modeling*, Cambridge, MA, MIT. pp. 291-333, 1989.

3.2 Analog VLSI Models of Mean Field Networks

Christian Schneider and Howard Card

Department of Electrical and Computer Engineering
University of Manitoba
Winnipeg, Manitoba, Canada, R3T 2N2

Abstract

Two compact analog CMOS synaptic circuits with in situ Hebbian learning have been developed and used to construct a Mean Field Network (MFN), which is a deterministic version of a Boltzmann machine. This network, consisting of 25 neurons and 625 synapses with local learning and weight storage is currently being fabricated in 3μm CMOS. Our investigations show that neural network architectures, such as the MFN, can be constructed from highly non-ideal analog CMOS components, because the adaptive ability of neural net architectures with learning allows the network to compensate for device variations.

INTRODUCTION

Analog CMOS VLSI is an excellent candidate for the implementation of large-scale neural networks, provided that the architecture of the neural system does not require functions that are inefficient to implement in silicon (Mead 1988, Shimabukuro, Reedy et al 1988, Murray 1989, Card and Moore 1989, Clark 1990). The architecture must be tolerant of non-ideal arithmetic operations, inaccurate timing, etc. It has been shown recently by Hinton (1989) and by Peterson and Hartman (1989) that fully-connected networks of neurons that perform weight updates according to a *contrastive Hebbian* learning rule can perform pattern classification tasks with similar generalization properties to backpropagation networks. These networks are called Mean Field Networks (MFNs) or deterministic Boltzmann machines (DBMs) (Hinton 1989). Our system-level simulations show that MFNs continue to learn and to function properly when constructed from components which only crudely approximate the functions required by theory. Two analog CMOS

VLSI for Artificial Intelligence and Neural Networks, Edited by J.G. Delgado-Frias and
W.R. Moore, Plenum Press, New York, 1991

circuits implementing synapses with in-situ Hebbian learning are described below. System-level simulation indicates that these circuits are suitable candidates for the implementation of neural architectures such as the Mean Field Network.

THE NEURAL NET MODEL

Our circuits implement a standard analog bipolar neural network model, where both neuron activations and weights may have values in the range $[-V,+V]$, and

$$\frac{dW_{ij}}{dt} = AV_i V_j - BW_{ij} \qquad (1)$$

$$V_i = f\left(\sum_j W_{ij} V_j\right) \qquad (2)$$

where (1) represents a common form of the Hebbian learning rule (see for example, Kohonen 1988), and (2) a weighted summation of neuron activations. Thus, the weight W_{ij} (the contribution of the jth neuron to the input of the ith neuron) gradually increases with time when V_i (activation of the ith neuron) and V_j (activation of the jth neuron) are correlated, and decreases when they are anti-correlated.

The current activation of neuron i is calculated from a linear weighted sum of the contribution of all neurons which synapse on neuron i (equation 2). The function $f(\cdot)$ is sigmoidal, with saturation values of $\pm V$. Note that the weight change operation of (1) (learning) typically occurs at $\frac{1}{100}th$ to $\frac{1}{10000}th$ the rate of network operation, represented by (2).

16 TRANSISTOR SYNAPTIC CIRCUIT

The circuit of figure 1 implements an approximation of the neural network described by equations 1 and 2. In the synaptic circuit of figure 1, W_{ij} is represented by the voltage on C (V_{ij}), and $\frac{dW_{ij}}{dt} \propto \frac{dV_{ij}}{dt} = \frac{I_{cap}}{C}$. The product $AV_i V_j$ is implemented with transistors $M_1 - M_{14}$. $M_1 - M_4$ perform the multiplication $AV_i V_j$, and $M_5 - M_{12}$ implement a cascode current mirror which ensures that I_{cap} is independent of V_{ij}. Figure 2a shows I_{cap} as a function of V_i and V_j (all plots are SPICE level 3 simulations of Northern Telecom's $3\mu m$ CMOS3): clearly the four transistor multiplier is far from linear. However, our system-level simulations indicate that this approximation to Hebbian learning is accurate enough for neural network architectures such as the MFN. Intuitively, it is not surprising that an adaptive circuit (in our case a neural network with learning capability) can learn to compensate for system imperfections. For example, this circuit can compensate for variations in the transconductance of M_{15} and M_{16} by learning a different weight V_{ij}. This ability to compensate for device variations is critical in analog VLSI systems.

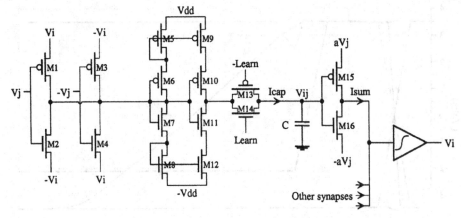

Figure 1. 16 transistor synaptic circuit.

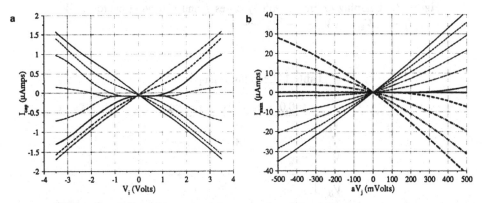

Figure 2. a) Learning current I_{cap} as a function of V_i, for various V_j. b) I_{sum} as a function of aV_j, for various V_{ij} ($a = 0.14$).

Figure 2b is a plot of the product $aV_j V_{ij}$, implemented by M_{15} and M_{16}. Note that a is a small constant, used to scale V_j to keep the two transistor multiplier (M_{15}, M_{16}) operating in the linear region. The input to the sigmoidal neuron amplifier is maintained at virtual ground.

The learning behavior of this circuit is illustrated in figure 3 and table 1, where two synapse circuits (figure 1) j and k are connected to neuron i. The system is stable until $t=0.9\mu s$, when both V_j and V_k switch sign. The result is that V_i also switches, since the ith neuron is correlated with the jth neuron and anti-correlated with the kth neuron. At $t=2.9\mu s$, V_j changes to a moderate negative value, but V_i only changes slightly since V_k

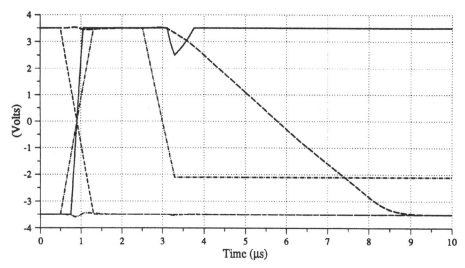

Figure 3. Learning example, with synapses j and k driving neuron i. V_i —, V_j —·—, V_k ----, V_{ij} ———, V_{ik} —··—

Table 1. Learning example

	$t=0.0$	$t=0.9\mu s$	$t=2.9\mu s$
V_i	−	+	
V_j	−	+	−
V_k	+	−	
V_{ij}	+		→ −
V_{ik}	−		

maintained its previous value. Now V_i and V_j are no longer correlated: thus V_{ij} gradually becomes negative as the new anti-correlation is learned. Note that the learning rate can be reduced by pulsing the *Learn* control signal (M_{13} and M_{14}) -- as the *on* portion of the duty cycle of the *Learn* signal is shortened, the learning rate in reduced.

36 TRANSISTOR SYNAPTIC CIRCUIT

The circuit described in the previous section has several problems: 1) inverted and non-inverted analog neuron outputs are required; 2) the neuron output must be scaled by a small constant; 3) the input to the neuron amplifier must be maintained at virtual ground; and 4) the learning multiplier characteristic (figure 2a) has a "flat spot" for small values

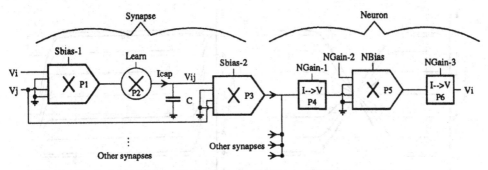

Figure 4. Synapse and neuron circuits.

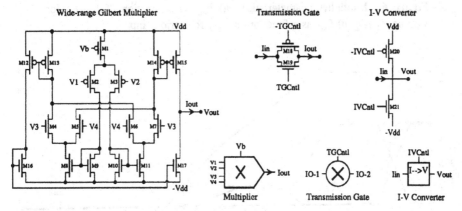

Figure 5. Schematics of circuit components.

of V_j (depletion-mode transistors would solve this problem). We have developed a second synaptic circuit which, at the expense of layout area, avoids these problems.

In the synaptic circuit of figure 4, W_{ij} is represented by the voltage on C (V_{ij}), and $\frac{dW_{ij}}{dt} \propto \frac{dV_{ij}}{dt} = \frac{I_{cap}}{C}$. The product AV_iV_j is implemented by multiplier P_1. The second term in (1) is a weight decay term, which has been set to zero ($B=0$) in this circuit. P_3 computes the product $V_{ij}V_j$, and current summation at the input to P_4 implements the summation in (2). P_4, P_5 and P_6 implement a neuron with a saturating sigmoidal output. In a typical network, such as the MFN, each neuron receives input from many other neurons in the network: thus each neuron is connected to many copies of the synapse circuit.

Transistor schematics of the circuit components are illustrated in figure 5. The multiplier is a wide-range Gilbert multiplier variant (Mead 1988), which multiplies two differential voltages and outputs a current. Note that unlike in Mead 1988, transistors in our multiplier are operating above threshold.

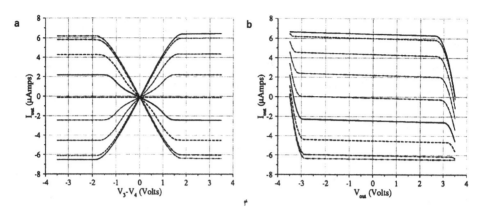

Figure 6. Multiplier characteristics, a) I_{out} as a function of V_3-V_4 for various V_1-V_2; b) I_{out} as a function of V_{out} for various inputs.

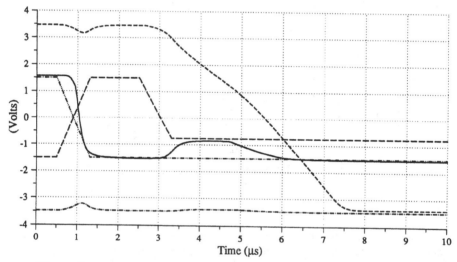

Figure 7. Learning example, with synapses j and k driving neuron i. V_i —, V_j ---, V_k —··—, V_{ij} ----, V_{ik} —·—·

Figure 6a shows that the multiplier is far from linear. However, as with the previous circuit, our system-level simulations indicate that this approximation to Hebbian learning (P_1) and weighted summation (P_3) is accurate enough for the MFN.

The learning example from the previous section is repeated here using the 36 transistor synaptic circuit; as before two synapse circuits j and k are connected to neuron i. Notice the similarity between figures 3 and 7: the two synaptic circuits exhibit essentially the same learning dynamics, despite substantial differences in the behavior of the components which make up the two circuits.

Table 2. Learning example. Note that $W_{ij} = -V_{ij}$, so a negative V_{ij} represents a positive correlation

	$t=0.0$	$t=0.9\mu s$	$t=2.9\mu s$
V_i	+	−	
V_j	−	+	$-\frac{1}{2}$
V_k	+	−	
V_{ij}	+		$\rightarrow -$
V_{ik}	−		

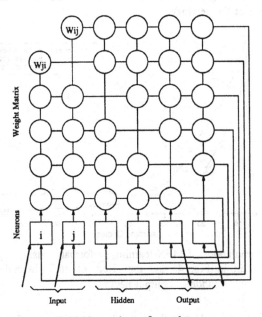

Figure 8. A Mean Field Network configured as a pattern associator.

MEAN FIELD NETWORKS

A Mean Field Network (Fig. 8) is a fully-connected neural network which uses a mean field approximation to replace the statistical neurons of a Boltzmann machine with continuous-valued functions. In the learning algorithm, multiplication replaces the collection of co-occurrence statistics. One of the advantages of this network structure is that, because neurons are not preassigned as input, output or hidden, the same network can be used to implement an associative memory, a classifier or a pattern associator.

The MFN employs "contrastive Hebbian learning" where the weight changes depend on the difference in the products of activations of neurons in a 'clamped' and an 'unclamped' phase. In the clamped phase, both the inputs and outputs of the network are held at the desired values. In the unclamped phase, only the inputs are held and the network is free to determine the output values. Weights are adjusted using the formula

$$\Delta W_{ij} = \varepsilon(V_i V_j - V_i' V_j') - BW_{ij} \tag{3}$$

where V_i is the clamped-phase activation of the ith neuron, calculated as in equation (2) and V_i' is the activation of the same neuron during the unclamped phase. ε determines the learning rate and B is the weight decay factor. It has been shown (Hinton 1989) that this learning rule results in gradient descent in an information-theoretic measure related to the error performance of the network.

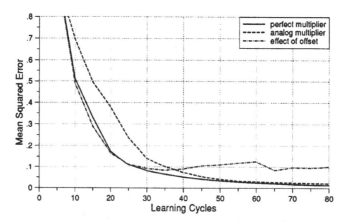

Figure 9. Simulations of MFN learning performance using a perfect multiplier, the circuit in Fig. 4, and the effect of an uncancelled systematic offset. (6 input, 16 hidden, 3 output neurons)

It was mentioned previously that the network can compensate for non-ideal behavior in the analog circuits by learning different weight values. Similarly, the imperfect behavior of the learning multiplier (Fig. 4, P1, P2) merely results in longer learning times (the effective ε varies) as long as learning is always in the right direction (Fig. 9). Note, however, that the multiplier characteristic in Fig. 6a shows a systematic offset for small values of $V_1 - V_2$ (V_i), and $V_3 - V_4$ (V_j) which causes I_{cap} to have the wrong sign.

Fortunately, the MFN learning rule (equation 3) calculates ΔW_{ij} as the *difference* between two imperfect multiplications. As long as the subtraction operation is reliable and the multiplier characteristic is monotonic, the multiplier offset does not affect the error rate of the network. To make the subtraction operation as accurate as possible, the sign reversal in the learning current I_{cap} for the unclamped phase is implemented as part of the capacitor charging circuitry instead of by exchanging V_i and its zero reference at the input to the differential learning multiplier.

IMPLEMENTATION DETAILS

The synaptic circuit of figure 4 requires one small addition to accommodate the two-phased contrastive Hebbian learning required for an MFN: $P2$ must be replaced by four transmission gates, which allow the output of $P1$ to be connected to either end of the weight storage capacitor C. The opposite end of the capacitor is connected to ground. Thus, during the clamped learning phase, I_{cap} flows into the positive terminal of C, and during the unclamped phase I_{cap} flows into the negative terminal of C (equation 3).

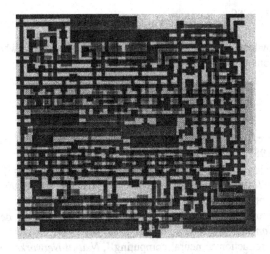

Figure 10. Layout of single synapse ($32440\mu\mu m^2$ per synapse).

A fully-connected 625 synapse, 25 neuron MFN has been submitted for fabrication in $3\mu m$ CMOS, with chip testing scheduled for September 1990. Figure 10 illustrates the layout of a single synapse of our MFN. This layout implies a density of 3000 *synapses* cm^{-2} in $3\mu m$ CMOS, and 20000 *synapses* cm^{-2} in $1.2\mu m$ CMOS technologies. These are very respectable synaptic densities, especially considering that they incorporate *in situ* learning computations.

CONCLUSIONS AND FUTURE WORK

We have demonstrated that compact analog VLSI circuits may be used in the implementation of neural network architectures, such as the Mean Field Network. The adaptive ability of neural net architectures makes them more tolerant of device and process variations than conventional analog circuits.

The time scales of these circuits are in the ns range for the network dynamics, and in the μs range for the learning dynamics. Tasks involving 100 training patterns for 100 epochs can be learned in $<1s$ and the capacitive charge leakage during this period can be reduced by modest cooling of the chip (Schwartz et al 1989). The training set is periodically repeated to refresh the weights, and this has the added benefit of compensating for component drift due to temperature, etc. It is intended to eventually incorporate small MF networks into all-analog systems, with analog sensory preprocessing (Mead 1988) and analog motor output, resulting in simple silicon 'animals'.

The synapse circuits described in this paper and a number of variations have been submitted for fabrication through The Northern Telecom/Canadian Microelectronics Corporation silicon fabrication service for universities, and will be tested in September 1990.

ACKNOWLEDGEMENTS

We gratefully acknowledge the contribution of Roland Schneider, who performed the system-level simulations of the Mean Field Network used in this paper.

REFERENCES

Card, H.C. and Moore, W.R., "VLSI devices and circuits for neural networks", *Int. J. Neural Systems*, 1989, Vol. 1, pp. 149-165.

Clark, J.T., "An analog CMOS implementation of a self organizing feed-forward network", *Proc. Int. Joint Conf. on Neural Networks*, IJCNN-WASH 90, M. Caudill, editor, 1990, Vol. 1, pp. 118-121.

Hinton, G.E., "Deterministic Boltzmann learning performs steepest descent in weight space", *Neural Computation*, Vol. 1, No. 1, 1989, pp. 143-150.

Kohonen, T., "An introduction to neural computing", *Neural Networks*, 1988, 1, pp. 3-16.

Mead, C.A., *Analog VLSI and Neural Systems*, 1988, Reading: Addison-Wesley

Murray, A.F., "Silicon implementation of neural networks", Proc. First IEE Int. Conf. on Artificial Neural Networks, 1989, pp. 27-32.

Peterson, C. and Hartman, A., "Explorations of the Mean Field Theory Learning Algorithm", *Neural Networks*, Vol. 2, pp. 475-494, 1989.

Schwartz, D.B., Howard, R.E., and Hubbard, W.E., "A programmable analog neural network chip", *IEEE J. Solid St. Ccts.*, 1989, 24, pp. 313-319

Shimabukuro, R.L., Reedy, R.E., Garcia, G.A., "Dual-polarity nonvolatile MOS analog memory (MAM) cell for neural-type circuitry", *Electronic Letters*, 1988, 24, pp. 1231-1232.

3.3 An Analogue Neuron Suitable for a Data Frame Architecture

W.A.J.Waller, D.L.Bisset, P.M.Daniell

Electronic Engineering Laboratories
University of Kent at Canterbury, CT2 7NT, UK

Abstract

This paper describes the VLSI realisation of a novel neural network implementation architecture which is geared to the processing of frame based data. The chief advantage of this architecture is its elimination of the need to implement total connectivity between neural units as hard-wired connections. This is achieved without sacrificing performance or functionality. A detailed description of the implementation of this architecture in 2μ CMOS, using a mixed analogue and digital building blocks, is given, together with details of system level design.

INTRODUCTION

One of the greatest potential benefits of using a neural network to solve some problem is the prospect of being able to realise the solution directly in hardware, thus giving a significant improvement in speed over any software based implementation. Therefore when designing hardware implementations of neural networks, it is important to consider the system wide constraints that might be imposed by an engineering environment.

Although these constraints will encompass problem specific limitations, they will also include the standard engineering concerns of cost and flexibility. If commonly available and therefore cheap VLSI processes can be used to implement neural networks, then this will enhance their attractiveness to engineers. With respect to neural networks, flexibility can be identified in a number of different ways:

a) The ability to build different sizes of neural network from some standard building block, (different numbers of neurons per layer, different numbers of inputs per neuron).

b) The ability to change the function computed by the neural units, (e.g. to control the non-linearity of the activation function).

VLSI for Artificial Intelligence and Neural Networks, Edited by J.G. Delgado-Frias and
W.R. Moore, Plenum Press, New York, 1991

c) To be able to construct different neural network architectures, (e.g. feedback, feed-forward, self organising).

It is important to consider these desired features when formulating a hardware implementation, and for VLSI implementations it is important that this flexibility can be achieved without any need for physical changes to the device.

Many different approaches have been taken to the implementation of neural networks in VLSI, but they often suffer from basic impracticalities when judged by engineering criteria. These can range from requiring large numbers of expensive devices to implement a network, to requiring all of the input data to be presented in parallel (Hirai *et-al* 1989, Eberhardt *et-al* 1989). The main problem facing the VLSI designer is the large increase in the number of synapse circuits required for each additional neuron (assuming total connectivity between layers). This has partially been addressed through the use of cross-and-bar arrays, however these suffer from the problem that they require the input data to be presented in parallel, and that the number of synapses in any particular device is strictly limited by the pin count. Clearly significant savings in terms of device area and pin count can be made if the numbers of physical synapses that need be implemented can be reduced. Akers has explored this through the design of limited interconnect networks (Akers *et-al* 1989). Akers tries to tackle the problem by constraining the neural network. The alternative is to look for implementation architectures that reduce the number of physical synapses required. A novel implementation architecture has been developed by the authors (Bisset *et-al* 1990), which solves this problem from the implementation point of view. This paper describes a 2μ CMOS device that realises this implementation architecture.

IMPLEMENTATION ARCHITECTURE

It has been noted that multiplexing holds the key to the efficient hardware implementation of neural networks (Bailey and Hammerstrom 1988). The problem is to find a multiplexing scheme that does not seriously affect overall system performance. In the general case where the fastest possible response is required, it is inevitable that any multiplexing scheme will result in a reduction in throughput over a fully parallel system. However it is possible to make use of the constraints in an engineering environment to design an efficient multiplexing scheme that does not affect system level performance.

When considering a multiplexing scheme, it is important to identify those parameters of the system which will give the greatest savings in implementation terms. For neural networks the most costly component is the synapse. A single transistor saved here may result in significant overall savings across a device. If significant numbers of neurons are to be integrated into a single device, then the largest saving that can be made by using multiplexing is to trade the time slots for synapses. This can only be done in environments which do not require an output for each data input, but where many data inputs constitute a *data frame*, and outputs from the neural network are only required after each frame of data has been presented to the network.

This provides for a trade-off between physical synapses and multiplexing slots. Figure 1 shows the functional diagram for a single neuron channel. Data and weights are

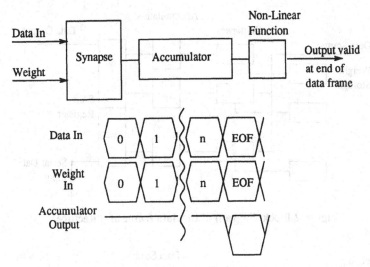

Figure 1 A single neuron in the data frame architecture

provided together and the output from the accumulator is valid at the end of each data frame. This output is now the weighted sum of the data in the frame and the weights for one neuron. This can then be passed through a non-linear function if desired. The architecture can easily be extended to many neurons since the data input is common to each neuron. Only the parallel provision of weights increases for each extra neuron. By providing a data multiplexer at the output, a serial data stream can be generated suitable for feeding into the next layer (see Figure 2). This gives the final form of the implementation architecture, which achieves the goals of reducing the number of physical synapses to one per neuron and reducing the pin count, while still allowing outputs to be generated at the same rate as the frame input. The architecture scales up without the need for significant increases in pin count or external system complexity, nor does it require its data to be presented in parallel. The architecture is also independent of the technology used to implement it, and is flexible with respect to the criteria laid out above (Bisset *et-al* 1990).

A REALISATION OF THE DATA FRAME ARCHITECTURE

This section describes an implementation of the data frame architecture in 2µ CMOS VLSI using a mixture of analogue and digital techniques. The design employs building blocks already available to the authors from previous work (Daniell *et-al* 1989). These consist of a pulse-stream synapse based on original work at Edinburgh (Murray *et-al* 1989). and reimplemented by the authors, together with associated support blocks, such as a voltage controlled oscillator, and analogue input and output pads. These building blocks were used because they are known to work, and their characteristics are well documented. They should be seen as a practical starting point for the design, rather than the essence of it. The use of these blocks also sets the representation of the network

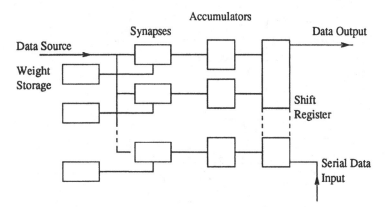

Figure 2 Block diagram of the data frame architecture.

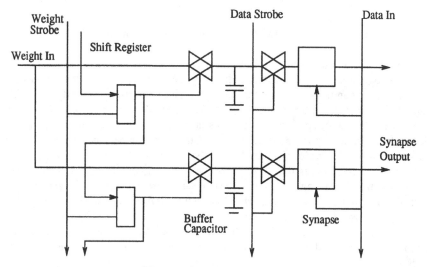

Figure 3 Input stage design.

values, in that the data and weight inputs will be required as analogue voltage levels, and the output from the synapse will be a variable frequency variable width pulse stream.

Because of the technology independence afforded by the architecture, further implementational savings can be made with particular realisations of it. In particular, the number of weight inputs required need not increase directly with the number of neurons. Weight values can be loaded onto the device faster than the synaptic multiplier can operate, so a saving in pins can be made by multiplexing the weights for a group of neurons through a single pin. Figure 3 shows the design for the input side of the device. The shift register has a single bit set and is used to clock each weight value through the transmission gate onto the first buffer capacitor, where it is stored during the time it takes to update all the weights in a block. Once the weights have all been loaded, they are appled simultaneously with the next data sample to the synapse circuit. The input capacitance of the synapse acts as a second buffer. During the computation time of the synapse the first buffers are loaded with the weight values for the next calculation. For this particular implementation, the synapse calculation takes about 2μ seconds. There are 32 neurons per block, and two blocks per device.

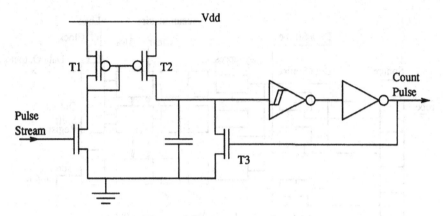

Figure 4 Charge accumulator.

The next problem is to accumulate the output of the synapse calculation over the whole data frame. Since the result of this calculation is represented as the area underneath a pulse stream, and this can be easily translated into a current, it might seem sensible to use a capacitor to accumulate this charge over the frame. Unfortunately the frame time is variable and long with respect to the charge holding ability of a VLSI capacitor. The circuit in Figure 4 neatly solves this problem by converting the pulse area into unit charge counts, which can be accumulated and held indefinitely by a digital counter. The current mirror (T1,T2) charges the capacitor in proportion to the area of the pulses coming from the synapse. As the voltage on this capacitor rises, it will eventually reach the upper threshold on the Schmitt inverter, which will then change state. This is then passed via another inverter to a discharge transistor (T3) which discharges the capacitor. The lower threshold on the Schmitt inverter, together with circuit delays, ensures that the capacitor will be fully discharged. The output of this circuit is then passed through a pulse stretcher and used to increment a counter. At the end of a frame this counter will contain the weighted sum value for that neuron over the data frame.

The final stage of the implementation is to convert the counter outputs back into a serial data stream, suitable for feeding to a similar device forming the next layer of the network. The first problem is that the number of pulses generated by the charge counting process is much larger than the required accuracy of the output value. In order to solve this, a larger counter than necessary is used (14 bits), and only the upper eight bits are passed on to the next layer. As the count is only valid at the end of a frame, and the next data sample must start a new accumulation, the counter outputs are loaded into a shift register from which they can be piped serially to the next layer during the next data frame. The transfer process is carried out using three signals: A HOLD signal that stops any further counting, (a final transition of the charge detector could occur causing a count to take place during the transfer of data to the shift register. This would lead to corrupt output value), a LOAD signal that is used to parallel load the shift register, and finally a CLEAR signal to clear the counter ready for the next data frame. This process currently takes place during a short frame blank period which must exist between data frames. The complete implementation is shown in Figure 5.

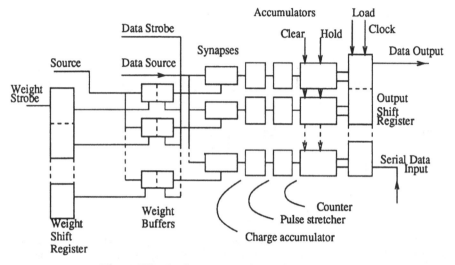

Figure 5 Device implementation block diagram.

One part of the neuron has not yet been implemented. As described, the device only outputs the basic sum-of-products values for each neuron. It does not include any non-linear terms, or activation functions. Because the data that passes between each layer is in a serial form, a single circuit can be used to perform a non-linear function between layers. In the current design this has been left external to the device. Figure 6 shows how the device fits into a system capable of implementing a fully connected neural network. For the current design the output data is in the form of a bit-serial signal controlled by an output clock. This represents sets of 8-bit values. The simplest way to pass these values through a non-linear function is to use them to address a look-up table attached to a digital to analogue converter, the output of which can then be feed to the next stage. By changing the contents of the look-up table the non-linear function can altered.

RESULTS

The devices are currently being fabricated, and therefore no test results from real devices are available. However considerable simulations have been carried out during the course

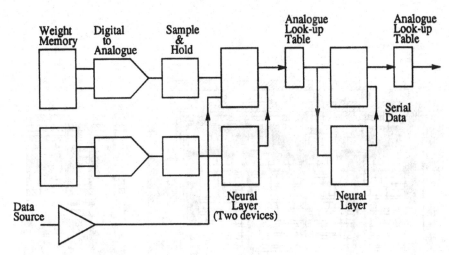

Figure 6 System level design.

of this design and these have shed some light on possible future improvements. They have shown that the pulse-stream synapse is not ideally suited to this architecture. This is partly because it was originally designed for an environment where the size of the synapse was a critical limiting factor in the design, and should be reduced in size at the expense of performance. In this design the speed of the synapse calculation is more important, since the size limitations are imposed by the digital parts of the design (see Figure 7). Furthermore the synapse used is unable to handle negative weights, nor does it have a particularly good accuracy. Its accuracy is estimated to be between 5-6 bits for the data input, and 3-4 bits for the weight values. Using a more conventional sub-threshold multiplier these figures could be significantly improved upon (Eberhardt *et-al* 1989). This implies that the overall performance of the device can be significantly improved if the synapse and its associated analogue circuits are re-designed.

Although a detailed discussion of the data frame architecture is outside the scope of this paper, it is interesting to note that the inability of the synapse to handle negative weights can easily be solved by splitting the calculation for each neuron between two physical neurons, one accumulating the positive sum, and the other the negative sum. If the two blocks in a device were used in this way to mirror one another, a simple adder circuit between layers would be sufficient to achieve negative weight operation.

If the device described in this paper were applied to a practical pattern recognition task using a standard television signal as a data source, it would be able to produce recognition results every frame (20ms). These recognition results could be made on images measuring approximately 100 pixels by 80 pixels. If the full 64 neurons were involved in this task a single device would be operating at some 25×10^6 connections per second. Hardware is currently under construction to demonstrate this capability.

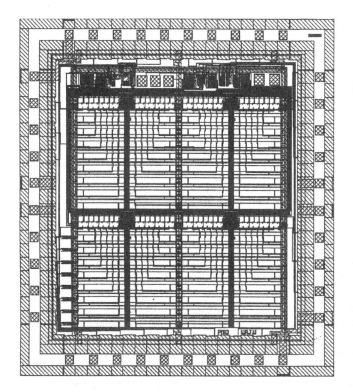

Synapse (72µ by 210µ

Digital Accumulator (622µ by 146µ).

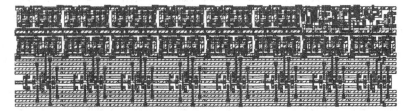

Figure 7 Device layout (4151µ by 4199µ).

CONCLUSIONS

This paper has presented one specific realisation of the data frame implementation architecture for fully connected neural networks. The design demonstrates that using a commonly available and cheap VLSI process, fully connected neural network devices can be implemented without the need to physically construct each synapse, and without sacrificing system level performance. This has been achieved by taking engineering type system level constraints into account, and limiting the format of the system input to that commonly available from data sources such as video and audio digitisers.

The design uses a mixture of analogue and digital building blocks to ensure an efficient use of available device area, allowing 64 fully connected neurons to be implemented on a single device of some $20mm^2$. The current design only uses 18 pins of the 40 available, and could clearly be fitted into a smaller package. The architecture allows expansion of the number of neurons per layer, as well as the number of layers, without significant expansion of pin counts or external circuit complexity at a system level, and most importantly, without saturating the available bandwidth of the device.

During the design and implementation of the device, a number of potential improvements to its design have been identified. Most important of these is the replacement of the current synapse with a fully analogue sub-threshold multiplier. It is hoped that these modifications will be included in the next iteration of the device, and that the hardware demonstrator currently under construction, will also be completed.

REFERENCES

Akers, L., Walker, M., Ferry, D., and Grondin, R., "A limited interconnect, highly layered synthetic neural architecture" in *VLSI for Artificial Intelligence*, Delgado-Frias, J.G., and Moore, W.R., Eds., Boston, Mass.: Kluwer, pp. *218-226*, 1989

Bailey, J., and Hammerstrom, D., "Why VLSI implementations of associative VLCNs require connection multiplexing" in *Proceedings of the first IEEE international conference on neural networks*, pp. 173-180, 1988.

Bisset, D.L., Daniell, P.M., and Waller, W.A.J., "A data frame architecture for implementing neural networks", Technical report in preparation, University of Kent, 1990.

Daniell, P.M., Waller, W.A.J., and Bisset, D.L., "An implementation of fully analogue sum-of-products neural models.", *1st International conference on artificial neural networks*. IEE, Savoy Place, October 1989.

Eberhardt, S., Duong, T., and Thakoor, A., "Design of parallel hardware neural network systems from custom analogue VLSI building block chips", *Proceedings of the International Joint Conference on Neural Networks* Washington, vol II, pp183-190, June 1989.

Hirai, Y., Kamada, K., Yamada, M., and Ooyama, M., "A Digital neuro-chip with unlimited connectability for large scale neural networks", *Proceedings of the*

International Joint Conference on Neural Networks Washington, vol II, pp163-169, June 1989.

Murray, A., Smith, A.V.W., and Tarassenko, L., "Fully-programmable analogue VLSI devices for the implementation of neural networks", in *VLSI for Artificial Intelligence*, Delgado-Frias, J.G., and Moore, W.R., Eds., Boston, Mass.: Kluwer, pp. *236-244*, 1989

3.4 Fully Cascadable Analogue Synapses Using Distributed Feedback

Donald J. Baxter, Alan F. Murray and H. Martin Reekie

Department of Electrical Engineering
University of Edinburgh, EH9 3JL

Abstract

We have solved the problems of cascadability and process variation for analogue VLSI neural networks. A synapse design is proposed, based on op-amp feedback, which avoids these problems. Other supporting circuitry which automatically determines bias voltages is also discussed. The circuits have been fully simulated and are now being fabricated.

INTRODUCTION

Analogue circuitry is much more sensitive to the problems of cascadability and process variations than digital logic. The massively parallel structures that form a neural network simply compound these problems. Also these problems are magnified as the scale of the network increases. Thus in any analogue neural design work these two problems must be addressed and solutions found.

In a recent paper (Murray 1990a) we reported the development of 4 and 3 transistor pulse stream synapse circuits (Figure 1). They are both based on the transconductance multiplier (Denyer 1981a, Han 1984a), which produces current pulses proportional to a weight voltage stored on a capacitor, at a frequency controlled by the presynaptic (sending) neural state. In the 3 transistor synapse the output current is pulsed while in the 4 transistor version the whole of the multiplier is switched in and out. This pulsing action is the basis of the pulse stream technique (Murray 1987a, Murray 1988a, Murray 1989a). The current pulses from a column of these synapses are summed and integrated using an op-amp "leaky integrator" circuit, (Murray 1990b) the output of which is used to control the pulse rate of a Voltage Controlled Oscillator (VCO).

VLSI for Artificial Intelligence and Neural Networks, Edited by J.G. Delgado-Frias and
W.R. Moore, Plenum Press, New York, 1991

PROBLEMS OF CASCADABILITY AND PROCESS VARIATION

The main attraction of the 4 and 3 transistor synapses is the small area which they occupy, potentially offering 1000's of synapses per chip. However, the SPICE simulations of these synapses revealed several problems. The first problem is with the switching characteristic of the 4 transistor synapse. Since in this synapse the whole of the transconductance multiplier is switched in and out, the capacitance of the transistors determines how quickly the circuit settles. Thus the large transistors which are required to reduce the output current range down means that this circuit will have a relatively long settling time. The 3 transistor synapse does not suffer from this problem as it is only the output of the transconductance multiplier which is being pulsed.

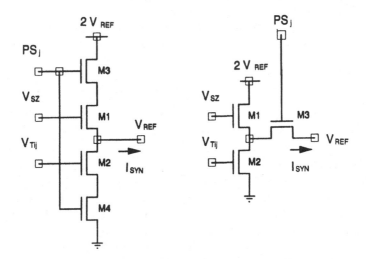

Figure 1   The 4 and 3 Transistor Synapse Circuits

The second problem is that the output is very sensitive to value of the voltage reference. This sensitivity is due to 2 factors. Firstly, the output current is the difference of two currents (I_{M1}, I_{M2}). Thus a small variation in the currents through M1 and M2 can cause a large change in the output current. Secondly, transistors M1 and M2 are in their linear region making the currents in them particularly sensitive to variations in the drain-source voltage. For these circuits to perform correctly this voltage has to be maintained to better than ± 5 mV.

This gives the following specifications for the op-amp in the "leaky integrator":

1 Gain must greater than 1000.

2 It must be able to drive a load capacitance of 50 pF (100 synapses at approximately 0.5 pF per synapse).

3 It must also have sufficient drive capability to maintain V_{REF} even when 30 μA (100 synapses at approximately 300 nA per synapse) is being input into the integrator.

While it perfectly possible to design a CMOS op-amp to meet these specifications, the resulting op-amp would be both large and power hungry. Further, if the number of synapses per neuron is increased to 200 the op-amp would have to be redesigned to meet the new requirements. It is this problem of needing to redesign the op-amp every time the network is scaled up that renders this type of synapse uncascadable.

Process variations cause more problems in analogue circuits than digital circuits. In digital circuit all that should vary will be the delay through the logic. Whereas in an analogue circuit like the transconductance multiplier, an output current representing the result of a multiplication can vary by a factor of 2 with process. Thus the operation of analogue circuits, the transconductance multiplier in particular, are effected to a much higher degree by variations in the process than digital logic.

These two problems mean that this particular synapse/neuron combination is neither truly cascadable or process independent.

THE NEW SYNAPSE DESIGN

Synapses Controlled By Op-amp Feedback

The new synapse circuit in Figure 2 solves these problems. It is effectively the 3 transistor, transconductance multiplier synapse, M1/M2/M5, with its own buffer stage, M3/M4. This buffer supplies enough current to balance the current output by the transconductance multiplier, under the control of op-amp feedback from the foot of the postsynaptic column. The analysis of a cascade of N of these synapses gives the following instantaneous input/output relationship.

$$V_{outi} = \frac{1}{N} \frac{\beta_1}{\beta_3} (\sum_{j}^{M_i} V_{Tij} - M_i (V_{SZ} - V_{REF})) + V_{BLEED} + V_{REF} \tag{1}$$

where

N - the number of synapses per neuron

M_i - the number of weights switched in for neuron i, as determined by the number of presynaptic pulses present.

B_x - the transconductance factor for transistor x. ($\beta_1 = \beta_2$ and $\beta_3 = \beta_4$)

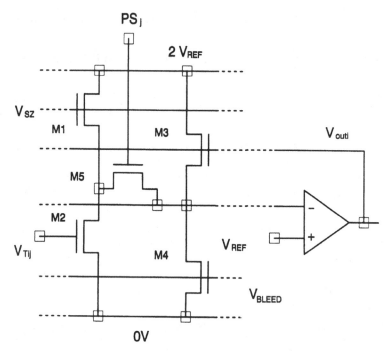

Figure 2 A Synapse Based on Op-amp Feedback

V_{outi} - the instantaneous neural activity for neuron i.

V_{Tij} - the synaptic weight from neuron j to neuron i.

V_{Tx} - the threshold voltage for transistor x. ($V_{T1} = V_{T3} = V_{T2} = V_{T4}$).

V_{SZ}, V_{REF} and V_{BLEED} are bias voltages which keep all the transistors in their linear regions.

Thus the output voltage represents a "snapshot" of all the weights switched in at a particular moment in time. In order to convert this "snapshot" into the neural activity the output of the feedback op-amp has to be integrated. Thus the op-amp is followed by a voltage integrator. The output of which is used to control a VCO with a sigmoidal response. This separation of the summing and averaging from the integration is quite useful, as it means that only a relatively small integration capacitor is required. Also, as the capacitor is not distributed amongst the synapses, they are much smaller. This makes this type of synapse/neuron particularly suitable for fully interconnected networks.

This synapse has several important advantages which ease the design of the feedback op-amp.

1   The op-amp does not sink or source substantial currents, as the distributed buffer stage in the synapse provides the current.

2   The op-amp only drives transistor gates and not a large integration capacitor.

3   As the buffer and the transconductance multiplier transistors are close together, they will be well matched. This means that the input/output voltage relationship above will not vary substantially with process.

To confirm that the op-amp would stay stable, the gain around the feedback loop was calculated theoretically and from SPICE simulations. The theoretical calculations gave a gain of 0.4 while simulation gave a gain of 0.33. Since both of these values were less than 1, the op-amp will remain stable in this configuration.

Thus this synapse represents a circuit which is easily cascadable as well as being more immune to the effects of process variation than the 4 and 3 transistor synapses.

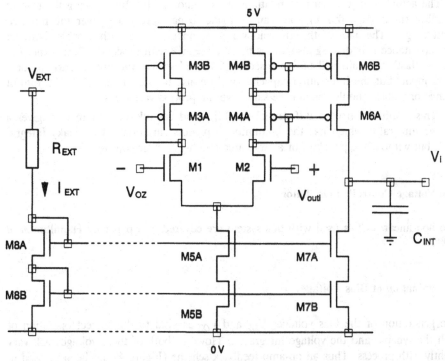

Figure 3   A Voltage Integrator Based on a Differential Amplifier and Cascode Current Mirrors

The Voltage Integrator

The obvious way to integrate the output of the feedback op-amp would be to use a standard "leaky integrator" circuit. However this would involve the need for a second op-amp per neuron. Thus a more compact solution to the problem was sought.

The answer was found in a combination of a differential amplifier and cascode current mirrors (Figure 3). The current though the cascode current mirrors is determined by an external resistor. This removes the effects of process variation from the output current range of the integrator. The differential amplifier steers currents down the two paths, M1/M3A/M3B and M2/M4A/M4B, according to the voltage difference between the differential amplifier's 2 input terminals. When these 2 inputs are at the same voltage, the current through transistors M3A/M3B ($I_{M3A/M3B}$) equals the current through M4A/M4B ($I_{M4A/M4B}$). Thus $I_{M4A/M4B}$ is half the value of $I_{M5A/M5B}$. At this point the current being supplied to the integrator should balance the current being removed. So $I_{M5A/M5B}$ should be mirrored on to the integration capacitor by half the ratio, that $I_{M4A/M4B}$ is being mirrored by, to achieve this balance condition.

The actual voltage to current relationship is sigmoidal, but by reducing the gain of the differential stage this sigmoid can be made to be more linear over the required input range. The gain of this sigmoid varies by about ± 5% with process, however the capacitance it is driving also varies by about ± 5% with process. Thus if the process is "fast" the gain will be increased by 5%, and so will the output current for a given input, but the integration capacitor will be also be 5% larger. Thus the rate of change of voltage should remain the same over all process variations.

This combination of a differential amplifier and cascode current mirrors gives a voltage integrator which has the immunity to process variations of a "leaky integrator", but without the penalties of a large area and high power consumption.

The Voltage Controlled Oscillators

The non-linear VCO's used with this system are covered in a paper by Hamilton *et al* (1990).

Determination of Bias Voltages

The generation of the bias voltages V_{SZ} and V_{OZ} is vital to the correct operation of both the synapse and the voltage integrator. However both of these voltages will vary slightly with process. Thus an op-amp feedback scheme (Figure 4) has been devised to automatically determine the bias voltages accurately while at the same time compensating for process variations.

These modules are the final pieces required to form a complete network (Figure 4).

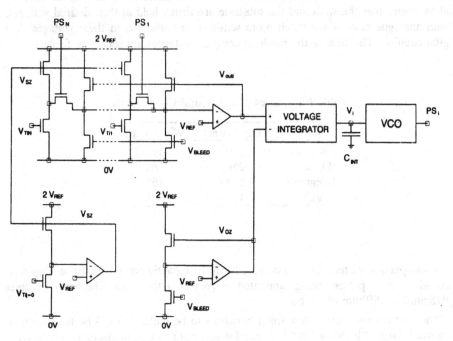

Figure 4 An Overview of the Complete System

VLSI IMPLEMENTATION

Particular care has been taken over transistor matching and guard rings. For example, in the voltage integrator, accurate current mirroring is required to divide a current by 4. Here 4 identical transistors were used in place of one transistor 4 times the width of the one the current is being mirrored to. This greatly improves the tracking of the current ratio with process. Also, in the op-amp the 2 input transistors are cross-coupled (Allen 1987a) to make sure that they are closely matched.

Throughout the design, extensive use has been made of guard rings to provide good connections to the substrate and the wells. So minimising the risk of latch-up and to ensure that the wells and the substrate are firmly held at their desired voltages. Again analogue circuits are much more sensitive to variations in these voltages than digital circuits. The sizes of the resulting component layout are shown in Table 1.

Table 1 The Sizes of the Neural Components

Part	Height(μm)	Width(μm)
Synapse	130	165
Op-amp	250	165
Integrator	200	165
VCO	165	165

These parts were then used to build a 10 by 10 synaptic array with 10 on-chip neurons which is at present being fabricated as part of a test chip. The array occupies 1.915mm by 1.650mm of silicon.

This test chip will also allow small networks to be built, and will be the precursor to a much larger "building block" device for applications in optimisation, robotics and pattern recognition.

CONCLUSIONS

Thus it is clear that the proposed neural circuitry offers a level of cascadability and process independence, for both the synapse and the neuron, that is very hard to match. This process immunity will allow us to build large networks out of many chips without worrying about if some of the chips are "fast" while others are "slow". Thus by solving the problems of cascadability and process independence we have opened the way to much larger hardware implementations of neural networks.

ACKNOWLEDGEMENTS

The authors acknowledge the support of the Science and Engineering Research Council and the EEC (ESPRIT) for funding, and Donald Baxter is grateful to SERC and Thorn-EMI for a CASE studentship.

References

Allen, P. E. and Holberg, D. R., *CMOS Analog Circuit Design,* Holt, Rinehart and Winston, New York, 1987.

Denyer, P. B. and Mavor, J., "MOST Transconductance Multipliers for Array Applications," *IEE Proc. Pt. 1,* vol. 128, no. 3, pp. 81-86, June 1981.

Hamilton, A., Murray, A. F., and Churcher, S., *Working Analogue Pulse Stream Neural Network Chips,* in this book.

Han, Il S. and Park, Song B., "Voltage-Controlled Linear Resistors by MOS Transistors and their Application to Active RC Filter MOS Integration," *Proc. IEEE,* pp. 1655-1657, Nov., 1984.

Murray, A. F. and Smith, A. V. W., "Asynchronous Arithmetic for VLSI Neural Systems," *Electronics Letters,* vol. 23, no. 12, pp. 642-643, June, 1987.

Murray, A. F. and Smith, A. V. W., "Asynchronous VLSI Neural Networks using Pulse Stream Arithmetic," *IEEE Journal of Solid-State Circuits and Systems,* vol. 23, no. 3, pp. 688-697, 1988.

Murray, A. F., "Pulse Arithmetic in VLSI Neural Networks," *IEEE MICRO,* vol. 9, no. 6, pp. 64-74, 1989.

Murray, A. F., Brownlow, M., Hamilton, A., Han, Il Song, Reekie, H. M., and Tarassenko, L., "Pulse-Firing Neural Chips for Hundreds of Neurons," *Neural Information Processing Systems (NIPS) Conference,* pp. 785-792, Morgan Kaufmann, 1990.

Murray, A. F., Baxter, D., Butler, Z., Churcher, S., Hamilton, A., Reekie, H. M., and Tarassenko, L., "Innovations in Pulse Stream Neural VLSI : Arithmetic and Communications," *IEEE Workshop on Microelectronics for Neural Networks, Dortmund,* pp. 8-15, 1990.

3.5 Results from Pulse-Stream VLSI Neural Network Devices

Michael Brownlow   Lionel Tarassenko   Alan Murray†

Department of Engineering Science
Oxford University, Oxford, OX1 3PJ, UK

†Department of Electrical Engineering
Edinburgh University, EH9 3JL, UK

Abstract

This paper describes a novel switched–capacitor design for the implementation of artificial neural networks in VLSI using the pulse–stream signalling mechanism and dynamic weight storage. Test results are presented from a small number of chips, paying particular attention to the synaptic weight linearity and storage time. The synaptic weights are fully–programmable and the VLSI chips can be used to process analogue sensor data in real time with an accuracy equivalent to 6 or 7 bits, as demonstrated in the robotics application described in the paper.

INTRODUCTION

As previously reported (Murray, Smith & Tarassenko 1989), we have been developing CMOS VLSI technology for the electronic implementation of artificial neural networks. With all of our designs, there is one (pseudo–analogue) multiplier per synapse and we can therefore exploit the full advantages, in terms of speed and fault–tolerance, inherent in the fine–grained parallelism of neural network architectures. We use a "pulse–stream" arithmetic system, the principles of which are briefly summarised below.

PULSE–STREAM NEURAL NETWORKS

The pulse stream signalling mechanism is analogous to that found in biological neural systems. The output of a neuron j (V_j) is represented as a train of pulses whose repetition rate (R) varies from $R = 0$, representing a state $V_j = 0$, to a rate $R = R_{max}$ corresponding to $V_j = 1$. The efficacy of the received pulse train at a neuron i is determined by the multiplication of the pre–synaptic neural state V_j by the synaptic weight (T_{ij}) from j to i which can be either positive (i.e. excitatory) or negative (inhibitory).

VLSI for Artificial Intelligence and Neural Networks, Edited by J.G. Delgado-Frias and
W.R. Moore, Plenum Press, New York, 1991

215

The response of a particular neuron i to all of its inputs is usually described by means of an internal neuron variable, termed the neural activity (x_i). The neural output V_i is a non–linear function f of the activity, i.e. $V_i = f(x_i)$. In an *analogue* model of a neuron, the neural activity can be described by a differential equation, as first proposed by Grossberg (1968):

$$\frac{\partial x_i}{\partial t} = -Ax_i + \sum T_{ij}V_j + I(t) \tag{1}$$

$$
\begin{aligned}
x_i &= \text{Neural activity} \\
A &= \text{Passive decay term} \\
V_j &= \text{Neural state} \\
I(t) &= \text{External input}
\end{aligned}
$$

From this equation it is possible to derive further simplified descriptions. For example, Murray and Smith (1988) have shown how Equation 1 can be reduced to the update equation proposed by Hopfield (1982) for feedback networks. In feedforward neural networks, equation 1 is replaced by a static evaluation of the neural activity whereby $x_i = \sum T_{ij}V_j$.

The original motivation for developing the pulse–stream technique was the desire to implement pseudo–analogue circuits on an essentially digital CMOS process. A number of pulse–stream designs have been published in the last two years (see, for example, Murray *et al* 1989) and another paper in this book (Hamilton *et al* 1990) reports on one of these designs. In this paper, we concentrate on the results which we have obtained with a switched capacitor variant of the pulse–stream technique (Brownlow, Tarassenko and Murray 1990).

ASYNCHRONOUS SWITCHED CAPACITOR NETWORK

Most analogue VLSI implementations of neural networks are built around summing amplifiers. The input voltages, which represent the neural states V_j, are converted to currents $T_{ij}V_j$, where $T_{i1} = 1/R_1, T_{i2} = 1/R_2$, etc... These currents are summed at the input of the amplifier and converted back to an output voltage $V_i = f(\sum T_{ij}V_j)$. This is essentially the circuit proposed by Hopfield (1984) and indeed a VLSI device with 512 such amplifiers has been built by Graf *et al* (1986). There are two main problems associated with this approach to building VLSI neural networks:

- The resistors available in VLSI technology are comparatively inaccurate (20–40% tolerance), depending on the method used, e.g. poly, diffusion, pinch, etc... Futhermore, there is no obvious method of generating negative synapse weights.

- More importantly perhaps, the limitations of existing technology are such that the resistors implementing the synaptic weights cannot be readily altered once they have been formed. This results in networks with fixed functionality and precludes the possibility of on–chip learning.

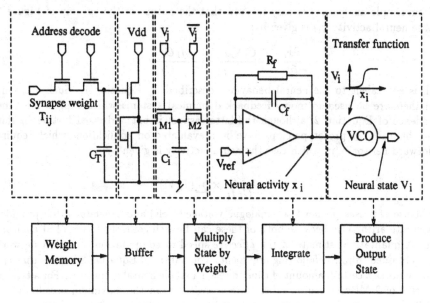

Figure 1. Asynchronous Switched Capacitor Synapse and Neuron

In the approach described in this paper, the concepts of pulse stream arithmetic and dynamic weight storage are linked with well understood switched capacitor techniques in order to implement networks which are fully programmable.

Consider the circuit shown in Figure 1. The feedback resistor R_f, is implemented as a fully–fledged switched–capacitor resistor consisting of a capacitor C_L, switched by a *global* two–phase non–overlapping clock signal (common to all neurons) of frequency f_L Hz. The capacitor C_f maintains feedback around the op–amp during the transitions of the clock signal. The usual implementation of the circuit of Figure 1 would require a separate clock signal for each input resistor in order to make each synapse programmable. This would require a significant silicon area and, as there will be several thousand synapses in a VLSI neural network, such an approach cannot be contemplated. The pulse–stream technique, however, provides a very elegant solution to this problem. Since the neural states V_j are encoded as pulse streams, we can use them here as the *clock signals* for the switched–capacitor synapses (M_1, M_2, C_i). The weight T_{ij} is then the *input voltage* to the switched cpacitor synapse; this voltage is stored on capacitor C_T and refreshed periodically from an external RAM via a D/A converter.

The synapses are fully-programmable, *in magnitude and sign*. To implement positive weights, the buffered synapse weight voltage is set to be less than V_{ref} and vice–versa for negative weights. The synapse is small ($65\ \mu \times 65\mu$), which implies that around 12,000 synapses could be integrated on a standard die. So far, a small number of prototype chips have been fabricated using a standard 2μ CMOS process, on a 3 mm $\times$ 3 mm die, of which only $780\mu \times 880\mu$ was used to implement 144 synapses and 12 neurons (ie. >200 synapses per mm^2). Digital control of the weight refresh circuitry also necessitated a small silicon overhead.

From simple analysis, it is easy to show that the output of the op–amp of Figure 1 (i.e. the neural activity x_i) is given by:

$$\frac{\partial x_i}{\partial t} = -\frac{C_i \sum T_{ij} V_j}{C_f} - \frac{f_L C_L x_i}{C_f} \tag{2}$$

which is equivalent to the neural behaviour described by Equation 1. Such a circuit could therefore be used to model feedback dynamical systems which exploit the time dependence of Equation 2, although the latter aspect is not addressed further in this paper. Instead, the prototype chips have been evaluated on applications which require feedforward networks, in which case the neural activity is given by:

$$x_i = -\frac{C_i}{C_L f_L} \times \sum (T_{ij} V_j) \tag{3}$$

The use of pulses (rather than analogue voltage levels) and capacitor *ratios* provides for accurate arithmetic because both of these can be well controlled in a VLSI environment. A qualitative estimate of the *effective* speed of computation of such a network can be obtained from the following argument. The nature of Equation 2 implies that the circuit requires a certain amount of time to reach a stable neural activity x_i. For a typical pulse rate of 2 MHz, a neuron takes $15\mu s$ to switch from the maximum possible value of $\sum T_{ij} V_j$ to the minimum or vice–versa. With of the order of 10,000 synapses on–chip (easily achievable on a standard 64 mm^2 die) this corresponds to a computational rate of just under 10^9 operations per second, since all synapses are operating *in parallel*. Such a calculation merely serves to emphasise the full parallelism of analogue implementations and is in no way meant to be used for making a direct comparison with digital processors with floating–point accuracy.

TEST RESULTS

When evaluating the prototype chips, the following parameters were investigated in particular detail: weight storage time, weight linearity, neural state linearity.

Weight Linearity

The synapse weight voltage, stored on capacitor C_T, is buffered by an unusual buffer circuit, consisting of an NMOS source impedance, *and an NMOS pull up device*. This circuit was used because realistic analogue VLSI neural networks will require of the order of *tens of thousands of synapses*. Area is therefore of crucial importance, and complementary device structures consume large quantities of silicon real estate. A complication of this unusual circuit form, however, is that the digital process has no facility for creating well conditioned capacitors of moderate value. MOS devices, biased into a suitable region of operation, were used as the storage elements. The combination of the inevitable body effect present in an NMOS device operating with a variable source potential greater than the local substrate potential and of the non–linear capacitance–voltage characteristics of the MOS storage device places a restriction on the available dynamic range of the weight voltage. The buffer transistor aspect ratios were chosen such that a reasonable approximation to a linear transfer characteristic between *applied* synapse weight and *effective* synapse weight could be obtained. The buffer transistors were designed with relatively large geometries so that the effect of length and width variations could be minimised. The storage capacitor was laid out in such a way as to minimise indirect cross–talk via capacitive coupling.

The experimental procedure for determining the linearity of weight storage consisted of applying a known neural state input *from a calibrated frequency generator*, and monitoring the neural activity as a function of the synapse weight for all synapses on the chip. An important feature of this design is that the synapse weights are fully–programmable and can be set to any value between ±1, with an accuracy determined by the external D/A. An averaged plot of *applied* vs *effective* synaptic weight, for a number of chips, is displayed in Figure 2.

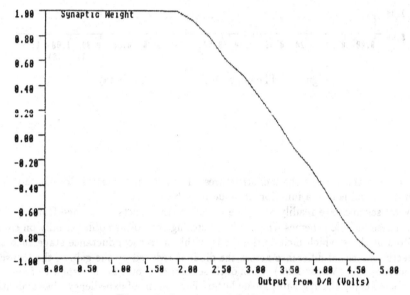

Figure 2. Synapse weight linearity

Weight storage time

The method of weight storage described above is obviously dynamic which means that the fundamental problem associated with it is that of leakage. There are two main mechanisms for the decay of the weight voltage: leakage through the reverse biased source–substrate diode and leakage through the channel of the address structure. Of these two mechanisms the major source of leakage is via the diode to the substrate. Both forms of leakage are unfortunately highly variable across the silicon surface, due to

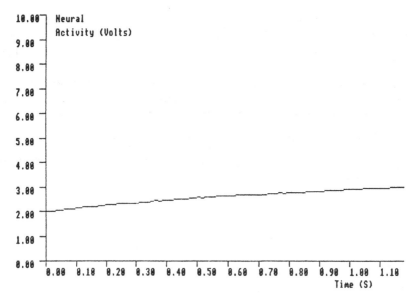

Figure 3. The effect of synapse weight decay

mismatches in the various channel structures. The leakage increases dramatically with temperature, and is also a function of diode back bias.

Several schemes are readily available to reduce the effects of leakage from dynamic nodes. These include schemes which rely on storing the voltage differentially on similar capacitors or those which include the diode within a transconductance stage such that the effective potential difference across the diode is reduced by the gain of the transconductance amplifier (Vittoz 1990). Both of these solutions come at the expense of area, the requirements being much greater in the latter. For reasons of expediency, the straightforward approach of an uncompensated channel transmission system was adopted. SPICE 2 simulations of the effects of weight leakage were at best a *very* crude approximation, since the crucial parameters required by the program are ill–conditioned and not provided by the manufacturer. It was to be expected that a variation in weight hold times would be apparent. The effects of weight decay were determined in a similar way to those of linearity, by monitoring the post–synaptic neural activity in response to a weight which was programmed and then allowed to decay.

Figure 3 shows the effect on neural activity of 12 synapses initially programmed with $T_{ij} = 0$ (which from Figure 2 corresponds to an applied voltage of 3.5V), each fed with a constant neural input. The average decay at each synapse can be approximated by dividing the neural activity rate of change by 12, and then also by the gain of the neuron, as set by the global clock frequency. This gives a decay rate at the synapse of

20–30 mV/s. Such a decay rate can be considered to be negligible since the external D/A converter updates each synapse at approximately 5ms intervals, with a weight voltage between 2 and 5V. With larger networks, which will eventually address the issue of on-chip learning, more research will be required into the weight storage problem but the dynamic principle will remain applicable if suitably modified.

Neural State Linearity

The neural state linearity is taken to be the linearity of the multiplication of a synaptic weight by a varying neural state. This was tested by applying a fixed weight to a synapse, and varying the pulse rate of the pre–synaptic neural state by means of an external pulse generator. The post–synaptic neural activity should then be proportional to the product of synapse weight voltage and neural state *frequency*.

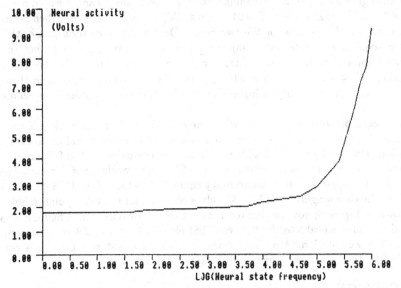

Figure 4. Neural state linearity

The results of this test indicated that a linear response could be achieved over a range of frequencies from 100kHz to 2MHz, as displayed in Figure 4, which is a plot of the recorded post synaptic neural activity against the logarithm of the neural state input.

APPLICATIONS

The switched–capacitor pulse–stream VLSI devices described in this paper allow us to perform *real time* pattern association or matching with analogue data. Most sensors give analogue data and the analogue–to–digital conversion stage often represents the main bottleneck in signal processing applications where the input data has a high dimensionality. In such cases, parallel analogue computation can have a clear advantage in terms of speed and efficiency, provided that the lower precision of analogue techniques is adequate for the given task. As an example of such an application, we have been developing a *localisation module* as part of a real–time autonomous robot navigation system based on VLSI neural network modules (Tarassenko, Brownlow and Murray 1990). The task of the navigation module is to determine the robot's position within a room from range readings given by a time-of-flight infra red range scanner mounted on the robot. In this section we report on results obtained with simulated range data using two of our 12-neuron chips.

For the purposes of simulation, the model room of Figure 5 was constructed and mapped out with 24 grid points. The room environment was "learnt" by recording a full range scan at each of the 24 grid points. Thus, for each grid point, the simulation programme generated the range readings which an ideal range scanner would have given every 30° (i.e. 12 range values). The 24 sets of analogue range values were then normalised and became the T_{ij} weights for the two chips. During the navigation phase, the most recently–acquired scan is fed as the input V_j values to the two chips which then compute in parallel, for all grid points, the distance between this scan and all the stored scans by evaluating the 24 $T_{ij}V_j$ scalar products. The robot's approximate position is then given by the neuron whose activity is highest and which therefore identifies the *nearest* grid point.

As an example, consider the case when the robot is at the point marked X on Figure 5. The scan recorded at this position is fed as a set of 12 input V_j values to each of the two chips. The results obtained with the chips were compared with a full simulation of the same matching procedure carried out on a SUN 3/80 workstation. In each case, the T_{ij} weights were quantised to 8–bit accuracy equivalent to that of the D/A converter used to refresh the chip weights. The $\sum T_{ij}V_j$ values obtained for each grid point in both cases are shown in Figure 6; note the limited range of the vertical axis. The figure shows that the scalar products evaluated by the two VLSI chips are within 1.2% of those computed on the SUN workstation. Most importantly, this means that grid point 9 is correctly identified by the hardware as being the closest to the robot.

CONCLUSION

One of the most important applications of analogue VLSI neural networks is likely to be in real time sensor data processing, for example networks which associate a given output (or motor) behaviour with certain types of input sensory data. The application described in this paper is an example of a network which uses a single–layer architecture with analogue range values as inputs. The precision obtained with our chips (equivalent to 6 or 7 bits) was achieved for two main reasons: firstly, the use of pulse coding techniques ensures that the transistors are always in well–defined operating regimes; secondly, the gain of the circuit is set by a capacitor *ratio*, C_i/C_f, which can be accurately controlled. Such precision will be more than adequate for signal processing with analogue sensors.

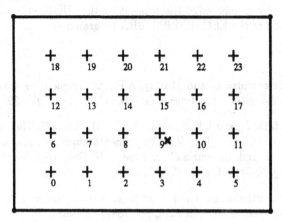

Figure 5. Simulated Test Environment

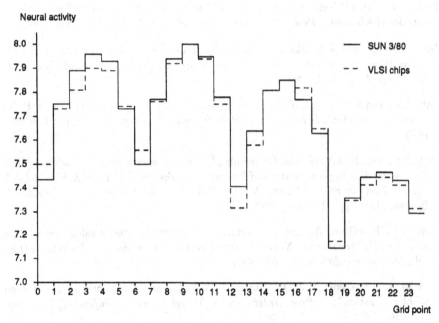

Figure 6. Mobile robot localisation with VLSI neural network chips

ACKNOWLEDGEMENTS

The authors gratefully acknowledge the support of the UK Science and Engineering Research Council and of the EEC (ESPRIT BRA programme).

REFERENCES

Brownlow, M.J., Tarassenko, L. and Murray, A.F., "Analogue computation with VLSI neural network devices", *Electronics Letters*, vol.26, pp. 1297–1299, 1990.

Graf, H.P., Jackel, L.D., Howard, R.E., Straughn, B., Denker, J.S., Hubbard, W.E., Tennant, D.M. and Schwartz, D., "VLSI implementation of a neural network memory with several hundreds of neurons", in *Proc. AIP Conference on Neural Networks for Computing*, Snowbird, pp. 182–187, 1986.

Grossberg, S., "Some Physiological and Biochemical Consequences of Psychological Postulates", *Proc. Natl. Acad. Sci USA*, pp. 758–765, 1968.

Hamilton, A., Murray, A.F., Reekie, H.M. and Tarassenko, L., "Working Analogue Neural Network Chips", in this volume.

Hopfield, J.J., "Neural Networks and Physical Systems with Emergent Collective Computational Abilities", *Proc. Natl. Acad. Sci. USA*, vol.79, pp.2554–2558, 1982.

Hopfield, J.J., "Neural Networks and Physical Systems with Graded Response have Collective Properties like those of Two–State Neurons", *Proc. Natl. Acad. Sci. USA*, vol.81, pp. 3088–3092, 1984.

Murray, A.F. and Smith, A.V.W., "Asynchronous VLSI Neural Networks using Pulse Stream Arithmetic", *IEEE J. Solid–State Circuits & Systems*, vol.23, pp. 688–697, 1988.

Murray, A.F., Smith, A.V.W. and Tarassenko, L., "Fully–programmable Analogue VLSI Devices for the Implementation of Neural Networks', in *VLSI for Artificial Intelligence*, Delgado-Frias, J.G. and Moore, W.R., Eds., Kluwer Academic Publishers, Boston, Mass., pp. 236–244, 1989.

Murray, A.F., Hamilton, A. and Tarassenko, L., "Programmable Analog Pulse-firing Networks', in *Advances in Neural Information Processing Systems*, Touretzky, D.S., Ed., Morgan Kaufmann, pp. 671–677, 1989.

Tarassenko, L., Brownlow, M.J. and Murray, A.F., "VLSI neural networks for autonomous robot navigation", in *Proc. International Neural Network Conference*, Paris, pp. 213–216, 1990.

Vittoz, E., Oguey, H., Maher, M.A., Nys, O., Dijkstra, E. and Chevroulet, M., "Analog Storage of Adjustable Synaptic Weights", in *Proceedings of 1st Int. Workshop on Microelectronics for Neural Networks*, pp. 69–79, 1990.

3.6 Working Analogue Pulse-Firing Neural Network Chips

Alister Hamilton, Alan F. Murray, H. Martin Reekie,
and Lionel Tarassenko‡

Department of Electrical Engineering
University of Edinburgh, EH9 3JL

‡Department of Engineering Science
University of Oxford, OX1 3PJ

Abstract

*The design of a programmable analogue pulse width modulation synapse is
described for use in pulse-firing neural networks. Results from working
VLSI devices are presented. A scheme for communicating large numbers of
neural states between chips is proposed. The design of process independent
pulse-firing neurons for use in networks and inter-chip communications are
given.*

INTRODUCTION

Pulse-firing neural networks are inspired by the biological exemplar of a neuron which
outputs voltage spikes at a rate determined by its level of excitation or activity. This
neuron model is relatively easy to implement in VLSI as a Voltage Controlled Oscillator (VCO) with constant pulse width output and a variable duty cycle controlled by an
analogue activity voltage, x_i.

Results obtained from working VLSI demonstrate the function of an analogue
synapse that implements the multiplication of neural state by synaptic weight. A
number of methods have been suggested to perform this function efficiently using
analogue circuit techniques and pulse stream arithmetic (Murray1990a, Murray1990b,
Murray1989a, Murray1990c). The approach taken in the work presented in this
paper is to use a *pulse width modulation* technique to multiply the presynaptic pulse
width by a factor in the range $0 \rightarrow 1$. By combining the presynaptic pulse and the output of the multiplier both excitation and inhibition can be achieved. Synapse outputs
are commoned together via distributed integrating capacitors which sum the synaptic
outputs to form the activity, x_i, input to neuron i. Weights are stored dynamically at
each synapse as charge on a capacitor. Weight values are refreshed from off chip via
an external RAM and Digital to Analogue converter.

VLSI for Artificial Intelligence and Neural Networks, Edited by J.G. Delgado-Frias and
W.R. Moore, Plenum Press, New York, 1991

The use of analogue circuit techniques here is only made possible if high precision is not required. The fact that biological neural systems are relatively slow and imprecise suggests that artificial neural networks may well be suited to analogue implementation. The advantage offered is that by careful exploitation of transistor characteristics complex functions may be performed using relatively few transistors, resulting in small circuit sizes. However, in the analogue domain, particular attention must be paid to variations in circuit performance due to process variations introduced during chip fabrication. This becomes an important issue when we try to communicate neural states between devices. VCO design is of particular importance in this respect. Feedback techniques have been employed in order to allow VCOs to operate independently of these variations.

The issue of communicating neural states between chips is considered. Clearly if we aspire to implement networks with large numbers of neurons it is impractical to allocate a single pin on a chip as a dedicated neuron input or output. A scheme for multiplexing neural states onto a small number of pins is required to allow fast inter-chip communication of neural states while not consuming vast areas of silicon in implementation. Such a scheme is described where the space between pulses is used to encode neural states and an asynchronous handshake controls data flow.

AN ANALOGUE SYNAPSE

Figure 1 shows the circuit diagram of the synapse circuit. A capacitor is used to store the synaptic weight value, T_{ij}, dynamically as an analogue voltage. This arrangement allows the synaptic weight to effectively set the power supply, V_{supply}, to the inverter formed by T1 and T2. Presynaptic pulses occur asynchronously at the input to this inverter, with a constant width Dt and a frequency determined by the state of the transmitting neuron. The length of the output pulse is determined by how long the discharge node spends below the threshold of inverter 1, which is in turn set by V_{supply} and hence T_{ij}. This circuit then, is effectively multiplying the width of the presynaptic pulse Dt by the synaptic weight T_{ij}. The relationship between the multiplier and synaptic weight voltage is linear over a 2V range.

The synaptic weight voltage range may be used to implement both inhibition and excitation using each presynaptic pulse to remove charge from an activity capacitor for time Dt, while each postsynaptic pulse, generated by the multiplier circuit, adds charge at twice the rate for time $Dt.T_{ij}$. In this way, a synaptic weight voltage of 2V, giving a pulse length multiplier of ½, gives no net change in neuron activity x_j. The synaptic weight voltage range 1→2V therefore gives a net reduction in neuron activity and is used to represent inhibition, the range 2→3V gives a net increase in neuron activity and is used to represent excitation.

A VLSI Test Chip

A chip has been fabricated in 2μm CMOS that demonstrates the functionality of the analogue synapse. It integrates 100 synapses, each occupying an area of 174x73μm, the restriction on chip complexity in this device is fundamentally one of pin count

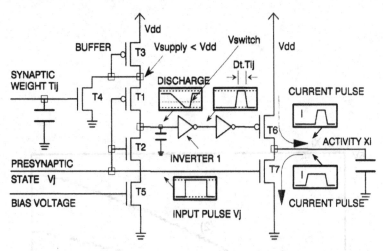

Figure 1 Programmable Pulse Width Modulation Synapse

rather than of area due to the large number of pins provided for test purposes. At present, the neural function is implemented in discrete components to allow maximum flexibility in the choice of pulse and neuron transfer characteristics.

The operation of the synapse can be demonstrated by the data from the test chip shown in Figure 2. All data has been sampled with a 6 bit analogue to digital converter. The lower graph shows the change in x_i when a constant duty cycle pulse stream is applied to the input of a synapse. Initially the weight is excitatory and x_i increases in a linear manner towards 5V. An inhibitory weight is then applied and x_i decreases linearly towards the minimum activity of 0V. The top graph shows the change in x_i when pulse streams of different duty cycle are applied to the input of the synapse. The synaptic weight is excitatory. The difference in slope of the two traces is due to the fact that twice as many pulses arrive at the synapse in trace (2) as compared to trace (1), and hence the slope of trace (2) is approximately twice that of trace (1).

IMPLEMENTING LARGE NEURAL SYSTEMS

Having demonstrated the operation of a programmable analogue pulse width modulating synapses, we are now in a position to consider the implementation of large neural systems. It has been estimated that, using this synapse, approximately 6400 synapses can be implemented on a 8mmx8mm die (Murray1990b). In order simply to get neural states on and off chip a multiplexing scheme is required since allocating one or more pins per neuron is clearly impractical. In addition, real applications of neural networks are likely to require larger arrays of synapses and neurons than can be integrated on a single chip. It is therefore crucial to the effective realisation of large, concurrent VLSI neural systems that the problem of inter-chip communication be solved.

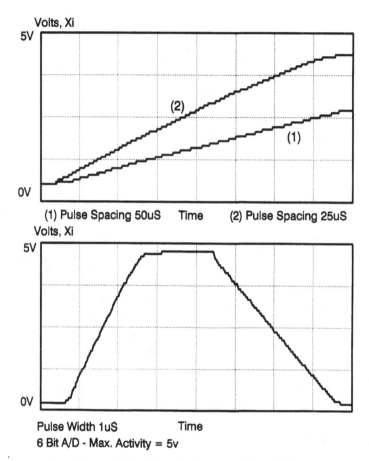

Figure 2 Test Results from working VLSI

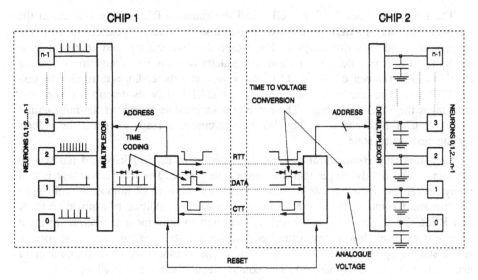

Figure 3 An Inter-Chip Communication Scheme

An Inter-Chip Communication Scheme

Information representing a neural state is encoded in the rate of occurrence of pulses at the neural output. However, the instantaneous neural state is also encoded in the space between pulses. The inter-chip communication scheme illustrated in Figure 3 encodes the neural state as a pulse whose width corresponds to the space between output pulses on a particular neuron, i, and transmits this information between chips. The receiver uses this time information to charge a capacitive storage node to a voltage dependent on the width of the encoded pulse. This stored voltage is used as a reference by the receiving VCO in order to regenerate the transmitted neural state. The lines Request To Transmit, RTT, and Clear To Transmit, CTT perform a handshake such that although the transmitting and receiving state machines may be asynchronous to one another, the multiplexor's movement through the sending and receiving neurons is synchronised between chips.

This scheme does not facilitate the transmission of a neural state of zero, where no pulses are being output by the transmitting neuron, nor does it allow a neuron that is being switched off, where only one pulse appears at the neuron output during the transmitting interval, to be transmitted. In order to overcome this limitation a time-out mechanism is introduced. The transmitting state machine starts the time-out when waiting for a pulse from the neuron to be transmitted. The DATA line is taken high by either the time-out expiring or the arrival of a pulse. If the time-out has expired it is assumed that a zero state is to be transmitted and DATA is taken low after a second time-out interval. However, if a pulse has taken DATA high then the transmitting state machine resets the time-out mechanism and awaits either a second pulse or the time-out interval to expire before taking DATA low again.

The handshake lines RTT and CTT and the common RESET line operate in the following manner. RESET is asserted to initialise the address pointers in both the transmitting and receiving chips and to reset the transmitting and receiving state machines to a zero state. The transmitter requests to transmit information by taking RTT low. The receiver on seeing RTT go low indicates its readiness to receive by taking CTT low. The transmitter now outputs the DATA pulse as described earlier and then takes the RTT signal high. The receiver acknowledges receipt of the information by taking CTT high and on seeing this the transmitter is ready to repeat the process for the next neural state.

This inter-chip communication scheme is elegant in its simplicity and has several advantages and disadvantages that are worth noting here. The main advantage is that many neural states can be transmitted and received on a small number of chip pins. The transmitter and receiver both require 3 pins each in addition to a single CLOCK and RESET pin. The hardware overhead required to implement the communication scheme is relatively low - the transmitter and receiver state machine comprise some 8 and 6 states respectively and the state machine size is independent of the number of neural states to be communicated. The communication scheme also allows easy interface to a host computer via standard microprocessor interface devices such as the Intel 8253 Programmable Interval Timer. The main disadvantages are the requirement for equal number of transmitting and receiving neurons and the relatively slow speed of transmitting neural states of zero.

If the DATA signal is used to represent some fixed fraction of the original pulse spacing information, the communication speed would be increased and greater use made of the bandwidth available on the communication link.

NEURON DESIGN

Two types of VCO have been designed - one with a sigmoid voltage to duty cycle characteristic, the other with a linear characteristic to act as a receiving neuron for use with the inter-chip communication scheme. In both cases the manufacturing process variations need to be compensated for so that all VCO's have a predefined pulse width output. These VCO's form part of a small neural network currently being fabricated in a test chip (Baxter1990a, Churcher1990a).

Non-Linear VCO

The circuit diagram for a non-linear VCO with a sigmoid voltage to duty cycle is shown in Figure 4. The duty cycle varies from 0% to 50% under control from the activity input, x_i. Transistors are chosen so that a duty cycle of 25% is achieved when x_i is equal to V_{ref}. By varying the current, I, charging capacitor, C, the pulse width can be set independent of process variation. In practice, a reference clock with 50%

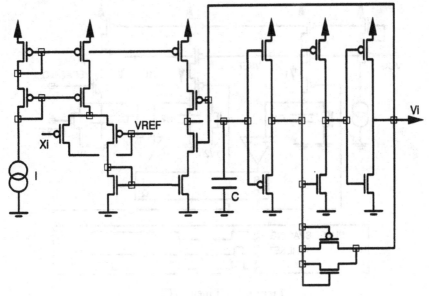

Figure 4 A Non-Linear VCO

duty cycle set to the required pulse width is used to compare against a reference VCO with $x_i = 5V$. A phase lock loop arrangement is used to vary the current, I, charging capacitor C in such a way that the VCO locks on to the reference clock. Current mirrors are used to set I and hence the pulse width to all other VCO's of this type on chip.

Linear VCO

The receiving VCO used in the inter-chip communication scheme is shown in Figure 5. The capacitor C3 is charged to a voltage proportional to the width of the pulse spacing signal. This voltage, held between successive updates of the input neuron, acts as a reference to a circuit which charges an identical capacitor, C2, at the same rate. Once the voltage on C2 reaches the reference voltage, the S-R latch toggles and C2 is discharged. Capacitor C1 now charges up until it reaches V_{ref}, the S-R latch toggles, and C1 is discharged. Capacitor C2 charges again and the process repeats itself. The transmitted neuron output state is hence regenerated on the receiving chip. The pulse width is controlled by the charging current, I, charging capacitor C1 to V_{ref}. An on chip feedback circuit adjusts the current, I, so that the pulse width matches an external reference clock.

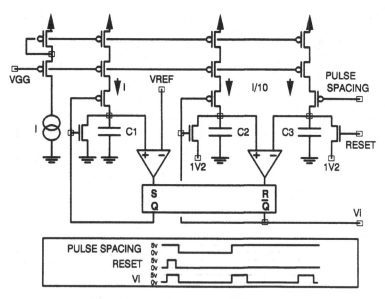

Figure 5 A Linear VCO

CONCLUSIONS

A programmable analogue pulse width modulation synapse has been fabricated and shown to work. A neuron design with sigmoid activity to duty cycle transfer characteristic and a novel inter-chip communication scheme has been designed and is currently being fabricated. The results from these test chips will allow us to implement large analogue pulse-firing neural systems. It is proposed to implement a Multi-Layer Perceptron architecture using circuit components based on those outlined in this paper. This will have 100 input neurons, 64 hidden layer neurons and 32 output neurons.

ACKNOWLEDGEMENTS

The authors are grateful to the UK Science and Engineering Research Council for its support of this work.

REFERENCES

Baxter, D. J., Murray, A. F., and Reekie, H. M., *Fully Cascadable Analogue Synapses Using Distributed Feedback,* in this book.

Churcher, S., Murray, A. F., and Reekie, H. M., *Pulse-Firing VLSI Neural Circuits for Fast Image Pattern Recognition,* in this book.

Murray, A. F., "Pulse Arithmetic in VLSI Neural Networks," *IEEE MICRO*, vol. 9, no. 6, pp. 64-74, 1989.

Murray, A. F., Tarassenko, L., Reekie, H. M., Hamilton, A., Brownlow, M., Baxter, D., and Churcher, S., "Pulsed Silicon Neural Nets - Following the Biological Lead," in *Introduction to VLSI Design of Neural Networks*, ed. U. Ramacher, Kluwer, 1990.

Murray, A. F., Brownlow, M., Hamilton, A., Han, Il Song, Reekie, H. M., and Tarassenko, L., "Pulse-Firing Neural Chips for Hundreds of Neurons," *Neural Information Processing Systems (NIPS) Conference*, pp. 785-792, Morgan Kaufmann, 1990.

Murray, A. F., Baxter, D., Butler, Z., Churcher, S., Hamilton, A., Reekie, H. M., and Tarassenko, L., "Innovations in Pulse Stream Neural VLSI : Arithmetic and Communications," *IEEE Workshop on Microelectronics for Neural Networks, Dortmund*, pp. 8-15, 1990.

3.7 Pulse-Firing VLSI Neural Circuits for Fast Image Pattern Recognition

Stephen Churcher, Alan F. Murray and H. Martin Reekie

Department of Electrical Engineering
University of Edinburgh, EH9 3JL

Abstract

Neural networks are identified as an effective means of performing pattern recognition on image data. To take advantage of the parallelism inherent in such architectures, an analogue CMOS VLSI circuit has been developed. This device consists of novel pulse-firing neurons and synapses. The neurons are current controlled oscillators, which deplete their own input activity whenever a pulse is fired, in a manner similar to biological neurons. The synapses use neural voltage pulses to create pulsed current outputs. The magnitude of these outputs is determined by the synaptic weight voltage. When configured as a multi-layered perceptron, the neural circuit will facilitate the "real-time" labelling of regions in segmented images.

INTRODUCTION

The problem of recognising patterns and objects in images, using "passive" detection techniques (i.e. video cameras) presents a major obstacle to the development of autonomous robotic systems. In order to perform "real-time" (i.e. video rate) recognition, a system must be able to pre-process large volumes of data very quickly, before classifying this information correctly by some means. These tasks may be somewhat "simplified" in industrial (e.g. assembly-line) applications, where lighting conditions can be carefully controlled, and *a priori* assumptions may be made about the objects to be recognised. However, they become almost intractable in the analysis of "natural" scenes, where the environment cannot be artificially manipulated. For this reason, the information provided by the pre-processing system is more ill-defined (or "fuzzy"). This fuzzy data imposes greater demands on the recognition algorithm, which must be more robust to variations in input information. The design of such algorithms is extremely difficult, and in some cases an algorithm might not even exist.

Artificial neural networks have a number of distinct advantages over algorithmic techniques, in the field of pattern recognition. Firstly, they have the ability to explore

VLSI for Artificial Intelligence and Neural Networks, Edited by J.G. Delgado-Frias and
W.R. Moore, Plenum Press, New York, 1991

several competing hypotheses simultaneously, thus giving them a major speed advantage over conventional methods, which generally perform this operation in a sequential fashion. Secondly, neural networks *learn* the mapping from data space to classification space; no complex algorithm need be devised. Finally, neural paradigms can operate on "fuzzy" data without suffering significant performance degradation (Lippmann 1987a, 1989a, Hecht-Nielsen 1988a). The main disadvantage of the neural network approach is the need to train networks, since this generally requires large sets of training data, and can be quite laborious (in instances where supervised learning techniques are employed).

Having identified artificial neural networks as a possible solution to the problem of image pattern recognition, the question of physical implementation must be addressed. With the exception of WISARD (a hardware system which has demonstrated fast image pattern recognition (Aleksander 1982a, 1982b)), most work in the area has hitherto relied heavily on computer simulations of neural systems. Whilst this approach is interesting in its own right, and an essential precursor to the development of dedicated hardware, the available computation rates are too low to make a real-time recognition system practicable.

To take full advantage of the parallelism offered by neural networks (which is the mechanism by which they attain their high speeds of operation), some form of dedicated hardware must be utilised. The two main contenders are silicon VLSI and optical implementations. Whilst neural systems have been demonstrated using lasers, holograms, and optical non-linearities (Wright 1988a), the technology is not yet as well established as are conventional electronic techniques. For this reason, despite the apparent advantages in speed and interconnect density, we have concentrated on hybrid analogue-digital silicon VLSI networks.

The ultimate aim of this work is to produce a hardware realisation of a Multi-Layered Perceptron (MLP), which will label regions in segmented images (i.e. "recognise" them). The network will be trained on the relative positions of, and the unary features (e.g. area, mean grey level) pertaining to, a set of regions obtained from image segmentations. This principle has already been proven by extensive software simulations of the MLP (Wright 1988b); the use of custom VLSI hardware will provide a real-time implementation of the network.

VLSI FOR NEUROCOMPUTING

We have reported the development of the so-called "pulse-stream" arithmetic system (Murray 1987a, 1988a, 1989a). In such implementations, a neuron is a variable oscillator, with an output pulse rate which represents its activity (Murray 1987a, 1988a, 1989a, 1988b, 1989b, 1990a), mirroring the behaviour of biological neurons. At the input of each neuron is an "activity column", which sums all of the post-synaptic activity into a particular neuron (see Figure 1). Each synapse stores a weight, which is used to determine the *proportion* of the input pulse stream (from the output of some other neuron) which will pass to the activity column (Murray 1990a). Pulses may be passed in the form of voltages (Murray 1988a), which are OR'ed together, or they may be passed as currents, which are summed as charge on a capacitor (Murray

1989b, 1990a). The use of voltage pulses was abandoned because information is "lost" in the OR'ing process, whenever two (or more) separate pulses were coincident. The law of charge conservation ensures that this situation does not arise, when summing current pulses at a single node.

This work continues the pulse-stream paradigm, and seeks to improve upon existing circuits, both in terms of electrical performance, and silicon area. More physically compact circuits, which have lower power consumption, will allow neural systems of greater complexity to be integrated on a single piece of silicon. Since these goals are,

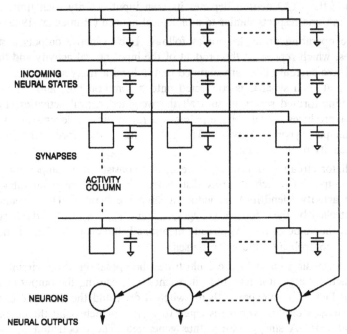

Figure 1 Generic Neurocomputing Architecture

by and large, conflicting, their attainment requires the development of new circuit forms, as opposed to direct evolution of existing hardware. The remainder of this section details two new circuits (a neuron and a synapse) which have been developed to meet these criteria.

Current Controlled Oscillator Neuron

Efforts within the group have hitherto centred on the use of voltage controlled oscillators (VCO's) as neurons. Practical systems have been implemented in silicon, but have suffered from a very fast transition from the "off" state to the "on" state. Early attempts to remedy this shortcoming have resulted in VCO's occupying a relatively large area.

In Hopfield net type structures, the number of synapses is of order n^2 (where n is the number of neurons) and synapses will dominate area calculations, in any VLSI implementation. Therefore, less of a premium is placed on reducing the neuron area. The emphasis changes, however, when dealing with MLP's. In this case, the number of synapses is closer to order n, so it becomes *comparatively* more important to reduce the area occupied by each neuron.

A new oscillator, which uses only one capacitor to determine both the pulse width and pulse rate, was therefore developed to obviate these problems. Because of the direct relationship which exists between the input current and the pulse rate, this neuron is actually a *current* controlled oscillator (CCO). When connected directly to a synaptic array, the CCO neuron depletes its own input activity each time a pulse is fired, and is in some respects similar to a biological neuron (Rumelhart 1986a).

The basic operating principles are as follows. Each synapse outputs a stream of current pulses, which represents the product of the input neural activity and the synaptic weight. These current pulses are summed onto a local activity summation capacitor. The capacitor at each synapse is connected onto a common bus, and the distributed capacitance thus formed serves to sum all the weighted neural activities (Figure 1). The oscillator produces digital voltage pulses at a rate which is dependent on this sum (i.e. the total post-synaptic activity). The pulse rate is therefore a measure of the aggregated activity of the neuron.

The oscillator circuit is shown in Figure 2, and consists of a comparator with hysteresis, the output of which controls distributed charge/discharge circuitry at each post-synaptic activity (dendritic) capacitor, feeding the neuron. The amount of hysteresis is controlled by the reference voltages, V_{ref} and V_{ref1}, whilst the discharge rate is dependent on the value of I_{PD}. As already mentioned, the charging rate of the dendritic capacitor is controlled by the synapse itself.

The waveform diagram in Figure 2 illustrates the operation of the circuit. The voltage on the activity capacitor rises until it reaches V_{ref}, causing the output of the comparator to go high. The synapse is then "switched off", and the dendritic capacitor is discharged (via I_{PD}) until its voltage is equal to V_{ref1}, at which point the circuit reverts to its original state. A single pulse is thus generated. The production of subsequent pulses requires that the activity capacitor recharges, so the pulse rate is determined by the charging rate (i.e the current supplied by the output of the synapse - the waveform diagram assumes that this is constant).

The simplicity of the circuit, in terms of transistor count/size, means a substantial reduction in area from previous forms. Furthermore, the efficient use of the dendritic capacitor to integrate post-synaptic activity, *and* to perform all the timing operations for the neuron, yielded significant area savings in the oscillator, albeit at the expense of some added complexity at the synapse. Low power consumption (predicted by SPICE simulations) bodes well for the instantiation of many such oscillators on a single integrated circuit, and the distributed nature of the dendritic capacitor/discharge circuitry allows for easy cascading of synapses, without significant degradation of oscillator performance. Finally, both pulse width and maximum pulse rate are adjustable, via variations in the reference voltages and the discharge current. This allows fabrication process variations to be compensated for, so minimising matching errors.

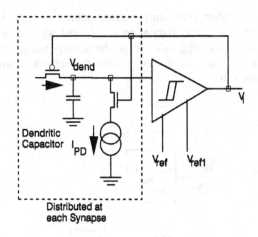

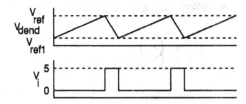

Figure 2 Current Controlled Oscillator Neuron
- Principles of Operation

Pulse Magnitude Modulating Synapse

Early pulse-stream synapses were relatively large (Murray 1987a, 1988a), in terms of silicon area. Furthermore, because of the way in which they modulated pulse width (in order to perform multiplication), they suffered from the slight disadvantage of requiring an input pulse of fixed duration (Murray 1989a). This meant that any new neuron design, which was to be used with this synapse, would have to generate pulses of the same width as previous neuron designs. Whilst not actually a fundamental problem, this fixed pulse width criterion does somewhat constrain future design work, and reduces overall system flexibility.

In order to circumvent these problems, a pulse *magnitude* modulating synapse was designed. As well as having a reduced transistor count, this circuit is fully compatible with existing neuron designs, and the current controlled oscillator. Figure 3 shows a schematic of the synapse, which operates as follows. The synaptic weight, which is stored (dynamically) as a voltage on a capacitor, controls a current source, which charges the post-synaptic activity capacitor whenever a pulse arrives from the transmitting neuron. Another (constant) current source is used to simultaneously remove charge from the capacitor. Excitation is achieved when a net flow of current onto the capacitor occurs, resulting in a rise in the activity voltage (Figure 3); inhibition is produced by a net removal of charge from the capacitor, with a concomitant reduction in the activity voltage.

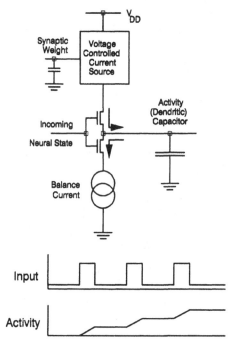

Figure 3 Pulse Magnitude Modulating Synapse -
Principles of Operation

The low transistor count means that, even with charge/discharge control circuitry required by the current controlled oscillator, the area occupied by the synapse is less than that of existing circuits. Extensive SPICE simulations have been very encouraging, with power consumption, cascadability, and process variation issues being adequately dealt with by the circuit.

VLSI IMPLEMENTATIONS

The purpose of this work is to produce a VLSI realisation of a multi-layered perceptron. The previous section described the basic concepts and operating principles of circuits which performed neuronal and synaptic functions. This section examines the circuits in more detail.

The circuit topologies shown in Figures 4 and 5 illustrate the neuron and synapse (complete with the distributed discharge circuitry required by the neuron) respectively. Extensive simulations revealed many "practical" phenomena, which had implications for the actual circuit implementations. These design issues are discussed briefly below.

Figure 4 shows the neuron circuit diagram. The voltages V_{ref} and V_{ref1} are the reference voltages, whilst V_{dend} and V_i are the input (from the dendritic capacitor) and output respectively. V_{DG} is simply a bias voltage which sets differential gain and slew rate.

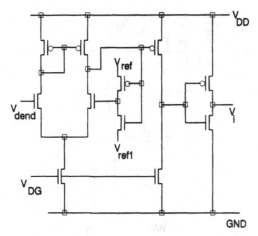

Figure 4 Neuron Circuit Diagram

It can be seen from Figure 4 that the reference voltage selection transistors (the mechanism by which hysteresis is achieved) are controlled by the output of the differential stage. It was originally intended that the control should be derived from the drive (inverter) stage, but the propagation delay incurred by such a scheme resulted in spurious oscillations (at the comparator output), whenever the input current (to the post-synaptic activity capacitor) was low. The problem was solved by using the output of the differential stage. Unfortunately, this created output instability at high values of input current, caused by excessive differential gain. Consequently, the differential stage was designed to have low gain, in order to maximise the range of operation of the circuit.

The synapse circuit is illustrated in Figure 5. Signals x and y are the synaptic weight addressing lines; T_{ij} is the synaptic weight refresh line. V_j is the incoming neural signal, whereas V_i is the output of the receiving neuron. The post-synaptic activity (i.e. the output) is represented by V_{dend} (see also Figure 4). V_{BAL} and V_{PD} control the balance and discharge currents respectively, whilst V_{GG} is the cascode bias voltage. The main problem with the synapse arose from the need to "mirror" the balance and discharge currents (see also Figure 3) to every synapse in the array. This requirement does not present difficulties in itself, but the fact that each "leg" in the respective mirrors must be switched on and off independently (by neuronal pulses) does. When a "simple" current mirror (Allen 1987a) was used, coupling of the switching transients

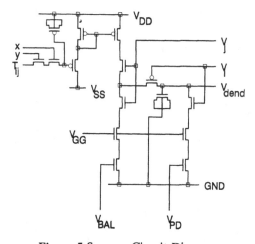

Figure 5 Synapse Circuit Diagram

(via parasitic capacitances) onto the common gate node, resulted in variations in the current flowing in other legs of the mirror. This effect is common to all large analogue circuits (i.e. it is not specific to neural networks), and was minimised by the use of cascode current mirrors (Allen 1987a), with the gates of the cascode transistors connected to a constant bias voltage.

Custom VLSI cells, for the circuits of Figures 4 and 5, formed an array of 10x10 synapses, feeding 10 neurons, to produce a network with overall dimensions of 1.4mm x 1.4mm. Since synaptic weights are stored dynamically (to be refreshed from "off-chip" RAM), address generation and decoding circuitry was also designed. Furthermore, an inter-chip communication scheme (Murray 1990a) was incorporated in the design, to facilitate the cascading of devices to form larger neural systems. At the time of writing, the designs have been submitted for fabrication as test devices, in 2.0μm double metal CMOS.

CONCLUSIONS

The use of multi-layered perceptrons for contextual labelling of regions in segmented images has been reported (Wright 1988b). This paper has detailed the design and development of analogue VLSI pulse-firing circuits, for the implementation of such neural networks. These circuits, in addition to having lower power consumption, are also more physically compact than previous circuit forms (the neuron uses 40% less area, and the synapse saves 5%). Using these sub-circuits, it would be possible to implement an MLP consisting of 89 input units, 16 hidden units, and 2 output units (the architecture proposed by (Wright 1988b)) on a piece of silicon measuring 6mm x 5mm. This calculation takes no account of any support circuitry which may be required. The neurons and synapses have been included, along with a self-timed inter-chip communication scheme, in a CMOS chip, which will allow final verification of the circuits. Additionally, it should be possible to cascade many such devices, to create a multi-layered perceptron capable of real-time scene analysis. At present, a VME interface is being designed, with a view to using a SUN workstation as a host machine for the neural network. This will allow full evaluation of the custom devices, and is an essential precursor to the development of a video-rate region labelling system.

ACKNOWLEDGEMENTS

The authors acknowledge the support of the Science and Engineering Research Council and the EEC (ESPRIT NERVES) for funding, and Stephen Churcher is grateful to SERC and British Aerospace for a CASE studentship. Finally, thanks are also due to Andy Wright (British Aerospace) and Lionel Tarassenko (Oxford University) for additional information and comments.

REFERENCES

Aleksander, I., "Memory Networks for Practical Vision Systems," *Rank Prize Fund International Symposium on the Physical and Biological Processing of Images*, The Royal Society, September, 1982.

Aleksander, I., Stonham, T. J., and Wilkie, B. A., "Computer Vision Systems for Industry," *Digital Systems for Industrial Automation*, vol. 1, no. 4, 1982.

Allen, P. E. and Holberg, D. R., *CMOS Analog Circuit Design,* pp. 219-239, HRW, 1987.

Hecht-Nielsen, R, "Neurocomputing : Picking the Human Brain," *IEEE Spectrum Magazine*, pp. 36 - 41, March, 1988.

Lippmann, R. P., "An Introduction to Computing with Neural Nets," *IEEE ASSP Magazine*, pp. 4 - 22, April, 1987.

Lippmann, R. P., "Pattern Classification using Neural Networks," *IEEE Communications Magazine*, pp. 47 - 64, November, 1989.

Murray, A. F. and Smith, A. V. W., "Asynchronous Arithmetic for VLSI Neural Systems," *Electronics Letters*, vol. 23, pp. 642 - 643, June, 1987.

Murray, A. F. and Smith, A. V. W., "Asynchronous VLSI Neural Networks Using Pulse-Stream Arithmetic," *IEEE Journal of Solid-State Circuits*, vol. 23, pp. 688 - 697, June, 1988.

Murray, A. F., Tarassenko, L., and Hamilton, A., "Programmable Analogue Pulse-Firing Neural Networks," *Neural Information Processing Systems (NIPS) Conference*, pp. 671 - 677, Morgan Kaufmann, 1988.

Murray, A. F., "Pulse Arithmetic in VLSI Neural Networks," *IEEE MICRO*, vol. 9, no. 6, pp. 64 - 74, 1989.

Murray, A. F., Brownlow, M., Hamilton, A., Han, I. S., Reekie, H. M., and Tarassenko, L., "Pulse-Firing Neural Chips for Hundreds of Neurons," *Neural Information Processing Systems (NIPS) Conference*, Morgan Kaufmann, 1989.

Murray, A. F., Hamilton, A., Reekie, H. M., Churcher, S., Baxter, D. J., Butler, Z. F., and Tarassenko, L., "Innovations in Pulse-Stream Neural VLSI Arithmetic and Communications," *IEEE Workshop on Microelectronics for Neural Networks, Dortmund, 1990*, 1990.

Rumelhart, D. E. and McLelland, J. D., in *Parallel Distributed Processing : Explorations in the Microstructures of Cognition Volume Two*, pp. 366-367, MIT Press, 1986.

Wright, W. A. and White, H. J., "Holographic Implementation of a Hopfield Model with Discrete Weightings," *Applied Optics*, vol. 27, pp. 331 - 338, 1988.

Wright, W. A., "Road Finding Neural Network," Technical Memorandum TM 1014, British Aerospace Sowerby Research Centre, 1988.

3.8 An Analog Circuit with Digital I/O for Synchronous Boltzmann Machines

Patrick Garda and Eric Belhaire

Institut d'Electronique Fondamentale - C.N.R.S. u.r.a. 22
Bat. 220 Université de Paris Sud 91405 Orsay France

Abstract

In this paper, we address the problem of designing a parallel system for the experimentation of arbitrary multilayered networks running the Boltzmann Machines algorithm. We present the Synchronous Boltzmann Machine, a new model recently introduced by Azencott (1989) and the functional analog cells its implementation requires. We then describe a fully analog cascadable chip set, already described, and introduce a new circuit which features internal analog computations and storage, and digital data I/O. We show how it can be used in a digital system performing the dynamical change of the network architecture.

INTRODUCTION

Many current neural nets experiments use multi-layered networks and the Generalised Delta Rule algorithm (Rumelhart *et al* 1986). Whereas the experimentation speed is insufficient, no cellular circuits have been realized for this algorithm, because neither its implementation nor its parallelization are obvious. On the other hand, Boltzmann Machines (Hinton and Sejnowski 1986) show a number of very attractive features, but the simulations of the model are desesperately slow. Mixed analog/digital implementations have been described (Alspector and Allen 1987a, Alspector *et al* 1987b, Kreuzer and Goser 1988), which are targeted towards fully connected networks.

In this paper, we describe the architecture of an analog circuit for multilayered networks running the Synchronous Boltzmann Machine algorithm, which uses internal analog circuits both for the computations and the storage, and digital data I/O. We show that it allows for the design of a digital system for the Boltzmann Machine experimentation, whose network architecture may dynamically change.

We present the Synchronous Boltzmann Machine, a model recently introduced by Azencott (1989) in the first section and we describe the functional analog cells it requires in a second section. We then review a chip set previously described in (Belhaire and Garda 1990), and

VLSI for Artificial Intelligence and Neural Networks, Edited by J.G. Delgado-Frias and
W.R. Moore, Plenum Press, New York, 1991

245

introduce a new circuit which features internal analog computations and storage, and digital data I/O. We show how it can be used in a digital system performing the dynamical change of the network architecture.

SYNCHRONOUS BOLTZMANN MACHINES

The Boltzmann Machine model has been introduced by Hinton and Sejnowski in 1985 (Hinton and Sejnowski 1986). It is an asynchronous model, where a single neuron updates its state at each iteration. However, in a parallel hardware implementation, it is natural for all the neurons to update their state simultaneously at each iteration. Therefore, a new model has been introduced by Azencott in 1989 (Azencott 1989a) to deal with this case. We describe now the operation of this model, which is called the Synchronous Boltzmann Machine.

Let $(u_i)_i$ be a set of *neurons*, x_i^n the *neuron state* of u_i at instant n (which may have values 1 or 0) and w_{ij} the *weight* between neurons u_i and u_j. Let V_i^n be the *action potential* of u_i after instant n, computed according to:

$$V_i^n = \sum_{j \neq i} w_{ij}\, x_j^n \tag{1}$$

All the neurons update their state simultaneously. Then the state of the neuron u_i at discrete time step (n+1) is tossed at random with the probability :

$$P(x_i^{n+1} = 0) = \frac{1}{1 + \exp(V_i^n/T)} \tag{2}$$

Now let us consider the learning process. For this we have to choose input, output and hidden neurons among the network of neurons. The weight update process is repeatedly performed for all the pattern associations, and for each of them, it consists in a clamped and a free phase. During each phase, the neurons update their state, and a cooccurrence counter is associated to each weight, which computes the following expression:

$$p_{ij} = \frac{1}{N} \sum_n [x_i^{n-1} x_j^n + x_i^n x_j^{n-1}] \tag{3}$$

During the clamped phase, a pattern is imposed both on the input and output neurons while the hidden neurons are left free, and the cooccurrence p_{ij}^+ is computed, whereas during the free phase, the input pattern is presented to the input neurons while the output and hidden neurons are left free, and the cooccurrence p_{ij}^- is computed. After these clamped and free phases, the weights are updated according to the rule (where η and T are two positive parameters):

$$\Delta w_{ij} = \frac{\eta}{T} (p_{ij}^+ - p_{ij}^-) \tag{4}$$

In a multilayer network, the neurons are grouped into layers. The input (resp. output) neurons compose the input (resp. output) layer, and the other neurons are distributed among several hidden layers. The neurons may also be numbered, and the state of the whole network is described through the *neuron state vector*, which is the vector of the states of all the neurons.

FUNCTIONAL CELLS

We are investigating an analog implementation of the Synchronous Boltzmann Machine. It consists in a chip set, which will be used for the realization of dedicated systems whose multilayered network architecture could eventually be dynamically changed. These chips are built out of functional cells, which implement the computations required by the equations (1), (2) (3) and (4), and store the variables they require. We describe the synaptic cell (computation of equations (1), (3) and (4), storage of cooccurrence and weight counters) in the first subsection, the neuron cell (computation of equation (2)) in the second subsection and the latching cell (storage of neuron state) in the last subsection.

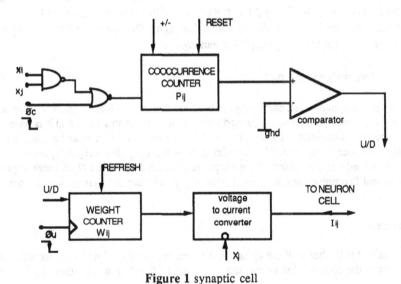

Figure 1 synaptic cell

Synaptic cell

Firstly, the synaptic cell is in charge of the computation of the cooccurrence counter according to equation (3), of the weight update according to equation (4), and of the storage of the cooccurrence and weight counters. A significant amount of chip area may be gained from replacing digital memories by analog ones. The weight and cooccurence memories may be carried out by capacitors at room temperature both in the learning and in the recognition phase.

In the former the resulting slow weight decay favours the learning (Alspector and Allen 1987a). In the later we use a suitable refreshing scheme: it is built out of an external digital memory (RAM), which is scanned in order to sequentially refresh the analog weight value. In this way we get a very small area on-chip storage without any specific technological developments such as circuit cooling or analog floating gates. A similar scheme has been described in (Eberhard 1988, Murray *et al* 1990). Of course some external hardware is required, but it is accessed sequentially and thus it does not introduce any bottleneck. Other refreshing schemes are introduced in (Vittoz *et al* 1990) for example.

The synaptic cell (figure 1) consists in an analog cooccurence counter p_{ij}, which is incremented during the clamped learning phase (where control signal $+/- = 1$) and decremented during the free learning phase ($+/- = 0$). An analog counter may be realized thanks to a switched-capacitor integrator; however we are investigating simpler circuits which could provide this function (Madani *et al* 1990). At each relaxation iteration, the counter is sequentially modified twice, by considering a value which is firstly $x_i^{n-1}x_j^n$ and secondly $x_j^{n-1}x_i^n$. For that purpose two wires, x_i and x_j, reach the synaptic cell and are fed to a nand gate whose output is connected to the cooccurrence counter through a latch controlled by the Cooccurrence signal Φ_c.

The output of the cooccurrence counter is fed into a comparator to determine the sign of $(p_{ij}^+ - p_{ij}^-)$. According to this sign the weight analog counter w_{ij} is incremented or decremented under the control of the weight Update signal Φ_u. Therefore this learning block actually implements the following simplified learning rule:

$$\Delta w_{ij} = \text{sign} (p_{ij}^+ - p_{ij}^-) \tag{5}$$

Moreover, the synaptic cell participates to the computation of the action potential according to equation (1). This computation is carried out by a distributed structure, and it is based on a single rail current summator. It consists in n voltage-to-current converters and a single current-to-voltage converter. In the synaptic cell storing the weight w_{ij}, the weight capacitor drives a voltage-controlled current source whose output is connected to the net N_i in order to provide on N_i a current I_{ij} representing the contribution $w_{ij} x_j^n$. The current I_{ij} is inhibited when $x_j^n = 0$.

Neuron cell

The neuron cell is in charge of the update of the neuron state according to equation (2), and it participates to the computation of the action potential according to equation (1). One of its inputs is the current I_i which is the sum $\sum_j I_{ij}$ of the currents I_{ij}, generated by each synaptic cell: this current I_i represents the action potential V_i.

The random tossing required by the Boltzmann Machine results in some troubles : the use of resistor thermal noise (cf Alspector and Allen 1987a) leads practically to correlated generators, as pointed out in (Kreuzer and Goser 1988) and confirmed experimentally by (Alspector 1988). On the other hand, the use of digital pseudo-random generators uses a lot of surface and leads also to some problems (Kreuzer and Goser 1988).

We investigate an original solution based on a uniform law random number generator: the binary neuron state is resulting from the comparison of the output υ_i of the uniform law generator to the sigmoïdal function $\varpi_i = 1/(1 + \exp(V_i/T))$ of the action potential V_i. The uniform law υ_i is built out of the integration of a sequence of unbiased independent binary values, which result from the sampling of an optical random physical system, the speckle of laser, which is made time independent by a suitable scheme described in (Lalanne 1989).

Finally the neuron cell has two inputs, the binary random samples and the current I_i representing the action potential V_i, and one output, the neuron state x_i. It consists (cf figure 2) in a current to voltage converter (from I_i to V_i), a sigmoïdal function, an integrator and a comparator.

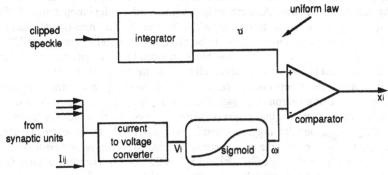

Figure 2 neuron cell

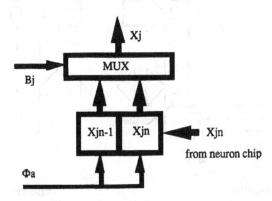

Figure 3 latching cell

Latching cell

The latching cell is in charge of the storage of the neuron state and its broadcast to a linear array of synaptic cells. It consists in a shift register, which stores the states x^{n-1} and x^n. These data are shifted in the shift register under the control of signal Φ_a when the next neuron state is valid. The signal B controls a multiplexer, which broadcasts either the value x^{n-1} (B = 0) or the value x^n (B = 1). (cf figure 3)

ANALOG I/O CHIP SET

Now let us describe the way the synaptic and neuron cells are grouped into chips for the implementation of arbitrary multi-layered networks. In order to keep on with the symmetry of the weights which is required by the Boltzmann Machine model while using an analog storage, a first design choice is to decide that each cooccurrence and weight counter should have a single physical representation. As each weight w_{ij} is used for the computation of the two contributions $w_{ij} x_i$ and $w_{ij} x_j$ to the potentials V_i and V_j, this means that the currents representing these two contributions have to be generated in a single synaptic cell. For this purpose, a second voltage-to-current converter is included into the synaptic cell of figure 1, resulting in a so-called bidirectional synaptic cell (cf Belhaire and Garda 1990).

Now in a multilayered network this occurs between two fully interconnected successive layers. This means that p neurons $(u_i)_{1 \leq i \leq p}$ of one layer are fully interconnected to q neurons $(v_j)_{1 \leq j \leq q}$ of the other layer. The interaction between these two sets of neurons is described by a matrix $(w_{ij})_{1 \leq i \leq p, 1 \leq j \leq q}$, and this suggests a matrix floor plan for the synaptic cells matrix.

Regarding the broadcast of the neuron states, one has to successively broadcast x_i^{n-1} and x_i^n on the wire x_i, and symmetrically x_j^{n-1} and x_j^n on the wire x_j. Therefore a latching cell is required for each row anf for each column of synaptic cells. These cells have to be included in the synaptic chip. (cf figure 4)

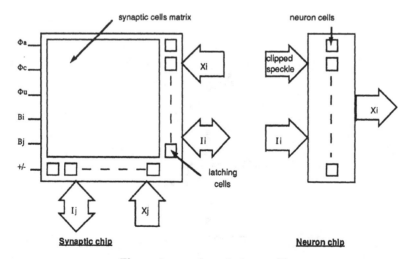

Figure 4 synaptic and neuron chips

However, we have shown in (Belhaire and Garda 1990) that the synaptic chips have to be cascadable in both directions. Moreover they should have a square shape (about 32x32 in a CMOS 2μ technology), and they should not include any neuron cell. Thus we need a separate neuron cells chip, which consists in a column of r neuron cells, where no synaptic cells are included. (cf figure 4) The synaptic and neuron chips have analog data I/O, therefore they are called an analog I/O chip set.

DIGITAL I/O CIRCUIT

Unfortunately, the previous chip set has also several drawbacks. When a neuron belongs to the input layer of a multilayer network, its state is always clamped by the environment, and it is thus useless to compute its potential V_j. Hence the second voltage-to-current converter could be omitted (as in figure 1) for all the neurons of the input layer, and some chip area could be saved. This synaptic cell could be used for all neurons, but for neurons belonging to hidden or output layers, this leads to two different physical representations of each weight. Therefore the symetry required by the Boltzmann Machine interaction may not be respected.

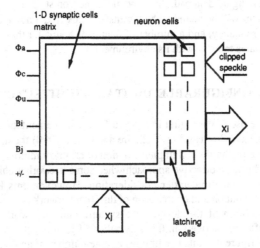

Figure 5 digital I/O circuit

On the other hand, the currents provided by different chips are affected by large fluctuations, and it is not experimentally proved that combining them will be practicable. Finally, the data I/O of the synaptic chip require (P+Q) analog pads and (P+Q) digital pads for a PxQ synaptic cells matrix, and the data I/O of the neuron chip require R analog pads and R digital pads for a R neuron cells column: this will limit the matrix size, or increase significantly the package cost, as the technology feature size decreases. These two remarks lead to the conclusion that one should give up with the cascadability of the analog I/O chip set.

Another circuit is depicted in figure 5, which features digital data I/O only: it consists in a matrix of PxQ synaptic cells as described in figure 1, together with a column of Q neuron cells, and the required latching cells. It includes a row of P digital input pads, which feed into the circuit the binary states of P input neurons. It also includes a column of Q digital output pads, which send out of the circuit the binary states of Q output neurons. It provides by itself the update of the states of the output neurons, computed thanks to the previous states of the input neurons. It also performs the update of the weights matrix leading from the input neurons row to the output neurons column.

The output neurons belong to the same layer, say the H layer. The input neurons belong to two layers, the one which is preceding the layer H in the multi-layer network and the one which is following it. Now this circuit is cascadable in a single direction only: several circuits may share the same input neurons whereas their output neurons may belong to the same layer H. As the number of synaptic cells in a row is the maximum number of input neurons, it will limit the size of the achievable layers. Therefore P will be chosen large and Q small. For example, a 1024 synaptic cells circuit could be shaped as a 128x8 matrix.

Observe that in this circuit the data I/O are digital, and that the neuron states update frequency (typically 300 kHz, max. 1 MHz) is expected to be significantly lower than the serial data transfer frequency achievable by a digital link (typically 10 MHz). Therefore, it will be possible and fruitful to transfer serially several input (resp. output) neuron states through each input (resp. output) pad. This will limit the pad number, thus simplifying the packaging of the chip in technologies with smaller feature size. Consider an example where 8 neuron states are transfered through each digital data pad: the same global neuron states transfer rate between the chip and its environment will be achieved by a transfer clock frequency 8 times faster that the neuron states update frequency, and a number of data pads 8 smaller than that of a chip using fully parallel neuron states transfer with its environment.

DYNAMICALLY CONFIGURABLE DIGITAL ARCHITECTURE

Now let us describe the use of the digital I/O circuit for the implementation of arbitrary multi-layered networks. We have discussed in (Belhaire and Garda 1990) the use of the analog I/O chip set (cf figure 4) for the hardwired implementation of arbitrary multilayered networks with a fixed architecture. This is an effective approach when some network architecture is known to be well-suited to the application under consideration. However, this knowledge will be acquired through the simulation and comparison of different network architectures.

This raises the question of the design of a system whose network architecture could dynamically change after its fabrication. It seems rather difficult to achieve this target with the analog I/O chip set of figure 4, as its use implies a large number of analog data multiplexing. But it is possible to devise such an architecture with the digital I/O circuit (cf figure 5 and previous section). This architecture is shown on figure 6. It consists in a column of the circuits of figure 5, an injection and broadcast module, and an interconnection network.

Let us describe the operation of this system. The new neuron states vector consists in the new states of the neurons belonging to the hidden and output layers, computed by the neural circuits, together with the states of the input neurons, provided by the environment. This neuron state vector is fed into the injection and broadcast module, which generates a message for each destination of each neuron state. These messages are then moved to their destination by an interconnection network. This interconnection network, which is fully digital, may be a circuit-switching network or a packet-switching network.

Observe that multiplexing the neuron states allows the reduction of the number of messages the interconnection network has to transfer. Notice also that all I/O within the system, and between the system and the environment, are digital; the control of the interconnection network is digital as well, and a digital interface to the analog control signals could also be provided.

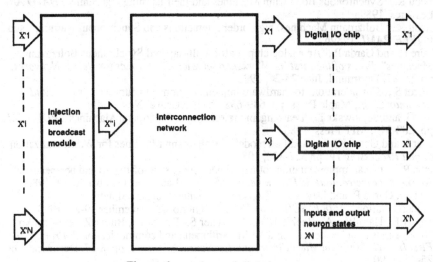

Figure 6 experimental digital system

CONCLUSION

In this paper, we have described the architecture of an analog circuit with digital I/O for multilayered Synchronous Boltzmann Machines, and we have introduced several original points. By following the Synchronous Boltzmann Machine model, we are getting considerable improvements in relaxation speed and in learning and recognition results. By using analog circuits both for the computations and the storage, we may improve the relaxation speed and the number of computing synaptic and neuron cells per chip. By designing circuits with digital data I/O, we provide an easy way of multiplexing the transfer of neuron states between chips. This leads to the design of a digital system whose network architecture may dynamically change, while keeping the advantages of internal analog computations and storage.

ACKNOWLEDGMENTS

This work has been supported by D.R.E.T. under Contract 87/292 and by C.N.R.S. under P.R.C.-A.M.N. and G.C.I.S. project RA. We thank Robert Azencott and Jérome Lacaille, from D.I.A.M.E.N.S. in Paris, Pierre Chavel and Philippe Lalanne, from I.O.T.A. in Orsay, Francis Devos, Kurosh Madani and Zhu Yi Min from I.E.F., for fruitful discussions.

REFERENCES

Alspector J. and Allen R., "A neuromorphic V.L.S.I. learning system", *Procs of the 1987 Stanford Conf. on VLSI*, MIT Press., pp. 313-349, 1987a

Alspector J. , Allen R., Hu V., Satyarayana S., "Stochastic learning network and their electronic implementation", *Procs NIPS 87* , AIP, pp. 9-21, 1987b

Alspector J., private communication, *22nd Asilomar Conf.*, Pacific Grove, Nov. 1988.

Azencott R., "Synchronous Boltzmann Machines and their learning algorithms", *NATO ARW*. Les Arcs, 1989a

Azencott R., "Boltzmann Machines: high-order interactions and Synchronous learning", sub. to *IEEE PAMI*, 1989b.

Belhaire E. and Garda P., "An analog chip set for multi-layered Synchronous Boltzmann Machines", *Procs of the First Int. Workshop on MicroElectronics for Neural Networks*, pp. 80-87, Dortmund, June 25-26, 1990

Eberhardt S., "Considerations for hardware implementations of neural networks", *22nd Asilomar Conf.*, Maple Press, pp. 649-653, Pacific Grove, Nov., 1988

Hinton G. and Sejnowski T., "Learning and relearning in Boltzmann Machines", *PDP Vol.1*, pp. 282-317, MIT Press, 1986

Kreuzer I. and Goser K., "A modified model of Boltzmann Machines for W.S.I. realization", *Signal Processing IV*, pp.327-330, 1988.

Lalanne P., "Optical implementations of neural networks : state-of-the-art and perspectives", *Journées d'Electronique de Lausanne*, pp. 251-264, Lausanne, October 10-12, 1989.

Madani K., Garda P. and Devos F., "Two analog counters for neural networks implementation", *16th ESSCIRC*, pp.233-236, Grenoble, September 19-21, 1990

Murray A.F., Hamilton A., Reekie H.M., Churcher S., Baxter D., Butler Z., Tarassenko L., "Innovations in pulse sream neural VLSI - arithmetic and communications", *Procs of the First Int. Workshop on MicroElectronics for Neural Networks*, pp. 8-27, Dortmund, June 25-26, 1990

Rumelhart D.E., Hinton G.E., Williams R.J., "Learning internal representations by error propagation", *PDP Vol.1*, pp. 318-362, MIT Press, 1986

Vittoz E., Oguey H., Maher M.H., Nys O., Dijkstra E., Chevroulet M., "Analog storage of adjustable synaptic weights", *Procs of the First Int. Workshop on MicroElectronics for Neural Networks*, pp. 69-79, Dortmund, June 25-26, 1990

4.1 The VLSI Implementation of the Σ Architecture

S.R. Williams and J.G. Cleary

Computer Science Department, University of Calgary
Calgary, AB, Canada T2N 1N4

Abstract

A description is given of a parallel computer architecture called Σ and its implementation as a full custom design in 2μm VLSI technology. The architecture is highly parallel, consisting of many simple processing elements heavily interconnected. The processing elements perform threshold computations on thousands of inputs. This architecture was inspired by research under the "neural network" banner and retains the highly interconnected nature of such systems. However, it differs from them in some key areas. The Σ architecture is digital, it provides greater functionality with respect to the type of threshold comparison done, the connection weights remain static for the duration of a problem, and its processing is deterministic. Communication between units is in single bit values which are heavily multiplexed to reduce the amount of physical interconnect and pinout.

THE Σ ARCHITECTURE

The Σ architecture was motivated by the need for a system suited to a number of areas that cannot be efficiently executed on conventional serial, or von Neuman, computers. Neural network research heavily influenced this architecture but rather than attempt to duplicate all their features, the Σ architecture focuses on achieving a large number of highly interconnected processors. Each processor is very simple, so that alone it is incapable of performing much meaningful computation, but collectively many such processors can be made to perform complex tasks.

A complete Σ system is composed of a conventional host computer and a number of identical chips, containing processing elements (σs). Each σ sums its inputs, and its output is a programmable linear comparison function of this sum against a programmable threshold. Each input is selected for summing by a weight of 0 or 1. The comparison performed can be either >, ≥, <, ≤, = or ≠ to the threshold. Within this scheme all the standard logic functions can be obtained and in addition so can more complex functions not easily expressed in boolean logic, for example "any three of some large set of inputs are true".

To achieve the degree of interconnection between the σs that is required by this architecture, each chip has 1000 inputs. This input pool is shared by all the σs on the chip. This allows any σ to compute results on anywhere from 1 to 1000 inputs. The inputs available

VLSI for Artificial Intelligence and Neural Networks, Edited by J.G. Delgado-Frias and
W.R. Moore, Plenum Press, New York, 1991

255

will depend on how the system is physically wired together – chip inputs originate as outputs from other chips, or occasionally from an external source, such as the host.

A σ weights the chip input set by a locally stored weight vector to arrive at a subset of inputs used in its calculation. The vectors form a connection matrix that prior to computation is programmed to described the connections between σs. With this programmable scheme, communication is configurable to a structure matching application requirements, thus accommodating a wider range of problems than a hard-wired pattern.

The host provides programming and control for the system including downloading programs for execution. Programming is done for each σ by setting the weights attached to its inputs, the form of threshold comparison to be done, the value of the threshold and the weight vector. The host also provides a way of injecting inputs into the system for processing. To intercept the final outputs of the system there is an interface back from the Σ system to the host.

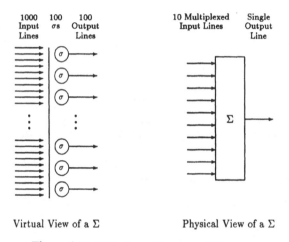

| Virtual View of a Σ | Physical View of a Σ |

Figure 1 Multiplexing of Inputs and Outputs

TOWARDS A VLSI IMPLEMENTATION

The architecture lends itself well to implementation in VLSI circuit technology. The repetition of the basic processing element hundreds or thousands of times immediately reduces the VLSI design complexity (see Fairbairn 1982) – a key consideration in managing the design of chips in excess of 100,000 transistors. In addition, due to the scale of integration possible, a VLSI implementation allows many of the σs to be integrated onto a single chip thereby minimizing system cost.

The decision of implementing the Σ architecture as a VLSI chip is not without cost. In a VLSI implementation where a large number of processors are interconnected, anything other than single wire interconnection is prohibitive. The VLSI design for the Σ architecture allows only single bit datum to be communicated between the σ units, and single bits are used as input weights. Thus the current design includes no provision for excitatory and inhibitory connection levels, instead the information in the connection matrix stores only whether there is or is not a connection between σs. This binary data limitation is not one of concept but rather a question of chip area.

The distributed nature of the system and the inherent large communication bandwidth is also a problem in VLSI since fewer I/O pins exist than inputs and outputs. This pinout problem is solved by heavily multiplexing the input and output signals on wires. Multiplexing also has the advantage of reducing the amount of interchip wiring. Multiplexing signals, particularly the inputs, influenced much of the chip design.

The current realization of the Σ design has 10 physical inputs to each chip, see Figure 1. The number of inputs seems right at 10, this is sufficient for most problems including mesh wiring patterns where an input can be received from each of 8 neighbors as well as a feedback from the Σ chips own output and an input for control and data from the host. An example of a complete Σ system is given in Figure 5.

Each physical input has 100 virtual bit streams multiplexed onto it for a total of 1000 inputs available to each chip. Each chip has a single physical output line. So that it can serve as an input directly to other chips it also has 100 output lines multiplexed onto it. The natural size for a chip would then be to have 100 σs each generating one of the virtual outputs. However, area limitations on the MOSIS process for which the design was targeted limited the number of σs to 20 per chip. The design however allows five of these chips to be combined to form a single Σ unit and to generate a single output line, see Figure 2.

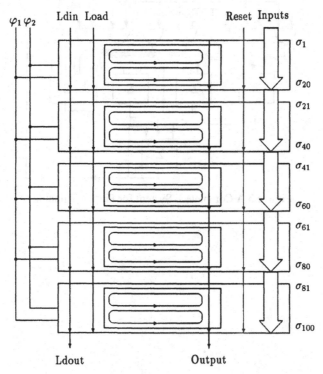

Figure 2 A Σ as 5 Cascaded Chips

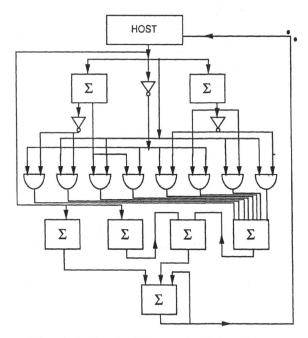

Figure 3 A Complete Σ System for Picture Thinning

APPLICATIONS

There exist many examples where a high degree of concurrency can be arranged by matching the processing elements to the natural structure of the data. The Σ architecture supports such processing through its many processing elements and a programmable connection matrix. For problems that need parallelism and the high degree of connectivity, they are primitive properties of the system and do not need to be grafted on top of an existing structure. The processing elements compute simple threshold functions on their inputs; sufficient processing power so that collectively they can solve interesting problems in areas of cellular automata, image processing and pattern recognition. Some examples are given by Sahebkar (1987) and Cleary (1986, 1987) including the n-queens problem; rule-based reasoning; string searching; shortest path; completion of a jigsaw; parallel thinning; playing tic-tac-toe and the game of life. Such applications exhibit properties of conflict detection, constraint propagation, pattern matching, decision making, feature extraction and reducing the search space.

Figure 3 shows how a complete Σ system can be configured. This example does parallel thinning for black-white pixel images (for the original description of the problem see Holt, Stewart *et al* 1987). It operates on a 10x10 pixel field. Sahebkar (1987) includes a more elaborate mesh design which can be scaled to any size field of view. The system makes use of some simple gates to do primitive operations on all the bits in a multiplexed line – one gate does the work of 100. The resulting system can do one parallel thinning operation on the entire field in 40μsec when clocked at 10 MHz.

VLSI DESIGN

The chip layout was done in the Electric CAD system. (Figures 4 and 5 give the floor plans of a σ and a Σ). Further details of the design are given by Williams (1990). The design obeys MOSIS's (conservative) 2μm double-metal process design rules. The number of transistors is in excess of 200,000 covering a 9200μm x 7854μm area. Fortunately, the overall structure of the design is more like that of a RAM than a CPU – inherent in the design is a great deal of repetition. This regularity makes the design viable as a full custom design, which was essential in achieving the layout density required for a single chip of this size.

The layout of a single σ can be divided into two parts: the storage of its connection weights, and the logic to compute the weighted summation and the threshold comparison. The weights are stored as bits circulating in 10 shift registers, one for each physical input stream. This provides a compact and simple storage scheme and allows convenient access to the values while accumulating the sums.

A serial adder accumulates 10 weighted inputs into a register holding a running total of the weighted sum. As each of the inputs is a 0 or 1 and each of the weights is similarly a 0 or 1, input weighting is equivalent to "and"ing the inputs against a mask of weights. To speed the threshold comparison it is done in parallel, and the weighted sum register is compared with zero. This requires the weighted sum register into which the weighted inputs are accumulated be initialized with the two's complement of the desired threshold. This negative threshold value is stored in a register. Another register, storing the comparison type, selects the σ output from the comparator results.

The calculation by a σ is a cumulative process. On each clock cycle, 10 multiplexed inputs are weighted and accumulated. After 100 cycles all inputs have been processed by the σs to

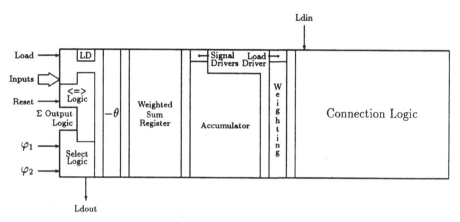

Figure 4 Floor Plan of a σ

yield an output. The weighted sum registers are re-initialized and the process repeats for the next batch of inputs.

The remaining chip circuitry interfaces the σs to the off-chip environment and provides a means to load the chip from an external source. A shift register is used to multiplex the σ outputs onto the output line: σ outputs are latched and shifted off-chip over the subsequent 100 cycles. During loading the connection weight registers, the weighted sum registers, the negative threshold registers, and the output function registers of the σs are linked together to form a load line. The floor plan of a complete Σ chip appears in Figure 5.

The inclusion of testability into any VLSI design is important to assure that no faults exist in individual chips due to fabrication errors. Additional circuitry is not needed to test a Σ chip for fabrication errors. For testing purposes the load line also serves as a scan path. Since all the internal registers are on this scan path the chip is 100% testable: every register can be controlled and observed.

Performance predictions and electrical characteristics for the layout were derived from SPICE simulations of the leaf cells found in the design. Although conservative timing estimates of the internal computation delays result in a clock frequency of 18MHz, the system is to be clocked at a much slower 10MHz rate. The clock speed is not limited by the processor speed, but by the power consumption of the chip. The problem is the number of registers switching at high speeds – the faster elements are clocked the more frequently the transistors switch, the higher the average current drawn, and the more power consumed. Table 1 compares the power consumption calculated for various chip components at clock frequencies of 18MHz and 10MHz. Ceramic chip packaging can dissipate a maximum power of 2.5 watts without special cooling requirements (see Glasser and Dobberpuhl 1985). Hence the clock speed is has been tuned down.

The results from the SPICE simulations further help in circumventing several potentially hazardous conditions from arising by ensuring the power and ground supply lines are of adequate width. Sufficiently wide supplies keep current densities below the metal migration limit and ensure that the supply rails have low resistance so that switching transients do not introduce significant noise.

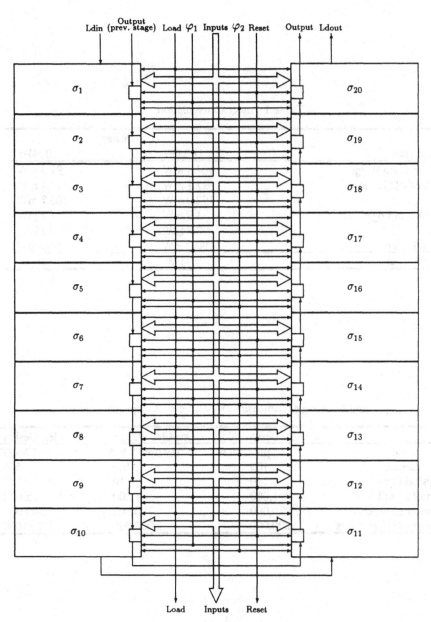

Figure 5 Floor Plan of a Σ

Table 1 Power Consumption

Component	Power 18 MHz	10 MHz
Connection Weight	164.3 mW	91.3 mW
Threshold Logic	27.7 mW	13.4 mW
σ	192.0 mW	106.7 mW
Σ Output Logic	1.9 mW	1.1 mW
Σ	3.84 W	2.13 W
Pad Frame	90.0 mW	50.0 mW
Chip Total	3.93 W	2.18 W

Table 2 Scaling of Dimensions for Different Σ Implementations

	Current Design	One Chip Design	Ideal Design
Fabrication	2 μm CMOS	0.9 μm CMOS	0.35 μm CMOS?
Multiplexing	100	100	500
Physical Input Lines	10	10	10
Virtual Input Lines	1,000	1,000	5,000
Number Connections	20,000	100,000	2,500,000
Number of Transistors	200,000	1,000,000	25,000,000

SCALING WITH TECHNOLOGY

As current state-of-the-art technology becomes more readily available and the fabrication technology further scales down this will open many avenues for design experimentation with the Σ architecture. First order scaling of the linear dimensions increases circuit density in an inverse square relation. Estimates indicate that it would be feasible to squeeze the full 100 σs of a Σ onto a single chip in a fabrication process of approximately 0.9μm (the current 20 σ design is for a 2μm process). The dimensions of the system are not cast in stone. Other designs may implement a different combination from the 1000 inputs and 100 σs presented here. The underlying architecture is flexible and easily extensible. Table 2 shows the comparison of the current Σ design with an ideal system that awaits further advances in technology. A VLSI design for such a scaled version shares many of the same principles and design ideas presented in this paper.

CONCLUSIONS

The arrival of VLSI technology has removed a fundamental constraint from computer architecture. Designers are no longer rigidly bound by the cost of processing logic. Ideas that were once impractical and only reasoned about are now within reach and can be built. Of the numerous possible parallel architectures, a system composed of simple processors such as the Σ is ideal for implementation using current VLSI technology.

ACKNOWLEDGEMENTS

This work was supported by the Natural Sciences and Engineering Research Council of Canada, and by the Alberta Microelectronics Centre. The authors also thank Masoud Sahebkar for many enlightening discussions and gratefully acknowledge his effort in programming a simulator and implementing a number of applications.

REFERENCES

Cleary, J.G. "Connectionist Architectures", Research Report 86/234/8, Department of Computer Science, University of Calgary, 1986.

Cleary, J.G. "A Simple VLSI Connectionist Architecture", *IEEE First International Conference on Neural Networks*, San Diego, pp 419-426, 1987.

Fairbairn, D.G.. "VLSI: A New Frontier for Systems Designers", *IEEE Computer*, vol. 15(1), pp. 9-24, January 1982.

Glasser, L.A. and Dobberpuhl, D.W., *The Design and Analysis of VLSI Circuits*, Addison-Wesley, Reading, MA, 1985.

Holt, C.M., Stewart,V., Clint, M. and Perrot, R.H., "An Improved Parallel Thinning Algorithm", Communications of the ACM, vol. 18(2), pp. 255-264, 1987.

Sahebkar, M., "An Analysis of Algorithms for a Connectionist Architecture", Project Report Department of Computer Science, University of Calgary , 1987.

Williams, S.R. "The VLSI Implementation of a Fine-Grained Parallel Architecture", MSc Thesis, also available as Research Report 90/391/15, Department of Computer Science, University of Calgary, 1990 .

4.2 A Cascadable VLSI Architecture for the Realization of Large Binary Associative Networks

Werner Poechmueller and Manfred Glesner

Institute for Microelectronic Systems
Technical University Darmstadt
Karlstrasse 15
D-6100 Darmstadt
Germany

Abstract

This paper presents the hardware realization of a binary associative memory. Two designs have been made to provide dedicated VLSI chips. A cascadable architecture allows to build up associative systems consisting of several thousand neurons. To keep costs low and reach a high storing density, standard RAM chips are used for weight storage. The realizable memory systems may be used for arbitrary fast associations or for classification tasks. Due to high speed performance of the hardware, real time problems may be solved.

INTRODUCTION

In many application areas, as e.g. image processing or speech recognition, classical sequentially operating systems are facing insurmountable limitations. These limitations are on the one hand the maximum data processing rate which principally can be augmented only by an increase of the clock frequency or word width of the system and on the other hand the necessary amount of software which has to be developed. In most of the information processing systems used today, software development is several times more costly than all the necessary hardware devices.

The application of neural network technology is promising in many areas demanding for an enormous amount of data to be processed in very short time. Due to their inhe-

VLSI for Artificial Intelligence and Neural Networks, Edited by J.G. Delgado-Frias and
W.R. Moore, Plenum Press, New York, 1991

rent prallelism, a great computational power may be achieved even with rather slow and simple processing elements. But this is only possible if this inherent parallelism of neural networks is really used by a fully parallel hardware architecture, whereas most of small applications and prototype sustems are still running on sequential machines, today. As a result of the high applicability of such parallel systems in many industrial real time tasks, manifold activities are going on not only to develop "academic" VLSI chips for the emulation of neural networks but also commercially available products for applications. Another interesting feature of neural network technology is that these networks are programmed during a training phase without further development of software. So the use of special software is confined to some tools which are necessary to provide an appropriate data preprocessing and to implement the network in its environment. Nevertheless, the problem how to provide the system with training data should not be underestimated. Usually, training data has a profound influence on the final performance of a neural network system which makes it necessary to chose training vectors very carefully and to perform many training cycles until a prototype system shows its optimal performance.

With this paper the Technische Hochschule Darmstadt (THD) wants to present a cascadable VLSI architecture for the emulation of a binary associative network. Due to cascadability one is not forced to implement a whole network on the area of one chip. Hence, large systems consisting of many chips for building networks of several thousand neurons are realizable.

BINARY ASSOCIATIVE NETWORK

Already during the 60s and 70s, authors like Steinbuch, Gabor, Rosenblatt, Longuett-Higgins, Kohonen, and others described associative memories. Generally, and associative memory performs a mapping $M : I \rightarrow O$ where I and O are the input and output set. The elements of I and O are vectors, whereby I contains vectors of length m and O contains such of length n. A linear mapping matix M, performing the desired mapping, only exists for a set of linearly independent input vectors I.

We used an associative memory as depicted in figure 1. The horizontal lines are the input lines where an input vector may be clamped to the memory. The vertical lines from the top of the whole structure down to the large circles are called sum lines. At the crossing of two lines there may exist a connection as indicated by a dot. So the connection matrix may be described by a 0–1–matrix. If a binary input vector i^x is presented to the memory, this vector is multiplied by the connection matrix. The result will be a sum vector containing integer values which is transmitted to threshold units, each performing the same threshold operation. After the threshold operation, a binary output vector is obtained. Principally, such a memory is able to map a set of linearly dependent input vectors onto a set of output vectors (problems are stated below). Using neural network terminology, the connection matrix is a matrix of synapses, the sum vector is the input vector to neurons, and the threshold devices are neurons. An appropriate

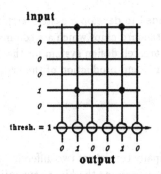

input

thresh. = 1

output

Figure 1 Binary Associative Memory

training procedure for the network is performing the outer product between input and desired output vectors which means for the training of N input/output pairs)

$$m_{jk} = \bigvee_{x=0}^{N} i_j^x \cdot o_k^x \qquad (1)$$

with m_j^k being an element of connection matrix M and j, k elements of the input vector and output vector respectively. The operator $\bigvee$ corresponds to the logical OR operation. Even in such a memory using nonlinear threshold operations, malfunctioning may occur which limits the effective storing capacity. Contemplating the situation, stated in Figure 2, it is not difficult to understand the cause of errors. In this example the information of a trained vector pair is lost because there exists a set of other trained input vectors whose ones completely cover the ones of the lost vector. Furthermore, the corresponding output vectors of this set of input vectors all have a one in a common column, whereas no one exists in the same column of the corresponding output of the lost input/output pair. To reduce the probability of such errors, it is necessary to use sparsely coded input and output vectors. Palm showed that the effective storing capacity of a binary associative memory with a $m \times n$ matrix may reach up to $m \cdot n \cdot ln2$ bit which means 68% of the potential storing capacity.

HARDWARE REALIZATION

At the beginning of the implementation of the above mentioned associative network there had been the following requests:

- A network consisting of several thousands of neurons must be realizable

- Chip design and the production of about 1000 chip shall be as cheap as possible

- Chip design must be fast

Due to these requests we decided to develop a system architecture with off chip weight storage using as many cheap standard chips which are commercially available as possible. Furthermore, we used a standard cell design system for the design of the needed ASICs. This also garanteed a fast design and production of the first prototypes.

The BACCHUS Concept

The associative network principally consists of two different types of components. On the one hand standard RAM chips containing the binary synaptic weights of the association matrix on the other hand dedicated VLSI chips (called BACCHUS chips) for the realization of the neuron functionality, e.g. the summation of the weighted inputs and the

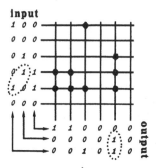

Figure 2 Example for Malfunctioning

threshold operation (see Figure 5). Due to the binary concept, only simple operations are necessary to evaluate the answer of the network to an applied input vector. The inner products between the input vector and all the memory columns may be simply calculated with a number of logical AND operations and summations. Thereby, every neuron contributes to perform the inner product between the input vector and its corresponding memory column. The evaluation of the inner product between the first memory column and the input vector is depicted in Figure 3, at which the dot corresponds to the logic AND opertion and the plus sign to the summation. Since elements of the input vector representing a zero do not contribute to the inner product, it is not necessary to take care for them. Therefore, it is absolutely sufficient to apply successively all the addresses of the "one positions" of the input vector to the correlation matrix memory and to accumulate the contents of each memory column in an accumulator belonging to that column, as shown in Figure 4. The input vector applied to the associative memory system contains two ones at the positions one and two. All the other positions (position zero and positions three to six) contain zeros. Now first, the address of the first one, address one, is generated and applied to the memory to read out line one (lines zero to seven from bottom to top). All the bits of this line are accumulated in their respective accumulators. Afterwards, the address of the second one, address two, is applied to the memory to accumulate the contents of line two. Thereby, the accumulators are realized in the dedicated BACCHUS chips. After the evaluation of all the input vector's ones the threshold operation may be done. A more hardware efficient way to solve the threshold detection is to preset every accumulator with the threshold value and to decrement the accumulators instead of incrementing them. The threshold of a memory column is reached if its accumulator contains a zero which is very easy to detect. This is the final evaluation concept realized by means of the BACCHUS architecture. With this architecture it is possible to evaluate all columns of the correlation matrix memory in parallel

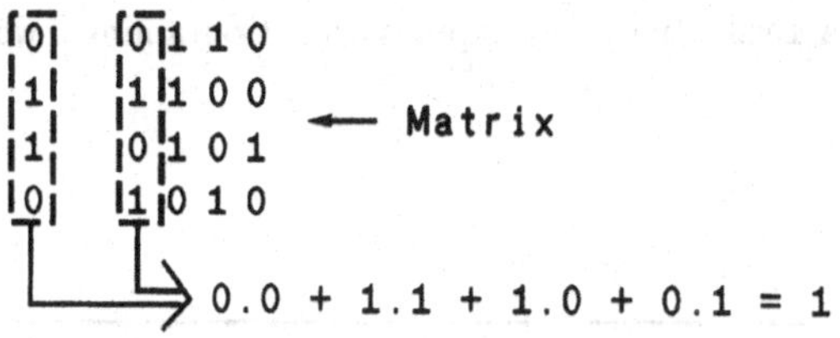

$$
\begin{bmatrix} 0 \\ 1 \\ 1 \\ 0 \end{bmatrix} \quad \begin{bmatrix} 0 & 1 & 1 & 0 \\ 1 & 1 & 0 & 0 \\ 0 & 1 & 0 & 1 \\ 1 & 0 & 1 & 0 \end{bmatrix} \longleftarrow \text{Matrix}
$$

$$
0.0 + 1.1 + 1.0 + 0.1 = 1
$$

Figure 3 Inner Product between Input Vector and First Memory Column

but all its lines sequentially. To guarantee a cheap chip fabrication it is necessary to limit the pin number. Therefore, the output of each neuron (e.g. accumulator or counter) is not fed to its own pin. Rather, there is a coder on each BACCHUS chip to generate the address of an active neuron (i.e. counter which reached the value zero) and an evaluation circuit to generate successively the addresses of active neurons. After the generation of its address, each active neuron is inactivated. Since the whole architecture has to be cascadable, each BACCHUS chip contains a ripple-in input and a ripple-out output to control the address generation of active neurons. If the ripple-in input receives a "low" signal the chip starts the address generation and after the evaluation of all its neurons it sets its ripple-out output to the "low" state to start the address generation of the next chip. The detailed BACCHUS concept is depicted in Figure 5. Two chip designs have been made and fabricated named BACCHUS I and BACCHUS II which are described in the following.

BACCHUS I

On the first BACCHUS design we realized 32 8 bit counters whose size is sufficient if the whole system is used with sparse coding of input and output vectors. Furthermore, it contains a 21 bit address bus, a bidirectional data bus, and some control logic to control the RAM chips. In addition to the address and data bus, it was necessary to have some

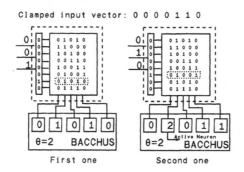

Figure 4 Evaluation of an Input Vector Containing Two Ones

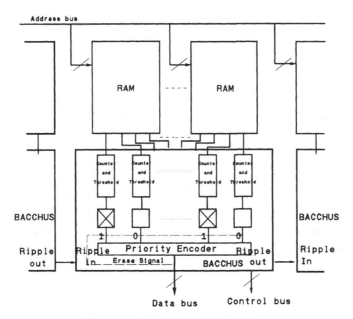

Figure 5 Detailed BACCHUS Concept

control pins and some pins for a small control bus resulting in a chip with 108 pins which was packed into an expensive 120 pin carrier. This was the main reason for the design of the improved BACCHUS II version. Some data of BACCHUS I:

- 10 MHz clock frequency

- 8.828 $mm \times$ 8.758 mm = 77.32 mm^2 area

- 5585 gate equivalents (22340 transistors)

- 108 pins

BACCHUS II

Since it was planned to produce a larger number of chips to mount some prototype systems, it was necessary to design a cheap chip version fitting into cheap small chip carriers. In BACCHUS II we took off the RAM control and combined the data and address bus to one 8 bit data/address bus. Furthermore, there are some functional improvements, as e.g. an asynchronous ripple logic which was synchronous on BACCHUS I. Some data of BACCHUS II:

- 10 MHz clock frequency

- 6.898 $mm \times$ 6.898 mm = 47.58 mm^2 area

- 5767 gate equivalents (23068 Transistors)

- 68 pins

The BACCHUS II architecture is depicted in Figure 6.

APPLICATIONS OF THE ASSOCIATIVE NETWORK

The correlation matrix memory may be applied in two different ways. First, it is possible to use it for arbitrary associations between arbitrary input and output vectors as mentioned in the introduction. But this mode of operation supposes sparsely coded vectors to keep malfunctioning low and to reach reasonable storing capacities. A second way to work with such a network is a more conventional approach where one training or sample vector is stored in each memory column. By means of a simple recall algorithm decreasing slowly threshold Θ of the memory neurons, a parallel nearest neighbour search between the currently clamped input vector and all the memory columns may be performed. If

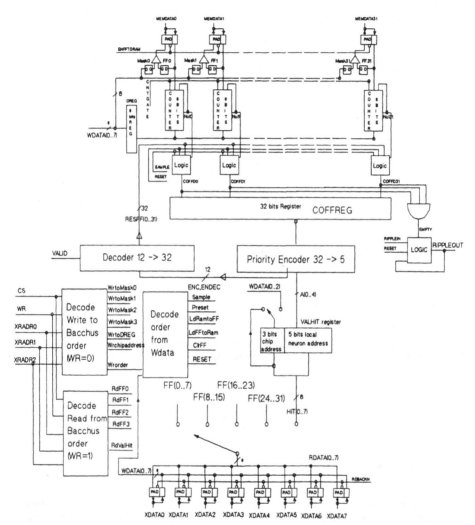

Figure 6 BACCHUS II Architecture

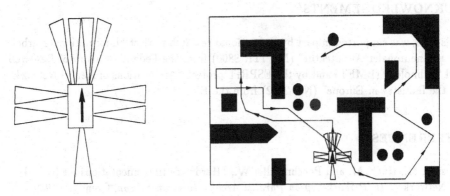

Figure 7 Autonomous Vehicle

the neurons are grouped into classes whereby each neuron belonging to one class carries the information of one sample vector of that class, such a network will be well suited for solving classification tasks. An advantage of this operation mode is that the whole potential storing capacity of the correlation matrix memory may be used. With small changes in the recall algorithm, parallel nearest neighbour classifiers may easily be realized. Since one neuron and one memory column is necessary for each training vector, problems appear if large amounts of training data shall be trained. In these cases iterative learning algorithms may help which are able to reduce the number of stored vectors. Figure 7 shows an application of the memory to an autonomous vehicle. Ultrasonic sensors provide the vehicle with information to the next obstacles in its environment. The vehicles task is to go straight on and avoid obstacles. About 500 vectors have been trained and stored. In Figure 7 a typical way pursued by the vehicle is depicted. With an iterative programming algorithm only 10% of the training set were stored and the vehicle showed almost the same behaviour as before.

FUTURE WORK

In our future work we will pursue the hardware development for the described associative network and its application. Concerning the hardware, a sea-of-gate design will be made by the end of this year to provide a commercial version of the BACCHUS chip which shall be used to build up some large prototypes, containing several thousand neurons each. On the software and application level we are interested in developing more sophisticated training algorithms for the classifier approach and to investigate how to combine the correlation matrix memory with other neural networks, since it may serve as a very large and fast data base.

ACKNOWLEDGEMENTS

This work was supported in part by the national research project "Informationsverarbeitung in neuronaler Architektur" (No. ITR 8800) from the Federal Ministry of Research and Technology (BMFT) and by the ESPRIT project "Applications of Neural Networks for the Industry in Europe" (No. 2092) from the EEC.

REFERENCES

Glesner, M., Huch, M. and Poechmueller W., "Hardware Implementations for Neural Networks", *IFIP Workshop on Parallel Architectures on Silicon*, Grenoble, 1989

Kohonen, T., *Associative Memory*, Springer, 1977

Kohonen, T., *Self-Organization and Associative Memory*, Third Edition, Springer, 1989

Palm, G., "On Associative Memory", *Biol. Cybernetics*, pp.19-31, 1980

Palm, G. and Bonhoeffer, T., "Parallel Processing for Associative and Neuronal Networks", *Biol. Cybernetics*, pp.201-204, 1984

Poechmueller, W. and Glesner, M., "Handwritten Pattern Recognition with A Binary Associative Memory", *IJCNN 90*, San Diego, 1990

Poechmueller, W. and Glesner, M., "Supervised Classification with A Binary Associative Memory", *ITG/IEEE Workshop on Microelectronics for Neural Networks*, Dortmund, 1990

Steinbuch, K., *Automat und Mensch*, Springer, 1963

4.3 Digital VLSI Implementations of an Associative Memory Based on Neural Networks

Ulrich Rückert, Christian Kleerbaum and Karl Goser

Bauelemente der Elektrotechnik
Universität Dortmund

Abstract

This paper is devoted to a digital special-purpose hardware implementation of an associative memory based on distributed storage of information. The cascadable semi-parallel architecture can be easily extended to large scale memories with several millions of storage elements. The memory has a matrix structure with binary elements (connections) and performs a pattern mapping or completion of binary input/output patterns. Though the memory concept is very simple, it has an attractive asymptotic storage efficiency of $0.69 \cdot m \cdot n$ Bits and the number of patterns that can be stored with low error probability is much larger than the number of columns (artificial neurons).

INTRODUCTION

In the last decade there has been an increasing interest in the use of artificial neural networks in various applications. One of these application areas, where the analysis of the perfomance of a neural network approach is comparatively advanced is associative memory. Neural networks are well suited for the implementation of associative correlation memories (Kohonen 1977). The idea is that information is stored in terms of synaptic connectivities between artificial neurons. The activities of the neurons represent the stored patterns. Many different models have been discussed in literature under such names as *"Lernmatrix"*, *"Correlation Matrix"*, *"Associative Memory"* etc. (Kohonen 1977).

VLSI for Artificial Intelligence and Neural Networks, Edited by J.G. Delgado-Frias and
W.R. Moore, Plenum Press, New York, 1991

Recent advances have been largely supported by simulations on conventional computers. However, if these models should offer a viable alternative for storing and processing information in large scale applications (e.g. pattern recognition) these systems will have to be implemented in hardware. Because of their regular and modular structure, neural networks are well adapted for VLSI system design. Implementing large numbers of individually primitive processing elements directly in VLSI hardware is intuitively appealing (Ramacher and Rückert 1990). There are two different approaches for supporting these models on parallel VLSI hardware (Treleaven 1989): *General-Purpose Neurocomputers* for emulating a wide range of neural network models and *Special-Purpose VLSI-Systems* which are dedicated to a specific neural network model.

This paper is devoted to a special-purpose hardware implementation of a very simple associative memory loosely based on neural networks. The memory has a simple matrix structure with binary elements (connections, synapses) and performs a pattern mapping or completion of binary input/output vectors. To the authors knowledge, this comparatively simple model of a distributed associative memory was first discussed by Willshaw *et al* in 1969. However, similar structures have been more generally discussed, e.g. by Kohonen 1977. The characteristics of the implemented model are described below.

The important aspect for VLSI implementation of this simple memory model is the close relationship to conventional memory structures. Hence, it can be densely integrated and large scale memories with several thousand columns (model neurons) can be realized with current technologies already. Furthermore, the regular topology results in a rigorous modularization of the system indespensible for a successful management of the design and test complexity of VLSI systems. In this respect a digital semi-parallel VLSI-architecture will be described and discussed later.

THE ASSOCIATIVE MEMORY CONCEPT

In general the basic operation of an associative memory is a certain mapping between two finite sets X and Y. In a more abstract sense these two sets may be regarded as questions and answers or stimuli and responses, both coded as vectors of numbers. The associative memory should respond with $\underline{y}^h$ to the input $\underline{x}^h$ for every pair $(\underline{x}^h, \underline{y}^h)$ stored in the associative memory. The paired associates can be selected freely, independently of each other. This operation is often called *pattern mapping* or *heteroassociative recall* (Kohonen 1977, Palm 1982). Further it would be convenient if the associative memory responds with $\underline{y}^h$ not only to the complete input $\underline{x}^h$ but also to sufficiently large parts of it. In other words the mapping should be fault-tolerant to incomplete or noisy versions of the input pattern. A special case of this functionality is the *autoassociative memory* where the stored pairs looks like $(\underline{x}^h, \underline{x}^h)$. Given a sufficiently large part of $\underline{x}^h$ the memory responds with the whole pattern (*pattern completion*). Besides the discussion of the fuzzy term "sufficiently large" the input can be any part of the stored pattern and it even can be a noisy version of $\underline{x}^h$. This operation is called the best match search in terms of pattern recognition.

Among the many different implementations of an associative memory in the field of neural networks the following simplest type is very attractive as well as effective in regard to VLSI implementation. The *Associative Memory* (AM) is a nxm matrix of binary storage elements w_{ij}, the connection weights. The input vectors $\underline{x}^h$ as well as the output vectors $\underline{y}^h$ take a binary form. The mapping is build up in the following way. The input vector $\underline{x}^h$ as well as the output vector $\underline{y}^h$ of every pair which should be stored in the AM (h=1, ... ,z) are applied to the matrix simultaneously. At the beginning all storage elements in the matrix are zero. Each storage element at the crosspoint of an activated row and column ($x_j^h = y_i^h = 1$) will be switched on, whereas all the other storage elements remain unchanged. This clipped Hebb-like rule (Palm 1982) programs the connection matrix, and the information is stored in a distributed way (Figure 1 a,b):

$$w_{ij}^h = w_{ij}^{h-1} \vee (x_j^h \wedge y_i^h) , \quad w_{ij}^0 = 0 , \ h = 1, ... ,z \quad (1)$$

The recall of the constructed mapping is done by applying an input vector to the rows of the matrix. For each column i we sum up the products of the input components x_j and the corresponding connection weights w_{ij}:

$$S_i = \sum_{j=1}^{m} x_j^h \cdot w_{ij} \quad (2)$$

The associated binary output vector is obtained by the following threshold operation (Figure 1c):

$$\tilde{y}_i^h = \left\{ \begin{array}{l} 1, \text{ if } S_i \geq Th \\ 0, \text{ otherwise} \end{array} \right. , \quad Th \in \mathbb{N} \text{ (threshold)} \quad (3)$$

Obviously, because of the above mentioned programming rule the memory matrix gets more and more filled (the connections will never be switched off). Consequently, the output might contain more '1's than the desired output pattern. The chance that this kind of error will occur increases with the number z of stored pairs. This fact causes the following quantitative questions:

    i) How many patterns can be stored in an AM?
    ii) How many bits of information can be stored in an AM?

Both questions were answered by Palm 1980. Summarizing his results, an AM has its optimal storage capacity C for sparsely coded input/output patterns.

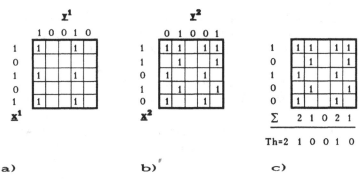

Figure 1 Programming two pattern pairs into an associative memory (a,b) and pattern mapping of an incomplete input pattern (c)

Therefore, the number l (k) of active components ('1') in the input (output) patterns should be logarithmically related to the pattern length (n,m). Asymptotically, the optimal storage capacity is given by (Palm 1980):

$$C(m,n,k,l,z) \longrightarrow \ln 2 \cdot m \cdot n \qquad (4)$$

for $n,m \longrightarrow \infty$ and parameters:

$$k = \log(n) \ , \ l = \log(m) \ , \ z \leq \ln 2 \ \frac{m \cdot n}{k \cdot l}$$

Hence, the storage capacity C is proportional to the number of storage elements n·m and the number of patterns z that can be stored is much larger than the number of columns (artificial neurons). For example, an optimum of C = 593.000 bits for n, m = 1000, z = 34.780 (k=2, l=9) can be stored in the AM under the constraint that on the average 90% of the information of the output vector of each pair is stored (Palm 1980). Figure 2 shows the storage capacity of an AM as a function of the number of stored patterns (z) and Table 1 as a function of the number of activated components in the input (l) and output (k) patterns, respectively.

Furthermore, it turns out that the AM works for pattern mapping applications in a more economic way compared to conventional methods (e.g. hashing) and other neural network models, if the number of patterns is large and their individual information content small (Palm 1986).

These results encourage a hardware implementation in VLSI of this simple associative memory model in situations where such a mapping is a more natural way of storing information than a listing. Especially, because the AM works the more effective the larger the matrix is.

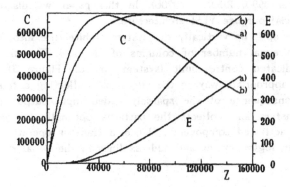

Figure 2 Storage capacity C in bits and the expected number E of additional ones in the output pattern as a function of the number of stored patterns z (m,n = 1000): a) k = l = 3; b) k = l = 4

Table 1 Number of patterns z that can be stored with an expected number of additional ones E<1 and the corresponding storage capacity C as a function of the parameters n, m, l (k=3)

m=n	l	z	C/m·n
1024	10	23.313	0.565
2048	11	96.012	0.591
4096	12	318.353	0.604
8192	13	1.182.378	0.613
16384	14	4.407.707	0.621

DIGITAL VLSI IMPLEMENTATION

We have designed different parallel VLSI architectures for an AM using digital, digital/analog and analog circuit techniques (Rückert *et al* 1987, Rückert 1990a, Rückert and Goser 1990, Rückert 1990b). In this paper we discuss a digital semi-parallel special-purpose VLSI architecture.

In general, we split up vertically the system architecture into "slices"; each slice manages an equal number of columns of the AM. The slices are controlled by a dedicated control unit (system control, Figure 3), distributing input data in an appropriate way to the slices and collecting output data from the slices. In consequence of the sparsely coded input/output patterns the control unit transfers and collects the patterns optimally by means of the addresses of the activated components. Hence, a transfer operation of a m-bit pattern takes only log(m) cycles and address lines in the serial case.

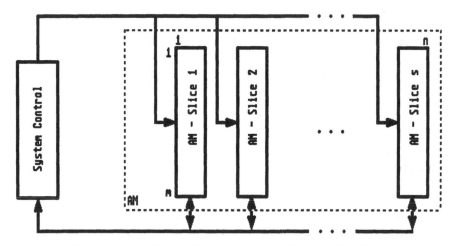

Figure 3 Partition of an Associative Matrix into slices

In the case of digital implementation the columns of an AM are controlled by a special *slice chip* comprising several very simple *processing units* (PUs). Each PU controls one column of the matrix and computes bit-serially the weighted sum (Equation 2) of the input pattern and the respective column. Because the input/output signals as well as the connection elements are binary, the basic building blocks of a PU are a counter and a comparator (Figure 4a).

The programming algorithm (Equation 1) for the connection matrix is realized by a simple OR-logic-Block and is incorporated on the chip, too. The

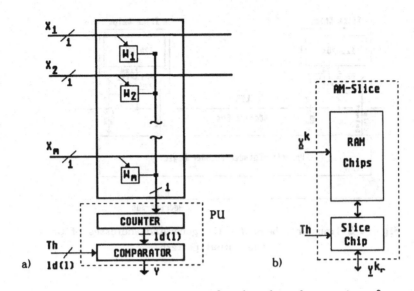

Figure 4 Basic building blocks of a digital implementation of an
Associative Matrix column (a) and slice (b)

connection matrix can be build up by conventional RAMs (Figure 4b).

In order to transfer the output pattern to the system control the addresses of the '1's in the pattern are generated locally in the slice chips by an additional priority-encoder. All slice chips are connected to a common bus and the access to the bus can be controlled by daisy-chaining or by an additional priority-encoder-logic (Figure 5). In case of the daisy-chaining method the time for transferring the output pattern is proportional to number of slice chips. In the other case the time is proportional to the number of ones in the output pattern. In both cases the transfer of the associated output pattern and the calculation of the weighted sum of inputs can be pipelined.

Up to now several standard-cell-designs comprising 32 PUs (e.g. 2 μm CMOS, 38mm^2, ≈20.000 transistors, 53 pads, 10MHz (Rückert 1990a)) and a full-custom- design comprising 128 PUs (2μm CMOS, 1cm^2, 48.000 transistors, Rückert 1990b) of a slice chip has been finished. Instead of realizing a whole chip in silicon we have first fabricated and tested successfully a single PU of the full-custom-design at the University of Dortmund (Rückert 1990b). The tested 6-Bit-PU is able to perform the calculations for the Equations (1)-(3) at least at a clock rate of 12 MHz. Optimization in respect to speed hasn't been done yet. Instead, we have concentrated ourselfs on a modular and testable design. Therefore, the PU is built up by six bit-slices which can be configured to a scan path for test reasons. An extension to a 8- or 16-Bit-PU

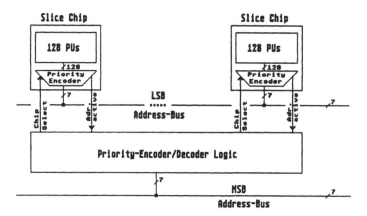

Figure 5 Transfer scheme for the generated addresses of ones
in the output pattern

is easily achieveable by duplicating the bit-slices.

Based on this facts, a 8192x8192-AM can be build up by a 64 MBit-dRAM
and 64 slice chips each comprising 128 PUs, for example. This AM stores
more than one million sparsely coded patterns with E<1 (Table 1), which
corresponds to a storage capacity of 40 Mbits. Such an implementation
performs a pattern mapping within 10µs. The association time is proportional
to the number of '1's in the input/output patterns (log(m)+log(n)) hence independent of the number z of stored pairs. Table 2 shows some time estimations
of the asociation time for a single pattern (t_A) and the programming time for
z pattern pairs (t_P) depending on the number of ones in the input (1) and
output (k), respectively. The estimations are based on test results of the
fabricated PU in combination with a static RAM (100ns cycle time).

With current submicron technologies it is possible to integrate 512 and
more PUs on a single slice chip. Hence, the limiting factor for the number of
PUs per chip is the pin count. Nevertheless, it is possible to have 256 PUs on
a slice chip at least. The important disadvantage of this digital approach up
to now is that most RAM chips have a one, four or eight bit organization
whereas a longer word length (≥16) is more appropriate for this approach. In
order to get the highest degree of parallelism the optimal memory organization
is m x u (m=number of matrix rows, u=number of PUs per slice chip). For the
above mentioned 8kx8k-AM, 1MBit-RAM chips with a 8kx128 organization are
required, for example. Therefore, the system architecture has to be slightly
modified in order to make effective use of currently available memory chips.
Work on this topic is been done in the moment.

Table 2 Association (t_A) and programing (t_P) time estimations as a function of the parameters n,m,k,l,z.

m=n	l	k	z	$t_A(\mu s)$	$t_P(s)$
4096	12	3	318353	4.4	2.7
	11	10	95395	5.5	0.7
8192	13	3	1182378	4.7	11
	13	10	354750	6.1	3.3
16384	14	3	4407707	5.0	44.1
	14	10	1322288	6.4	13.2

DISCUSSION

Though the AM system concept is comparatively simple, it has very attractive features in regard to other associative or neural network VLSI implementations:

* the asymptotic storage capacity is 0.69·n·m bits
* the number of sparsely coded patterns that can be stored in an AM is much larger than the number of columns (artificial neurons)
* the number of operations during association is only O(log(n)·m) instead of O(m·n) and the operations are very simple (counting)
* the simpler circuit design requires less silicon area

Because of the modular and regular structure of the proposed architecture, the implementation of very large AMs (n,m≥10000) is feasible. This aspect is very important for practical applications where the AM has to be extended to a useful number of storage elements. Work on possible applications of an associative memory of this type is done at the moment by different research groups, e.g. in the field of speech recognition, scene analysis and information retrieval.

Comparing the approach presented above with alternative hybrid solutions (Rückert 1990), we can call on efficient software tools for a fast, reliable and even complex digital system design. For the memory matrix we can use standard RAM chips employing the highest density in devices. In general, the matrix dimensions (n,m) can be extended by using additional RAM chips. An important disadvantage up to now is that most RAM chips have a one, four or eigth bit organization whereas a longer word length (≥16) is more appropriate for a high degree of parallelism. Nevertheless, even if we cannot utilize the full parallelism inherent in the memory model the storage capacity and association speed of the proposed architecture is sufficient for many applications.

ACKNOWLEDGEMENTS

The authors thank the DFG (Deutsche Forschungsgemeinschaft) and the EC (ESPRIT-Project NERVES) for financial support.

REFERENCES

Kohonen, T.,"Associative Memory: A system-theoretical approach", Springer Verlag, Berlin 1977.

Palm, G., "On Associative Memory", *Biol. Cybernetics 36*, pp. 19-31, 1980.

Palm, G., "Neural Assemblies", Springer Verlag, Berlin 1982.

Palm, G., "On Associative Memories", in *Physics of Cognitive Processes*, E.R. Caianiello, E.R., Ed., World Science, pp. 380-420, 1986.

Ramacher, U., Rückert, U., "VLSI Design of Artificial Neural Networks", Kluwer Academic 1990.

Rückert, U., Kreuzer, I., Goser, K., " A VLSI Concept for an Adaptive Associative Matrix based on Neural Networks", *1st Int. Conf. on Computer Technology, Systems and Applications*, Hamburg, pp. 31-34, 1987.

Rückert, U., "VLSI Implementation of an Associative Memory based on Distributed Storage of Information", in: Almeida, L. B., Wellekens, C. J., (Eds.) "Neural Networks", *Lecture Notes in Computer Science*, no. 412, Springer Verlag, Berlin 1990.

Rückert, U., "VLSI Design of an Associative Memorie based on Distributed Storage of Information", in: Ramacher, U., Rückert, 1990.

Rückert, U., Goser, K., "Hybrid VLSI Implementation of an Associative Memory based on Distributed Storage of Infomation", Proceedings of the *1st Int. Workshop on Microelectronics for Neural Networks*, University of Dortmund 1990.

Treleaven, P. C., "Neurocomputers", *Int. Journal of Neurocomputing*, Vol.1 89/1 pp. 4-31, 1989.

Willshaw, D. J., Buneman, O. P., Longuet-Higgins, H. C., "A Non-Holographic Model of Associative Memory", *Nature 222*, no. 5197, pp. 960-962, 1969.

4.4 Probabilistic Bit Stream Neural Chip: Implementation

Max van Daalen, Pete Jeavons and John Shawe-Taylor

Royal Holloway and Bedford New College
University of London
Egham, Surrey, UK

Abstract

In this paper, we describe a proposed hardware implementation for a novel neural network chip. Our design uses probabilistic bit streams to represent the real valued quantities processed by the network. We show that the use of this representation means that each neuron requires only very simple digital circuitry to perform the weighted combination of the inputs and calculate a suitable activation function. The fully digital nature of the design allows the use of well established CMOS VLSI techniques. The mathematical theory supporting the operation of this device is dealt with in a companion paper.

INTRODUCTION

One of the major constraints on hardware implementations of neural networks, is the amount of circuitry required to perform the multiplication of each input by its corresponding weight (Goser *et al* 1989). This problem is especially acute in digital designs, where parallel multipliers are extremely expensive in terms of transistors, and hence consume large areas of silicon. Adopting an equivalent bit serial architecture, significantly reduces this complexity, but still tends to result in large and complex overall designs.

One solution that is currently receiving a lot of attention (Mead 1989, Schwartz 1988) is to implement neurons using analogue techniques. Using this approach the circuitry required to perform the multiplications becomes relatively uncomplicated. It is however much more difficult to design robust analogue circuitry, with the required dynamic range and signal to noise ratio. The design tools currently available for analogue integrated circuitry do not begin to approach the power and sophistication of the tools available for

VLSI for Artificial Intelligence and Neural Networks, Edited by J.G. Delgado-Frias and W.R. Moore, Plenum Press, New York, 1991

digital integrated circuitry. An analogue design must also be able to tolerate the wide variations that can occur in transistor parameters, across a given die.

The approach presented in this paper tackles the problem by using a novel approach to the representation of the signals processed by a neural network. In this design, real valued signals are represented by *probabilistic bit streams*, where the number represented is the probability of any bit within the stream being set to '1'. If two real values are represented by two independent random bit streams in this way, then the product of the two values will be represented by the logical AND of the two bit streams. Hence, by using this representation the multiplication of real values may be achieved using very simple circuitry: a single AND gate.

The technique of using probabilistic bit streams in this way may be seen as a further extension of the idea of using pulse stream arithmetic in a neural network, which has been successfully implemented by Murray and his co-workers (Murray 1989). The essential difference is that calculations using pulse streams still require some analogue circuit elements. Using the probabilistic bit stream technique we are able to design a chip which uses only simple digital circuitry to implement a standard feed-forward neural network, as described below. Hence this technique is able to exploit fully the strengths of existing digital VLSI technology. The idea forms the basis of the design of a chip produced by Neural Semi-conductor Inc. (Tomlinson *et al* 1990). The current work, however, uses the idea in a new way, which makes the basic neuron more powerful and still allows for cascading of layers of neurons.

In our design the use of probabilistic bit streams enables each neuron to calculate a suitable activation function using very simple circuitry. In fact, the activation function is obtained by using the interaction of the probability distribution of the input bits, and the probability distribution of a threshold value, in the following way: the weighted input bits to each neuron are summed using a simple counter and the final total is compared to a preloaded threshold value. The result of this comparison determines the output of the neuron, which is a single bit forming part of a probabilistic bit stream representing the result of the activation function.

With this simple circuitry, various different activation functions can be obtained depending on the choice of the probability distribution for the threshold value. For example, a linear activation function may be obtained by using a uniform probability distribution for the threshold value, and a sigmoid activation function may be obtained by using a step-function probability distribution for the threshold value. A detailed analysis of these results is presented in a companion paper (Shawe-Taylor *et al* 1990).

Another of the problems facing VLSI neural networks is the high degree of connectivity between the individual neurons. The use of probabilistic bit streams and time multiplexing has made it possible to design a neuron that behaves as if it has many inputs from other neurons, but in fact has only one physical connection. For this reason, the physical connectivity between the neurons in the design we propose is very straight forward. This allows the number of neurons per chip to be very high, as they can be packed onto the silicon in tightly spaced regular structures.

THE OVERALL NETWORK ARCHITECTURE

A block diagram of the basic layout of a group of neurons on a chip, all sharing the same input, is illustrated in Figure 1. Depending on the size of the package available, there may be several such groups accommodated on a single chip.

Associated with each bit arriving on the shared input line to each neuron, there is a unique signed weight value. The probabilistic bit streams representing the absolute values of these weights are generated off-chip, by circuitry described below. One bit from each of the streams representing the weights is distributed to each neuron via the dynamic shift register labelled W, drawn down the right hand side of the Figure 1. The corresponding sign bits for each weight are also generated off-chip, using the convention that a value of '1' represents a positive sign. These sign bits are distributed to each neuron via the dynamic shift register labelled S. Each neuron has associated with it one element of each shift register, W and S.

Each neuron also has associated with it a section of another shift register, that is used to load it with a threshold value. The input line to this shift register is labelled T_{in} in Figure 1, and the connections between successive sections are indicated in the Figure by the links between successive neurons. The threshold values, which are represented as normal binary integers, are loaded into this shift register whenever the neuronal thresholds are updated. The loading of threshold values is performed by the external support logic, and may be carried out in parallel with the loading of the weight and sign bit shift registers.

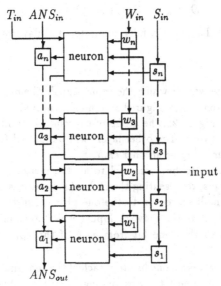

Figure 1 Layout of a group of neurons within a chip

For each input bit arriving at the group of neurons, the sign and weight shift registers, S and W, have to be completely loaded with their appropriate bits, one for each neuron in the group. The dynamic shift registers W and S are therefore the fastest operating circuit elements within the design, so it is important that they operate at the maximum possible speed. The loading time for these shift registers ultimately determines the overall speed of the chip. To maximise this, these shift registers can be split up into sections, allowing them to be loaded in parallel. This does however soak up additional pins on the chip, and make the external housekeeping circuitry more complicated, so some compromise must be reached.

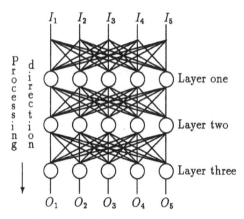

Figure 2 Layout of a fully connected multilayer network

In order to explain the way in which the input signals themselves are organised we shall assume that the neurons are configured as a fully-connected multi-layer feed-forward network, as illustrated in Figure 2. The group of neurons shown in Figure 1 will form a single layer within this network. The other layers will be formed from similar groups of neurons, either on the same chip or another chip.

In order for each neuron to be connected to all the neurons in the previous layer the probabilistic bit streams, representing the real valued outputs of the neurons in this previous layer, are time multiplexed on to the one physical input. (In the case of the first layer in the network, it is the network inputs which are multiplexed.) The time multiplexing is arranged so that one bit from each of the appropriate bit streams is presented in turn.

When the neuron has processed one bit from each of the time multiplexed probabilistic input streams, together with one bit corresponding to each weight and one bit for each sign, it produces one bit of its probabilistic output stream. The details of the internal processing to compute this output bit are dealt with in the next section. The output bit produced by each neuron is passed to another shift register, labelled ANS, shown on the left hand side of Figure 1. Using this shift register the results may be clocked out and passed to the next layer of the network. It is important to note that on every *neural cycle*, each neuron produces only one bit. This bit is latched and transfered to the next layer, via the shift register ANS, whilst the original neuron processes the next bit of all the input values. The serial output of the shift register ANS automatically produces input bits for the next layer in the correct time multiplexed format.

In this architecture the number of logical inputs to a particular neuron will be equal to the number of neurons in a layer. Taking the network illustrated in Figure 2 as an example, there are five neurons in each layer, so in the implementation we have described each neuron will receive five sequential logical inputs. The number of neurons in a layer may be increased very simply by combining groups of neurons together and passing the same input stream to all of them. The output shift registers from all the groups that have been combined may be simply joined together and will still contain the correct sequence of bits to be fed to the next layer. The number of logical interconnections in the fully-connected network increases with the square of the number of neurons in each layer, but because of the high degree of parallelism the speed of operation of the physical device decreases only linearly with the size of each layer. This means that very large networks of neurons can be constructed using the hardware we describe whilst maintaining a high processing speed.

The final output bits, from the neurons in the last layer, are accumulated by external support circuitry, and then converted back from probabilistic bit streams to real values.

THE ARCHITECTURE OF AN INDIVIDUAL NEURON

The main elements of a single neuron are shown in Figure 3. The operation of the three shift register elements, SR_w, SR_s and SR_a which conduct the weights and signs to the neuron, and then carry away the result, have already been discussed in the previous section.

Once the required inputs have been assembled at the neuron the first step in the processing is to multiply each input value by the corresponding weight value to obtain a weighted input value. The multiplication of the input bit by the weight bit is carried out by the single AND gate shown in Figure 3. This simple multiplication operation is one of the primary advantages of the use of probabilistic bit streams to represent the real valued signals, as mentioned in the introduction.

The next phase of the processing within each neuron is the summation of all the weighted inputs. However, before the product bit emerging from the AND gate can be summed by the counter, the sign bit corresponding to the weight must be taken into account. One solution to this problem, would be to use an up/down counter. With this scheme, positive weighted input values would increment the counter by one, and negative weighted input values would decrement the counter by one. In order to simplify the circuitry we prefer to avoid the use of an up/down counter and use a normal binary counter instead. To do this we offset the counter contributions so that contributions are always positive but positive weighted input values contribute more than negative weighted input values. The actual counter contributions, are shown in Table 1.

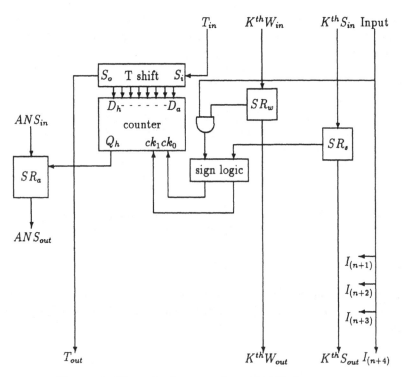

Figure 3 The main elements of a probabilistic neuron

Table 1 Contribution to counter, for signed weighted inputs

Result of AND	Sign Bit	Net Contribution	ck_0 clock signal	ck_1 clock signal
1	0	0	0	0
0	0	1	1	0
0	1	1	1	0
1	1	2	0	1

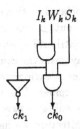

Figure 4 Random logic to control the counter operation

From this table, it can be seen that the counter simply has to be able to increase its value by 0, 1, or 2, depending on the input values. To increase the counter value by 0 we do nothing. To increase the counter value by 1 we simply clock the counter from the least significant stage, by setting clock signal ck_0 to '1'. Finally, to increase the counter value by 2, we clock the counter from the second least significant stage, by setting clock signal ck_1 to '1'. The two required clock signals, are generated by the *sign logic* box shown in Figure 3. The simple random logic required to perform this function is shown in Figure 4, which also includes the *input-weight* AND gate from Figure 3.

After the counter has summed the offset weighted input bits from the probabilistic input streams its value is compared against the threshold in order to produce an output bit. To reduce the circuitry required we do not in fact latch the threshold value, and compare it with the accumulated counter value, instead we use an appropriate value to initially offset the counter. This value is chosen so that the counter will overflow into its top bit if the chosen threshold has been reached. The output from the neuron may then simply be taken from the most significant bit of the counter.

Once the output bit has been obtained and passed to the output shift register, the counter is reset to the required offset value and the operational cycle repeats for the next bit of each input stream.

HARDWARE IMPLEMENTATION

The neural network design presented in this paper has been developed with the express aim of making its implementation in conventional VLSI very straight forward. As we have shown, the circuit design is uncomplicated, and allows the neurons to be easily packed next to each other in a very regular structure, with simple interconnections.

The shift registers that load the weight and sign bit are in continuous operation, thus allowing the use of simple dynamic circuitry. The threshold shift register may also be dynamic, so long as its counter sized segments are loaded into the counters without delay once it is full.

The counter at the heart of each neuron is straight forward and may be implemented as a simple ripple counter, with the additional clock signal, ck_1, ORed into the second stage. The major constraint on the implementation of the counter is that the maximum ripple time must be less than the time between the arrival of succesive input bits at the neuron.

The size of the counter, and the associated section of the threshold value shift register, depends on the maximum number of inputs per neuron. During each operational cycle, as described above, each input may contribute a maximum of 2 to the total count. In addition to this, the threshold value may offset the counter by any amount up to the total possible input contribution. The counter in each neuron must therefore be able to count up to a value which is four times the number of inputs, without overflow. This means that by using a ten bit counter it is possible to have up to 256 inputs to each neuron. In the fully-connected multi-layer architecture we have assumed above, the maximum number of inputs to a neuron is equal to the maximum number of neurons in a layer. Hence a ten bit counter in each neuron will allow up to 256 fully-connected neurons in each layer.

Finally, each neuron contains weight and sign logic, which consists of two AND gates and an inverter, as shown in Figure 4. This is clearly trivial to implement in silicon. It is very likely that in the final transistor design, some of these components could be even further simplified by making use of existing signals and circuitry.

The number of neurons per chip, and the number of pins that can be allocated to the various shift registers, will obviously depend on the size of die used in the final construction. We estimate that a neuron with a ten bit counter requires approximately 250 transistors. Using widely available and reliable fabrication techniques it is straightforward to contruct a device containing 60,000 densely packed transistors, with a shift register clock speed of 50MHz. This would allow us to integrate 240 neurons of the type we have described.

We now give an estimate of the time required for each operational cycle of a device of this type. We shall assume that the 240 neurons form a single group, with a single shared input, so that for each input bit delivered to the neurons the shift registers for the weight and sign bits must each be loaded with 240 bits. We shall further assume that these shift registers are both divided into 20 segments, using a total of 40 pins on the chip. Each segment may be loaded in parallel with the appropriate 12 bits, taking a total of 240ns, at a clock speed of 50MHz. If the 240 neurons form a complete layer of the network, then they will receive 240 inputs during each operational cycle, from the neurons in the previous layer. Hence the total time required to produce each output bit is 240 times 240ns, or $58\mu s$. As more layers are added to the network, this processing time will not increase, although the initial *pipeline delay* will increase in steps of $58\mu s$ per extra layer.

The actual useful speed of the device obviously depends not only on this processing speed but also on the desired accuracy in the output values and the length of the probabilistic bit streams required to achieve this accuracy.

An alternative method of construction, that is currently being investigated, is to use a large programmable gate array. A typical device familily is the Plessey ERA series. Using currently available devices it would be possible to integrate 200 neurons of the type we have described, running at a maximum clock speed of 40MHz. Devices up to 10 times bigger are due to become available in the near future, and these could be used to provide complete layered networks on a single chip.

EXTERNAL SUPPORT LOGIC

The external circuitry has to provide the running network with a continuous supply of probabilistic bit streams. Real values may be transformed to probabilistic bit streams by using them as thresholds for a random noise source: the binary output of the threshold comparitor is the required bit stream. To achieve the required bit rate this process has to be carried out very carefully, if truly random operation is to be preserved. The circuitry required to implement this process is beyond the scope of this paper, and is discussed in a companion paper (van Daalen 1990).

If the network is not required to adapt by changing its weights during the course of operation then probabilistic bit streams corresponding to the weight and sign values may be calculated before the network starts processing and the resulting bits stored in video RAMs. Video RAMs are readily available components which are extremely convenient for this purpose, as they allow bit parallel values to be loaded in the usual way, but read out serially at very high speeds via built-in shift registers.

The inputs to the network, are not known at run time, so they have to undergo probabilistic conversion in real time. These input streams then have to be multiplexed before being passed into the network. In the example given in the previous section the bits forming the input bit stream need to be delivered to the neurons at intervals of 240ns, which is a rate of 4.17MHz.

At the outputs of the network the reverse operation has to be carried out to convert the multiplexed bit streams back into real values. To achieve this, the bit streams must first be demultiplexed and then passed to some averaging circuit, such as a counter. Once again, the use of video RAM is very convenient here since the bits may be assembled in the correct format and then serially shifted out via the RAM's shift register to the averaging circuit.

CONCLUSION

We have shown in this paper that representing real valued numbers by probabilistic bit streams allows a neural network to be implemented using very simple circuitry. We have also described how the use of time multiplexing allows fully connected multiple layer networks to be conveniently implemented using this circuitry. Time multiplexing is particularly suitable when the inputs being processed are inherently serial, as for example video input data.

The design for each individual neuron, as described in this paper, is extremely compact and regular, thus allowing many hundreds of neurons to be packed onto a single chip. The design also allows chips to be easily cascaded, so as to increase the width of layers within a network, with only a linear decrease in the speed of processing.

These chips can also be cascaded in layers with the output bit streams of one layer being fed directly as inputs to the next layer. In this way the operation of the whole network is synchronised and the extra layers only add a pipeline delay to the time required for an accurate output to be assembled.

REFERENCES

K. Goser, U. Hilleringmann, U. Rueckert and K. Schumacher, "VLSI Technologies for Artificial Neural Networks", *IEEE Micro* 9, pp. 28-44, 1989.

Carver Mead, *Analog VLSI and Neural Systems*, Addison-Wesley, 1989.

A. F. Murray, "Pulse Arithmetic in VLSI Neural Networks", *IEEE Micro* 9, pp. 64-74, 1989.

D. B. Schwartz and R. E. Howard, "A Programmable Analog Neural Network Chip", *Proc. IEEE Custom Integrated Circuits Conference*, IEEE Press, 1988.

John Shawe-Taylor, Pete Jeavons and Max van Daalen, "Probabilistic Bit Stream Neural Chip: Theory", *Technical Report*, RHBNC, London University, 1990.

M.S. Tomlinson, Jr., D.J. Walker and M.A. Sivilotti, "A Digital Neural Network Architecture for VLSI", *IJCNN*, San Diego, II pp. 545–550, 1990.

Max van Daalen and John Shawe-Taylor, "Generating real time probabilistic bit streams", *in preparation.*

4.5 Binary Neural Network with Delayed Synapses

Tadashi Ae[†], Yasuhiro Mitsui[†], Satoshi Fujita[†] and Reiji Aibara[††]

[†] Faculty of Engineering, Hiroshima University
[††]Research Center for Integrated Systems, Hiroshima University

Abstract

Although the neuron with sigmoidal function is usually used to construct the neural network, it is difficult to be fabricated within the chip. The neural network with only binary neurons (in short, the binary neural network) is less powerful than the general neural network (Bruck and Goodman 1987). The binary neural network, however, can be easily fabricated because of hardware simplicity. To increase the power of the binary neural network, we propose the binary neural network with delayed synapses, where the delay inserted into synapse is variable and controllable.

We demonstrate a CMOS chip design of the binary neural network with delayed synapses. Using 2μm design rule, 64 neurons can be realized in a plane of 12.4mm×12.5mm, where four bits are used for 16 different weights and delays of each synapse, respectively. Moreover, the memories of the weight value and the delay time need another plane of the same size. As a result, the total configuration requires two planes and we conclude that the 3-D CMOS technique is most appropriate to realize it.

We also demonstrate a high-speed sorter which is originally designed by a Hopfield neural network with sigmoidal function (Hisanaga et al.), and a network for finding the shortest path as examples.

INTRODUCTION

The Hopfield neural network is syntactically represented as the set of n functions ;

$$x_1 = f_1 (x_1, x_2, \cdots, x_n)$$
$$x_2 = f_2 (x_1, x_2, \cdots, x_n)$$
$$\vdots$$
$$x_n = f_n (x_1, x_2, \cdots, x_n)$$

VLSI for Artificial Intelligence and Neural Networks, Edited by J.G. Delgado-Frias and
W.R. Moore, Plenum Press, New York, 1991

295

,where f_i ($i = 1,2, \cdots ,n$) is implicitly given as

$$\frac{du_i}{dt} = - \frac{u_i}{\tau_i} + X_i \tag{1}$$

$$X_i = \sum_{j=1}^{n} T_{ij}x_j - \theta_i \tag{2}$$

$$x_i = \frac{1}{1 + \exp\left(-\dfrac{u_i}{\lambda} \right)} \tag{3}$$

The binary neuron is just as the case of $\lambda \to 0$, i.e., the case where the equation (3) becomes the threshold function. For the binary neuron, each value of input and output is given as either 1 or 0. The value of synapse (interconnection) between binary neurons is an integer, whereas it is a real number for the general case.

The binary neural network is less powerful than the general neural network. The binary neural network, however, can be easily fabricated because of hardware simplicity (Ae *et al.* 1989a, 1989b, 1990). To increase the power of the binary neural network with smaller increasement of hardware, we propose the binary neural network with delayed synapse where the delay inserted into synapse is variable and controllable. In this paper, we focus on the configuration with feedback, i.e., the Hopfield neural network.

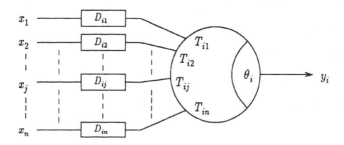

Figure 1 Binary neuron with delayed synapses (BN.DS)

The synapse with variable time-delay is realized by the Schmitt-trigger circuit, which is known to play a role of sigmoidal function of a kind of Hopfield neural network (Smith and Portmann 1989). A class of Hopfield neural networks with sigmoidal function can be transformed into a binary neural network with delayed synapses, where each delay time is provided directly by the optimization problem to be solved.

THE BINARY NEURON WITH DELAYED SYNAPSES

To increase the power of the binary neural network, we propose *the binary neuron with delayed synapses* (in short, BN.DS). The binary neuron with delayed synapses is shown in Figure 1, and is given as

$$y_i = \begin{cases} 1 & \text{if } X \geq 0 \\ 0 & \text{if } X < 0 \end{cases} \qquad X = \sum_j T_{ij} x_j - \theta_i \qquad (4)$$

(x_j : input, y_i : output, T_{ij} : weight for input x_j, θ_i : threshold). Though this neuron is binary, the delay (D_{ij} : delay for input x_j) is introduced in synapse.

THE HOPFIELD NEURAL NETWORK CONSTRUCTED BY BN.DS

The Hopfield neural network is known to be effective for solving optimization problems (Hopfield and Tank 1985). We focus on the Hopfield neural network constructed by BN.DS, i.e., *the binary neural network with delayed synapses* (in short, BNN.DS) in this paper. The BNN.DS is fully interconnected with BN.DSs. The important feature of this network is to have two variable factors, i.e., the weights and the time-delays. We use usually weight T_{ij} for feasibility, and time-delay D_{ij} for optimality.

DESIGN EXAMPLES

The function to realize the binary Hopfield neural network, i.e., the summation and multiplication can be implemented in the digital hardware, but this would require a complex multiplier-adder circuit at the input of each neuron, resulting in a large circuit even for a modest number of neurons. On the other hand, using the analog computation, we can achieve a multiplication with a single resistor, and the summing

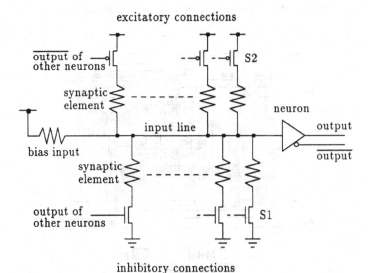

Figure 2 Circuitry of the designed circuit of a neuron

of currents is accomplished on the input wire of the amplifier (Graf *et al.* 1988, Aibara *et al.* 1990). Then the implementation of BNN.DS described here uses a mixture of analog and digital complementary metal oxide semiconductor (CMOS) IC technology.

We describe a CMOS circuit implementing BNN.DS that consists of an array of 64 simple neurons with their inputs and outputs fully interconnected through a matrix of synaptic elements.

Figure 2 shows the circuitry of an implemented neuron. The inverted and noninverted outputs going into the connection matrix are used to control excitatory and inhibitory connections. The input voltage of an amplifier is determined by the sum of the currents flowing into the node. Thus ,the voltage is an analog measure of the sum of the contribution of all other amplifiers connected to the input line. The output lines of the amplifiers do not feed current directly into the input line, but, instead they control switches S1 and S2. This method reduces the amplifier load and the capacitance of the output line.

A neuron in Figure 2 consists of three inverters connected in series that work as one amplifier unit. The circuit of a neuron using CMOS inverters and its layout are shown as in Figure 3 and Figure 4, respectively.

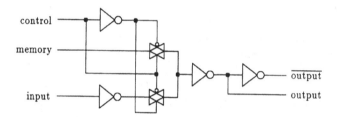

Figure 3 Circuit of a neuron using CMOS inverters

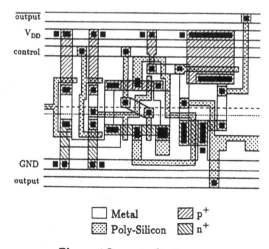

Figure 4 Layout of a neuron

Each connection between two amplifiers consists of the synaptic elements, and all of the elements are programmable. A synaptic element in Figure 2 consists of two parts, i.e., the resistive part and the delay part.

The resistive element

The circuitry of a resistive element and its layout are shown as in Figure 5 and Figure 6. Four memory cells control switches and by setting of each memory this resistive element can have 16 different values, and the content of these memory cells determines the type of connection. One of three connections can be selected: an excitatory (switches on excitatory side enables), an inhibitory (switches on inhibitory side enables), or an open (both disabled) state.

The delay element

The circuitry of delay element is shown as in Figure 7. The time-delay is determined by the value of variable resistor and the circuitry of variable resistor is shown as in

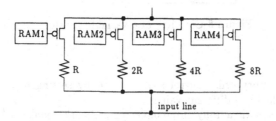

Figure 5 Circuitry of a resistive element

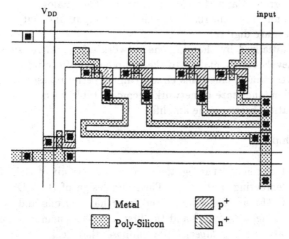

Figure 6 Layout of a resistive element

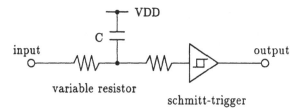

Figure 7 Circuitry of a delay element

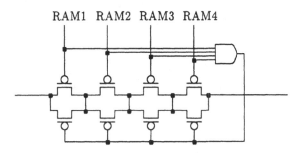

RAM1 RAM2 RAM3 RAM4

Figure 8 Circuitry of a variable resistor

Figure 8. Four memory cells control switches and by setting of each memory the delay element can have 16 different values.

Since n neurons with a fully interconnected network require n^2 connections, a BNN.DS includes the total of 64×64 elements with such synapses, and the main part of the chip area of network layer will be occupied by the array of connections.

The amplifier used here has a high gain and works essentially as a threshold element between the ground and the supply voltage. The analog computation is used only within the connection matrix in the network; input and output data, and all other control signals are digital.

The circuit is initialized by charging the network using control signal in Figure 3 with the voltage levels corresponding to the components of the initial state. But the state of all 0's is restrained, since this circuit cannot perform association in this case. For the computation, the state of network becomes stable without any external control or synchronization between the amplifiers.

The 3-D CMOS chip

With the current technology of integrated circuit, the circuit of BNN.DS occupies a large area for implementing in 2-D IC. Then our design of BNN.DS is extended on two layered 3-D IC (Figure 9). The second layer has neurons and synapses except memories (called *the network layer*) and the first layer has memories for neurons and synapses (called *the memory layer*). We suppose that it is fabricated in CMOS technology with 2.0-micrometer design rules, and that the chip size is in about 12.4mm×12.5mm.

APPLICATIONS

The high-speed sorter

Let set $A=\{a_1, a_2, \cdots, a_n\}$ be a set of positive integers that differ from each other, where n be the number of the elements of the set A. Network A' for the primitive block for sorting is shown as in the Figure 10. The value of delay, i.e., $D_1, D_2, \cdots, D_n$ correspond to the value of $a_1, a_2, \cdots, a_n$. In the initial state, all output of neurons in this network is 0. Then, the external input I becomes 1. As a result, k neurons become 1 in turn depending on the length of delay, that is, network A' is a circuit to output k-th smallest numbers among the set A.

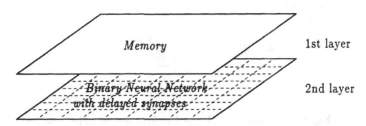

Figure 9 Two-layered 3-D IC Chip

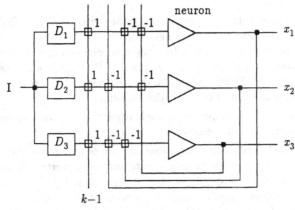

□ 1 : connection with weight 1

□ -1 : connection with weight -1

Figure 10 Network A' in the case of $n=3$

A sorter is constructed by combining $n-1$ Network A's. The sorter of increasing order is shown as in Figure 11. In this figure, $N_1 \sim N_{n-1}$ denote Network A's with $k=1 \sim n$, respectively. Given the set A as inputs, each network N_k picks out k smallest elements, have value 1, and others have value 0. At this time, comparing states of N_k and N_{k-1}, the states of neurons corresponding to the k-th smaller element are just only difference. Therefore, by comparing all states of these network using an exclusive OR (in short, ex-OR), the ex-OR corresponding to the k smaller element has just only value 1, and others have value 0. That is to pick out the k-th smaller element of the set A. Hence, by doing so for all $k=2, \cdots, n$, the sorter can sort elements of set A.

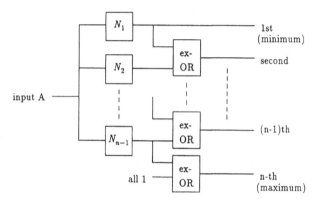

Figure 11 A sorter with the Hopfield neural networks

The neural network for finding the shortest path

In this section, we demonstrate organization of the network N' for finding the shortest path and state the behavior of this network.

Suppose that the directed graph G (for example, Figure 12) has no edges of negative length and source s and sink t are designated. We organize the neural network N' (for example, Figure 13) for finding the shortest path from s to t.

The way of mapping from G to N' is the following;

1. Each neuron of N' corresponds to each edge of G. Two neuron s and t are added for the source and the sink.

2. The bidirectional excitatory connections are composed as follows; neuron s <-> neurons which correspond to edges outgoing from vertex s, neurons which correspond to edges into one vertex except s and t <-> neurons which correspond to edges outgoing from the corresponding vertex except s and t. The strength of connection takes $+1$ respectively and the delay of synapse corresponds to the length of corresponding edge of G. For example, if there are edges $[i,j]$ and $[j,k]$ with $length(j,k)=l$, the strength $T_{ij,jk} = T_{jk,ij} = +1$ and the delay $D_{jk,ij} = l$.

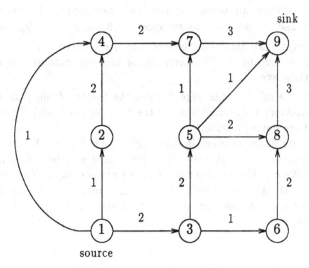

Figure 12 Directed graph G

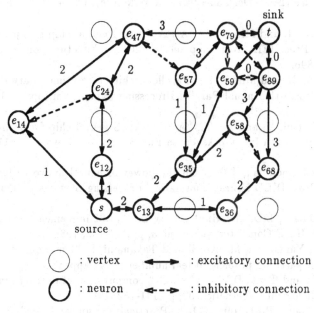

Figure 13 Neural network N'

3. The bidirectional inhibitory connections are composed between neurons corresponding to edges incoming to a vertex. The strength of connection takes -n. That is, if there are edges $[i,k]$ and $[j,k]$, the strength of connections $T_{ik,jk} = T_{jk,ik} = -n$, and the delay of this synapses are 0, i.e. $D_{ik,jk} = D_{jk,ik} = 0$.

4. The (unidirectional) inhibitory connections are composed from neuron t to all other neurons except s. The strength of this connections takes -2, and the delays of these synapses are 0.

In Figure 12 the label on the edge denotes the length of edge. In Figure 13 the label on the excitatory connection denotes the value of delay and the inhibitory connections from t are not represented.

The initial state of the network is that only one neuron s is 1, and other neurons are 0. First, neurons on the shortest-path tree rooted at s become 1 in turn of distances from s (We call this behavior *the forward propagation*). Next, when the neuron t becomes 1, the inhibitory connections from t turns active. Then the shortest path from s to t only remains active, that is, at the state of "1". (called *the backward propagation*).

REFERENCES

Ae, T. and Aibara, R., "A neural network for 3-D VLSI accelerator", *VLSI for Artificial Intelligence* (Ed. J.Delgado-Frias and W.Moore), pp.247-254, Kluwer Academic Pub., 1989a.

Ae, T., Aibara, R. and Mitsui, Y., "A RAM-based neural chip for optimization problem solver", Proc. IFIP Workshop on Parallel Architectures on Silicon, pp.80-99, Grenoble, 1989b.

Ae, T., Aibara, R. and Mitsui, Y., "Parallel architecture using binary Hopfield neural networks", Proc. 4th Annual Parallel Processing Symposium, pp.168-180, Fullerton, 1990.

Aibara, R., Mitsui, Y. and Ae, T., "A 3-D CMOS neural chip for optimization problem solver", Proc. 8th Int. Workshop on Future Electron Devices, pp.113-116, Kochi, 1990.

Bruck, J., and Goodman, J.W., "On the power of neural networks for solving hard problems", Proc. IEEE Neural Information Processing Systems Conference, Denver, 1987.

Graf, H.P., Jackel, L.D. and Hubbard, W.E., "VLSI implementation of neural network model", IEEE Computer, vol.21, no.3, pp.141-152, 1988.

Hisanaga, Y., Yamashita, M., Ae, T. and Takanami, I., "On Hopfield neural network for solving set partition problem of real numbers", (to appear).

Hopfield, J.J., and Tank, D.W., ""Neural " computation of decisions in optimization problems", Biological Cybernetics, 52, pp.141-152, 1985.

Smith, M.S., and Portmann, C.L., "Practical design and analysis of a simple "neural" optimization circuit", IEEE Trans. Circuit and Systems, vol.36, no.1, pp.42-50, 1989.

4.6 Syntactic Neural Networks in VLSI

Simon Lucas and Bob Damper

Department of Electronics and Computer Science
University of Southampton, SO9 5NH, UK

Abstract

Syntactic neural networks (SNNs) are an important new paradigm for neural computation. Their power stems from the existence of an underlying grammar which allows natural expression of time-varying patterns. In this paper, we are primarily concerned with the implementation of SNNs in VLSI. Their benefits for this purpose, compared to more common neural architectures, include sparse connections, fast learning and – for those nets based on a non-stochastic grammar – a simple and elegant digital realisation. We illustrate this with an example application; a dynamic signature verification system. Results are presented for a software simulation in which learning proceeds off-line. Hardware implementation is straightforward, requiring only a small number of RAMs, shift-registers and adders.

INTRODUCTION

In this paper, we argue that syntactic neural networks (Lucas and Damper 1989a, 1990a) are a new and important neural computing paradigm. As such, we are concerned with their ease of implementation in silicon.

Syntactic neural networks (SNNs) are characterised by their direct relation to an underlying formal grammar – hence, the name. Because SNNs are a complete paradigm, there are many different versions. However, they all have the advantages of fast (non-iterative) learning, simple modular structure and sparse connections between the modules. The latter property is particularly attractive as far as VLSI is concerned. Further, the simpler forms of SNN have compact silicon realisations while still performing useful functions.

This paper is structured as follows. First, we outline the basic features of SNNs as they affect their application and implementation. These features include a modular structure, whereby the basic components of the net – which we call *local inference* (or *parsing*) *machines* – can be interconnected in various ways according to the problem at hand. We describe both the macrostructure of the various nets as well the microstructure of the local machines. Then, by

VLSI for Artificial Intelligence and Neural Networks, Edited by J.G. Delgado-Frias and
W.R. Moore, Plenum Press, New York, 1991

305

way of an example drawn from pattern recognition, we describe a particular SNN designed for dynamic signature verification and show how it can be implemented using currently-available VLSI technology. Initial results are comparable with other signature verification systems reported in the literature.

SYNTACTIC NEURAL NETWORKS (SNNs)

Formal grammars provide an efficient way of describing (and recognising) long, complex patterns. Useful abstractions are represented by non-terminals in the grammar; the production rules which combine these symbols allow the structure implicit in all information-carrying signals to be modelled explicitly. It is precisely this type of structure that most connectionist models so obviously lack. This observation has inspired us to promote syntactic neural networks (SNNs) – based on an underlying formal grammar – as a new neural computing paradigm (Lucas and Damper 1989a, 1990a).

The grammars embodied in the SNNs may be stochastic or non-stochastic context-free. Learning may be *supervised* or *unsupervised*, and *on-line* (self-organising) or *off-line* (pre-programmed). Non-stochastic SNNs require only AND and OR gates to model the production rules, and shift-registers to implement delay elements; hence, they are straightforward to implement in silicon. Stochastic SNNs (where each production has an associated probability) require multipliers, adders and delays, and are just possible with current analogue VLSI such as the pulse-stream technology developed by Murray (1989), and now commercially-available (Tomlinson *et al* 1990).

In the off-line case, the SNNs simply act as parsers for the pre-learned grammar. In the self-organising case, they become adaptive parsers constantly changing the grammar rules and probabilities in response to new inputs. While it is relatively straightforward to describe this adaptive process mathematically and implement it in software (Lucas and Damper 1990c), difficulties arise in silicon implementations of the learning rules i.e. deciding *how* the weights should be adjusted. Due to the local nature of the adaptations, however, this is less of a problem than with error back-propagation, for example. Also, storing the changing weight values is a difficulty, although progress in this area is evident (e.g. Card and Moore 1989).

Previous connectionist implementations of context-free parsers have required $O(n^3)$ neurons (Fanty 1986), where n is the maximum pattern length. By introducing delay elements (so making the network *temporal*), we reduce this growth to $O(n^2)$ without any loss of function and only a negligible reduction in speed. By restricting the grammar to be *strictly-hierarchical* (Lucas and Damper 1989a), we reduce the growth further to $O(\log n)$.

We have so far applied SNNs to a variety of problems, including isolated character recognition (Lucas and Damper 1990c), cursive script recognition (Lucas and Damper 1989b), signature verification (Lucas and Damper 1990b) and text-phonetics translation (Lucas and Damper 1990d). Results so far suggest that even non-stochastic, strictly-hierarchical SNNs are very useful pattern discriminators.

MACROSTRUCTURE

SNNs have a modular architecture. The design of the modules (microstructure) is therefore largely independent of the way we connect these (macrostructure). The modules correspond to local 'fragments' of grammar, and are known as *local parsing machines* (LPMs) if they are constructed according to a grammar that has been pre-learned, or *local inference machines* (LIMs) if they are able to acquire and parse their own grammar. Thus, the LPM architecture is a subset of the LIM architecture. The macrostructure depends on two factors; the class of grammar we wish to parse/infer, and whether we require a temporal or non-temporal network.

In all cases, the number of inter-module connections grows only in proportion to the number of neurons, instead of the *square* of this number for more conventional fully (or highly) connected networks, such as Hopfield nets and multi-layer perceptrons (MLPs). Clearly, this is of major significance for VLSI implementation.

Temporal versus Non-Temporal SNNs

There are essentially two approaches to parsing (recognising) context-free grammars. The first is to augment a finite-state automaton with a stack to create a pushdown automaton. The second is to construct a parsing matrix where each element, or table entry, covers a particular span of the input. (This is called chart parsing if the matrix is held in sparse form.)

The matrix method is more appropriate for pattern recognition applications, as argued in Lucas and Damper (1990a). To implement this in connectionist form, we may use a non-temporal or temporal network. The temporal case allows for a more efficient implementation; we now represent the parse-matrix as a time-varying vector. Thus, at time-step t the outputs of the LIMs represent column t of the parsing matrix, with the previous outputs of columns $1 \ldots t - 1$ stored in the time-delays. This saves on the number of LIMs by a factor of n over the non-temporal version.

Their position-invariance property makes temporal SNNs ideal for inferring useful abstractions from continuous signals; they are therefore the natural choice for continuous speech or cursive script recognition. Conversely, the greater precision of the non-temporal SNN may be utilised to good effect in the recognition of isolated sequential patterns. This paper concentrates on the more parsimonious temporal models.

Strictly-Hierarchical versus Full Context-Free Grammar

There exists a trade-off between the power of a grammar and the cost of the VLSI implementation of its equivalent SNN. Full context-free grammars are relatively powerful but prohibitively expensive for long input strings ($O(n^2)$ neurons). For this reason, we often choose to work with a simpler version, the strictly hierarchical context-free grammar, which scales in a more attractive manner ($O(\log n)$).

In this case, the set of non-terminals is partitioned into a number of subsets $S_1 \ldots S_n$, and only productions of the form $A_{i+1} \rightarrow B_i C_i$ are allowed, where the subscript denotes membership of the ith subset. This greatly reduces SNN complexity; compare Figures 1 and 2. The results presented below show that even nets based on this simple formalism can achieve useful performance.

MICROSTRUCTURE

The microscopic structure of the LPMs (assuming off-line learning) depends on the details of the grammar (e.g. stochastic or non-stochastic, ambiguous/unambiguous, attributed or non-attributed).

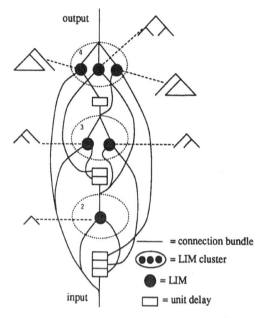

Figure 1. The full-CFG temporal SNN for patterns up to length $n = 4$. The growth function is $O(n^2)$ both in terms of neurons and connections. The LIMs (or LPMs) are labelled with their corresponding parse-spans.

Below, we look at three types of LPM with reference to the type of grammar they parse. Also, we consider the more interesting case of the local inference machine (LIM) which allows the construction of adaptive connectionist parsers – machines that learn their own grammar on exposure to their environment.

The Local Parsing/Inference Machine

The LPM parses a very simple local grammar. Referring to Figure 3, A denotes the set of outputs while B and C are the two input-sets. The grammar parsed has productions of the form $a \rightarrow b\ c$, where $a \in A$, $b \in B$ and $c \in C$. In the LIM case, the parsing structure needs to be augmented with a mechanism for updating the connection weights – see Lucas and Damper (1990a).

Non-Stochastic, Unambiguous Grammar

Here we are concerned that the grammar is *locally* unambiguous. This means that, for each local fragment of grammar, there is only one non-terminal for any given right-hand-side. If this condition holds, then for any given input pair (assume only one input from each input-set may be active at any time), we have at most one output symbol. If we have only one LIM for each span, as in the strictly-hierarchical case, then in any connection bundle (see Figures 1 and 2),

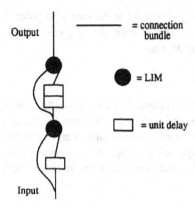

Figure 2. The strictly-hierarchical temporal SNN for $n = 4$. Network size grows as $O(\log n)$.

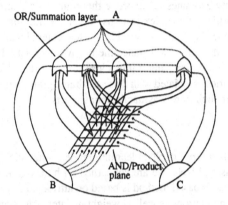

Figure 3. The structure of the local inference/parsing machine.

at most only one of the logical connections may be active. This allows binary encoding of the activations. If a connection bundle has 2^n logical connections, only n physical connections are needed.

We may also apply this binary encoding to the design of the local parsing machine, and implement it in a RAM (or ROM) look-up table. For a locally unambiguous grammar G such that $|B| < 2^m$, $|C| < 2^n$ and $|A| < 2^b$, we require a $2^{m+n} \times b$-bit memory.

Non-Stochastic, Ambiguous Grammar

If the locally unambiguous condition does not hold, or we require a more powerful grammar than strictly-hierarchical, then binary encoding of the symbols becomes inappropriate. We now require a wire for each symbol to be transmitted in a given connection bundle. The local parsing machines must now produce more complicated outputs, with a number of output symbols present at any given time, rendering impossible the simple RAM implementation. We may still use off-the shelf technology, however, in the form of a programmable logic array (PLA). The LPMs map very directly onto the PLA architecture, since in both cases we have (logically) an AND plane followed by an OR plane.

Stochastic Grammar

If the grammar is stochastic, it will (typically) also be locally ambiguous, so the LPM architecture must be at least as complicated as the non-stochastic, locally ambiguous case. The fact that we must deal with continuous probability estimates complicates things further. The LPM now consists of a multiplication layer followed by a summation layer. VLSI implementation of the stochastic SNN is probably feasible using pulse-stream technology, but not yet economically attractive.

Attributed Grammars

There exist at least three good reasons for dealing with attributed grammars (Knuth 1968): to counter poor probability estimates, to improve the grammatical inference process, and to allow more efficient modelling of complex patterns. When the training set is small, probability estimates become unreliable. We may counter this to some extent by augmenting the grammar with a set of attributes, and defining a distance metric over this set. Then, if an unexpected symbol occurs we may be more forgiving if it is 'close' to an expected symbol than if it is not. However, the distance metrics associated with these attributed grammars make them much more difficult to implement than their purely syntactic counterparts.

Self-Organising SNNs

Lucas (1990a) describes two types of SNN learning modes – statistical and cluster-based. In implementing self-organising SNNs, we are concerned with how to realise these adaptation-rules in hardware. The cluster-based method is based on attributed grammars, and must therefore deal with distance computations as well as weight updates. The statistical method reduces to a simple form of Hebbian learning, and allows more straightforward implementation. The remainder of this paper deals only with the simplest form of SNN, where each local grammar is non-stochastic and unambiguous.

APPLICATION: DYNAMIC SIGNATURE VERIFICATION

In this section, we show how even the simplest SNNs can out-perform conventional statistical methods when applied to the important practical problem of dynamic signature verification. We further show that the VLSI implementation of these simple SNNs is straightforward, as shown in Figure 4.

Signature Verification

Hand-written signatures are a widely-accepted form of personal identification, used especially in financial transactions. Our first attempt at signature-verification with SNNs was reported in Lucas and Damper (1990b). Although we obtained a zero error rate (compared with a few per cent with a proprietary statistical system tested on the same data), those results need qualifying in the following ways:

- The model for each user was trained on the *entire* set of signatures from that user. Thus, the generalisation ability of the SNNs was not tested at all.

- The networks became very large, employing tens of thousands of neurons.

- The inferred grammars were ambiguous; this would require the use of PLAs instead of RAMs to implement the local parsing machines.

By contrast, the work described below tests the generalisation ability of the SNNs, which in turn have a compact and elegant implementation.

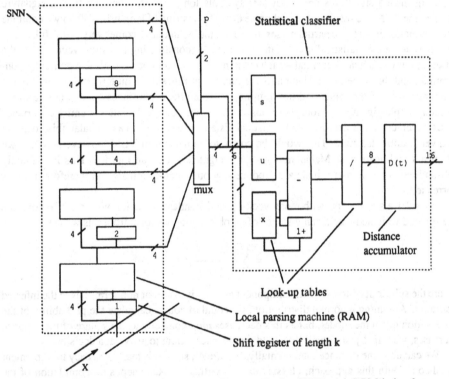

Figure 4. SNN-based signature verification system. In the SNN, each LPM is implemented as a 256 × 4-bit RAM. For each position in the input, X, the output of each RAM is in turn gated through the multiplexor to the incremental statistical classifier. The 4-bit output is combined with the 2-bit selector to produce a unique 6-bit address for each non-terminal. This address accesses the lookup tables for μ_i (u), σ_i (s) and x_i (x). Each time x_i is accessed it is automatically incremented. The required division is also done in RAM (/) – this output is the change in distance, as specified in the text; the distance accumulator adds this value to the previous estimate to yield output D(t).

Signal Capture and Representation

Signatures were captured on an *x-y-t* digitising tablet. Thus, at each point in time, we know the whereabouts of the stylus in terms of its x and y coordinates. This type of data is not directly suitable for input to an SNN, which requires a string of symbols. This can be obtained by some simple pre-processing; we track the pen's movement and represent relative motion by one of eight direction vectors (i.e. $N, NE, E \ldots$). Thus, we retain the *order* in which the signature strokes were produced but not the exact *timing* information. The incorporation of timing information would make the task of the forger yet more difficult.

Implementation

As a trade-off between verification performance and cost of implementation, we choose to use a 4-layer strictly-hierarchical SNN. However, this can only parse strings of length 16. Typical vector-quantised signatures are about 500 symbols long. Thus, when we feed a signature through the SNN, the result is a partial parse of each substring of length 16. When we combine the information in all these partial parses, however, the technique becomes very powerful. Here, we apply a simple statistical combination method by constructing a feature vector from the observations of each non-terminal – each element of the vector corresponds to a particular non-terminal, and the value of the element is the number of times that non-terminal occured in the 'running parse' of the input. During training, we count the occurrences of each non-terminal in each sample signature. From these observations, we could calculate the entire covariance matrix, then use some well-founded statistical distance measure such as Mahalanobis, to arrive at a verification decision. This would be costly to implement in VLSI, however, so here we adopt a simplification of Mahalanobis – the weighted Euclidean metric. This is definitely sub-optimal, since non-terminals are produced by other non-terminals and therefore must be correlated.

Consider a single class with mean vector μ and standard deviation vector σ. To compute the squared weighted Euclidean distance of an observation vector x from this we use:

$$D = \sum_{i=1}^{|N|} (\frac{\mu_i - x_i}{\sigma_i})^2$$

where the subscript denotes the ith component and N is the set of non-terminals in the inferred grammar. Assuming a normal distribution, we could of course calculate the probability of the observation given the model, but as this decreases monotonically as the square of the distance increases, we might just as well threshold the distance output to arrive at a decision.

We calculate the distance incrementally, (Figure 4), since this method is easy to implement in silicon. With this approach, classification is virtually instantaneous on completion of the signature. Note that the output is given by the distance accumulator. Initially, $x_i = 0 \; \forall \; i$, since no non-terminals have been observed. The distance accumulator is loaded with a pre-computed value for this zero-vector. As each LPM delivers its output, a counter for the output non-terminal is incremented. We calculate the difference that this change should have on the overall distance. This may be done using a relatively small lookup-table, since the change in value of this figure depends only on the change in the number of standard deviations from the mean of the newly-observed symbol. We can see this by considering the ith component of the distance:

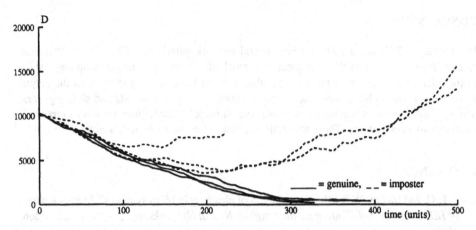

Figure 5. The variation of the squared weighted Euclidean distance estimate as the input is processed for typical signatures, both valid and imposters. All begin with the same value i.e. the distance from the zero vector to the class mean. Each non-terminal corresponds to a feature-vector dimension. As non-terminals are observed, the distance measure changes accordingly. For the first few time-units the system is unable to distinguish the genuine from the imposter signature, but as we approach the signature's final length, so the difference becomes clear.

$$D_i = (\frac{\mu_i - x_i}{\sigma_i})^2$$

By considering the difference in going from $x_i = k - 1$ to $x_i = k$, we arrive at the change in the distance, ΔD_{ik}, for $x_i = k$:

$$\Delta D_{ik} = \frac{2(k - \mu_i) - 1}{\sigma_i^2}$$

To implement this in hardware simply requires an adder (to compute the difference of x_i and the mean), an incrementer to keep count of x_i and four RAMs, one each to look-up x_i, μ_i and σ_i, and one to compute the division. Great precision is not necessary. Figure 5 shows how the output, D, changes as the input is processed, for a few, typical genuine signatures and imposters.

Results

We have tested a software simulation of the system on a database of approximately 1800 signatures, gathered from 15 users. When trained on all the signatures from each user, the error rate was 3.4%, compared with 6.5% when only the first 20 were used to initialise the system. These figures are in line with results reported in a recent survey of dynamic signature verification techniques (Parizeau and Plamondon 1990). The SNN error rates are about half those obtained in comparable cases with a proprietory statistical system (Lucas 1990b) on the same database.

CONCLUSIONS

In summary, SNNs are a powerful new neural network paradigm. They are practical for silicon implementation in their simplest, non-stochastic form. The non-overlapping nature of the inferred sub-grammars makes it possible to adopt binary coding to transmit the output activations, allowing for a very efficient representation using only RAMs and shift-registers. The stochastic versions require a 1-wire per neuron output coding, since we wish to transmit continuous-valued outputs. These are realisable, but not yet commercially viable.

REFERENCES

Card, H.C. and Moore, W.R., "Implementation of plasticity in MOS synapses", in *Proceedings of IEE International Conference on Artificial Neural Networks*, pp. 33–36, IEE, London, 1989.

Fanty, M.A., "Context-free parsing with connectionist networks", in *Proceedings of AIP Neural Networks for Computing Conference No. 151.*, pp. 140–145, Snowbird, UTAH, 1986.

Knuth, D.E., "Semantics of context-free languages", *Journal of Mathematics and Systems Theory*, 2, 127–146, 1968.

Lucas, S.M., *Connectionist Architectures for Syntactic Pattern Recognition*, PhD Thesis, Univeristy of Southampton, 1990a.

Lucas, S.M., "Recent Progress on the VERISIGN Project", *Confidential Report to British Technology Group Limited*, London, 1990b.

Lucas, S.M. and Damper, R.I., "A new learning paradigm for neural networks", *Proceedings of IEE International Conference on Artificial Neural Networks*, pp. 346–350, IEE, London, 1989a.

Lucas, S.M. and Damper, R.I., "Using stochastic context-free grammars for modelling and recognising cursive script", *IEE Colloquium on Character Recognition, Digest No. 1989/109*, IEE, London, 1989b.

Lucas, S.M. and Damper, R.I., "Self-organising temporal networks", *Proceedings of IEEE Workshop on Genetic Algorithms, Neural Networks and Simulated Annealing Applied to Problems in Signal and Image Processing*, IEEE, Glasgow, 1990a.

Lucas, S.M. and Damper, R.I., "Signature verification with syntactic neural nets", *Proceedings of the IJCNN-90*, Vol. 1, pp. 373–378, IEEE, San Diego, CA, 1990b.

Lucas, S.M. and Damper, R.I., "Syntactic neural networks", *Connection Science*, 2, pp. 199–225, 1990c.

Lucas, S.M. and Damper, R.I., "Text-phonetics conversion with syntactic neural networks", to appear in *Proceedings of ESCA Workshop on Speech Synthesis*, Autrans, France, 1990d.

Murray, A.F., "Pulse arithmetic in VLSI neural networks", *IEEE Micro*, July, pp. 64–74, 1989.

Parizeau, M. and Plamondon, R., "A comparative analysis of regional correlation, dynamic time warping and skeletal tree matching for signature verification", *IEEE Transactions on Pattern Analysis and Machine Intelligence*, 12, pp. 710–717, 1990.

Tomlinson, M.S., Walker, D.J. and Sivilotti, M.A., "A digital neural network architecture for VLSI", *Proceedings of IJCNN-90*, Vol. 2, pp. 545–550, IEEE, San Diego, CA, 1990.

4.7 A New Architectural Approach to Flexible Digital Neural Network Chip Systems

Torben Markussen

Microelectronics Center, Building 348
Technical University of Denmark
DK-2800 Lyngby
<torben@dc.dth.dk>

Abstract

This paper presents the design considerations for a neural network chip system. Various network sizes may be obtained by the connection of several chips. The chips are programmable to perform simulation of different network topologies and training algorithms.

Realistic design sizes are made feasible by restricting the implementation of network connectivity, and designing with hardware constraints in mind.

This work should result in a prototype design within 1990.

INTRODUCTION

The artificial neural networks are under constant evolution in the literature. Several neural network topologies and training algorithms has been developed to perform different classification tasks.

The two most popular networks today are:

- The Hopfield net (Hopfield, 1982), a feed-back network with the simple Hebb training rule.

- The multi-layer feed-forward network (perceptron) with the more complicated back-propagation algorithm (Rumelhart and McClelland, 1986).

The tasks performed by these two algorithms differs widely, but recent implementations of neural network structures normally falls between these two.

Future development of neural network structures is assumed to reuse the basic mechanisms of known algorithms.

VLSI for Artificial Intelligence and Neural Networks, Edited by J.G. Delgado-Frias and
W.R. Moore, Plenum Press, New York, 1991

315

Neural networks on silicon

The development of VLSI circuits for neural networks has moved in two directions:

- Special purpose chips, with a large number of neurons, fast switching time and no possibility of learning.

- General purpose chips or chip sets, that offers a number of configurations and training algorithms to the user.

The former is often realized by analog hardware, while the latter requires digital implementations.

THE AIM OF VLSI IMPLEMENTATION OF NEURAL NETWORKS

The main purpose of this work is to construct digital neural network chips, which are capable of handling several network topologies and network training algorithms. Furthermore they should offer a reasonable span of operations for future algorithm development.

The chips should be independent of additional hardware for calculations.

If these requirements are to be fulfilled, the topology part and the algorithmic part of a network specification must be as independent of the hardware as possible.

The chip system acts as a tool, offering basic operations common to most neural networks. It will act as a peripheral device, exchanging data with the environment, and with no need for external computation. Operations are specified by external software as micro instructions.

There is a number of considerations to be taken in VLSI design. The main obstacles are:

- Limited area on *one* chip. The fabrication of large networks with the properties mentioned above on a single chip is impossible.

- The number of pins on a chip is limited for economical and practical reasons.

Desirable VLSI features related to neural networks would be:

- The neurons (or the processing elements representing them) should be identical for easy repetition, and placement by abutment.

- The behaviour of a single chip should be independent of the number of processing elements it contains. This includes fixed I/O bandwidth between the PEs.

- The coupling of chips should be like coupling of processing elements. That is, the interface between processing elements and the interface between chips should be functionally identical.

The possible appearance of such a system is shown in Figure 1.

The cost of fixing the I/O bandwidth, which is caused by the fixed pin number, is an increase in data transfer time to and from the system with increasing neuron count.

If we assume that the I/O bandwidth is as large as the host processor system's, the problem is irrelevant.

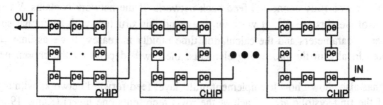

Figure 1. The flexible connection strategy of a fixed I/O bandwidth neural network chip system.

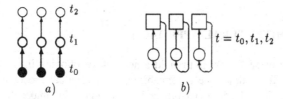

Figure 2. *a*) The "physical" viewpoint of a three layer network. *b*) Model of a time-simulated network. ○ indicates the processing elements. □ are latches to hold calculated values.

PRINCIPLES

There are two methods in the construction of neural networks. The first is to assign *one* network unit (neuron) to *one* ressource (processing element) as depicted by the three-layer example in Figure 2a. At t_0 calculations are performed by the black neurons to generate inputs to the neurons in the next layer, beginning their calculations at t_1, and so on. If the circuit processing elements are dedicated to only one "physical" neuron, and no pipelining is used, the utility of the processing elements is in fact only 1/3 because of the critical path.

The second method is to assign several neurons to each ressource, so that neuron layers will be simulated in time (Figure 2b). A three layer network can be simulated by a processor array, where one processing element performs the calculation of three corresponding neurons (one in each layer). The processor efficiency will be near 100 %.

A fast processor array is presented for calculation of the back-propagation algorithm by Pomerleau et. al. (1988). This Warp array is dependent on external weight storage and calculation power.

Our aim is to construct a chip architecture which is feasible for the construction of neural networks in small microcomputer systems.

Sun-Yuan Kung has proposed a neural network based on a ring-systolic array structure, where neurons are simulated in time (Kung, 1988b; Kung and Hwang, 1989). Neuron states are circulated through the processing elements in one direction.

Kung derives the systolic architecture for a Hopfield net by full matrix-vector multiplication (Kung, 1988b). Implementations of a similar architecture has been done by Weinfeld (1988).

This becomes a fully connected feed-back network. If the network contains N neurons, the number of weights are N^2. If we want to expand this structure with additional neurons, the number of parameters and the calculation time rapidly increases. If we assume weights to be stored locally in the processing elements, these will depend on the chosen network size.

Kung has also shown how to implement multi-layer feed-forward networks with a matrix version of the ring-systolic array (each of the rows represents one layer) (Kung, 1988a), or using the single ring systolic architecture (Kung and Hwang, 1989). Here, the number of neurons in each layer is also allowed to become a multiple of the number of processing elements. One layer is then calculated in a "hunk" serial way.

Again, additional neurons in each layer will result in an increasing size of the processing elements and an increase in calculation time.

A NEW ARCHITECTURAL APPROACH

The idea of the present work is to build a network functioning in a neuron-parallel, layer-serial manner. To facilitate the expandability, the individual processing elements will not grow by connection of additional processing elements. To make this possible, restricted interconnection strategies has to be considered.

Limited interconnection strategy

Most implementations done in hardware offers the possibility to construct fully connected feed-back networks, or feed-forward networks where a single unit is connected to all other units in the surrounding layers.

However, it is propably not necessary to have these oversized connection schemes. Of course the number of parameters will decrease with fewer connections. Insufficient number of parameters normally causes network overloading, if too many training patterns are presented, though a well trained network would still act reasonably well (Markussen, 1990).

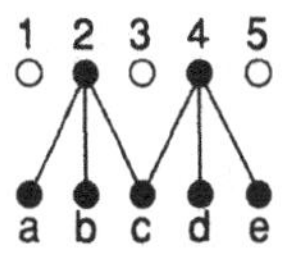

$$\rightsquigarrow \quad \begin{array}{c} \begin{array}{ccccc} a & b & c & d & e \end{array} \\ \left(\begin{array}{ccccc} \bullet & \bullet & 0 & 0 & \star \\ \bullet & \bullet & \bullet & 0 & 0 \\ 0 & \bullet & \bullet & \bullet & 0 \\ 0 & 0 & \bullet & \bullet & \bullet \\ \star & 0 & 0 & \bullet & \bullet \end{array} \right) \end{array} \begin{array}{c} 1 \\ 2 \\ 3 \\ 4 \\ 5 \end{array}$$

Figure 3. Limited interconnection scheme formulated by a weight matrix (• means non-zero entries). Inputs are only evaluated from a subset of all neurons. This reduces the number of parameters in the system. If the outermost processing elements are connected, the ⋆ entries are also nonzero.

In Figure 3, two layers in a possible feed-forward network are shown. One neuron in the upper layer is dependent of only three neurons in the lower layer (only the connection of two neurons are shown). The weight matrix of the upper layer is also shown to contain several zero elements.

This reduces the number of calculations being done by the individual neurons. Also it decreases the physical size of the weight storage held by the single processing elements.

When the number of parameters is determined and built into hardware, the aim is to utilize the given ressources 100 %.

Local interconnections

As the architecture is intended *not* to depend on the fully connected neural network structures, the one way communication link of the ring systolic architecture will not be satisfactory. If a neuron state has to be communicated to its neighbour PE, it is not necessarily practical to shift the state through *all* other processing elements.

We have to make short bi-directional connections instead. A model is shown in Figure 4.

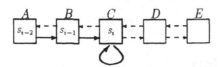

Figure 4. The processing element C collects data from the neighbour PEs. The first calculation is made of internal data. Meanwhile new data (other neuron states) is pipelined from the other neurons. This task is performed simultaniously by all other processing elements. In a two dimensional scheme data is evaluated from four directions.

The number of shifts in each direction (2 in Figure 4) necessary to collect data corresponding to the connection scheme, will be termed *reach out* (RO). The RO value is configurable, and determines the actual connectivity.

I/O communications

The signals discussed in the former section will be defined as the *local* communication signals. Other important signals are the *global* I/O communication signals, which contains the new input patterns to be evaluated by the network, and the results calculated.

The local communications may only occupy a fragment of the total communication time available between PEs. The global communications could use the same channels when the local communications are idle.

Two-dimensional connection schemes

In Figure 5 a possible connection scheme is shown. Here the processing elements are arranged in a rectangular array and each PE is connected to its four neighbours.

The structure will be able to simulate networks with 16 neurons in each of a number of layers.

Links between the PEs are data busses of a certain width. If we assume the bus (combined local and global) to be 8 bit wide, the total number of pins on the chip would be 128.

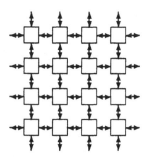

Figure 5. To justify two-dimensional connection of the processing elements, a huge number of I/O pins is required on each side of the chip. The processing elements would also be more complex in order to exploit the available bandwidth. That is, as data requires multiplications, a number of multipliers must be available in each PE.

Alternative connection scheme

In order to reduce the processor complexity, and lighten the connection to other chips, accepting the reduction in processing speed, the strategy shown in Figure 6 is considered.

In this architecture the PEs are only connected to two neighbour units. The data propagates serial through the PEs. It may not be necessary to let data flow in both directions at the same time.

Again, if it is assumed that the global data is 8 bit wide, this will now require a total number of only 16 terminals on the chip. The number is independent of the number of processing elements on the chip. Interconnection to similar chips is performed straight forward.

The architectural considerations of Figure 6 was chosen as the foundation of the present work.

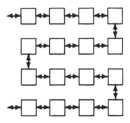

Figure 6. The one-dimensional connection scheme requires more pipelining to achieve speed, but saves I/O pins for connections to other chips. An important feature is that the number of pins is fixed, independent of the number of PEs.

Advantages of separating local and global communications

If Figure 6 is extended to a huge number of neurons the I/O communication will increase. It will perhaps *not* be possible to fit in a load of new inputs or retrieving of outputs in the period of one calculation.

A problem will occur with the network configuration dependent scheduling between global communication and local PE communication (the communication of states between the PEs).

To overcome this problem an alternative (or rather an extension) to the structure proposed, is shown in Figure 7. This structure separates the communications in two channels; one for global I/O communications, and one for the local inter-communication.

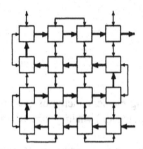

Figure 7. Seperated serial communication. Thick arrows are the data paths used to distribute the output and input values to the network. The thin arrows are used for local communications between PEs. The widths of the busses are independent. The problem of communication scheduling between the global and local values is now removed.

The local communication channel can now be parallel or serial as required by the processor arithmetics and is independent of the global I/O data transfer. It is also unnecessary to support bi-directional global communications.

The architecture is a double serial structure. In Figure 7 the global and local communications are shown perpendicular to each other, but the designer should feel free to choose the most reasonable strategy related to feasible layout.

The connection to other chips is still possible. The number of pins is increased a little, but the connections can still be done without additional hardware.

In addition it also becomes simple to connect the outermost PEs of the system.

As is seen we end up with the structure of Figure 1.

THE PROCESSING ELEMENT

As mentioned, functioning of the whole system has to be controlled by micro programs, stored outside the chips. The micro program language executes operations like *shift* states one position, *add* or *multiply* two specific numbers etc.

The efficiency by which simulations are performed is based on the possibilities offered by the controller hardware, to fully exploit the parallelism within a single processing element.

The processing element is the heart of the neural network chip. One can determine the complexity of the PE from the requirements of the training algorithms.

It must be considered, whether the processing elements should share arithmetic ressources or not. In this work all the operations are performed in each PE in parallel, because this gives the easiest expansion to larger systems and the highest possible calculation through-put. If the pipelining and time scheduling of the processor operations are done well, none of the arithmetic units will be idle anyway.

As we know from the literature (e. g. Lippmann (1987)), the different algorithms requires different complexities of arithmetic ressources.

Common to the simulation phase of neural networks, is the ability to perform large summations of products:

$$net_j = \sum_i w_{ji} o_i$$

The complexity of a processing element increases (number of registers, complexity of arithmetic units and demands for precision) when generality in respect to training algorithms is supported.

The present design will support the following training algorithms immediately:

- No training (Loading of parameters)

- Hebb rule (Feed-back networks)

- Delta rule (Perceptrons)

- Back-propagation (Multi-layer feed-forward nets)

A rough outline of a processing element is shown in Figure 8.

The processing elements are optimized towards features of the neural network equations, which allows us to save silicon area in the final design.

As an example there is no circuit dedicated to the calculation of the activation function used by the back-propagation algorithm (see Figure 8). While all neurons are calculating their output states, no other internal calculations can take place anyway, since further calculations depends on the output (e. g. before calculation of subsequent layers).

The logistic activation function:

$$f(net_j) = \frac{1}{1 + e^{-net_j}}$$

is often used with the back-propagation algorithm, but it is too complicated to calculate for the present processing element in its original form. Good results has been achieved

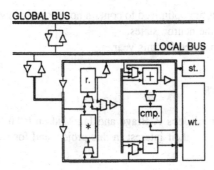

Figure 8. Schematic of the internal organization of a processing element. It is expected to implement about 20 registers and a weight storage of maximum 64 entries. Estimated PE area: 10mm² in a 2μ process. In the final design the subtractor may be saved.

(Markussen, 1990) by approximations made with piecewise second order polynomials (Ouali *et al.*, 1989).

To get output values between 0 and 1 we use the approximation:

$$
f(net_j) = \begin{cases}
O^+ & \text{if } net_j \geq \theta_j \\
-\alpha_j(r_j - \text{abs}(net_j))^2 + 1 & \text{if } 0 \leq net_j < \theta_j \\
\alpha_j(r_j - \text{abs}(net_j))^2 & \text{if } -\theta_j < net_j < 0 \\
O^- & \text{if } net_j \leq -\theta_j
\end{cases}
$$

where O^+ and O^- indicates the values to assign if net_j exeeds the treshold value θ_j. α_j is a fraction between 0 and 1, and $r_j \geq \theta_j$.

The implementation is intended to use fixed point arithmetics, with a 16 bit precision.

To end up with a VLSI design which is process independent, the processing elements may be built as module generators.

CONCLUSION

In this paper a digital architecture for neural networks has been proposed, which will not cause an explosive increase in size and complexity of the PE, dependening on the network size.

The first thing that has been done to overcome the problems is to reduce the number of parameters. This is in fact a violation of the major part of the neural network equations proposed in the literature, but simulations shows that good results still can be achieved.

The number of pins are fixed by localized communications in a one-dimensional architecture to make extensions of the network easier. The easy expandability is of great importance, if an economical and physical realistic chip design is wanted.

Various training algorithms will be supported as a set of sub-operations, controlled by micro programs, and common operations can be combined to form future algorithms.

The processing elements are optimized to contain no special hardware to perform isolated operations, as to calculate the neuron states.

A prototype design is planned for this year.

ACKNOWLEDGEMENTS

The author would like to thank Jens P. Brage and Jan Madsen from the Design Automation Group at the centre (DAG) for their interest in this project and for helpful discussions.

REFERENCES

Hopfield, J. J., "Neural networks and physical systems with emergent collective computational abilities", In *Proceedings of the National Academy of Sciences 79*, pages 2554–2558, 1982.

Kung, Sun-Yuan and Hwang, Jenq-Neng, "Neural Network Architectures for Robotic Applications", *IEEE Transactions on Robotics and Automation*, 5(5):641–657, October 1989.

Kung, S. Y., "Parallel Architectures for Artificial Neural Nets", In Bromley, Keith, Kung, Sun-Yuan, and Swartzlander, Earl, editors, *International Conference on Systolic Arrays*, pages 163–174, Computer Society Press, May 1988a.

Kung, S. Y., *VLSI Array Processors*, Prentice Hall, 1988b.

Lippmann, Richard P., "An Introduction to Computing with Neural Nets", *IEEE ASSP Magazine*, 4:4–22, April 1987.

Markussen, Torben, *Digital VLSI Architectures for Neural Networks*, Master's thesis, Technical University of Denmark, Microelectronics Center, August 1990.

Ouali, J., Saucier, G., and Trilhe, J., "Customizable Neural Networks in Silicon", In *IFIP Workshop on Parallel Architectures on Silicon*, pages 18–31, Institut National Polytechnique de Grenoble - France, December 11-13 1989.

Pomerleau, Dean A., Gusciora, George L., Touretzky, David S., and Kung, H. T., "Neural Network Simulation at Warp Speed: How We Got 17 Million Connections Per Second", In *IEEE International Conference on Neural Networks, vol. 2*, pages II–143–II–150, Sheraton Harbor Island, San Diego, California, July 24–27 1988.

Rumelhart, David E. and McClelland, James L., editors, *Parallel Distributed Processing. Explorations in the Microstructure of Cognition. Volume 1: Foundations*, MIT Press, 1986.

Weinfeld, Michel, "A fully digital integrated CMOS Hopfield network including the learning algorithm", In Delgado-Frias, J. G. and Moore, W., editors, *VLSI for artificial intelligence*, Kluwer Academic, Oxford, 1988.

4.8 A VLSI Implementation of a Generic Systolic Synaptic Building Block for Neural Networks

Christian Lehmann and François Blayo

Laboratoire de Microinformatique
EPFL, CH-1015 Lausanne, Switzerland

Abstract

Designing hardware requires a thorough decomposition of the conceptual models to be integrated as well as extensive analysis of all the functional parameters they involve. Together with an introduction to artificial neuron models, we briefly explain, in this paper, why artificial neural networks are good candidates for silicon integration although they still require much theoretical thoughts.

Analysis at the conceptual level and integration at the logic and gate levels, conducted in parallel, are intended to lead to a digital VLSI realization of Hopfield's and Kohonen's models. This paper develops an original architectural approach using semi-specialized recurrent systolic arrays building blocks to be combined in general neuro-emulators starting with those two well known models. These implementations are primarily intended to be used as preprocessing stage to real-time computing.

INTRODUCTION

Biological neurons have the ability to process a large amount of rough information and inexact knowledge which allows living beings to control their behavior in an ever changing environment. This ability probably derives from the fact that the animals' brain involves distributed representation and parallel processing (Rumelhart 1986). Today's computers, even though they can overpower the biological brain in many precise tasks, lack this ability to process even the simplest rough data whence the deceptions with symbolic AI approaches. Hoping to overcome the high level representation limitation, computer engineers together with a large range of scientists have developed models for parallel distributed processors similar to the brain's: the artificial neurons.

A model for artificial neurons has been proposed by Mc Culloch and Pitts (1943), of which various connecting networks where proposed. This model stayed the almost unchanged basis

VLSI for Artificial Intelligence and Neural Networks, Edited by J.G. Delgado-Frias and
W.R. Moore, Plenum Press, New York, 1991

325

of most artificial neural network (ANN) models until today. We have emphasized our study on two well known models developed by Kohonen (1984) and Hopfield (1982). The work described in this paper relates mostly to those models.

A discussion on hardware integration followed by a short description of ANNs at the conceptual level will be given next. It will then be shown how a theoretical effort on structural and functional analysis of the existing models can lead to a better understanding and determination of generic computing elements, the GENES's family, we wish to develop. The architecture of the systolic network and synaptic cells which will constitute the neuro-emulator will also be described.

FROM SOFTWARE SIMULATIONS TO REAL WORLD UTILIZATIONS

Today, the artificial neural networks are studied by mathematicians, physicians, biologists and computer science engineers throughout the world. Since their models include many heuristic parameters, they require a heavy simulation process from which theory is being built. Such software simulations have serious limitations for they emulate parallel neuronal matrices on sequential machines: the time required for the result to be evaluated depends on the number of neurons being simulated. Only a fairly low number of neurons and, for this reason, only simple academic problems can efficiently be simulated on cheap personal computers or require expensive calculators. However, simulated networks allow for much flexibility and can be combined with high level user-interfaces which favor simulated experiments.

Meanwhile, a straightforward application domain of ANNs is found in the controlling part of artificial automata which must cope with a wild or semi-domesticated environment such as industrial factories. However, although these models are intended to process rough information, there is a tricky rule which seems to apply to most of them, that is they require a preprocessing stage prior to any computation they perform. Since there are, in the brain areas dedicated to sensory inputs, a hierarchy of neural layers (Alexandre et al. 1988) part of which could be identified as preprocessing, we can assume that some particular ANNs can be used efficiently as preprocessing blocs (Fig. 1). Cottrell has shown (1989) why the auto-organizing Kohonen model was one of them.

Because ANNs will probably be part of real-time computer systems and because there is a need to study larger and more complex networks, fast hardware neuro-emulators, *neuro-accelerators*, are now being developed. Most of them, however , still use standard architecture based systems as add-on cards to host computers (Guerin 1987). They are fairly expensive since they require many elements and a complex board organization.

The last step in integration is to realize true parallelism on VLSI chips using digital or analog technologies. The most appealing implementation would require optical or analog technologies. These can be very size efficient but, unfortunately we consider that they are not yet well mastered enough to be used. We emphasize therefore our work on the more mature digital technologies.

True parallelism and full interconnected networks usually lead to virtual connections via broadcasting busses or synaptic matrices implementations. This integration process can follow two strategies, either specializing a chip to emulate one type of model and aiming at one specific application, such loosing the flexibility but resulting in optimally sized integration, or producing

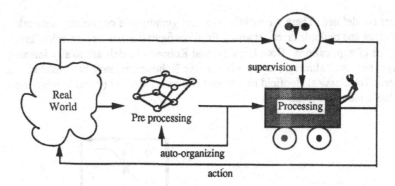

Figure 1 Data flow in a real time, real world configuration

a general neuro-emulator aiming at several applications and conserving part of the simulators' flexibility but consuming wide silicon areas.

Our approach will be close to the second one and based on the synaptic matrices implementation. An ideal synaptic element would be able to compute many different models and such behave like a small microprocessor. However, because we intend to build large networks, we need to strongly reduce the size of these elements. Therefore, it is not possible to integrate fully general synapses but only some specific functions, general enough to be used in more than one model, but specialized enough to be kept in a small area. Such *generic* elements will be combined to produce different networks or even multiple network configurations .

ARTIFICIAL NEURAL NETWORKS MODELS

In order to introduce the problem, let us identify the structural and functional elements we have to work with and describe the neuron models, the networks and the phase of computations involved.

The simple neuron model, as depicted in Figure 2, widely used, is derived from neuro-biologists' observations. It consists of a neuron body which computes the weighted sum of input values or neighbor neurons' activation values (x), the neuron activation potential (p), followed by the application of a non-linear and threshold function (σ) often described as a sigmoïdal function. These can be expressed in the following matricial form:

$$p = Wx \tag{1}$$

$$y = \sigma(p) \tag{2}$$

where W is the synaptic matrix.

When intended to be used in specific applications, the network models require a first *structural definition* phase where connections between neurons, learning algorithms and special parameters are defined. There are mainly two configurations of connecting networks: single layer networks and multiple layer networks. Each configuration has its own behaviors, theories and domains of applications. Both Hopfield and Kohonen models are totally interconnected single layer networks although, as we will see, the Kohonen net may be considered as being two layered. The classical Hopfield model uses two states neurons (0 and 1) while Kohonen's network has continuous responses.

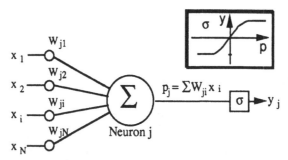

Figure 2 The artificial neuron model

The following phase, *learning*, involves the modification of the neurons' interactions through the adaptation of the synaptic weights. The learning is here the data driven counterpart of the classical and symbolic programming phases. The large variety of learning algorithms found in the literature (Lippmann 1987) can be divided in two classes whether they are supervised (external agent dictating correctness) or unsupervised (self-organizing) (Fig. 1). The learning phase involves comparisons of values, scalar products, matrix-vector products and modification of the weights through subtractions, and scalar multiplications as well as computation of the neurons' non linear functions generally expressed by the following expression from Rumelhart:

$$\mathbf{W}(k+1) = \mathbf{W}(k) + g(\mathbf{p}(k),\mathbf{t}(k)) \ h(\mathbf{y}(k),\mathbf{W}(k)) \tag{3}$$

where g() and h() are two functions respectively of the neurons' activation potential (**p**), calculated as in equation 1, and a taught input (**t**) and of the post sigmoïdal output value (**y**) and previous synaptic weight (**W**).

Let us take again the example of Hopfield network synaptic weights which are defined by the application. The weights are often modified according to the classical Hebb type learning rule:

$$W_{ji}(k+1) = W_{ji}(k) + (2y_j(k)-1)(2y_i(k)-1) \tag{4}$$

In Kohonen's network only the synaptic weights leading to the neuron with the strongest response (**y**) and its neighboring *bubble*, are updated every time a new prototype input (**x**) is presented to the network according to the following rule:

$$W_{ji}(t+1) = W_{ji}(t) + \alpha(t)(x_i(t)-W_{ji}(t)) \text{ if } y_j \in \text{bubble}(y_k) \tag{5}$$

The networks, once structure and interactions are frozen, will produce responses to given stimuli during the so-called *recall phase*. The computation required here is a matrix-vector product in addition to the same neuron function as in equation 2.

$$y(t) = \sigma(Wx(t-1)) \tag{6}$$

Of course the computational phases are only conceptually separated and may be interleaved or concurrent in practical models.

Since the two models we have taken as examples have different behaviors, they have different properties and may be used in different applications. The Hopfield net is mainly used as an CAM (Content Addressable Memory) or associative memory while the Kohonen net is used to map a N-dimensional space in a more tractable 2-dimensional one.

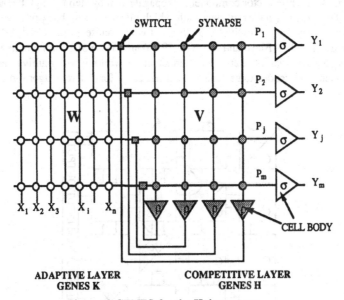

Figure 3 GENES for the Kohonen net

NETWORK MODELS ANALYSIS AND GENERIC ELEMENT SYNTHESIS

"The neuron interconnecting pattern is perhaps the most distinguishing characteristic of a neural model" (Treleaven et al. 1989). However, a closer analysis of these structures reveals amazing similarities: the Kohonen net can be viewed as having two different weight layers, the adaptive layer in which the learning takes place (equation 5) and the competitive layer defining the competitive interactions between neurons. This second layer's schedule shows similarities to the Hopfield's recall phase.

For this reason, we are now able to divide Kohonen's model into two architectural structures (Fig. 3): GENES K, able to modify weight matrix **W** according to expression 5, and GENES H, in which recurrent iterations on a pre-loaded synaptic **V** matrix allow the building of the bubble, where **V** is the lateral coupling matrix which determines competition between neurons. Both subsystem have compatible data flow and structure as explained below and in more details by us in NERVES project deliverables (1990). The second part of this network can of course also be used for the application of Hopfield's model itself.

GENERIC SYNAPTIC NETWORK ARCHITECTURE

The architecture of the fully interconnected network we propose is inherited from a classical systolic matrix-vector product network: the synaptic matrix components are set into the systolic array synaptic cells while vector components propagate step by step through the array. It adds to this systolic stream, a recurrent data path which allows a flow back of the result to be combined iteratively and recursively. Such a network architecture, called APLYSIE, has already been described by Blayo and Hurat (1989). While APLYSIE was completely dedicated to Hopfield's binary model, our derived cell architecture, working with multivalued vector and matrix coefficients is intended to be used as a generic block for different algorithms.

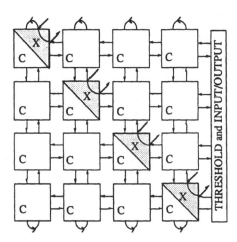

Figure 4 GENES HN, 4x4 network

Figure 4 shows the dataflow in the network. Values move in the four cardinal directions, starting from a prior loading on the diagonal. When reaching the North or South borders, they instantly rebounds in the other direction. The neuronal functions are located on the East side of the synaptic matrix from where the resulting neuronal response is reintroduced in the matrix. This response value will meet the former value on the diagonal cells where they will be compared and combined to start a new iteration.

This recurrent systolic dataflow will be the base of all GENES's family elements which will now be described in more details.

PERFORMANCES

In such a network, a complete 24 bits iteration, composed of a matrix-vector product and vector's return to their initial location, can be computed in 2x24xN clock cycles, N being the network's size, i.e. the number of neurons. Calculating 13 million Connections Per Second (CPS), and 3000 neural Updates Per Seconds (UPS) for 128 neurons working with a 20MHz master clock could be sufficient for some real-time applications (De Man et al. 1987). However full performances of this architecture are only achieved when using pipelined vectors, which is bound to happen when processing real-time data. In such a case, the network would calculate in parallel 2xN matrix-vector products and therefore produce one every microsecond, independently of the network's size, leading to the calculating power of 1 MUPS with a 100% pipeline load.

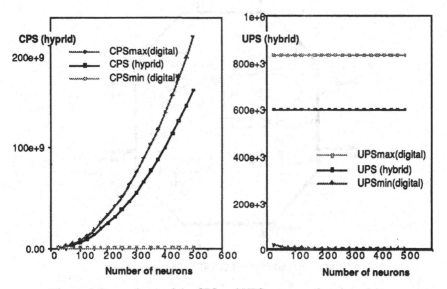

Figure 5 Comparisons of the CPS and UPS rates as a function of the number of Neurons in fully interconnected networks.

Figure 5 compares our performances with a similar architecture developed by Rossetto (1990) using hybrid technology. We see here that both these architectures will require efficient interfacing mechanisms to be able to follow the high bandwidth of their outputs. Therefore, the study of their interconnection toward full system integration will be our prime interest in the future.

GENERIC SYNAPTIC CELL

We have integrated those synaptic cells, analyzed in the conceptual level, in a first VLSI design. Let us describe in more details the cells' functions in relation with the constraints and requirements they must follow.

Architecture

In the network, each cell performs the same instruction. The architecture of a GENES H8 cell, dedicated to the generalized Hopfield model and containing 8 bits registers (24 for the partial sum), is shown in figure 6.

Let us point out the physical resources required during the learning and recall phases of models of concern.

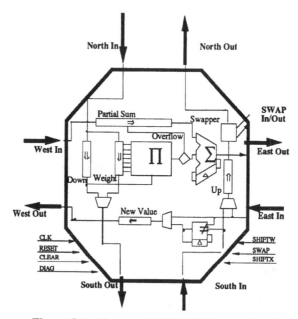

Figure 6 Architecture of GENES H8 synaptic cell

First of all, we must consider the storage resources required. Each synapse stores one synaptic coefficient updated during the learning phase or loaded during the initialization phase. Throughout both learning and recall processes, inputs and partial results flow back and forth in the recurrent network. The synapse's partial sums, coming form West, computs the matrix-vector product, to be exited to East. In Kohonen's network, the coefficients may be modified by adding to a selection of them part of the difference between the current value of the coefficients and the prototype input (not depicted in figure 7).

While the network is iterating, there must be a mean to detect the stabilization of the output values. In our architecture, the synapses are also in charge of detecting the identity of the current value ($x(k)$) coming from South and of the preceding value ($y(k)=x(k-1)$) arriving from the East side. A comparator, located on the crossing of East and South inputs performs this convergence detection.

In addition, in the diagonal cells, stable vectors can be swapped inside and outside the chip at any time in order to introduce and extract values of vectors.

A time-size tradeoff had to be made concerning the multiplication of input vectors by the synapse coefficients which was implemented as serial-parallel multipliers. This choice has the important property to deliver a partial result for each clock cycle.

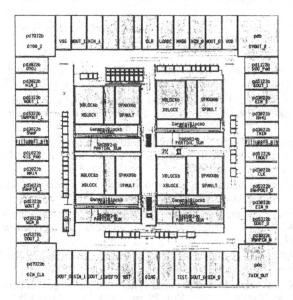

Figure 7 Layout of the GENES H8 2x2 chip

Implementation

Once the architecture has been defined, there is still different hardware implementation possibilities, several matured technologies. We have chosen the smallest CMOS technology available in our lab (2μ) and used a bit serial stream to reduce the size of the computing elements. Optimized static registers (16 transistors) have been used to allow easy step by step testing. 8 transmission gates logic full adders (14 transistors) build the heart of the serial/parallel multiplier. A first 2x2 chip (Fig. 7) has been realized and sent to foundry in June. Each cell contains 1300 transistors on a 0.7 mm^2 area. Test logic allows individual testing of cells.

We are now able to start experiments with multi-chips interfacing as well as communications with conventional hardware.

CONCLUSION

From the parallel study of how ANN models' low level computational blocks can be combined to build complex neuro-emulators and how these generic elements can be efficiently integrated on silicon we proved once again that theory brings better practical conceptions. The analysis we have started will be extended to many other algorithms, for instance Perceptron (Rosenblatt 1958) or back-propagation (Rumelhart et al 1986). The implementation of the first element of the GENES's family will be achieved during the first half of this year. An experimentation board will be designed before the end of 1990, after terminating analyses of the interfacing mechanism and further study of the neuron block, which description was left out of this paper.

REFERENCES

Alexandre, F., Burnod, Y., Guyot, F., Haton, J.P., "La colonne corticale: nouvelle unité de base pour des réseaux multicouches", in *Proceedings of NeuroNîmes '88*, pp. 21-33, 1988.

Blayo, F., Hurat, P., "A VLSI systolic array dedicated to Hopfield neural network", in *VLSI for Artificial Intelligence*, Delgado-Frias and Moore Eds., Kluwer Academic Publishers, pp. 255-264. 1989.

Blayo, F., Lehmann, C., "GENES: a systolic multivalued output network for simulation of various connectionnist models", in *ESPRIT BRA NERVES no 3049 task D1, 1st deliverables*, Dortmund, June 1990.

Cottrel, M., "Analyse mathématique d'un modèle du cortex cérébelleux: effet des liaisons inhibitrices", in *Annales CARNAC*, EPFL, Lausanne, 1989.

De Man, H., Rabaey, J., Six, P., Claesen, L., "Computer aided synthesis of digital signal processing ASICs", in *Proceedings of Journées d'électronique*, pp. 121-137, Lausanne,1987.

Guerin, A., "CRASY: un calculateur de réseaux adaptatifs systolique. Application au calcul neuro-mimétique", Thèse DI, INPG-ENSERG, Grenoble, 1987.

Hopfield, J. J., "Neural networks and physical systems with emergent collective computational abilities",in *Proc. Natl. Acad. Sci.*, Vol. 79, pp. 2554-2558, April 1982.

Kohonen, K., "Self organization and associative memory", Springer Verlag, Berlin, 1984.

Lippmann, P., "An introduction to Neural Networks", in *IEEE ASSP Magazine*, Vol. 3, No 4, pp. 4-22, April 1987.

Mc Culloch, J.,Pitts, "A logical calculus of the ideas immanent in nervous activity", in *Bulletin of mathematical biophysics*, Vol. 5, pp 115-133, 1943.

Rosenblatt, F.,: "The Perceptron: a probabilistic model for information storage and organization in the brain", in *Psychological Review*, Vol. 65, pp. 386-408, 1958.

Rossetto, O., Kreuzer, I, Jutten, C., "Analog VLSI Synaptic Matrices as Building Blocks for neural Networks", in *IEEE Micro*, Vol. 9, No 6., pp. 56-63, Dec. 1989.

Rumelhart, D. E., Mc Clelland, J.L., Eds., "Parallel distributed processing: explorations in the microstructure of cognition". Vol. 1: foundations. MIT Press, 1986.

Treleaven,P., Pacheco, M. and Vellasco, M., "VLSI Architectures for Neural Networks", in *IEEE Micro*, pp. 8-27, December 1989.

4.9 A Learning Circuit That Operates by Discrete Means

Paul Cockshott and George Milne

Department of Computer Science
University of Strathclyde, Glasgow, Scotland

Abstract

Since biological neural systems are assumed to operate by means of techniques that are at least partly analogue, this creates a disjunction between the domain of neural nets and existing binary circuit technology. An alternative is to produce a non-biological neural net model that is suitable for implementation on digital hardware. Using the ideas of back propagation, cellular automata and the process algebra CIRCAL, the authors have investigated a model suitable for VLSI fabrication.

DIGITAL OR ANALOGUE

Existing computer technology is overwhelmingly digital. More specifically, it is overwhelmingly based upon two-valued logics. Information is transmitted in terms of electrical voltages with voltages above a certain threshold being taken to represent a 1 and those below it to represent a 0. Although multi-valued logics have been proposed for computer use they have not attained more than a very limited use.

The underlying reason for this choice of digital techniques is the ability of digital number system to represent numbers for an implementation cost that is logarithmic in the range to be represented. The implementation cost of an analogue system of encoding grows more steeply with the range of values to be represented. Similar arguments of economy applied to the number base lead to two as the natural choice. If you want to perform computations on numbers up to N, it is cheaper to represent these in binary and use O log_2 (N) components than it is to represent these in some base $x>2$ and use $Olog_x(N)$ components.

Since biological neural systems are assumed to operate by means of techniques that are at least partly analogue, this creates a disjunction between the domain of neural nets and existing binary circuit technology. Neural net theories deal with idealised abstractions of neurons in which the neurons are assumed to be able to take on one of two possible activation levels. This is not a problem for implementation in binary logic but the representation of synapses creates difficulties.

Synapses are generally considered to allow various strengths of linkage between cells. The probability of activation of a cell becomes the weighted sum of the inputs

VLSI for Artificial Intelligence and Neural Networks, Edited by J.G. Delgado-Frias and
W.R. Moore, Plenum Press, New York, 1991

on its synapses. The weights in question are analytically modelled as continuous variables. They are continuous in that they can taken on a real-numbered range of values, and they are variable in that they can alter with time as a network adapts to its environment. Natural nervous systems also incorporate a very high degree of interconnectivity. This combination of attributes is very different from what we are used to in digital electronics.

PLANAR OR 3D

Digital VLSI is characterised by the planar disposition of cheap binary logic elements which contrasts strongly with the three dimensional disposition of semi-analogue elements seen in nerve tissue. It is worth stressing the significance of the 3D organisation of nerve tissue. If one considers the example of vision, the 3D organisation of the retina, optic nerves, visual cortex, etc., allows for a pipeline of image processing stages each of which acts on a 2 dimensional data-set. This is simply not available to us with current VLSI techniques. Here one is limited to a very small number of layers of interconnect, usually two to three, such as pictured in figure 1.

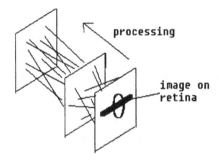

Figure 1 3D organisation of nervous tissue allows successive planar processes to be pipelined.

This has an direct effect on the feasible degree of connectivity between cells. Regular tesselations allow each cell to have three, four or six neighbours (see Figure 2). If one attempts to go beyond simple tesselations of the plane and achieve a higher degree of connectivity one has to throw away active components for wires. These wires can be considered as cells that just relay information; if they are counted in this way one finds that the mean degree of interconnect remains bounded by the regular tesselations.

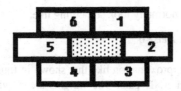

Figure 2 Planar geometry limits a VLSI cell to six neighbours

Two approaches have been taken to overcome the discrepancies between biological and VLSI systems:

a) analogue neural nets are simulated on computers using floating point arithmetic;
b) attempts are made to construct circuits working on analogue electrical principles.

The first technique suffers from limited parallelism, whilst the second is unable to take advantage of existing circuit technology. Computer simulation has the great advantage of being easy to do, computers with floating point arithmetic are readily available and easy to program. Provided that one is willing to wait long enough, one can simulate an arbitrary degree of interconnection by time multiplexing access to stored-weight parameters. Analogue circuits on the other hand hold out the promise of being much cheaper than hardware floating point for the limited accuracy that is needed for neural nets. Despite this they remain constrained by the limited connectivity imposed on all VLSI solutions.

NON-BIOLOGICAL NETWORKS

An alternative is to produce a non-biological neural net model that is suitable for implementation on digital hardware. This should meet the following constraints:

a) the components should operate by discrete means;
b) it should be suitable for planar silicon construction.

A two valued system can be viewed as a coarse approximation to a continuous one. If we view a neuron abstractly as a unit that has:

1. a vector of afferent signals $A = \{a_1, a_2, ..., a_n\}$
2. an efferent signal E
3. a vector of synaptic weights on its afferent signals $W = \{w_1, w_2, ..., w_n\}$
4. a firing function f such that $E = f(A, W)$

then by a suitable choice of the firing function and W we can construct a binary valued approximation. We will assume that the afferent signals, efferent signal and weights can take on the values 0 or 1.

A firing function would normally look something like:

if A.W > threshold then 1 else 0

This suggests a binary approximation like that shown in figure 3. In this the firing function is provided by an AND gate. The weights are provided by the use of an exclusive OR gate XORing a stored weight bit with the

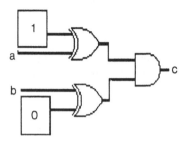

Figure 3 Simple binary approximation to a neurone

Learning

In order for this model to learn it is necessary to provide some means of modifying the weight control bits that are fed into the XOR gates which act as synapses. An obvious technique would be to use a back propagated 'target' signal. Each cell would then appear as shown in Figure 4

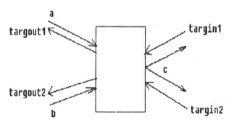

Figure 4 Adding back propagation signals

As signals propagate forwards (from left to right), the cell takes two inputs (**a,b**) and generates an output (**c**). In order to allow the horizontal composition of successive layers of cells with the same number of cells in each row, a fan-out of 2 is required. Thus the inputs of two cells in layer **N+1** will be derived from each cell in layer **N**. The target signals are what the next layer 'wants' its inputs to be.

If a cell finds that it is generating an output that the next layer does not want, then it can either change its own behaviour or it can ask the layer behind it to alter its behaviour. We will model this in CIRCAL, a process algebra adapted to the description of hardware.

Descriptions in CIRCAL

The CIRCAL process algebra is a language for describing and specifying the behaviour of digital hardware and other complex, concurrent systems. It is constructive in nature in that the behaviour of a system of interlinked components may be established from the behavioural descriptions of the components using suitable operators in a hierarchical manner. In this paper we are using CIRCAL as a hardware description language in which we specify the behaviour of two learning circuits.

CIRCAL is described in detail in (Milne 1985) and models of digital hardware created in it are given in (Milne 1989). We will introduce the CIRCAL operators in what follows and will explain their meaning informally; a formal presentation of them appears in the previous references.

Each CIRCAL process has a sort associated with it and this specifies the set of labelled ports through which a component may interact with other components. Components have their behaviour described by a CIRCAL process or term which is constructed out of the CIRCAL operators and the labels taken from a particular sort. The sort which corresponds to the input/output parts of figure 4 is the set {a,b,c,targin1,targin2,targout1,targout2}, for example .

Process algebras such as CIRCAL are based on the concept of synchronised interaction. If label **a** is in the sort of the process which corresponds to a particular component then a synchronised interaction, or communication, may occur with other processes via **a** if all participant processes are in a state where **a** is the next action they all wish to perform. An action is a non empty set of labels taken from the processes sort and this represents simultaneous synchronisation through a number of ports:

The CIRCAL operators may be described informally as follows:

Guarding: The process **mP** describes a component which wishes to perform action **m** and on so doing evolve into a new process **P**. For example process {a,b}P wishes to participate in an action which involves synchronisation on the port labelled by **a** simultaneously with a synchronisation on the **b** port. This process then evolves into process **P**. Notice that the set-theoretic {} brackets are used to indicate simultaneity of actions while processes such as that identified by **P** can be thought of as being in state **P** following a successful synchronisation on guard {a,b}.

Choice: For processes **P** and **Q**, then **P+Q** represents the process which can perform either the actions belonging to **P** or those belonging to **Q**, the choice being governed by other processes in its environment which are composed by the concurrent composition operator. For example, process {a}R + {b}S may synchronise with other processes and may evolve to **R** following a successful **a** synchronisation and S following a **b** synchronisation.

Nondeterminism: For processes **P** and **Q** then **P** + **Q** represents the process which can perform either the actions belonging to **P** or to **Q**. Unlike the choice operator the environment has no control over whether the actions will belong to **P** or to **Q** and the nondeterministic choice is made internally.

Composition: For processes **P** of sort L and **Q** of sort M then process **P*Q** of sort L M represents the behaviour of the components modelled by **P** and **Q** as they interact with each other and further processes. When action labels occur in the sorts of both processes then synchronisation must occur between the appropriate guarded terms; otherwise the actions belonging to **P** or to **Q** may occur asynchronously.

Two further operators constitute the core of the CIRCAL process algebra as presented in (Milne 1989). As termination and abstraction are not utilised in the examples in this paper we can safely avoid mentioning them.

Learning Circuit Descriptions in CIRCAL

The whole cell given in figure 4 can be treated as a process:

process cell of sort {a,b,c targin1,targin2,targout1,targout2}

which is formed by the composition of four sub-processes as shown in figure 5.

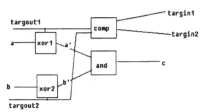

Figure 5. Use of 4 sub processess to make up the cell

In CIRCAL we would write this as

cell<= xor1 * xor2 * comp * and

where ***** is the process composition operator, **and, xor1, xor2, comp,** and **and** are the CIRCAL processes which correspond to the respective logical components.

In what follows assume that ~ is a prefixed negation symbol.

process and of sort {a',b',c}
The behaviour of this is a simple combinatorial AND and needs no further description.

The XOR processes on the other hand are able to alter their behaviour. The process **xor1** which represents the first Xor gate when its weight bit is 0 is capable of evolving into **xor1b** (where the weight bit is 1), as described below.

process xor1,xor1b of sort {a,a',targout1,~a,~a',~targetout'}

```
xor1<= {a}{a'}xor1+{~a}{~a'}xor1+
        {a,targout1}{a}xor1+
        {~a,~targout1}{~a}xor1+
        {~a,~targout1}{~a}(xor1+xor1b)+
        {a,~targout1}{a}{xor1+xor1b}
```

```
xor1b<= {a}{~a'}xor1b+{~a}{a'}xor1b+
        {~a,targout1}{a}xor1b+
        {a,~targout1}{~a}xor1b+
        {a,targout1}{~a}(xor1+xor1b)+
        {~a,~targout1}{a}{xor1+xor1b}
```

This indicates that if an **a** and a **~targout1** occur at the same time then the system evolves non-deterministically (the + operator) into either state **xor1** or **xor1b**. In the latter, any input on **a** is negated on **a'**.

The **comp** process is used to decide what the inputs to the **and** process ought to be. If both of the signals (**targin1,targin2**) are 1, then the values on the **targouts** obviously echo this. If the **targin** signals are both 0 then three patterns of input to the AND gate are compatible (00,10,01) and the **targout** pair can legitimately take on any of these. Ideally they should take on each with equal probability. If the **targin** signals differ then we should get a 50% superposition of the two previous states. We can describe this as follows:

```
process comp,comp00,comp11,compe
    of sort {targin1,targin2,targout1,targout2}
    comp<={targin1,targin2}comp11+
        {~targin1,targin2}compe+
        {targin1,~targin2}compe+
        {~targin1,~targin2}comp00
    comp11<={targout1,targout2}comp
    comp00<=1/3{targout1,~targout2}comp+
        1/3{~targout1,targout2}comp+
        1/3{~targout1,~targout2}comp
    compe<=1/2 comp11 +1/2 comp00
```

Notice the introduction of probabilities on the guards of the nondeterministic choices of **comp00** and **compe**.

Simulations of networks based on this model have proved capable of learning to associate pairs of binary patterns with each other, including traditonally 'hard' problems in which the output pattern depends upon the parity of the input pattern.

The cells dealt with above can implement any of the four following two input boolean functions:

```
c= a and b
c= ~a and ~b otherwise ~c = a or b
c = ~a and b
c = a and ~b
```

Given that there are in principle 16 possible 2 input boolean functions an obvious extension of the technique is to use cells capable of implementing any of these. An example is shown in figure 6.

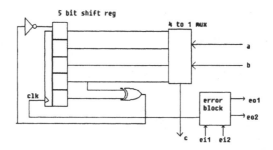

Figure 6 Universal 2 input logic block

A Counter Model

The logic block is implemented using a four to one bit multiplexor, the two inputs to the logic block, **(a,b)** are used as select lines. When an appropriate truth table is supplied as input to the multiplexor, a particular two input boolean function is effected. A 5 bit shift register with negated XOR feedback can be cycled through all possible 4 bit binary patterns on its lower 4 bits. If these are used as input to the multiplexor, then by pulsing the **clk** input an appropriate number of times any one of these may be reached.

The error block acts to adjust the truth table and handle the back propagation as follows:

> **process error,error1,error2,error3 of sort{ei1,ei2,eo1,eo2,clk}**
> **error <={ei1}error1+{ei2}error1+{ei1,ei2}error1**
> **error1 <=p error2 & (1-p)error3**
> **error2 <= {clk}{~clk}error**
> **error3 <= 0.5 {eo1}error & 0.5{eo2} error**

In words: with probability p an error on **ei1** or **ei2** will cause the shift register to be clocked, otherwise, one or the other of the error outputs will be activated.

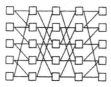

Figure 7 A possible regular connection net

It would be expected that networks using these counter cells would learn faster than the simple XOR based cells. This has in fact been found to be the case. Simulation of this model of cell, organised in regular connection nets such as shown in figure 7, showed marked improvements in speed of learning when compared to the previous model based on AND and XOR gates We do not have hard figures for the speed improvement, but subjectively it seemed to be about 4 to 8 fold in terms of

CPU run time. This is not necessarily convincing since the relative efficiencies of the two simulation programs may bias the results. We hope to obtain more objective results once the models have been implemented in hardware.

Implementation with CALS

We are currently working on implementing the model on a cellular array processor using Configurable Array Logic (CAL) chips (Gray and Kean 1989). These chips allow dynamic reconfiguration of logic cells using multiplexors whose select lines are controled by static RAM cells. They can implement any digital logic network. It is hoped that they will provide a suitable tool for experimenting with digital learning circuits.

References

Gray, J. P. and Kean, T. A. "Configurable Hardware: A New Paradigm for Computation", in Advanced Research in VLSI, Proc. Decennial Caltech Conference on VLSI, Pasadena, Ca., March 1989. (MIT Press 1989).
Milne, G. J. "CIRCAL and the Representation of Communication, Concurrency and Time", ACM Trans. on Prog. Lang. and Systems, Vol. 7, No. 2, April 1985.
Milne, G. J. "Timing Constraints: Formalizing their Description and Verification". Proc. 9th Int. Conf. on Computer Hardware Description Languages and their Applications (CHDL '89), Washington D.C., July 1989, (North-Holland), 1989.

4.10 A Compact and Fast Silicon Implementation for Layered Neural Nets

F. Distante, M. G.Sami, R. Stefanelli, G. Storti-Gajani

Dipartimento di Elettronica, Politecnico di Milano
P.zza L. da Vinci 32, I-20133 Milano, Italy

Abstract

In this paper we present an architecture for implementation of artificial layered neural networks. The building blocks of the architecture are simple processing elements properly interconnected to a number of shift registers which provide the processing elements with data and weights. The paper concentrates on optimization of the architecture with respect to the three main parameters of silicon area requirements, computational latency and throughput.

INTRODUCTION

A number of silicon implementations have been presented in recent literature for various structures of neural nets; common requirements are:

a. silicon efficiency — in particular, with reference to the problem of mapping the very high connectivity involved in neural net models, while taking into account the limitations due to silicon technologies;

b. operation speed — to achieve the requirements deriving from point *a*, a measure of serialization is often introduced against the intrinsic parallelism of neural nets;

c. flexibility — namely, the possibility of mapping a number of different neural graphs onto a given silicon device.

While analog implementations can meet the first two requirements (see e.g. Tank and Hopfield 1986), the third one is typical of *digital* architectures. Here, we will discuss a digital architecture that grants all three requirements listed above, and that is very well suited to silicon implementation.

The solution here examined is in the same line as those presented by Kung 1988, Kung and Hwang 1989, Treleaven *et al* 1987, Blayo and Hurat 1989, Ouali *et al* 1989, in

VLSI for Artificial Intelligence and Neural Networks, Edited by J.G. Delgado-Frias and
W.R. Moore, Plenum Press, New York, 1991

which connectivity is provided by the use of suitable shift registers transferring information *sequentially* between devices emulating the various neurons. In such architectures, the high connectivity characterizing neural nets is satisfied by transposing in time the data transfers from source to target neurons.

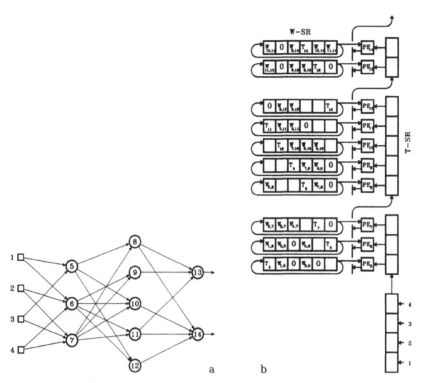

Figure 1.a A small three layered net
b Net 1.a realized with the basic architecture

In particular, we refer to the architecture discussed in Distante *et al* 1989a and 1989b (see Figure 1).

1. each *neuron* is implemented by a processing unit (evaluation logic and generation of the output signal) and a *weight shift register* $(W - SR)$ in which weights associated with the connections from "source" neurons are stored in suitable order;

2. a *transmission shift-register* $(T - SR)$ forwards the incoming signals (from the external sensors or from a previous layer) to all neurons;

The structure is well suited to support implementation of *completely-connected layered nets*, often called *Back-propagation nets* due to the requirements of the generalized delta rule learning algorithm typically adopted for such nets (see Rumelhart *et al* 1986); these constitute a class widely advocated for applications, e.g., in the area of pattern classification (see e.g. Gevins and Morgan 1988). In this structure, "neural elements" consisting each of a pair $PE - W - SR$ are organized in groups corresponding each to a layer of the neural net. Firing signals form the previous layer (or from the input sensors) are fed sequentially to the various PEs on the $T - SR$ associated to the layer. The ordering of the weights in the $W - SRs$ (and the initial setting of the registers) must match the incoming data so that when the datum coming form the ith neuron of the previous layer is input to the PE associated with the jth neuron of the present layer, $W_{i,j}$ is input to the same PE through its related $W - SR$ (see the ordering in figure 1.b, mapping the net in figure 1.a). To achieve correct sychronization, all $W - SRs$ in the system must have the same length — namely, that corresponding to the layer with highest indegree. Referring to figure 1.b, null weights correspond to "missing" links in a non-completely connected net, while "void" positions account for the extra weight slots that must be inserted in smaller layers to grant correct synchronization of operation. The solution is valid both for *parallel* and for *serial* implementation of the processing elements and, therefore, for corresponding organizations of weights in the $W - SRs$. The design is mapped with obvious ease onto silicon, consisting as it does of well-assessed building blocks with simple and regular interconnections: on the other hand, the speed that can be achieved is rather low. This solution becomes also relatively inefficient in terms of silicon utilization if the difference between cardinalities (and thus indegree) of the various layers is relevant.

In this paper we will present an alternative architecture which, stemming from the previously described one, optimizes both latency and silicon area requirements.

THE ARCHITECTURE

The architecture here presented is based on two considerations:
1. the area requirements of the processing element are far lower than those of the $W - SRs$ (in general, the number of neurons in each layer will be very large); thus, we can afford a reasonable increase in the complexity of the individual processing element, if this is balanced by better operation speed;
2. *pipelining* can be exploited to optimize latency and throughput over a number of subsequent data sets.

Each neuron appearing in figure 1 is now organized with a number K of *pseudo-neurons* (PNs) each consisting of:
- a *processing element* containing an arithmetic unit, an accumulator, a shift register supporting transfers between the various PNs of each neuron (the example in figure 2 refers to $K = 3$ and to the adoption of serial arithmetics).
- a pseudo-$W - SR$ ($PW - SRs$); weights are stored in the $PW - SRs$ in an ordered way, as shown in figure 2. The ordering of weights in the $PW - SR$ follows the same reasoning adopted in the previous section considering that what was a single neuron (pair $PE - W - SR$) has now become a set of K pseudo-neurons (pairs $PN - PW - SR$). Instead of a single $T - SR$, now a set of K registers is introduced, each feeding one of the PNs and each connected to the *subset of source neurons* whose synaptic weights are stored in the corresponding $PW - SR$.

The input signals must be staggered in time over the K $T - SRs$ so that the timing

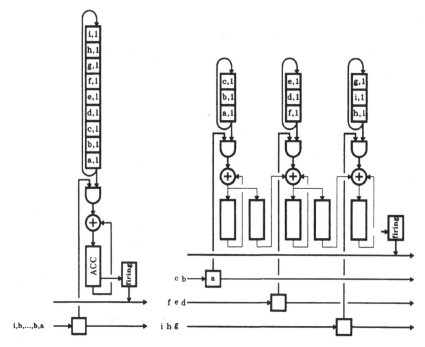

Figure 2 Structure and connection of pseudo-neurons

sequence shown in figure 3 is achieved; thus, the following mode of operation is obtained during the subsequent time slots:

t.s.1: $PN1$ accumulates $a \times W_{a,1}$;

t.s.2: $PN1$ accumulates $a \times W_{a,1} + b \times W_{b,1}$; $PN2$ accumulates $d \times W_{d,1}$;

t.s.3: $PN1$ accumulates $a \times W_{a,1} + b \times W_{b,1} + c \times W_{c,1}$; $PN2$ accumulates $d \times W_{d,1} + e \times W_{e,1}$; $PN3$ accumulates $g \times W_{e,1}$;

t.s.4: $PN2$ receives the contents of the buffer of $PN1$ and thus accumulates $a \times W_{a,1} + b \times W_{b,1} + c \times W_{c,1} + d \times W_{d,1} + e \times W_{e,1} + f \times W_{f,1}$; $PN3$ accumulates $g \times W_{e,1} + h \times W_{h,1}$;

t.s.5: $PN3$ receives the contents of the buffer of $PN2$ and therefore it accumulates the total value $a \times W_{a,1} + \ldots i \times W_{i,1}$; at the end of this time slot, $PN3$ generates the output signal f_1 *of the whole neuron 1.*

Consider now *one* layer l of cardinality L where each neuron receives I input signals. Assume that the I input signals are time-multiplexed onto K input lines (note that K must be a factor of I so that each input line receives strings of equal length; if this is not possible, input signals must be properly "padded" so as to fulfill this requirement). An example of how our architecture can support such a layer is shown in figure 4, where $L = 20$, $I = 12$ and $K = 3$.

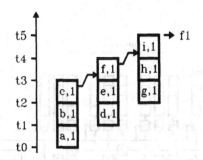

Figure 3 Timing sequence for $K = 3$

The length of each $PW - SR$ is constrained to be $r = I/K$. This in turn determines the number of neurons (i.e. group of pseudo-neurons) that can fire on the same output bus: no more than r neurons can fire on the same bus to avoid conflicts on it. Thus if more than r neurons are required by a layer, they will have to be organized in "rows", each row operating in parallel with the other ones (see figure 4).

Each neuron is split into K (here three) pseudo-neurons: the $T - SR$ is also transformed into K $PT - SR$s so as to match the number of incoming lines.

From the above, the number of neurons that can be accommodated in a layer is obviously a multiple of r. Since in our example we have a 20 neuron layer and $r = 4$ (number of neurons per row), we must have $R = 5$ rows of neurons.

Operation of the 5 rows of r neurons is now described. In figure 5 the timing diagram for all input and output lines is shown for three subsequent presentations of $12 = K \times r$ input signals. In each row of figure 4 delays in the $PT - SR$s are used to grant synchronization. In this way conflicts will not arise on the firing bus: each neuron *in a given row* receives a complete set of 12 inputs at subsequent time steps. Output delays skew the outputs as in figure 5, granting correct input to a subsequent layer.

CHARACTERISTIC PARAMETERS AND LATENCY

We analyze now the influence of the characteristic parameters (i.e. K, r and R) on architecture efficiency, evaluated in terms of area requirements and latency.

Regularity of the design would require for all layers to have the same number of $PT - SR$s, i.e. K should be a constant for all layers. I (the maximum indegree of the layer) and L (the cardinality of the layer) are fixed by the neural net graph. All the other parameters characterizing the layer can then be computed, that is:

- the number of pseudo-neurons constituting a neuron is equal to K;
- the length of the $PW - SR$ is

$$r = \left\lceil \frac{I}{K} \right\rceil \qquad (1)$$

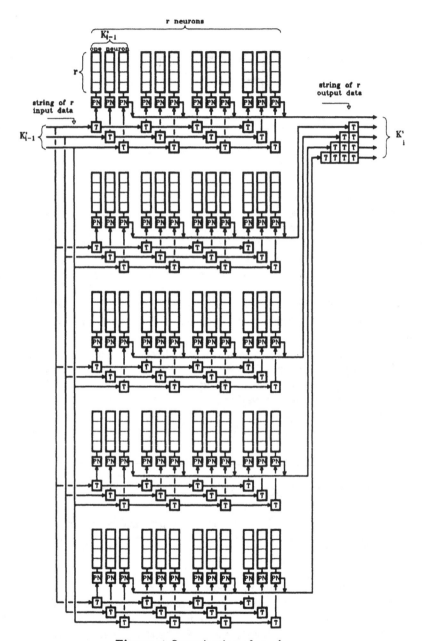

Figure 4 Organization of one layer

- the number of rows of neurons is

$$R = \left\lceil \frac{L}{r} \right\rceil \tag{2}$$

Let's now translate this into an example to stress some characteristics. Suppose we have five layers such that:

$$L_1 = \left\{ \begin{array}{l} L = 80 \\ I = 50 \end{array} \right., \; L_2 = \left\{ \begin{array}{l} L = 66 \\ I = 80 \end{array} \right., \; L_3 = \left\{ \begin{array}{l} L = 53 \\ I = 66 \end{array} \right., \; L_4 = \left\{ \begin{array}{l} L = 69 \\ I = 53 \end{array} \right., \; L_5 = \left\{ \begin{array}{l} L = 4 \\ I = 69 \end{array} \right. \tag{a}$$

This example fulfills the basic requirement that $I_i = L_{i-1}$ which means that the maximum indegree of layer of level i cannot be greater than the the cardinality of layer of level $i - 1$.

The problem is now that of choosing the values of the characteristics parameters so to optimize the latency of the system, seen as the main figure of merit. To obtain the formula which determines latency consider that a neuron will fire

$$r + (K - 1)$$

time slots after it has received the first input: r instants are required to recirculate the $PW - SR$, $K - 1$ to ripple the partial sums through the other pseudo-neurons.

After the first neuron in a row has fired, its signal is forwarded to the next layer which can start its operation. The latency of the whole system composed by n layers will thus be:

$$\sum_{i=1}^{n} (r_i + (K_i - 1)) \tag{3}$$

If we want to keep K fixed for all layers we have to express r as a function of K. Considering equation (1), equation (3) becomes then:

$$\sum_{i=1}^{n} \left(\left\lceil \frac{I_i}{K_i} \right\rceil + (K_i - 1) \right) \tag{4}$$

Since I is fixed by the problem, the value of K minimizing the global latency must be selected. Results for example (a) are given in Table 1 and Table 2.

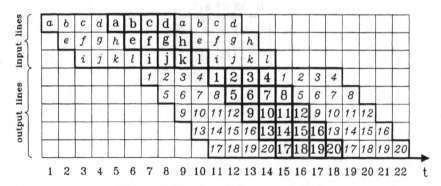

Figure 5 Skewing of the output values

Table 1 Latency for increasing values of K

K	1	2	3	4	5	6	7	8	9	10	11	12	13	14	15	16	17	18	19	20
Latency	318	163	114	93	82	76	74	73	72	75	77	79	83	84	89	94	96	99	104	109

Table 2 Parameters of all the net's layers (K fixed)

	L	I	K	r	R
L_1	80	50	9	6	14
L_2	66	80	9	9	8
L_3	53	66	9	8	7
L_4	69	53	9	6	12
L_5	4	69	9	8	1

Table 3 Parameters for all layers (r fixed)

	L	I	K	r	R
L_1	80	50	6	9	9
L_2	66	80	9	9	8
L_3	53	66	8	9	6
L_4	69	53	6	9	8
L_5	4	69	8	9	1

Keeping K fixed yields a regular architecture from the point of view of number of $PT - SRs$ required by each layer but:

1. some additional logic is required to match the number of output lines of a layer to the (fixed) number of input lines of the next one; this matching, obviously implies also an appropriate "reshuffling" of data;
2. the length of the $PW - SRs$ varies from one layer to another (being K fixed, the value of r depends on I which is, in principle, different for each layer). This implies that a *common* synchronization of all $PW - SRs$ is not possible: either each layer has its own shift signal properly timed in dependence of the length on the $PW - SRs$ of the layer, or some additional logic must process the global shift signal, adapting it to the characteristics of each layer.

The above requires an area and control overhead which practically invalidates this solution, nevertheless they give a clue on what could be an effective solution. In fact, it appears evident that the second consideration does not apply in case r, instead of K, is constant. In this case a global shift signal would be sufficient and could be broadcast to all $PW - SRs$ of the system. The drawback stressed by the first consideration would also disappear in case r was fixed: our aim is that the number of output lines of layer $i - 1$ match the number of input lines of layer i. Referring to figure 4, the number of output lines of a layer is equal to the number of rows R of PNs, while the number of input lines is equal to the number K of $PT - SRs$ per row. What we wish to obtain is thus that:

$$K_i \equiv R_{i-1}$$

This equivalence in true in case the net is fully connected and r is fixed since, applying equations (1) and (2)

$$K_i = \frac{I_i}{r} = \frac{L_{i-1}}{r} = R_{i-1}$$

The advantage of having r fixed is then obvious. We must now transform equation (3) in function of r instead that of K:

$$\sum_{i=1}^{n} \left(r + \left\lceil \frac{I_i}{r} \right\rceil - 1 \right) \tag{5}$$

This new equation identical to (4) substituting r for K_i; this relevant result allows us to state that *latency is invariant with respect to the two different approaches.* Applying equation (5) to the previous example, Table 3 is obtained.

The choice of having K rather then r fixed will thus take into account only architectural and not performance considerations. While in this paper we presented the lower area requirements of the "fixed-r" solution, it is presently under study a modification of the "fixed-K" alternative which, though requiring more area, allows a grater flexibility in terms of dynamic configuration of the structure. Throughput is, in both solutions, equal to $1/\max_i r_i$, obviously for the fixed-r solution throughput is simply $1/r$.

CONCLUDING REMARKS

In this paper we presented two different optimization approaches for a basic structure capable of supporting implementation on any feed-forward, multi-layered neural net.

The basic structure is an extension of the one presented in Distante *et al* 1989b. The concept upon which it is based exploits the non correlation of data input to the same neuron which allows parallel computation by a set of *pseudo- neurons* each working onto a subset of input data. Only one of the *PN*s will cumulate partial results and forward the firing signal towards the next layer. This operational concurrency leads to split the other building blocks, such as the shift registers containing the weights and those providing for data transfer (respectively Weight Shift Registers — $W - SRs$ — and Transmission Shift Registers — $T - SRs$) into sets of Pseudo $W - SRs$ ($PW - SRs$) and Pseudo $T - SRs$ ($PT - SRs$).

The cardinality of these sets are related one to the other and to the problem-specific parameters (i.e. the number of input signals to the net and the number of neurons per layer). The two optimization approaches make use of these relation to obtain two different architectures yielding the same computational latency but with different area requirements. Though it could seem that the solution requiring less area should be chosen, it is presently under study an extension of the other solution which, while less compact than the first, should allow a greater flexibility in terms of dynamic configuration (i.e. adaptability to a greater number of classes of neural networks) of the system.

REFERENCES

Distante F., Sami M.G., Stefanelli R. and Storti-Gajani G., "Alternative approaches for mapping neural networks onto silicon", *Proc. 2nd Workshop on neural networks and parallel processing*, Vietri sul Mare, Italy, 1989a

Distante F., Sami M.G., Stefanelli R. and Storti-Gajani G., "Multistage interleaved architectures for implementation of neural networks", *Proc. ICS 89*, Santa Clara, CA, pp.279-285, 1989b

Gevins A.S. and Morgan N.H., "Applications of neural network (NN) signal processing in brain research", *IEEE Trans. on ASSP*, vol. 36-7, pp.1152-1161, 1989

Blayo F. and Hurat P., "A reconfigurable WSI neural network", *Proc. IEEE Int'l conf. on WSI*, San Francisco, pp.141-150, 1989

Kung S.Y., "Parallel architectures for artificial neural nets",*Proc. Int'l Conf. on systolic arrays*, San Diego, pp.163-174, 1988

Kung S.Y. and Hwang J.N., "Digital VLSI architectures for neural networks", *Proc. ISCAS 1989*, Portland, Oregon, pp.445-448, 1989

Ouali J., Saucier G. and Trilhe J., "A flexible, universal wafer scale neural networks", *Proc. 3rd IFIP workshop on WSI*, Como, June 6-8, 1989

Rumelhart D.E., Hinton G.E. and Williams R.J., "Learning internal representations by error propagation", *Parallel Distributed Processing*, vol. 1, MIT Press, 1986

Suzuki Y. and Atlas L.E., "A study of regular architectures for digital implementation of neural networks", *Proc. ISCAS 1989*, Portland, Oregon, pp.82-85, 1989

Tank D.W. and Hopfield J.J., "Simple neural optimization circuits...", *IEEE Trans on CAS*, vol.33, n.5, pp.533-541, 1986

Treleaven P.C. *et al*, "Computer architectures for Artificial Intelligence", *Lecture notes in computer science*, vol.272, pp.416-492, Springer Verlag, 1987

5.1 A Highly Parallel Digital Architecture for Neural Network Emulation

Dan Hammerstrom

Adaptive Solutions, Inc.
Suite 340, 1400 Compton Drive
Beaverton, Oregon 97006-1999 U S A

Abstract

This paper discusses a new VLSI architecture for emulating neural networks. It consists of a SIMD array of simple DSP like processor nodes. By using low-precision arithmetic, an optimized PN architecture, and simple broadcast communication, a large number of processors can be placed onto a single piece of silicon, thus allowing cost-effective, high-performance network emulation. The resulting architecture allows the emulation of arbitrary neural network function, including powerful on-chip learning, and non-neural network data pre-processing and post-processing.

INTRODUCTION

The motivation for the architecture described in this paper was to develop inexpensive commercial hardware suitable for solving large, real world classification problems with neural networks. From the beginning we have believed that such an architecture must be flexible enough to execute any neural network algorithm, and work cooperatively with existing hardware and software.

The early application of neural networks will be in partnership with existing technologies, both hardware and software. Neurocomputation will succeed to the extent that it merges cleanly with existing computer structures. It is an enhancing, not a replacing technology.

The basic architecture consists of an array of simple, low-precision processor nodes laid out in a 1-dimensional array. Broadcast communication is used throughout, as well as SIMD control. The resulting system provides cost-effective, high-performance neural network emulation, and will enable the solution of a number of real world, real-time data processing problems.

DESIGN GOALS

We designed this architecture to meet the following criteria:

VLSI for Artificial Intelligence and Neural Networks, Edited by J.G. Delgado-Frias and
W.R. Moore, Plenum Press, New York, 1991

- *Adaptability*, or on-chip learning, is fundamental to the widespread application of neurocomputing technology. Practically every application can be improved by the ability to learn or adapt to a noisy environment, and many applications require such adaptability. Hence, our primary design goal was to develop an adaptive system that learns efficiently on-chip, at high speed, and does so with standard CMOS technology and without extra, off-chip hardware.

- *Flexibility* is a necessary characteristic of any general purpose neurocomputing engine. Flexibility enables a system to utilize any neural network algorithm. Our architecture succeeds in this goal by being programmable. "Programmability" implies digital implementation. Consequently, the first major decision was that this would be an all-digital implementation.

- *Cost Effectiveness* is a requirement for proliferating neurocomputers into real-world applications.

  There are several ways to reduce the cost of silicon implementation. The first is to use an inexpensive, mass producible silicon process. We used standard CMOS.

  The second is to use digital technology which is generally much more tolerant of manufacturing deviations than analog technology. Also, the semiconductor industry has greater experience with digital VLSI.

  Third, silicon area requirements must be made as small as possible. Here we begin to work against the other goals, and trade-offs are required. For example, the "multiplier" per synapse that many analog systems utilize, and which provides much of the speed of analog networks, can consume significant silicon area when precision requirements are increased and flexible weight update functionality is added to each weight site (Holler et al. 1989). By choosing a "shared" digital update, where the arithmetic hardware is shared over some number of connections, we can reduce the "per synapse" area to that of a few memory cells.

  The use of shared arithmetic hardware significantly reduces silicon area requirements. And, by reducing the precision of the computation to the limits required by the algorithms, the cost of digital update remains reasonable.

  A digital implementation also provides for the arithmetic precision requirements of many existing algorithms. Baker and Hammerstrom (1989), and others, have shown that 8 bits are sufficient for most algorithms, though sometimes 16 bits of precision are necessary for weight representation during neural network learning for certain algorithms such as back-propagation. In CMOS analog technology, these levels of precision are difficult and expensive to attain. Our architecture matches the precision requirements of the task of emulating a large range of neural network models, and it does so without excessive and expensive ALUs.

  Another reason for using digital techniques is the ability to multiplex scarce metal interconnect, thus saving significant silicon area. Bailey and Hammerstrom (1988) have shown that multiplexed communication allows for more cost-effective implementation in silicon of complex, high fan-out connectivity. Such multiplexing is much easier with digital communication.

- *Speed* increases are achieved by increasing concurrency in the computation. Ideally one would like to utilize all the parallelism that is available in a neural network model, including the parallel computation of all synapses, as one sees in biological systems. This is one of the strengths of analog based neurocomputation. However, the number of connections is an $O(n^2)$ cost, where n is the number of processing nodes. By using shared digital computation, we have traded off some speed for flexibility, precision, and lower cost per connection. Yet, by making the individual processors as small as possible, one can place a large number onto a single piece of silicon. So ultimately the speed sacrificed is minimal.

And it is clear from the performance numbers that feed forward performance is good enough for many real time applications. And more importantly so is the learning performance.

- *Systems integration* involves both hardware and software. By using programmable processors, multiplexed digital input and output, and by providing significant flexibility on chip, we have made the architecture interface more like existing computational devices and thus have eased the task of integrating this architecture into a complete system. In addition, the use of a separate sequencer simplifies the interface of neurocomputer arrays to existing computer structures.

By using state-of-the-art technology and innovative architectural techniques, we provide adaptability and flexibility while delivering very high performance in both learning and non-learning operation. Our goal is to create an architecture that has a reasonably straightforward silicon implementation and is sufficiently general purpose that it could be considered a "microprocessor" of neurocomputing.

THE ARCHITECTURE

The basic architecture consists of a number of simple, digital signal processor-like PNs (Processor Nodes), operating in a SIMD (single instruction stream, multiple data stream) configuration. Broadcast interconnect is used to allow inexpensive, high performance communication. The PN architecture is optimized for traditional neural network applications but is general enough to implement every neural network algorithm that we have examined (learning and non-learning) and many feature extraction computations, including classical digital signal processing, pattern recognition, and rule processing (fuzzy and non-fuzzy).

A group of PNs, which we call a layer, takes a vector, multiplies it by a matrix of weights and creates a new vector (of possibly different dimension). Any neural network structure can be created by this fundamental operation. Totally connected networks such as a Hopfield network use the output vector as the next input. Feed-forward networks can be thought of as several layers feeding each other successively.

More than one network element or node can be emulated by a single PN. Each element is represented by state in the PN and is called a CN or Connection Node. In the basic architecture, one PN maps each CN. In those cases where there are more PNs than CNs, idle PNs will result. In cases where there are more CNs than PNs, the vector can be folded such that each PN emulates more than one CN. In this case, each PN is time-shared by several CNs. Another type of multiplexing is where each PN emulates several CNs, each from a different layer in a network.

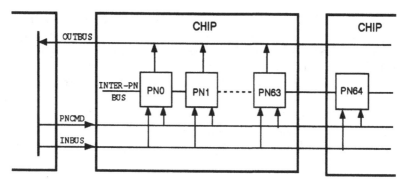

Figure 1 Multi-PN Configuration

Intercommunication is performed via simple broadcast. Each input vector element is broadcast on the global INbus, and each PN has a row of the weight matrix in its memory and does a multiply and accumulate. Thus after all input elements have been broadcast, each CN will have computed an element of the output vector, and collectively they yield the entire output vector. The basic broadcast communication is ordered, that is, each input vector element appears, in order, for one clock on the input bus. This leads to a simple and inexpensive communication structure.

PN BASIC ARCHITECTURE

There are 64 PNs on each chip, and 4K bytes of weight memory in each PN. Each PN has two input buses: INbus (8 bits) and PNCMD (31 bits), and one output bus, OUTbus (8 bits). There is also an inter-PN, one dimensional, nearest neighbor bus (2 bits each direction).

One possible system configuration is to connect chips to form a single PN array, Figure 1, though other structures are possible. The OUTbus goes into the sequencer and the INbus and PNCMD bus come out of the sequencer. The sequencer contains the program that both sequences program execution within the sequencer, and controls what commands are broadcast on the PNCMD bus. The user can indicate whether data from the system memory are placed sequentially on the INbus, and whether the data on the OUTbus are written to the board's memory or fed back around to the INbus. This data wrap around can be used to implement recursive networks. Feedforward networks can be implemented by computing one layer at a time. In this case, one layer transmits its outputs while the next layer in the network computes its output.

As shown in Figure 2 there are 8 internal units connected via control signals and data buses. The INbus and PNCMD bus enter the PN through the inUNIT (input unit). There is some minor decoding on the PNCMD bus which then becomes a group of individual control signals that propagate to the various units. The most important buses connecting the various units are the 16 bit A bus and B bus.

Here is a brief description of the 8 units in each PN and their operation:

1. *inUNIT:* (input unit) The inUNIT decodes the PNCMD bus and routes it to the other units. It also contains the conditional execution flag (xflag) and the logic for

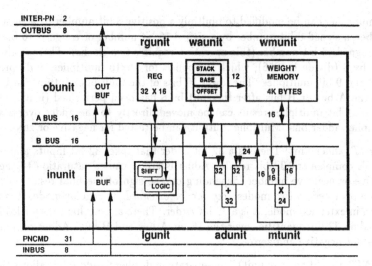

Figure 2 PN Architecture

conditionally setting and clearing the xflag. The 8 bit INbus goes into the inUNIT and its data can be placed onto the lower 8 bits of the A bus or B bus, or it can be held for a clock and combined with the next 8 bits on the INbus to form a 16 bit quantity to be placed on the A bus or B bus. (All data transfer is low byte first.)

2. *lgUNIT* (logic-shifter unit) The lgUNIT contains a shifter and a logic operation unit, both operate on 16 bit quantities. The shifter takes input from the A bus and the logic unit takes as input the output of the shifter and the contents of the B bus. The shifter can shift left or right by 1, 4, or 8 places. The logic unit can do AND, OR, or XOR on its two inputs. In addition, the shifter and the logic unit can pass data through intact, allowing the programmer to use one or the other, or to use the lgUNIT as a temporary register. There are also some additional shift modes for such things as arithmetic shifting, etc. The output can be tested for negative or zero. If an overflow occurs during a left shift, saturation to the maximum value occurs (either positive or negative, depending on the sign of the quantity being shifted). There is also a 1's counter for the least significant byte of the logic output. This value can be fed directly into the adder over a special 4 bit bus. This counter value is used in 1 bit weight mode to accumulate the AND of an 8 bit input vector and an 8 bit weight vector - 8 bits then are processed each cycle. Also, XOR can be used to obtain Hamming distance. There is a technique that allows for zero-error bias bit truncation during a right shift (patents pending).

3. *rgUNIT* (register unit) There is a register file that contains 32 16-bit registers. The register file can be read or written from either bus, however, it is single-ported. Some of the register locations are aliased for special functions including control or mode registers. The control registers contain mode bits that change the data width or other features of computation and operation.

4. *mtUNIT* (multiplier unit) The mtUNIT contains a 9x16 bit two's complement multiplier. The multiplier produces a 24 bit output. Using mode bits, the precision of

the multiplier can be modified to multiply a positive 8 bit number by a signed 16 bit number, a signed 8 bit number by a signed 16 bit number or a signed 16 bit number by a signed 16 bit number (this operation requires two clocks). There is also a shift right by 8 (divide by 256), which is implicit for 16x16 multiplies, and optional for the 8 and 9 bit multiplies. The lower 16 bits of the multiplier output can be placed onto the A bus or B bus after the shift by 8 has been performed (if it is enabled), or the 24 bit multiplier result can be moved directly to the adder over a separate multiplier-adder bus. Multiplier output can be tested for negative or zero.

5. *adUNIT* (adder unit) There is a 32 bit adder that takes 32 bit inputs and produces a two's complement 32 bit result. Adder overflow causes saturation to the largest positive or negative number, depending on the sign of the final result. The adder can be operated in two modes: *regular* or *extended*. In regular mode, it is a 16 bit adder, in extended mode, it is a 32 bit adder. There are mechanisms for loading and unloading 32 bit quantities over the 16 bit A bus and B bus. Adder output can be tested for negative and zero.

6. *waUNIT* (weight address unit) The separate multiplier to adder bus allows the PN to be operated in a chained mode, which also requires a regular stream of addresses to be generated for the weight memory. The waUNIT contains its own adder for adding the contents of the stride register to the current weight address. As a result we have arbitrary striding through memory for those programs that have more complex data structures per network connection.

7. *wmUNIT* (weight memory unit) The weight memory is addressed by the waUNIT. Memory can be accessed in either 8 bit or 16 bit mode. 16 bit mode access is to even addresses only, the least significant bit of the address is ignored. 8 bit accesses can be signed or unsigned (where the sign bit is extended to 16 bits when being placed onto the A bus or B bus). 8 bit writes to memory saturate to the maximum 8 bit value (positive or negative) if the 16 bit value being written is larger than 127 positively or negatively. The waUNIT also has hardware support, called the Virtual Zeros mechanism (patents pending), for the efficient representation of sparse connectivity.

8. *obUNIT* (output buffer unit) The obUNIT contains the arbitration logic for access to the Inter-PN bus and the OUTbus. Both 16 and 8 bit values can be transmitted. 16 bit values require 2 clocks to transmit over the 8 bit OUTbus. The Inter-PN bus is 2 bits, requiring 4 clocks for an 8 bit transfer and 8 clocks for a 16 bit transfer. The obUNIT arbitration and transmission mechanism operates separately from, but is synchronized with, the SIMD control to allow PNs to both transmit and do accumulation simultaneously (patents pending). This capability is required when outputs of a layer are fed back as inputs to the next layer. There are a number of arbitration modes including a mechanism for determining the maximum value in an array of PNs (patents pending) for networks requiring winner-take-all and best-match functionality.

There are several hardware supported data formats, these are:

8 bit signed (7 mantissa+sign) and unsigned: 8 bit data can be read from memory with or without sign (if there is no sign, it is assumed to be positive). Byte input/output ignores the sign. No other units recognize 8 bit data. Signed or unsigned 8 bit is determined by mode setting.

16 bit signed (15 mantissa+sign) and unsigned: The adder always assumes a sign bit, unless extended mode is asserted, then the lower 16 bit input or output is unsigned. The right (16 bit) side of the multiplier always expects a sign bit.

32 bit signed (31 mantissa+sign): In extended mode, the adder output and input can be extracted as a 32 bit signed integer by extracting the upper signed portion and the lower unsigned portion. None of the other units recognize this data type.

SEQUENCER BASIC ARCHITECTURE

The sequencer contains the program store and sequencing logic. It also has input and output buffers for directly accessing a host memory when operated as a coprocessor. Once the program is loaded, sequencing begins. 32 bits of the 64 bit program word contain sequencing, literal, and file input-output commands, 31 bits represent commands to be presented directly to the PN array, one bit is reserved for future use.

The sequencer (patents pending) has several basic command groups:

1. Sequencing: the sequencer supports unconditional and conditional branching, and a single level (one deep stack) call and return. Conditional branching tests one of the 8 loop registers for zero (these also automatically decrement the register) for loop control. Conditional branching also tests the OUTbus for a zero least significant bit, whether the OUTbus is being driven, or whether the current value on the Inter-PN bus is zero.

2. INbus Control: the INbus can take data from a number of sources: a host's system memory, parallel I-O port from off the board, or the constant register in the sequencer, which can be loaded in the same way as the loop counter registers. The constant register allows literals to be taken from the program directly into the PN array.

3. OUTbus Control: the OUTbus data can be directed either back around to the INbus, or to a direct parallel output port, or into an array in the board dRAM.

A SIMPLE VECTOR PROGRAM

It is instructive to give an example of a basic vector inner product loop. The following program has each PN compute a vector inner product. Input vector elements are presented one at a time on the INbus. Each PN in the array executes the same instruction, but each has its own weight vector.

The machine instructions are:

```
        # main loop
        LOOP N;
        { IN inA memB mul addaddL muladdR incbase; }
        addaddL muladdR;
```

The "LOOP N" tells the sequencer that the code enclosed in brackets is to be repeated N times. The second line is the inner loop. The "IN" indicates that the sequencer should place the next input byte from the input stream onto the INbus (broadcast into the PN array).

The remaining commands on the second line are PN commands:

- inA - loads the current contents of the INbus onto the least significant byte of each PN's 16-bit A bus (in this case the upper 8 bits are a sign extension of the eighth bit).

- memB - takes the most recently read weight data from memory (assume here 16 bits) onto the B bus.

- mul - multiplies the contents of the A bus and B bus. The result of the multiply will be available in the next cycle.

- addaddL - takes the result of the previous add and uses it as input to the left side of the adder.

- muladdR - routes the output of the previous multiply into the right side of the adder. The result of the add will be available in the next cycle.

- incbase - causes the weight offset or stride to be added to the weight memory base address.

The third line is used to empty the pipe, adding the last multiply into the accumulating sum. Now a 32 bit inner-product result is available at the adder output.

A SIMPLE MAPPING

Figure 3 shows how a simple two layer network may be mapped to the array. CN0-CN3's outputs have already been computed. In the first clock CN0's output is transmitted onto the OUTbus. It is then reflected back around in a broadcast manner on the INbus by the sequencer to all PNs, which compute one connection for each CN in the second layer. Each first layer CN output is broadcast in turn. In this manner n^2 connections are computed in n clocks - an efficient use of expensive metal interconnect.

PHYSICAL REALIZATION

The first silicon realization of this architecture has 64 PNs, each PN has 4,096 bytes of weight storage. Thus, one chip can store the weights for 262,144 (256K) 8 bit connections, 131,072 (128K) 16 bit connections, or 2,097,152 (2M) 1 bit connections. Chained mode allows each PN to perform a multiply-accumulate per clock, which means the computation of one connection per clock per PN for 8 and 16 bit weights. At 25 MHz, the maximum performance in non-learning mode is 1.6 billion connections computed per second per

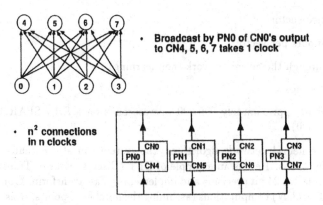

- Broadcast by PN0 of CN0's output to CN4, 5, 6, 7 takes 1 clock

- n^2 connections in n clocks

Figure 3 A Simple Feedforward Network Mapping

TABLE 1 Back-Propagation Learning Speed

System	Learning Rate
Adaptive Solutions (8 chips):	1,940 MCUPS
Adaptive Solutions (1 chip):	257 MCUPS
Cray 2 (Rosenberg and Blelloch):	7 MCUPS
Connection Machine 2 (Zhang et al.):	40 MCUPS

chip, assuming all PNs are utilized. For 1 bit weights, the maximum performance is 12.8 billion connections computed per second, since 8 connections are computed each clock.

PERFORMANCE

The entire NetTalk network (203 input nodes, we used 64 hidden nodes, and 21 output nodes) can be put onto a single chip, and can be trained using the standard back-propagation algorithm over the approximately 76,800 element training set reported by Sejnowski and Rosenberg (1986) in about 6 seconds, which translates to 187 MCUPS (learning rate). This number assumes 15 passes through the original 1,024 word corpus of informal speech, with an average of 5 letters per word. We have simulated this with both floating point and 16 bit integer weights and have found virtually no difference in number of epochs to converge or in final error rate.

The following table (McCartor 1990) shows the performance of general back-propagation learning. The Adaptive Solutions' implementation uses 16 bit integer weight values, while the other implementations use either single or double precision floating point.

An advantage of programmability is that we can implement a wide range of parallel algorithms. For example, our architecture can emulate every network algorithm that we have studied. In implementing Kohonen's LVQ2 (Kohonen et al. 1988) algorithm (single chip), which uses the more complex Euclidian distance measure, we have the following performance capabilities:

- 960 reference vectors

- 256 8 bit inputs per vector

- one pass through the entire network (non-learning)

- 242 microseconds

- as opposed to approximately 900,000 microseconds on a SUN SPARCstation 1 (a ratio of 1:4,000)

In addition to neural network algorithms, the system can also execute a number of preprocessing functions. Here is an example of DFT (Discrete Fourier Transform) times. Note, the Motorola has 24 bit precision and implements a Fast transform. Our architecture performs a DFT in $O(N)$ computations (assuming the number of points, N, is proportional to the number of PNs), an FFT implementation requires $O(NlogN)$ computations.

TABLE 2 Discrete Fourier Transform Performance

Chip	32 point, complex	256 point, complex
Adaptive Solutions	5.4 microseconds	328 microseconds
Motorola 56000	68.1 microseconds	713 microseconds

REFERENCES

Bailey J. and Hammerstrom D., "Why VLSI implementations of associative VLCNs require connection multiplexing", *Proceedings of the 1988 International Conference on Neural Networks*, 1988.

Baker T. and Hammerstrom D., "Characterization of artificial neural network algorithms", *1989 International IEEE Symposium on Circuits and Systems*, pp. 78-81, 1989

Motorola Corporation. "Digital signal processors: competitive analysis", *Technical Report*

Kohonen, T., et al., "Statistical pattern recognition with neural networks: Benchmarking studies", In *Proceedings of the 1988 International Conference on Neural Networks*, pp. 161-168, June 1988

Zhang, X., et al., "An efficient implementation of the back-propagation algorithm on the connection machine CM-2", D. Touretzky, Ed., *Advances in Neural Information Processing Systems 2*. Morgan Kaufman, San Mateo, CA, 1990

Holler, M., Tam, S., Castro H. and Benson R., "An electrically trainable artificial neural network (ETANN) with 10,240 floating gate synapses", *Proceedings of the IJCNN*, 1989

McCartor, H., "Back-propagation implementations on the Adaptive Solutions neurocomputer chip", *Neural Information Processing Symposium*, Denver, 1990.

Sejnowski, T. and Rosenberg, C., "NetTalk: A parallel network that learns to read aloud", Technical Report JHU/EECS-86/01, The Johns Hopkins University Electrical Engineering and Computer Science Department, 1986

5.2 A Delay-Insensitive Neural Network Engine

C.D. Nielsen*, J. Staunstrup* and S.R. Jones**

* Department of Computer Science
Technical University of Denmark
DK-2800 Lyngby, Denmark

** Department of Electrical and Electronic Engineering
The University of Nottingham
Nottingham NG7 2RD, England

Abstract

This paper presents the design of a digital delay-insensitive neural network engine. Delay-insensitive circuits are asynchronous and works correctly regardless of delays caused by logic elements and wires. They are data driven which means that their operation speed is determined by average processing times in contrast to the worst case as in synchronous circuits. Since a delay-insensitive circuit does not include any global control signals, e.g. clocks, it will work as fast as the operation conditions and data allow, regardless of the size of the circuit. These features are very attractive for realizing large neural networks. The architecture of the engine is based on a systolic toroidal network, which is well suited for a delay-insensitive implementation.

INTRODUCTION

Delay-insensitive circuits are asynchronous, i.e. not controlled by a global clock. They are data driven which means that their operation speed is determined by *average* processing times in contrast to the *worst case* as in synchronous circuits. Therefore, delay-insensitive circuits are potentially very fast. They can operate as fast as the technology, implementation, operating conditions, and specific input data allow. Furthermore the absence of a global clock has performance advantages because the problems caused by the distribution of a clock signal (e.g. skew) is avoided.

These properties of delay-insensitive circuits make them attractive for realizing neural networks. First of all, the absence of a global clock signal makes it possible to construct very large neural networks with delay-insensitive components, because there will not be any problem with clock skew. Secondly, the potential high performance of delay-insensitive circuits is needed to build large efficient neural network engines. Finally, in a neural network

Supported by a Nato grant for international cooperation and by the Danish Technical Research Council.

VLSI for Artificial Intelligence and Neural Networks, Edited by J.G. Delgado-Frias and
W.R. Moore, Plenum Press, New York, 1991

367

there is no separation of data and control, the current state implicitly controls the computation. This fits nicely with the approach we use for designing delay-insensitive circuits where data and control are mixed to avoid delay dependencies between control logic and the data path.

The main disadvantage of delay-insensitivity is the increased design effort, because the circuit must operate correctly regardless of time delays caused by wires and logic elements. This can only be overcome by using special delay-insensitive structures and rigorous design strategies.

This paper describes the development of a delay-insensitive toroidal neural network engine. In the following section the algorithm underlying the design is described. Secondly, we discuss the principles of delay-insensitivity and the application to the toroidal neural network. This forms the basis for our implementation of the delay-insensitive neural network. We describe the control structure applicable for delay-insensitive circuits and how they are applied to perform the different operations of the network. A small implementation example is presented. Finally we discuss the interface issues in relation with combining synchronous and delay-insensitive circuits.

ALGORITHM AND ARCHITECTURE

The architecture of the neural network engine is based on the systolic ring network proposed by Kung and Hwang (1988). We use the Hopfield network as a starting point for our design, as most other structures may be derived from this. In this paper we consider the implementation of the recall phase only. A design which includes learning is currently under development for a synchronous system (Jones and Sammut 1990). The learning phase has not yet been included in the delay-insensitive implementation.

The neural computations are performed as consecutive vector-matrix multiplications, where the vector represents the state of the neural network, and each element in the matrix represents one communication line between two neurons with a corresponding input weight. If there is no connection between two neurons the weight is zero. This multiplication is formulated as:

$$u(k+1) = W a(k)$$

where $a(k)$ represents the current state vector and W the weights matrix. A new state vector can be calculated from the result of the vector-matrix multiplication, $u(k+1)$, by applying an activation function, F:

$$a(k+1) = F[u(k+1), u(k)]$$

F is a nonlinear function, normally the sigmoid function, applied to each element in the vector.

These computations may be performed in two phases:

- First the inner products of all inputs and their corresponding weights for all neurons are computed:

$$\begin{pmatrix} u_1(k+1) \\ u_2(k+1) \\ u_3(k+1) \end{pmatrix} = \begin{pmatrix} w_{11} & w_{12} & w_{13} \\ w_{21} & w_{22} & w_{23} \\ w_{31} & w_{32} & w_{33} \end{pmatrix} \begin{pmatrix} a_1(k) \\ a_2(k) \\ a_3(k) \end{pmatrix}$$

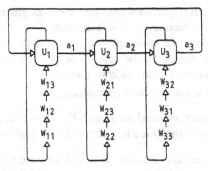

Figure 1. Data flow in toroidal neural net

- These are fed to the update functions in each of the neurons and all the outputs are calculated.

This algorithm may be mapped to a ring network of simple processors passing state vector elements from one to another, see Figure 1. Each state vector element $(a_j(k))$ circulates, as it meets processors consecutive elements of the inner product $(w_{ij}a_j(k))$ are computed and accumulated. When the state vector has completed a full cycle, $u(k + 1)$ is known. Each processor now locally computes $a(k + 1)$ using the activation function F. The weights w_{ij} are stored locally in processor i and supplied to the multiplier in a cyclic manner.

Because of the two-dimensional torus like data flow, this architecture has been named *toroidal neural network*

The toroidal architecture supports a variety of interconnection schemes including the most general, where all neurons are connected with each other. It is possible to support other interconnection schemes by setting the appropriate input weights in the matrix to zero.

This is also the case for layered networks (e.g. perceptrons). The layers may be placed side by side in the ring with the input weights programmed accordingly. To complete a computation it is necessary to make the ring cycle once for each layer in the network.

Another approach is to make each neuron emulate a column of neurons, i.e. one neuron from each layer. After each cycle the neurons are reconfigured to emulate the next layer in the network. This approach only requires the number of processors corresponding to the largest layer in the network. It must be possible to reconfigure dynamically during operation, i.e. both the input weights and the parameters for the activation function must be stored locally for each processor.

The network needs to be able to perform the following functions:

Reset	Force the whole network to a well known state.
Initialize	Initialize the activation function in each neuron.
Input	Input the initial state vector to the main ring.
Process	Circulate the state vector elements and calculate the inner product for each neuron.
Update	Perform the activation function in all neurons and place the new state elements in main ring. The Process/Update cycle may be repeated multiple times in between each Input/Output.
Output	Output final result from main ring.

In a synchronous network these operations may be viewed as global *modes* which all processors enters and leaves simultaneously. In a delay-insensitive network it is impossible to ensure that all neurons perform the same operations simultaneously, different parts of the network may be in different modes, but because of the inherent synchronization the result will be the same. This is discussed in the following sections.

The proposed architecture has the following advantages:

- It can perform fully interconnected networks. Therefore it is possible to emulate the whole range of interconnectivity models, simply by programming the weights.

- It is possible to emulate layered neural networks with more neurons than processors by programming each processor to emulate multiple neurons.

- The system is a ring network. This implies simple and localized interconnections between processors. This is attractive for VLSI implementations.

- The ring architecture yields a low I/O bandwidth independent of the number of processors in the ring. This fact is of course dependent on the way the local memory is implemented, i.e. *on chip* versus *off chip*.

- High degree of parallelism and high total interprocessor bandwidth for local communications.

- Relatively simple processors.

In the next section, the general principles of delay-insensitivity are introduced. These guide the design of the delay-insensitive realization of the architecture just described.

DELAY-INSENSITIVE OPERATION

A delay-insensitive circuit operates correctly regardless of arbitrary signal and gate delays. This excludes circuits using global control signals, for example a common clock. Therefore, delay-insensitive circuits are by definition asynchronous. The computation is controlled by the data flow instead of control signals. This means that data to a processor can be input as they arrive and output is produced as soon as internal computations have completed.

The speed of a synchronous circuit is determined by the worst case computation time. For example, in a clocked circuit all inputs are processed with the same clock period. If different data requires different execution times, the clock period must be long enough to accommodate for the longest (worst case) execution time. Consider, for example, a simple ripple-carry-adder. In a traditional synchronous realization, the clock period must be long enough to allow for the worst case carry ripple, even though only very few inputs will cause this ripple to occur. Alternatively, a delay-insensitive ripple-carry-adder operates with the maximum speed that the current inputs allow. Such an adder can be constructed by combining delay-insensitive full-adders (Seitz 1979). Each full-adder obeys the following signal convention:

- The carry output, c_i, is generated as soon as it can be calculated (i.e., when two inputs are equal).

- The sum output, s_i, is generated when all inputs (i.e. a_i, b_i and c_{i-1}) are ready.

The worst case delay of this adder is determined by the longest ripple-carry-path, i.e. bound by the number of stages in the adder, n. It has been shown, however, that the carry ripple is on the *average* of length $log_2 n$ (Seitz 1979), so the *average* delay in the delay-insensitive adder is bound by $log_2 n$.

This same principle may be used in many contexts, from the sub-cell level to the system level. Consider a sparsely interconnected neural network (e.g., a perceptron). In the proposed architecture, it is emulated with a sparse weights matrix, as no connection is represented by a weight equal to zero. A delay-insensitive design can take advantage of the potential speed up arising from the fact that multiplications with zero are very fast.

The benefit of a delay-insensitive design is higher performance and improved scalability, because clock skew is not a problem regardless of how many processors that are connected. However, the design of reliable delay-insensitive circuits is a difficult challenge. Unless one is very careful, circuits will have hazards and other problems which causes the circuit to mal-function. To illustrate the potential problems, consider a simple AND gate: $y = AND(a, b)$. Assume that the current state of (a, b) is $(1, 0)$ and that is changes to $(0, 1)$. In a properly operating circuit y should remain 0. However, if b changes much faster than a, there could be an intermediate state where (a, b) is $(1, 1)$, causing y to become 1. Therefore, this realization of an AND gate cannot be used, since a delay-insensitive circuit must function correctly regardless of delays in the wires carrying a and b.

Problems, such as the one just described, can be avoided by proper design. Several, design techniques for delay-insensitive circuits have been proposed, for example by Alain Martin and his group (Martin et al 1989). They have demonstrated their technique by producing a working delay-insensitive RISC microprocessor. We are using a different technique based on a high level behavioral description language called "Synchronized Transitions" (Staunstrup and Greenstreet 1990). Many properties, including delay-insensitivity, may be checked on source programs written in "Synchronized Transitions". Those programs meeting a set of delay-insensitivity conditions can be systematically (or even automatically (Hulgaard and Christensen 1990)) turned into delay-insensitive circuits which are guaranteed to be free from hazards and similar problems. The circuits will operate correctly regardless of delays in wires and gates. It is, for example, immaterial whether a wire connecting two processors is very short (on chip) or very long (for example, an off chip connection).

The conditions ensuring delay-insensitivity are very restrictive, and therefore, hard to satisfy. Fortunately, some very important architectures like a pipeline and a ring can be designed, so that they meet the conditions. In the ring, computations progress as circulating waves. The rising edge of the wave corresponds to computing a new result, the falling edge corresponds to resetting in preparation for the next computation. For proper operation, it must be ensured that the rising edge of a wave never overtakes the falling edge of any other wave. It is this property of the computation which makes it possible to meet the restrictive conditions for delay-insensitivity. When generalizing the ring to a torus, Figure 2, it is still possible to meet the delay-insensitivity conditions. The torus has waves circulating on rings in two dimensions. For proper operation waves and crests must meet each other in the intersecting nodes. Hence, we conclude that it is possible to construct a delay-insensitive torus. However, it is not possible to control this torus with global control signals. This excludes a common "mode" signal indicating the overall state of the torus (process, update,

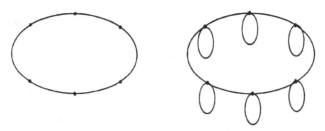

Figure 2. A ring and a torus

reset, io, etc.). To make the design delay-insensitive global control signals must be avoided. In the next section, it is described how this can be achieved for the delay-insensitive neural net engine.

THE DELAY-INSENSITIVE NEURAL NETWORK ENGINE

The ring architecture described in the previous sections is very well suited for a delay-insensitive realization. As illustrated above, it is possible to build delay-insensitive rings. However, the control signals used in the synchronous version must be avoided, because they represent a centralized delay dependence. It is, for example, vital that all processors in the synchronous circuit are in the same mode (update, process, ...). In a delay-insensitive circuit one cannot assure that control signals such as the mode arrive simultaneously at all processors. On the contrary, the circuit must work properly regardless of the delay on the wires connecting the processors and the differences in speed of the processors. Global control signals can be eliminated in the following ways (Nielsen 1990):

- Merge of the control and data paths. This can be done by tagging each data element with a special control token. Each piece of data is followed by a control signal, which determines the operations to be performed on that specific piece of data.

- Distribution of the control to each of the processors in the ring. This limits the dependencies between the processors to the passing of data between adjacent processors.

The control of a larger system may utilize both methods, possible in combination, depending on the origin of the control. The delay-insensitive neural network engine has been designed using this approach.

Functional Description

To comply with the specification given by the algorithm discussed above, the network needs to be able to perform the following operations:

- *Initialization* of the update function in each processor.

- *Input* and *Output* of state variables from the network.

- *Process*, each processor receives a state element from the main ring and a corresponding weight element from the local memory. The product is calculated and accumulated and the state element is sent on to the next processor in the ring. This process is repeated for all elements in the main ring.

- *Update* of the state variables in the main ring. After a full cycle of processing, each processor applies the update function to the local inner product and replaces a state variable in the main ring with the result.

- *Reset* of the network at start up.

Initialization, Process and *Update* is controlled locally in each neuron. *Input* and *Output* is controlled by a single I/O-unit which opens and closes the main ring when necessary. *Reset* is controlled externally by the only global signal in the network. This signal does not follow a delay-insensitive protocol.

Each processor has access to a local memory containing weights, elements to control the operation of the update function and tokens to control the operations performed on the memory data. The input from the local memory determines the next operation to be performed by the processor:

Memory input	Processor operation
weight $\neq 0$	Perform multiply-accumulate operation
weight $= 0$	Bypass multiply-accumulate operation
update token	Apply update function
update element	Reconfigure update function

The update function in each neuron is implemented as a table-look-up unit, where the entries are supplied from the local memory. This approach is relatively fast and easy to configure to approximate any activation function. The exactness of the update function depends on the number of entries in the table. By programming the contents of the local memory it is possible to dynamically reconfigure the content of the table-look-up unit. As the operation of the neural network is data dependent it is possible to reconfigure even though other processors are still computing and passing on state elements. Inputs to the reconfiguring processor will, if necessary, queue up until normal operation is resumed. This ability to reconfigure dynamically enables each of the processors to emulate more than one neuron in layered networks. Instead of having one processor for each neuron, it is only necessary to apply the number of processors corresponding to the largest layer in the network.

The input and output of the state elements in the ring is controlled by a front end processor attached to the I/O-unit. This unit tags the circulating state elements with a token telling the processors whether it is a newly input element in the ring. These tokens together with the control signals from the local memory enable the processors to determine the correct behavior according to the current input data from the main ring and the memory; when a processor encounters a new state element and an update token simultaneously, it knows that an I/O-operation has happened since the last update token, and hence, the value in the accumulator is invalid and should be cleared.

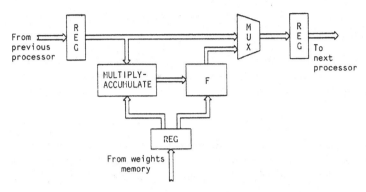

Figure 3. Structure of a delay-insensitive neuron processor

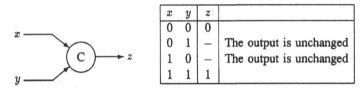

x	y	z	
0	0	0	
0	1	–	The output is unchanged
1	0	–	The output is unchanged
1	1	1	

Figure 4. Muller-C element

IMPLEMENTATION

The structure of the processor is shown in Figure 3. It is very similar to a corresponding synchronous implementation, except that all the components are delay-insensitive.

The communication of data uses the so-called *return to zero* protocol, where an element is implemented with dual-rail coding, where each bit of information, x, is coded on two lines, $x.t$ and $x.f$:

$x.t$	$x.f$	x	
FALSE	FALSE	E	(Empty)
FALSE	TRUE	F	(False)
TRUE	FALSE	T	(True)
TRUE	TRUE	-	Illegal

To ensure proper operation, it is very important that no blocks complete calculations until all its inputs are defined, i.e. the circuit needs to be able to hold its outputs until this happens. Therefore, Muller C-elements, Figure 4, (and variants of this) are heavily used in the design.

As an example, consider the implementation of the circuit controlling the output multiplexer. Depending on the control signal, $Insert$, the multiplexer has to either insert an element in the ring or pass the existing element in the ring on to the next processor. This is controlled by the two signals $Update$ from the local memory and New from the main ring.

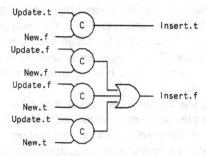

Figure 5. Delay-insensitive implementation

The function of the control circuit is shown in the following table. Only the entries where the circuit generates a new value are shown.

Update	New	Insert		
E (00)	E (00)	E (00)	Empty input produces Empty output	
F (01)	F (01)	F (01)	Pass	Process (old element)
F (01)	T (10)	F (01)	Pass	Process (new element)
T (10)	F (01)	T (10)	Insert	Update (old element)
T (10)	T (10)	F (01)	Pass	Update (new element)

This circuit may be implemented with one C-element for each entry where the circuit shall produce a non-Empty output as shown on Figure 5. This implementation is dependent on the fact that the rest of the circuit follows the return to zero protocol.

Interface to Synchronous Systems

Each processor needs access to a vector of weights. The size of this vector grows with the size of the network, so it must be anticipated that a significant amount of memory is needed to store the weights. The best performance is achieved by storing the weights on chip. However, the area used for storage reduces the area available to the processor. This means fewer processors on each chip which again means lower performance. This suggests storing the weights in separate chips, which also makes it possible to use standard memory chips. However, these are clocked, which creates another problem namely interfacing a delay-insensitive circuit with a conventional clocked circuit. A similar interface is needed to do I/O. Such an interface has an inherent problem with metastable behavior. The only way to reduce the probability of metastable behavior is reducing the speed, which means lower performance.

Hence, the decision about where to store the weights is a compromise which must be made to obtain the best performance. This compromise depends on detailed information about the chosen technology.

Implementation Status

The delay-insensitive neural network was designed using the hardware design language "Synchronized Transitions" (Staunstrup and Greenstreet 1990). This language facilitates a behavioral description of a high level specification as well as the lower levels down to gate level. This approach enables formal verification of the design with respect to functionality, delay-insensitivity, and implementation. This is necessary because delay-insensitive circuits differ from traditional synchronous circuits in that it is impossible to verify the correctness of the design by exhaustive simulation.

A prototype chip using this approach has been sent to fabrication in June 1990. The major goal of this chip is to gain experience with the design method and the testing of delay-insensitive circuits. Therefore, the prototype is simplified in several ways, most significantly by using a word width of 4 bits only and a simple update unit. Furthermore, the prototype has additional circuitry to exercise the delay-insensitive operation.

CONCLUSIONS

We have designed a delay-insensitive neural network engine and a prototype is currently under fabrication. This design has confirmed our belief in the suitability of using delay-insensitive circuits to realize neural networks. By using a systematic design method it is our experience that design of delay-insensitive circuits is manageable although it is still more complicated than designing synchronous circuitry.

REFERENCES

Henrik Hulgaard and Per H. Christensen, "Automated Synthesis of Delay Insensitive Circuits," Master's thesis, Department of Computer Science, Technical University of Denmark, 1990.

Simon Jones and Karl Sammut, "Toroidal Neural Network: Architecture and Processor Granularity Issues," in *Proceedings from ITG/IEEE Workshop on Microelectronics for Neural Networks, NeuroMicro'90, Dortmund*, 1990.

S.Y. Kung and J.N. Hwang, "Parallel Architectures for Artificial Neural Nets," in *IEEE International Conference on Neural Networks*, volume 2, pp. 165–172, 1988.

A.J. Martin, S.M. Burns, T.K. Lee, D. Borković and P.J. Hazewindus, "The Design of an Asynchronous Microprocessor," in *Proceedings of the Conference on Advanced Research in VLSI*, Caltech, 1989.

Christian D. Nielsen, "Design of Delay Insensitive Circuits using Synchronized Transitions," Master's thesis, Department of Computer Science, Technical University of Denmark, 1990.

Charles L. Seitz, "System Timing," in *Introduction to VLSI Systems*, C. Mead and L. Conway (eds.), pp. 218–262, Addison Wesley, 1979.

Jørgen Staunstrup and Mark R. Greenstreet, "Synchronized Transitions", in *Formal Methods for VLSI Design*, Jørgen Staunstrup, editor, North-Holland/Elsevier, 1990.

5.3 A VLSI Implementation of Multi-Layered Neural Networks: 2-Performance

Bernard Faure and Guy Mazaré

IMAG-LGI Groupe Circuits
46 avenue Félix Viallet, 38031 Grenoble cedex, France

Abstract

This paper presents a VLSI cellular array dedicated to the processing of neural networks. Each cell of this array computes the algorithms devoted to a neuron of a back-propagation neural network. Our approach consists in permitting only integer computations and limiting the number of synaptic weights/connections a cell must manage. If necessary, the topology of the neural network is locally changed with the introduction of sub-neurons and so related partially connected sub-layers. These changes in the topology add new degrees of freedom in the weight space and then increase the number of training epochs necessary to obtain a behaviour similar to that of the initial network. In recall mode, a 64 x 64 cellular array runs the NETtalk text-to-speech network 4 times faster than the Warp, a 20 node systolic array which uses a layer-based parallelism, 52 times faster than the Connection-Machine-1 which uses a synaptic parallelism and more than 2600 times faster than a Vax 780 without any parallelism.

INTRODUCTION

One possibility to increase the computing power necessary to neural network computations is to use a parallel machine. In large grain architectures, subsets of the neural network are processed by a single powerful processor. The neural network mapping, which must minimize interprocessor data transfers and take advantage of the parallelism to be efficient, is a hard work and, most of the time, the robustness and fault tolerance features of the neural network are lost because the resulting map has got nothing to do with the initial network topology. The best way to preserve these remarkable features of neural networks is to try keeping the initial network map. The description of neural networks as sets of simple processing units highly interconnected allows us to map them over a parallel fine grain architecture, providing this architecture is able to handle high connection rates. The one-neuron-per-processor association, which first comes in mind, allows the use of a cascadable architecture of identical processors.

Such an architecture can be composed of a large bidimensional array of processors which are reduced to simple automata, called cells, performing the simple algorithms of a neuron : both,recall and back-propagation learning. To avoid the handling of a huge number of physical links, we propose a communication system based on message transfers between processors enabling the logical connection between a given cell and potentially any other cell in the array without the need for global information. The messages are passed from one cell to one of its neighbours until they reach their destinations ; their paths are set dynamically by each passed-through cell. The cells are fully asynchronous and each of them is physically linked to its four immediate neighbours through buffers that allow the parallel transmission of the messages.

Back-propagation neural networks, described by Rumelhart et al (1986), Lipmann (1987) and Le Cun (1987) as sets of neurons arranged in layers of different sizes, with only inter-layer connections most of the time, lead to a disorganized parallelism that can be efficiently handled by this cellular array and its communication system.

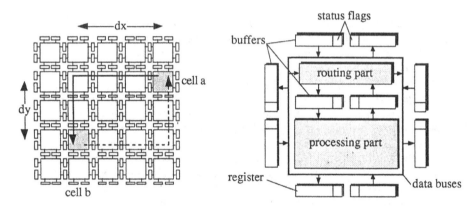

Figure 1 The cellular array   **Figure 2** The cell functional diagram

THE CELLULAR ARCHITECTURE

The proposed architecture consists of a N x M array of asynchronous cells, all identical. Each cell performs a simple local function and is physically connected to its four immediate neighbours through 8 parallel unidirectional buffers, one for each way of the four directions. The ability for each cell to be logically connected to any other cell of the array and to the outside world is handled by a parallel message transmission mechanism distributed among the cells. Figure 1 sketches a 5 x 5 array : the plain arrow highlights the path followed by a message emitted by the cell a to the cell b while the dotted arrow shows the path for a message emitted by the cell b to the cell a.

An important feature of this array is that it is dedicated to fit a particular application : the elementary cell can have the minimum silicon surface for a given task. The cell performs two concurrent tasks and thus is divided in two asynchronous hardware parts : *the routing part,* dedicated to the message transmission, which reads a message from an input buffer, selects an output buffer according to the destination of the message, updates its routing field and stores the new message in the selected output buffer if empty, otherwise, it holds the message in its input buffer and selects another input ; *the processing part* which emulates the neuron, that is, processes both the recall and the back-propagation learning algorithms (Figure 2).

The status flag included in each inter-cell buffer is a flip-flop mechanism that disables the two cells sharing this buffer from acceding it concurrently and then destroying the message stored in its register. The processing and the routing parts of the cell communicate between themselves through two unidirectional buffers that behave as the 8 external inter-cell ones.

To be handled by the communication system, a message must hold a data field containing the information necessary to the processing parts of the cells in order to compute the application mapped on the array : a value (e.g. the activation of a neuron) plus 4 control bits indicating the type of the value carried (e.g. neuron activation, gradient or initial weight) and a routing field containing information needed by the array for the proper transmission of the message : the relative displacement dx and dy from the current to the destination cell (Figure 3).

routing field   data field

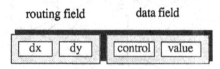

Figure 3. The message structure

This relative displacement fully describes the path followed by the message (figure 1). If dx is positive (resp. negative), the message is passed eastward (resp. westward) along the X axis and dx is decremented (resp. incremented) by 1 until it becomes null. When dx is null, the message is passed along the Y axis. If dy is positive (resp. negative), the message is passed southward (resp. northward) and dy is decremented (resp. incremented) by 1 until it becomes null. When both dx and dy are null, the message has reached its destination cell can be passed to the processing part. This communication policy allows a better use of the peripheral cells by draining the excess of messages off the cells located at the center of the array.

THE ALGORITHMS IMPLEMENTED IN THE CELL

In such a fine grain architecture that can be composed of thousands of elementary processing units, the compromise surface versus time is critical. Due to the high number of computations that have to be done, we must simplify the functions used, limit the data path width and decrease the memory requirements at the lowest level possible (Faure and Mazaré 1989).

How a cell emulates a neuron

The processing part of a cell performs the computations of the neuron in a different order from the standard series : it sums the weighted incoming inputs, computes its activation and outputs a weighted activation on each downstream path during the recall phase. During the learning phase, the cell updates each weight of the downstream links with its related incoming gradient, weights and sums the incoming gradients, computes and outputs its own local gradient on each upstream link. This new order in the series of computations is equivalent to the standard model of the neuron if, on the one hand, we consider that the cell generates the activation of a neuron n in the layer j and weights the inputs of all the neurons m in the layer j+1 it is linked to and if, on the other hand, we set the value of the weights of the neurons in the output layer to 1 and disable their updating (figure 4). This allows the immediate processing of any incoming message (the sum is updated as soon as an input message is present) and introduces an important output delay (necessary for the multiplication of the weight by the activation). While the processing part weights the neuron activation, once the routing part has cleared its output buffer, the other cells can transmit its previous output message.

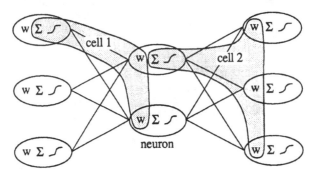

Figure 4 Two cells and their assigned neurons

We have suppressed the second order momentum in the weight update, we use a linearly interpolated transfer function, its derivative is computed from the linear interpolation. The absolute values of all the data handled by the processing part of a cell range from 2^1 to $2^{-(n-2)}$, n being the resolution of a cell, $n \geq 16$ bits (see below).

The effects of the limited connectivity

We have simulated the cellular array and the neural networks mapped on it for evaluating the minimum number of connections a cell could support without changing too much the behaviour of the neural networks. Because each cell/neuron stores the addresses of all the cells/neurons it is logically connected to, we have studied the mapping of the different neural networks on different arrays of cells which have a connectivity (that is a fan-in and a fan-out) of 2, 4, 8, 16, 32 and 64 in order to obtain the best compromise time versus surface.

Because of the linear interpolation of the transfer function and the absence of the second order momentum, the neural network may not support the round-off errors generated by the spreading of a neuron over more that one cell if the input sub-trees only evaluate a partial weighted sum of the inputs (as suggested in Faure and Mazaré 1989). The weight update value can be completely suppressed or if that weight update value is set to the lowest value that can be carried by the precision, the high oscillation rate introduced prevents any learning.

In order to bypass the limited connectivity, we introduce partially connected sub-layers in the initial topology (that is adds more degrees of freedom in the neural network weight space) by assigning a complete sub-neuron with its own non linear transfer function and its own weights to each cell in the input and output sub-trees that are necessary to implement a neuron of the initial network. To perform this task, we have developed a mapping program that, given an initial neural network topology, creates automatically an augmented network map for a given cell connectivity. It uses a simulated annealing algorithm that tries to balance the load and assign the i/o units to the cells at the periphery of the array. Its creates 4 files of initialization messages for the cells to which the neural units have to be assigned with information on their effective connectivity, their initial weights, the addresses of the cells they are logically connected to... During the initialization phase, the messages of the 4 files are sent concurrently to the peripheral buffers of the 4 edges of the array and are carried by the communication system to their destination cells. This initialization by message transfers can be an easy way to alter the structure of the mapped neural network during its life : we can deassign cells and/or connections, add cells and/or connections without initializing the whole array.

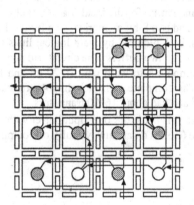

Figure 5 A map of the "xor" net   **Figure 6** A map of the "patt" net

Figure 5 shows one of the maps automatically created for the exclusive-or network (a 3-layered network with 2 units in the input layer, 2 in the hidden layer and 1 in the output layer) by this program for an array of cells which connectivity is 2 (each processing part can have a maximum of 2 inputs and 2 outputs). The bias unit is changed into the 3 white cells/neurons of figure 5. The 3 threshold weights are now 4 : the 3 original ones plus the input weight for the created neuron. If the original weights are w_1, w_2 and w_3, the new ones w'_1, w'_2, w'_3 and w'_4 and f a non linear function, we have :

$$w_1 = w'_1, \quad w_2 = f(w'_2, w'_4) \quad \text{and} \quad w_3 = f(w'_3, w'_4)$$

Figure 6 shows one of the maps automatically created for the character pattern recognition network (a 3-layered network with 25 units in the input layer, 60 in the hidden layer and 25 in the output layer, studied by Wang in 1989) by this program for an array of cells which connectivity is 8. A square represents a cell of the array, a dark point represents a mapped neuron (an assigned cell), the gray-scaled pattern of a particular square represents the load of the routing part : the darker the square, the more messages it has to handle.

THE DESIGN OF THE CELL

The CMOS layout of the routing part has been designed by Karabernou (1989). It allows up to 4 message transfers in parallel with a 40 ns delay from buffer to buffer, at a clock speed up to 20 MHz. This routing part is made of 4 buses, 4 input buffers augmented with 4 copies of a small circuitry that allocates the buses, updates the routing field of the message, clears the status flag of its input buffers and sets the one of its output buffers. The resulting circuit had less than 7000 transistors and was 9 mm^2 ; the buffers could store messages with 8 bits of data, 4 control bits and a routing field of 8 bits for both dx and dy (that is an addressing range of 16 x 16 cells). The flexibility of the design allows us to parametrize this routing part and generate rapidly a new layout for any size of any field of the message.

Concurrently, Mhiri (1989) has also designed a simplified version of the processing part. All the data being 8-bit twos complement integers, it was reduced to a twos complement 11 bits adder (multiplications were performed by additions and shifts) for the handling of round-off errors since we wanted the 8 bits of data to be correct, had two 8-bit memories : one for the 16 (dx, dy) pairs and another for the 8 synaptic weights, both required by the 8 logical links it handled. The i/o interface to the routing part was reduced to two buffers. The circuit had about 9000 transistors for a surface of 16 mm^2, could compute a forward pass in 29 μs and a backward pass in 55 μs at a 10 MHz clock speed. The complete cell, including 4 external buffers, the processing and routing parts, was 25 mm^2 and had about 16000 transistors.

Figure 7 shows the data path of the processing part. It is made of : one input buffer with a status flag that only stores the data field of the message (dx and dy are always null), one output

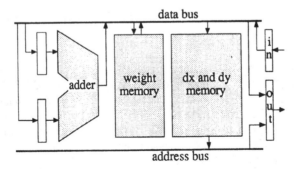

Figure 7 The data path of the processing part

buffer with a status flag that stores the data and routing fields of the message, a memory of 8 words storing the synaptic weights, a memory of 16 words for storing the values of dx and dy for the downstream and upstream connected cells, a twos complement integer adder and one extended accumulator for the multiplication.

THE PERFORMANCES OF THE ARRAY

We have simulated the behaviour of the cellular array for the Exclusive-or ("xor" : a 2-2-1 units, 3 layers network), Little Red Riding Hood ("lrrh" : a 6-3-7 units, 3 layers network, introduced by Jones and Hoskins in 1987), numeral pattern classification ("num" : a 45-9 units, 2 layers network which, given a 9 x 5 pixel image of a numeral, outputs its decimal value in a 1 out of 10 coding), character pattern classification ("char" : a 45-26 units, 2 layers network which, given a 9 x 5 pixel image of a character, outputs its value in a 1 out of 26 coding) and Character pattern recognition ("patt" : a 25-60-25 units, 3 layers network which, given a 5 x 5 pixel image of a character, outputs a 5 x 5 pixel image of the recognized prototype). NETtalk (a 203-60-26 units, 3 layers network), introduced by Sejnowski and Rosenberg (1987), was only tested for speed purposes but not for the accuracy of the memorization process. The initial neural networks were preprocessed, that is augmented if necessary (depending on the connectivity of a cell), and mapped on the array by the mapping program which also generates the initial random weights. The results presented in this section are compiled from 5 simulations of each neural network for every cell connectivity.

Memorization of the training set

The effects of the restrictions of the VLSI implementation - low precision and low connectivity - were functionally simulated with Occam on a Transputer-based system and with Pascal on a Vax 6310 for different arrays of cells having a maximum connectivity of 2, 4, 8, 16, 32, 64 and without any connectivity limit. We have compared the 16-bit precision-limited integer computations against the 32-bit floating point computations. The augmented networks emulated by the cellular array can memorize all the presented patterns most of the time.

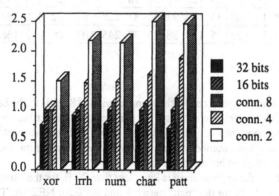

Figure 8 Relative number of learning epochs

Figure 8 shows for each tested example the times factor of the number of learning epochs needed to store all the patterns of the training set (related to an unchanged topology with 16-bit precision-limited integer computations) for 32-bit floating point (32 bits) and 16-bit precision-limited integer (16 bits) computations and for augmented networks mapped on precision-limited cells with a connectivity limited to 8, 4 and 2 (resp. conn. 8, conn. 4 and conn. 2).

Unrestricted 32-bit floating-point computations (with a true sigmoid transfer function) require between 20 and 35 % less epochs than precision-limited ones. The overhead introduced by the creation of sub-layers is around 10 % for all the examples mapped on cells whose maximum connectivity is 8 and smaller for higher connectivities. For all the examples but the exclusive-or mapped on the cellular array, given a cell has a maximum allowed connectivity of 2, the learning process requires between 2.2 and 2.5 times more epochs. The number of added learning steps depends on the initial neural network topology (wide layers demand more learning steps) and on the effectively mapped topology : the more the sub-layers introduced, the more the learning steps.

Speed

During the simulations, we have assumed that a cell is able to transmit a message in 40 ns from any input buffer to any output buffer (Karabernou 1989) and that the messages are processed by the outside world at the array speed. Table 1 shows from left to right, for each neural network, the times in μs taken for loading the network map onto the array, recalling one pattern and learning one pattern. Vertically is the connectivity of the considered cell.

Table 1 Loading, recall and learning times in μs

	xor			lrrh			num			char			patt			NETtalk		
2	3	3	40	7	5	100	23	5	101	34	7	306	53	19	883	not simulated		
4	3	3	21	6	6	58	18	5	56	29	7	75	45	17	547	96	91	1630
8	3	3	22	11	10	56	23	11	65	33	11	74	47	23	189	99	41	269
16	3	3	24	7	10	51	23	12	82	39	18	118	51	34	324	142	51	356
32	3	4	26	8	11	65	33	17	92	56	31	228	81	52	405	186	84	512
64	3	4	27	7	15	57	15	18	98	15	37	245	103	100	602	166	191	1498

In table 1, we can notice that a cell with a connectivity of 8 leads to the best performances most of the time. With a lower connectivity, the parallelism is larger but the communication times become more important than the processing times. A higher connectivity lowers the parallelism and decreases the number of message paths : much more messages use the same paths which introduces high transmission delays.

The recall activity of the cellular array is low : less than 20 % for the "num" network, 25 % for the "char" network, 15 % for the "patt" network and 10 % for NETtalk. The performances can be improved by forcing each cell to send acknowledgement messages to its connected cells in the upstream layer. This allows the possible pipe-lining of multiple pattern recalls. The recall activity of the cellular array averaged over all the examples which was 17.4 % can be almost doubled to 29 % with the introduction of acknowledgement messages. The simulations have shown that there is no need for an efficient mapping : see Faure and Mazaré (1990).

COMPARISONS WITH OTHER APPROACHES

To be run, NETtalk requires a 167 x 167, 97 x 97, 65 x 65 or 59 x 59 array with respectively 27800, 9317, 4175 and 2112 cells assigned to neurons, depending on the connectivity of the basic cell used to build the array : 2, 4, 8 and 16 respectively (Faure and Mazaré 1990).

The performances obtained for NETtalk can be compared with those of other machines (Pomerleau et al. 1988). The 65 x 65 array of cell with a connectivity of 8, 4175 of which are neural units, rated at 335.6 MCPS in recall mode (Millions of Connections Per Second), is more than 3 times faster than the Connection Machine 2 (104 MCPS), 4 times faster than the 20 nodes Warp (80.0 MCPS), 12 times faster than Saic's Delta Board and HNC's Anza-Plus simulator (27.5 MCPS), 52 times faster than the Connection Machine 1 (6.5 MCPS with one synapse per node) and more than 2600 times faster than a Vax 780 (0.125 MCPS).

The same array, rated at 51.5 MCUPS in learning mode (Millions of Connection Updates Per Second), is a little bit faster than the CM-2 (40 MCUPS), nearly twice faster than the Warp (32 MCUPS), 20 times faster than the CM-1 (2.6 MCUPS), 5 times faster than Delta and Anza-Plus (11 MCUPS) and more than 1000 times faster than a Vax 780 (0.05 MCUPS). This learning speed must be handled with caution : the learning trials are not equivalent, our cellular array may require more trials (sometimes up to 2.5 times more) than the other machines in order to obtain a configuration of weights that gives the neural network a similar behaviour.

CONCLUSION AND FUTURE WORK

The work described herein is part of a larger project : *a massively parallel asynchronous cellular array*. Our research team has already studied and designed dedicated cells for logical simulation (Objois et al. 1988) and image reconstruction (Lattard et al. 1990). We are now studying how to process data flow graphs (Payan 1990) and developing a general purpose parallel accelerator based on the idea of this cellular architecture (Rubini et al 1990). The processing part of each cell is composed of one 8-bit processor and 256 bytes of memory. We plan to produce a one-cell chip with a routing part able to address 64 cells in each of the four directions (8 bits for both dx and dy), which we will assemble in a small array.

Some simulations that have been done for this accelerator show it can simulate the neural network applications presented in this paper with an average activity more than twice the best activity obtained with the application specific accelerator, but at a speed 10 times slower. This indicates that the specificity of the cell is an important factor for the fine grain parallelism to be efficient in time critical applications such as neural networks. However, a general purpose accelerator is more cost effective for a small research team and more useful for the study of a wide range of distributed algorithms.

REFERENCES

Faure, B. and Mazaré, G., "A VLSI implementation of multi-layered neural networks", in *VLSI for Artificial Intelligence*, J. Delgado-Frias and W. Moore, Eds., Kluwer, 1989.

Faure, B. and Mazaré, G., "A VLSI asynchronous cellular architecture for neural computing : functional definition and performance evaluation", *3rd International Conference on Industrial and Engineering Applications of Artificial Intelligence and Expert Systems*, Charleston, South Carolina, pp. 838-847, July 1990.

Jones, W. P. and Hoskins, J., "Back-propagation : a generalized delta learning rule", *BYTE Magazine*, vol. 12, n°.10, pp. 155-162, 1987.

Karabernou, M., "Etude et réalisation d'un mécanisme d'acheminement de messages dans un réseau cellulaire", DEA de microélectronique, Université de Grenoble, France, June 1988.

Lattard, D., Faure, B. and Mazaré, G., "Massively parallel architecture : application to neural net emulation and image reconstruction", *Application Specific Array Processors*, S.-Y. Kung, E. E. Swartzlander Jr., J. A. B. Fortes and K. Wojtek Przytula, Eds., IEEE Computer Society Press, 1990.

Le Cun, Y., "Modèles connexionistes de l'apprentissage", Thèse d'informatique, Université de Paris 6, France, June 1987.

Lipmann, R. P., "An introduction to computing with neural nets", *IEEE ASSP Magazine*, n° 4, pp. 4-22, April 1987.

Mhiri, M., "Réalisation de la partie traitement d'un réseau cellulaire asynchrone pour une application de réseaux de neurones", DEA de microélectronique de l'INPG, Grenoble, France, June 1989.

Objois, P., Ansade Y., Cornu-Emieux, R. and Mazaré, G., "Highly parallel logic simulation accelerators based upon distributed discrete-event simulation", in *Hardware Accelerators for Electrical CAD*, T. Ambler, P. Agrawal and W. Moore, Eds., Adam Hilger, 1988.

Payan, E. and Mazaré, G., "Programmable highly parallel architecture : functional definition and performance evaluation", in *Parallel Processing in Neural Systems and Computers*, R. Eckmiller, G. Hartmann and G. Hauske, Eds., North-Holland, 1990.

Pomerleau, D. A., Gusciora, G. L., Touretzsky, D. S. and Kung, H. T., "Neural network simulation at Warp speed : how we got 17 million connections per second", *IEEE International Conference on Neural Networks*, vol. 2, pp. 143-150, San Diego, California, July 1988.

Rubini, P., Karabernou, S. M., Payan, E. and Mazaré, G., "A network with small general processing units for fine grain parallelism", *International Workshop on Algorithms and Parallel VLSI Architectures*, Pont-à-Mousson, France, pp. 197-200, June 1990.

Rumelhart, D. E., Hinton, G. E. and Williams, R. J., "Learning internal representations by error propagation", in *Parallel Distributed Processing : Explorations in the Microstructure of Cognition, Volume 1 : Foundations*, D. E. Rumelhart and J. L. McClelland, Eds., MIT Press, 1986.

Sejnowski, T. J. and Rosenberg, C. R., "Parallel networks that learn to pronounce English text", *Complex Systems*, n° 1, pp. 145-168, 1987.

Wang, S., "Réseaux multicouches de neurones artificiels : algorithmes d'apprentissage, implantations sur hypercube, applications", Thèse d'informatique de l'INPG, Grenoble, France, September 1989.

5.4 Efficient Implementation of Massive Neural Networks

James Austin, Tom Jackson and Alan Wood

Advanced Computer Architecture Group
Department of Computer Science
University of York, YO1 5DD, UK

Abstract

This paper discusses the issues relating to the implementation of massive neural networks. The discussion is placed in the context of applications for an uncertain reasoning system based on neural networks and applications in computer vision. It is shown how a binary neural network, ADAM, may be used to implement scalable architectures that manage the resources of the system efficiently. It is shown how systems that do not totally integrate all functions, but use standard components may result in more effective implementations.

INTRODUCTION

Current research on the implementation of neural networks by dedicated hardware places its emphasis on networks with continuous weights, and on systems of multiple layers of units (MLN) typically incorporating back error propagation learning algorithms (Rumelhart 1986). While the long term success of such endeavours is likely, the implementation problems to be faced in the short term relate both to the computation taking place in each neuron and the learning algorithm used. Because the weights are continuous in MLNs it is necessary both to store these weights, and to provide some means of performing the weighted sum of the inputs. This raises the need for the implementation of multipliers which, typically, in digital form are large with respect to the rest of the circuit. This leads to problems with the integration of large neural networks in VLSI (Mead 1989).

The problems involved in providing feed-forward computation in multi-layer networks are small compared with those involved in a dedicated implementation of back-propagation learning. These problems lead many people to ignore the implementation of this aspect of the network's performance which, unfortunately, is one of the most time consuming processes in network operation. This results in systems which cannot be used, for example, in applications that require real time adaptive performance. This paper considers the implementation of very large neural networks, and concentrates on the use of a neural network, ADAM, that incorporates binary weights and simple learning rules, thus overcoming the problems above.

VLSI for Artificial Intelligence and Neural Networks, Edited by J.G. Delgado-Frias and
W.R. Moore, Plenum Press, New York, 1991

The paper discusses why very large neural networks are required in real world problems. In particular the focus of our work is in the implementation of reasoning systems which operate on uncertain data. A generic project, Architectures for Uncertain ReAsoning (AURA), is investigating the architectures of such systems. Our initial application domain is the development of systems which may be used in visual scene understanding.

The first part of the paper discusses the need for very large neural networks; it then discusses how the problems are being solved by the use of the ADAM network. A number of different implementations are then discussed.

MOTIVATION

The need for neural networks with a large number of units is present in a number of application domains. An ideal application area for neural networks is Computer Vision. Consider problems where the whole image is to be recognized directly by a neural network, for example, in face recognition for passports. This would typically require large numbers of inputs to a network which, in turn, may be used to classify many thousands of faces. If orientation and scale invariance is required one approach is to train many views of the example patterns (Austin 1989a) again raising the need for large networks. In general scene analysis many different networks will be required for different levels of processing (Austin 1987), giving rise to the possibility of many large networks.

Underlying our interest in applying neural networks to scene analysis and image processing is their use in dealing with highly uncertain data. Computer vision problems typically need to handle uncertainty, either at the initial stages of processing (unreliable edge detectors) or at higher levels involved in object matching. This is not the only domain where efficient techniques are needed for dealing with uncertain data, one highly beneficial area is in safety critical systems, where reliable methods for dealing with uncertain data related to plant monitoring and control would be required.

To meet this need we are developing architectures for uncertain reasoning (AURA). We hope to define a generic architecture which is applicable in a wide variety of domains, a particular emphasis is on systems that can support some level of guaranteed performance. This and other issues are discussed below, but when considering neural network based architectures the following issues are of importance:

1   Providing scalable solutions.

2   Providing reliable and predictable solutions.

3   Providing systems that are cost effective and manage resources efficiently.

The AURA Approach

The AURA project (Austin et al 1990) involves the use of neural associative memories to process and reason on uncertain data. The approach has similarities with the approach taken by Hinton (Hinton 1981) for the implementation of semantic networks. However, at the time Hinton's work was carried out when networks which could learn to classify non-linearly separable problems were not available. In addition, no consideration was given to applying associative memory techniques for uncertain reasoning.

The AURA approach is basically rule-based, using the associative memory to map pre-conditions onto post-conditions. An essential aspect is that the data is represented as patterns in order to exploit the ability of neural-based associative memories to do partial pattern match. By expressing data as patterns, the uncertainty in the responses from the network and in the data presented to the network is exhibited in the corruption of patterns that otherwise represent certain data. This corruption is typically expressed as a mixture of a number of possible patterns when the system is not certain which is correct and as corruption of a single pattern when the system is not confident of any single response. For example, if the system were absolutely sure of a fact A, then the pattern used to store this fact would be clearly represented. Any uncertainty in A would be represented as a corruption of this pattern.

The optimal representation of the data A in a pattern is the centre of the study of how these systems will perform. Any data presented to the system must be efficiently mapped to a pattern-based representation. This raises the need for a pre-processing system in any implementation of such a system, its role being to perform this mapping.

In practice each piece of information presented to the associative memory is combined into a 'knowledge frame'. This frame has separate pattern slots that hold patterns arising from different sources. Their position indicates a semantic category for the data. For example the two categories for representing a red ball would be shape and colour, this would be given different slots in the knowledge frame on the input to the memory, as shown in figure 1.

Figure 1 Example of a knowledge frame for 'red ball'

The function of the associative memory is to recognise the patterns within the frames as pre-conditions of rules stored in the memory. The essential feature of the memory is that it is capable of performing a partial match on the input fields. On finding the closest match the memory outputs the post-condition of this which is stored in the memory. This is the basic form of the system which is currently under study at York (Jackson 1989, Beale et al 1990). It is clear that this approach raises a number of interesting possibilities which are under investigation. This work and the need to implement techniques for image processing (Austin 1989b) has led us to investigate efficient architectures for the implementation of neural networks.

The type of network we require must be scalable to allow us to apply the system to real-world problems. In practice it is likely that a large number of knowledge fields and associations will be required. Training of the network must be rapid to allow the system to be used in a development environment. Typically a user of such a system would not want to wait for long periods of time for the system to learn a new rule. For any reasonable application some understanding of the expected performance of the system would be necessary, and almost essential if applied to safety critical applications.

All the considerations above tend to preclude the use of networks which incorporate gradient descent learning. Whenever this is applied, the networks scale badly (slow learning rates), are difficult to analyze and are complex to implement. To overcome these problems our approach exploits a network, ADAM, developed at York over the last few years (Austin and Stonham 1987).

THE ADAM MEMORY

The Advanced Distributed Associative Memory (ADAM), has been under development for some time and has been applied to a variety of classification problems. A full description of its function may be found in (Austin and Stonham 1987) and in (Beale and Jackson 1990). A short review is given here.

The network's principal features are its fast learning rate and its ability to store large numbers of associations efficiently. The memory scales well with a training time which is almost linear in the number of patterns to train. To achieve this the memory uses binary weights within a two stage correlation matrix memory and uses binary Hebbian learning. However, to enable good recognition properties a set of logical decoders are used to pre-process the input data. To enable efficient storage the memory uses a special coding scheme which also allows simple recall.

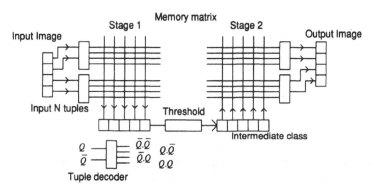

Figure 2 The ADAM memory

The operation of the memory is as follows. As shown in figure 2 the input data (binary in the above example, but which may be generalised to non-binary inputs (Austin 1988a)) is fed to a set of logical decoders. These apply a simple binary decoding to the tuples of size N fed from the input array. The form of mapping from the input array to the decoders effects the operation of the system and is covered in more detail below. The decoders partially ortho-gonalise the input pattern to enable the use of a linear classifier to be successful on non-linearly separable problems. The classification is achieved using simple correlation matrix memories with binary weights and functions in exactly the same way as the Willshaw network (Willshaw 1969) except in how the stored patterns are thresholded during recall. The memory acts as a two layer network with the pattern to be recalled being placed on the output of the second memory. The first layer of units are forced to take on a pattern made up of K points set to one for every new association presented. This allows successful recall by thresholding this layer of outputs to recover exactly K elements set to one (K-point thresholding). This is then passed to the second memory that uses a threshold set to K to recover the stored associated pattern. Because both training and recall requires only a single presentation of the input pattern, it is very rapid.

Implementation in hardware can take a number of forms as will be discussed later. However, it will be clear that the input decoders and the binary memory are effectively a random access memory. Thus, implementation can be very simple. The addition of dedicated summing units and a thresholding unit is all that is needed to complete the implementation. However, due to paging problems implementation is not as simple in practice.

The analysis of the performance of the network has been achieved due to the simplifying nature of the K-point coding and the use of N-tuple sampling. The classification abilities draw on other work which has analyzed the performance of N-tuple based classification systems which allow the prediction of recognition success. Other work has enabled the prediction of the number of patterns that can be stored by the network (Austin and Stonham 1987). Currently, work is in progress studying the fault tolerant properties of the network.

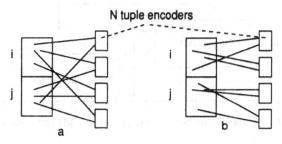

Figure 3 Mapping of knowledge fields on to N-tuples

The Relationship between ADAM and AURA

We intend to fully exploit ADAM for reasoning on uncertain data as discussed above. An important factor in this case is the use of the N-tuple decoders that pre-process the data. When the network is applied to knowledge frames the decoders are able to perform logical OR and AND functions between the different fields. Furthermore, the careful mapping of the input lines to the decoders provide varying degrees of coupling between the knowledge fields. For example figure 3a shows how the N-tuple groups must be mapped to provide a strong coupling between the knowledge fields, the grouping shown in figure 3b shows a weak coupling between the fields. In effect the former performs an AND function between the fields the latter performs an OR function. This provides the capability to implement complex but necessary relations between the knowledge fields. Furthermore, the effect has important consequences for the way weights are paged in to the memory in implementations of the system. It is interesting to note that the coupling between fields need not be a complete AND function - partial coupling is possible allowing varying degrees of interdependence between the categories represented by each field. These effects are not the issue of this paper and will not be developed further here.

IMPLEMENTATIONS

The section above has described why there is a need for large neural networks and how we propose to exploit the ADAM network in architectures for uncertain reasoning. The remaining part of this paper explores the difficulties that arise in the implementation of very large networks. The first part considers the general architectural features of the AURA system, then the problem of dealing with large numbers of weights is discussed. A number of implementation strategies currently under development are then discussed.

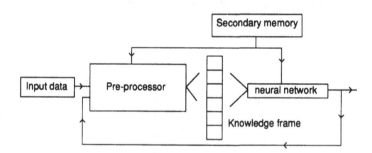

Figure 4 The relationship between pre-processor and neural network.

Architectural Considerations

In both the applications in computer vision and those in uncertain reasoning it is clear that some form of pre-processing of the data is required before the data is presented to the neural network. In any consideration of a dedicated implementation of a system to undertake both applications this must be taken into account. In the present work it is likely that large amounts of data will be passed to the neural network after pre-processing. This raises the need for a tightly coupled front-end processor which does not restrict the flow of information between the pre-processor and the neural network engine.

A high level form of the system is shown in figure 4. The exact architecture depends strongly upon what pre-processing is needed. In image processing this is likely to be operations such as normalization, skeletonisation and erosion etc. In knowledge processing it will be required to map textual inputs onto pattern-based representations. In the former case we are considering a CLIP style of architecture (Wood 1980). The SIMD architecture would provide high performance with excellent communication band-width between the two stages. In addition, the Clip architecture has been used to process relational structures (Wood 1986), making extensive use of its global propagation properties (Wood 1988). It is thus expected that an extension of these concepts will provide an additional knowledge processing capability outside the domain of image processing. Currently we are investigating the front-end architectures via transputer simulation studies. The work on the back-end neural network is discussed in the following sections.

MEMORY PAGING

A successful implementation of a neural network must consider how that network is to be used. The above description has shown what features are need for our application. For example, the application will involve any user of the system in a comparative study of different network configurations for different tasks. This will involve large amounts of loading and re-loading of the network memory and tuple mapping functions. It is also highly likely that the size of any cost effective dedicated network will be smaller than the requirements of some users. To allow large implementations to be cost effective it is likely that the resource will be shared among a number of users. These requirements imply the need for some method for efficiently paging network memories, in a similar fashion to that used in many conventional computer systems.

The architectures of many dedicated neural network implementations make the process of weight memory paging difficult to achieve. This arises because the memory and processing in neural networks are distributed, losing the address-based memory space. Without this, multi-level memory hierarchies involving caches, paging and segmentation cannot be used. It now becomes difficult to identify when a new page of data should be brought in from secondary memory. This ultimately leads to expensive and inefficient solutions to flexible neural network systems. The ways in which ADAM allows such an implementation to be efficiently achieved will now be discussed.

Paging in ADAM

ADAM resolves many of the problems discussed above by using conventional memories to implement the weight storage. This allows the output of the decoders to feed directly into a memory hierarchy consisting of caches, MMU's etc. However, a major problem with this arrangement is the memory access pattern that arises in any application of ADAM. Unfortunately, due to the way addresses are sampled over the input fields there is no 'working set' developed by the system. Access to memory covers the whole space attached to the knowledge fields via the tuple function. Any cache implementation would have a very low hit rate. This aspect also raises doubts about the possibility of an efficient implementation in a conventional processor that employs data caching. This results in the need for a simpler architecture, which contains no hard-wired cache system. An architecture that maximises the band-width between the network weight memory and the secondary storage is preferable. The way to achieve this is by employing memory interleaving systems.

Currently we are investigating an efficient implementation of ADAM in order to identify where integration would be useful, and to provide an initial accelerator for our simulators. The basic architecture of this is shown in figure 5. In this we have implemented a simple 2-way memory interleave. We are developing dedicated summing and thresholding functions to allow data to be directly summed and subsequently thresholded from the memory without the intervention of the processor. Our initial simulations have shown this to be the main bottleneck in the recall process of the system. The processor will mainly be involved in data passing, however, for a non-binary input pattern this will be used to perform grey scale N-tuple processing (Austin 1988b).

This sub-system is designed to run in parallel with others. Our immediate aim is to couple it to a VME bus and provide front-end processing from another processor on this bus.

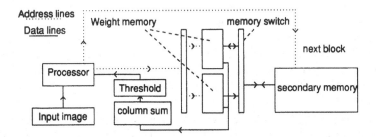

Figure 5 Implementation of a complete processor

Compiled ADAM

The above scheme is designed to implement an AURA system that can achieve high speed recall and training of the ADAM network. The architecture has resulted from a view of ADAM that considers separate N-tuple decoders and correlation matrix memories. However, an alternative view of ADAM taken at the conceptual level leads to a completely different instantiation in hardware. Because ADAM uses binary weights and logical decoders, once trained it can be seen to be evaluating a large number of Boolean expressions. Consider the simple example in figure 6.

The trained network evaluates the Boolean expressions $A = Q_0.\bar{Q}_1 + \bar{Q}_2.Q_3$ and $B = \bar{Q}_0.Q_1 + Q_2.\bar{Q}_3$. The expression uses + to represent summation, i.e. the responses of tuples for Q_0 and Q_1 are summed with those for Q_2 and Q_3. It is useful to note that this is a conventional way to view N-tuple processing (Stonham 1985).

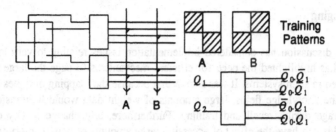

Figure 6 A Trained network as a set of Boolean expressions

This alternative view of a trained network allows us to consider alternative implementations based on approaches that efficiently evaluate large Boolean expressions. In parallel with the work in neural networks a project is involved in developing an architecture, VGLAD, for evaluating very large numbers of boolean expressions at high speed (Austin and Morgan 1989). This device has been used to implement trained memories and has been able to achieve a speed-up of 45× compared to a pure software implementation. This solution achieves an execution of a recall by firing a pre-determined control pattern to VGLAD. Thus network memory evaluation is controlled by the selection of the correct control pattern.

This approach is very similar to many of the current implementations of MLNs where training takes place off the dedicated processor, the weights effectively compiled on a simulator then transferred to the execution device (for example, the Intel 80170 neural network chip (Intel 1990)).

In our system some of the nodes executing neural networks would be implemented on VGLAD, others which require high speed adaptation of weights would exist on the processor based technology. This would provide a balance between speed and flexibility.

VLSI Implementation

Although we are considering an implementation with some functions implemented in dedicated ICs we believe that the size of neural networks we are using and the practical difficulties in implementing efficient paging mechanisms rule out the possibility of total integration. However, it is interesting to note the implementation of the BACHUS network (Goser et al 1989) is very similar to the implementation that could be used to implement ADAM. However, because of the similarity of ADAM to conventional RAM implementations, dedicated ADAM implementations could be produced very easily. This would use the address decoders in the RAM as the N-tuple pre-processing stage, an addition of a set of counters to implement the summing function and a special N-point threshold circuit would produce a custom implementation that could exploit the density of current memories to place many millions of binary neurons on one chip. Training could be achieved by providing a non destructive write to memory lines.

High Level Paging

The foregoing discussion has considered implementation issues relating to very large neural networks and has highlighted the need for efficient mechanisms to page the large number of weights required in such systems. It was shown that because the mapping of tuples is partially random over the knowledge fields, large amounts of weight data would be transferred from secondary storage during recall and training. Furthermore, any change in any one of the knowledge fields can have the effect of accessing large amounts of new memory thus requiring new network memories to be brought in. This effect is highly dependent on the mapping of tuples between the different weight arrays. Earlier it was shown how two tightly coupled knowledge fields would effect each other. Now it will be clear that access to knowledge fields defines which page should be brought in to the weight memory. An efficient paging system in this case knows which knowledge fields are tightly coupled and which are not. If a tightly coupled knowledge field is changed during processing, the weight memories of it and all its coupled knowledge fields will need to be brought in from secondary memory. Thus the data required by such a system can be predicted and resources allocated accordingly.

CONCLUSION

This paper has described how a neural network implementation is being developed for reasoning on uncertain data and for image processing. It has shown how the issues relating to the implementation of massive neural networks are being addressed in the work. Training times are being attacked using a binary neural network with a simple learning rule. Management of the weight memories is being implemented using conventional memories under control of the reasoning system. The paper has shown how it may be possible to provide a novel architecture for the processing of real world problems of realistic size.

REFERENCES

Austin, J. "ADAM: A Distributed Associative Memory For Scene Analysis", pp. IV-285 in *Proceedings of First International Conference on Neural Networks*, ed. M.Caudill, C.Butler, IEEE, San Diego (1987).

Austin, J. "Grey Scale N-tuple Processing", pp. 110-120 in *Pattern Recognition : 4th International Conference, Cambridge, UK*, ed. Josef Kittler, Springer-Verlag, Berlin (1988a).

Austin, J. "Image Pre-processing with a Generalised Grey Scale N Tuple Operator", YCS 102, University of York, UK. (1988b).

Austin, J. "An associative neural architecture for invariant pattern classification.", pp. 196-200 in *Proceedings of first IEE international conference on artificial neural networks, London.*, IEE (1989a).

Austin, J. "High Speed Invariant Pattern Recognition using Adaptive Neural Networks", pp. 28-32 in *Proc. IEE Conf. on Image processing and its applications.* (1989b).

Austin, J. and G. Morgan, "VGLADs : The efficient implementation of binary neural networks", in *Proceedings of Parallel Architectures on Silicon Workshop, Grenoble* (1989).

Austin, J. , T. Jackson and A.M. Wood, "Architectures for Uncertain Reasoning", in *Proceedings of INNC-90 Paris* (July 1990).

Austin, J. and T.J. Stonham, "An Associative Memory for use in Image Recognition and Occlusion Analysis", *Vision and Image Computing* 5(4), pp. 251-261 (1987).

Beale, R. and T. Jackson, *Neural Computing an introduction*, Adam Hilger (1990).

Beale, R. , T. Jackson and J. Austin, "Uncertain Reasoning in Associative Networks : A Conceptual Approach", Advanced Computer Architecture Memo 20 (1990).

Goser, F. et al., "VLSI technologies for artificial neural networks.", *IEEE Micro*, pp. 28-44 (Dec 1989).

Hinton, G. and J.A. Anderson, *Parallel Models of Associative Memory*, Lawrence Erlbaum Associates, Hillsdale, New Jersey (1981).

Intel. *80170NW Electrically trainable analog neural network data sheet*, Intel (1990).

Jackson, T. "Uncertain Reasoning in Neural networks", *ACAG memo19*, Advanced Computer Architecture Group, Department of Computer Science, University of York. (1989).

Mead, C. *Analog VLSI and Neural Systems*, Addison-Wesley (1989).

Rumelhart, D.E. and J.L. McClelland, *Parallel Distributed Processing: Explorations in the Microstructure of Cognition*, MIT Press, Cambridge Mass (1986).

Stonham, J. pp. 231-272 in *Advanced Digital Information Systems*, ed. I. Aleksander, Prentice Hall International (1985).

Willshaw, D.J. , O.P. Buneman and H.C. Longuet-Higgins, "Non-Holographic Associative Memory", *Nature* 222, pp. 960-962, June 7 (1969).

Wood, A.M. "The CLIP4 Array Processor", *J. British Interplanetary Society* 33, pp. 338-344 (1980).

Wood, A.M. "Higher Level Operations using Processor Arrays", pp. 91-105 in *Evaluation of Multicomputers for Image Processing*, ed. L. Uhr, K. Preston Jr., S. Levialdi, M. Duff, Academic Press (1986).

Wood, A.M. "Intermediate-level Vision, Relations and Processor Arrays: An Application of Clip4 to Image Sequence Analysis", pp. 157-170 in *Parallel Architectures and Computer Vision*, ed. I. Page, Oxford University Press (1988).

5.5 Implementing Neural Networks with the Associative String Processor

Anargyros Krikelis

Aspex Microsystems Ltd.
Brunel University
Uxbridge UB8 3PH, United Kingdom

Michael Grözinger

Department of Electrical Engineering and Electronics
Brunel University
Uxbridge UB8 3PH, United Kingdom

Abstract

The rebirth of activity in the area of neural computation is stimulated by the increasing frequency with which traditional computational paradigms appear to inefficiently handle fuzzy problems of large dimensionality (e.g. pattern recognition, associative information retrieval, etc.) and the technological advances. Indeed, with the huge strides in VLSI and WSI technologies and the emergence of electro-optics, massively parallel systems that were unrealisable only a few years ago are coming within reach.

The paper details the efficient implementation of two neural network models (i.e. Hopfield's relaxation model and the back-propagation model) on a massively parallel, programmable, fault-tolerant architecture, the ASP (Associative String Processor), which can efficiently support low-MIMD/high-SIMD and other parallel computation paradigms.

Indeed, the paper describes the mapping of the two neural networks, details the steps required to execute the network computations and reports the performance of the ASP implementations which achieved computational rate of Giga-interconnections/sec (i.e. 10^9 interconnections per sec).

INTRODUCTION

The research reported in this paper is motivated by practical considerations regarding the implementation of ANN (Artificial Neural Networks), one of them being the suspicion of serious problems with the direct implementation of the summing-plus-thresholding and the

VLSI for Artificial Intelligence and Neural Networks, Edited by J.G. Delgado-Frias and
W.R. Moore, Plenum Press, New York, 1991

399

hill-climbing learning procedures that dominate most current work in the field. The paper proposes a massively parallel processing approach to ANNs that bypasses some of the limitations inherent in the continuous analog framework and benefits from the availability of a mature technology.

The ASP (Associative String Processor) architecture (Lea 1988) is proposed as a general purpose parallel computer alternative for the implementation of ANNs. The ASP architecture is based on programmable fault-tolerant massively parallel processing modules which efficiently support low-MIMD/high-SIMD parallel computing system design methods for the rapid development of a broad range of application specific information processing systems (e.g. computer vision, databases, engineering and scientific simulations, etc.).

The ASP architecture provides an exceptionally comprehensive cover of both numeric and symbolic processing by mapping application data structures to a common string representation supporting content-addressing, parallel processing and a dynamically-reconfigurable rich-in-connectivity inter-processor communication network.

The paper details the efficient implementation using the ASP architecture of two very common models of neural networks, i.e. including Hopfield's relaxation model (Hopfield 1982), and the well understood back-propagation model (Jones and Hoskins 1987).

THE HOPFIELD MODEL

Some classes of physical systems have a dynamic behaviour which can be used as an error-correcting content-addressable memory. These systems can be described by a set of coordinates, which represent the point in the state space where the system is at some point in time. In the dynamic behaviour of those systems there are stable points, which can be conceived as the information saved in a content-addressable memory. The system is placed at some point in the state space, which is a distorted part of the desired information, and the system is left on its own until it has settled down at a stable point. Then the information can be read out of the system.

The Hopfield model (Hopfield 1982) is based on this idea, where the model consists of neuron like nodes. Each node can be in one of two states V_i, $V_i = +1$ means maximum firing rate or $V_i = -1$ means not firing. Each node is connected to all other nodes via synaptic weights, which represent the strength of a synaptic interconnection. The state of a node in the model changes when the weighted sum of input signals reaches a value that is below a threshold (new state is -1 *not firing*) or above a threshold (new state is +1 *firing*), where each node operates asynchronously. This can be expressed as follows:

$$
v_j^{t+1} = \begin{cases} +1 & \textit{if } (\sum_i t_{ij} \, v_i^t - \theta_j) \geq 0 \\ -1 & \textit{if } (\sum_i t_{ij} \, v_i^t - \theta_j) < 0 \end{cases}
$$

Information is stored from a set of state patterns S^k, ($k = 1..P$), each state can have the synaptic weights.

Natural parallelism of the Hopfield model

In order to implement the Hopfield net on a parallel computer architecture the natural parallelism in the network structure needs to be worked out. There must be a distinction between the training or storing phase and the retrieval phase in the operation of this content-addressable memory.

During training the values of the synaptic weights are determined, where each state to be stored is multiplied with each of its elements. So the operations are N scalar-vector multiplications per pattern, where N is the number of nodes in the Hopfield net. This is done for each pattern and the result vectors are accumulated in each column of the net, to get the

virtual node with synaptic inter - connections

synaptic inter - connection

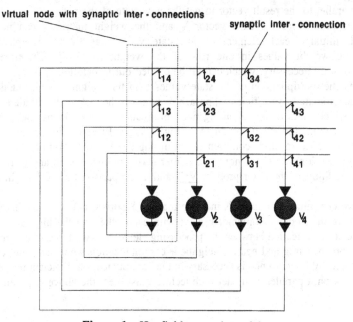

Figure 1. Hopfield network model

value 0 or 1, respectively. Each synaptic weight is calculated using the following expression:

$$t_{ij} = \sum_k (2S_i^k - 1)(2S_j^k - 1)$$

Figure 1 shows a Hopfield net with 4 nodes. The information capacity in the network is limited. If too many states are stored the number of errors in retrieving data increases. A good measure is to keep the number of states below 0.15 times the number of nodes N in the network (Hopfield 1982).

The N scalar-vector multiplications of all elements of a state pattern with the state pattern vector can be performed in parallel. The result of this operations can be conceived as a matrix of intermediate weights. For each state pattern such an intermediate matrix is calculated. In order to get the final weight matrix all transitional matrices are accumulated. The inherent sequential computation in the training of the Hopfield net is that after one set of scalar-vector multiplications for one state pattern the intermediate matrix is added to the previously obtained results. All the elementary scalar additions of one matrix addition can also be computed in parallel.

After training the net can be used as content-addressable memory, where the key information is stored as start state in the nodes of the network. Then the state vector $\underline{V} = [v_1, v_2, .. , v_N]^T$ is multiplied with the weight matrix T. A hard-limiting non-linearity is then applied in parallel to the result vector to get the new state of the net.

The outer product of the state vector $\underline{V}$ and the weight matrix $\underline{T}$ can not be fully parallelised. Initially, each element of the state vector has to be multiplied with its corresponding weight values in one row of the weight matrix $\underline{T}$. Therefore $N*(N-1)$ multiplications are necessary, which can all be carried out in parallel.

Following the multiplication of the state values with the weights, the products in all net nodes are accumulated. An efficient approach to perform the task is the divide and conquer method, in which pairs of neighbouring node products are added in parallel. The method allows the accumulation of all products in $\log_2 N$ steps. Effective implementation of the method requires efficient node communication during the accumulation phase.

The only operations which do not require inter-node communication are a multiplication by +/-1, an addition in the outer product $\underline{V}*\underline{T}$ and a comparison for the hard-limiting non-linearity.

The above computational analysis indicate that the Hopfield net is a very highly parallel network where the nodes communicate a lot with each other, so the highest demands are made on the communication between the processing elements. Two types of communications are needed, broadcasting and nearest neighbour communication with increasing distance. A very high degree of concurrency is necessary in the communication. Efficient implementation of the network on a parallel computer architecture must meet the above requirements.

Computational speed-up by a parallel implementation

A network implementation based on sequential computer architectures requires $N*(N-1)$ multiplications and N-1 additions. In addition, N-1 comparisons are necessary to get the new state of the net. In the parallel implementation only one step for the multiplications and a comparison, respectively, and $\log_2 N$ steps for the divide and conquer approach of the summation are required. However, communication slots are necessary to transfer information between the processing elements storing node information.

According to the above assumptions, it is possible to compare the sequential implementation with the parallel one. The relative speed up S_r can be estimated if the assumption is made that each operation takes the time t_p. The following expression can be derived:

$$S_r = \frac{T_{Seq}}{T_{Par} + T_{Comm}} = \frac{2N(N-1) + N}{2N + \log_2 N + T_{Comm}}$$

Mapping the model on the ASP

Initially, the above described natural parallelism needs to be mapped on the applied parallelism of the ASP. Since the ASP is a fine-grain massively parallel SIMD architecture each weight of the weight matrix is stored in an APE. For the mapping to have a regular structure the weights in the diagonal, which are all zero, are also stored in an APE. The state of a node can be coded in one bit and is located in the left most of the weight APEs in each segment. Figure 2 shows the schematic mapping of the net in Figure 1 on an ASP substring.

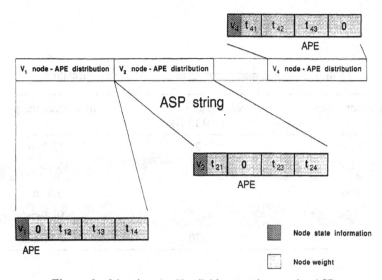

Figure 2. Mapping the Hopfield network onto the ASP

The mapping is chosen such that all weights of a virtual node are located as close as possible to each other. This pays off when all additions in the divide and conquer accumulation can be done in parallel without any conflicts in communication. Broadcasting can be done via the parallel data bus each state at a time. The segment links are to constrain the communications on each virtual processing node, which comprises the weights and a state of an element.

The maximum number of neural elements in the network that is possible in such a mapping is constrained by the size of the data register. It must accommodate the synaptic weight, the sum during the accumulation and some overhead needed during the calculations. The weight field in the data register needs to be wide enough for the maximum value that a weight can have. The same applies to the sum field. From this space needed and the width of the data register it is possible to calculate the maximum number of neural nodes of an implementation on the ASP. For example, a 64-bit Data Register can support a network model with 1800 nodes. If, in this case, more than 1800 nodes are requested one weight node has to be distributed over several APEs, which then form a virtual APE.

Implementing the network on the ASP

This mapping was used to implement the Hopfield net in the ASP programming language, which is basically Modula-2 with special constructs to control the ASP. The implementation was tested on a simulator for the ASP, which reports detailed performance results. The implementation was for 8 nodes. However, it is possible to extrapolate the calculation time

Table 1. Hopfield model storing mode - ASP implementation

Number of nodes N	Number of patterns (< 0.15 N)	Time to store the patterns
16	2	19.3 µs
64	9	250.2 µs
256	38	3.8 ms
1024	153	59.4 ms
1800	270	183.5 ms

to any number of nodes and patterns. It shall be distinguished between training and retrieval phase in the operation of the network. Table 1 shows the time to store a certain number of states in a network with N nodes.

The performance of the ASP in retrieving data shall be expressed in the time to calculate a new set of states and from that and the number of connections in a net the number of interconnections that are calculated per second can be derived. Table 2 illustrates these figures.

The mapping of the Hopfield net can be done very easily and in such a way that the resources the ASP provides, like the processing elements and the interprocessor communication network, are utilised as much as possible.

Table 2. Hopfield model state calculation mode - ASP implementation

Number of nodes N	Number of patterns (< 0.15 N)	Time to calculate a set of states	General performance in interconnections per second
16	2	20.4 μs	$1.25 \ 10^7$
64	9	70.3 μs	$5.81 \ 10^7$
256	38	267.5 μs	$2.4 \ 10^8$
1024	153	1.10 ms	$9.5 \ 10^8$
1800	270	1.98 ms	$1.6 \ 10^9$

THE BACK-PROPAGATION MODEL

A fully connected, three-layer feed-forward (Jones and Hoskins 1987) network containing a total of 137 nodes and 4195 weighted connections. The input domain used is all English alphabet letters which are mapped into a 7-by-9 grid of pixels. As these 63 cells are selected as the input to the net, the first layer, or input layer, contains 63 nodes one per input pixel. Further, an input can only take on the value zero or one corresponding to the cell being off or on, respectively.

The output layer is selected to have 27 nodes, a node for every alphabet letter and a node to indicate no letter recognition. The hidden layer was chosen to be 45 nodes after some experimentation to identify a configuration which provide faster network settling.

While the input nodes can only take on values of zero or one due to input considerations, the values at both the hidden and output nodes are positive 12-bit fixed point numbers (12 bits to the right of the decimal point) and range from 0.0 to 0.999755859. The output node with the largest value is selected as the total net output. If two or more nodes have the same value, they are all selected. Because the net is expected to output a value greater than zero and greater than the smallest non-zero value (i.e 0.00024414), an additional constant-valued node was added to the output layers. The constant-valued node is selected if the value of all other nodes are lees than or equal to it. The node is used to signal an internal network error condition and is not included in the count of 137 total nodes.

Two additional special nodes, one on the input layer and one on the hidden layer, are used in the network model. These are constat-valued nodes, named bias nodes, which supply an offset or bias to the discriminant function at the node layer to which the node connects. These nodes have no input connections but do have weights and connections to the next node layer and for all practical purposes act as just another node on the layer (thus appearing as 64 input nodes and 46 hidden nodes). The value of these nodes is considered to be one (actually 1.0 in input, 0.999755859 on hidden) so that the value of the weights connections are the actual bias for the discriminant function.

The net model used is a fully connected net, i.e. each node on a layers is connected to all nodes (excluding the bias nodes) on the next layer. Attached to each connection is a weight which is multiplied by the node value to provide the value arriving on the connection to the destination node. Weights in the implementation are assigned 16-bit fixed point numbers, ranging from -8.0 to +7.999755859 (4 bits to the left of the decimal points and 12 bits to the right). Following the standard net training techniques, these weights are adjusted to provide a *trained network*. In the used mapping, each weight of zero would map a non-connection.

Back-propagation execution algorithm

The ASP architecture offers massively parallel processing power which is better utilised for the implementation of the back-propagation model if a unique processor cell (i.e. APE) is assigned to each nodal interconnect as well as assigning an APE for each node, thus utilising a total of 4332 APEs.

The network is executed by following the standard feed-forward operations. These processing steps are described below.

If j is a network layer, then the value of a node k of the layer is defined as

$$x_{kj} = f(\sum_{i=1}^{N} w_{ik} * x_{ij-1} - \beta)$$

where f() is the non-linear function of equation (2); N is the number of nodes on the previous level (j-1); w_{ik} is the weight connecting nodes i and k; x_{ij-1} is the value of node i on the previous level; and β is the bias (or value of the weight on the connection from the bias node to node k).

(1) *Set input data in input nodes*. In the execution algorithm this involves thresholding the 8-bit input pixels to values of one and zero and loading the data to APEs designated as input nodes. In training, a fixed input with a known correct output is used.

(2) *Broadcast the input data to the corresponding weights and multiply*. Since there is a separate weight for the connection from each node of the input layer to each hidden node, the input node values are spread across the APEs representing the nodal interconnects of input and hidden layers. The employed scheme enables simultaneous (i.e. parallel) computation of the multiplication in equation (1) for all nodes.

(3) *Accumulate the input values arriving at every hidden node and apply the non-linearity function*. The results from step 2 are summed across all (including the bias) corresponding APEs. All hidden nodes are summed simultaneously in the ASP system. These sums are used in a pseudo sigmoid function (f(x) in equation (2)) to provide the hidden node value. The desired sigmoid function is f(x) = 1/(1 + e^{-x}). But for easy implementation this function was coded as a group of conditionals which simulate the sigmoid function as follows:

(4) *Repeat steps 2 and 3 for the output layer*. Similar computation as in steps 2 and 3 is executed using the values obtained in step 3 for the hidden and output nodes.

(5) *Determine the network output*. The values of all output nodes are compared those with the maximum value are identified. When this node (or nodes) is identified, the letter corresponding to the node becomes the network output.

Back-propagation training algorithm

For the training phase, the implementation algorithm is based on Kohonen's (Jones and Hoskins 1987) heuristic approach, which achieves performance improvement through self-

$$f(x) = \begin{cases} 0.999755859, & \text{if } x \geq 4.0 \\ 0.00024414, & \text{if } x \leq -4.0 \\ \dfrac{2x+17}{16}, & \text{if } 1.0 \leq x \leq 4.0 \\ \dfrac{x+7}{16}, & \text{if } -4.0 \leq x \leq -1.0 \\ \dfrac{2x+5}{4}, & \text{otherwise} \end{cases}$$

organisation.

The back-propagation algorithm involves adjustment of the weights based on the difference between the ideal and the computed (during the execution for a known input) node values. The equation below expresses the required weight adjustment:

$$w_{ij}(t+1) = w_{ij}(t) + \mu * \gamma_j * x_i$$

where w_{ij} is the weight on the connection from a node i to node j on the next layer; μ is a gain term; γ_j is the error term expressed in equations (4) and (5) and x_i is the value of node i.

For the case of the hidden-to-output node level the error term is:

$$\gamma_j = y_j * (1 - y_j) * (d_j - y_j)$$

where y_j is the value of output node j and d_j is the desired value for the output node.

For the input-to-hidden node level:

$$\gamma_j = x_j * (1 - x_j) \sum_k \gamma_k * w_{jk}$$

where k is over all nodes in the layer above node j.

The steps for the execution of the training phase of the back-propagation implementation are detailed below:

(1) *Perform the execution algorithm steps.* The computation, with the exception of the last step, described for the execution phase of the network are performed with input data which produce a known output.

(2) *Compute the error on the output layer.* In an ideal situation the network output value for the known output layer node would be 0.999755859, with all other nodes would hold the value 0.0.

(3) *Broadcast the error and multiply.* The calculated error is broadcasted from the output nodes over hidden node values. The node values are then multiplied by the node value and the gain (μ).

(4) *Modify the weights of the hidden layer.* The weight values are added to the corresponding products from step 3 to produce new weights for the next execution iteration.

(5) *Calculate the error for the hidden layer.* The error value of the output layer is multiplied by the weights and summed for all hidden nodes. This sum is then multiplied with the corresponding hidden node variance.

(6) *Repeat steps 3 and 4 for the input layer.*

Following the above steps the network has had one iteration of training for the given input. Typically many interactions are performed for all possible outputs.

Implementation of the described back-propagation model using ASP simulators indicate a performance of *1.2 * 10^7 interconnection/sec*.

CONCLUSIONS

From the small set of neural computation models reported in this paper it is difficult to state definite conclusions for the suitability and the impact of the ASP in the filed of neural computing.

It is indicative though, considering the demonstrated flexibility of mapping complex neural models, the efficient support of intricate interconnection patterns, its simple scalability and the demonstration of its computational flexibility in other demanding application fields (e.g. computer vision, signal processing and database management) that the ASP appears to be an appropriate vehicle for easy development, testing and demonstration of neural network models. Indeed, its simulated performance of *Giga-interconnections/sec* (i.e. *10^9 interconnections/sec*) signify that the ASP outperforms in many cases other, including dedicated, neural computational systems.

References

Lea, R. M., "The ASP: a cost-effective parallel microcomputer" *IEEE Micro*, pp. 10-29, October 1988,.

Hopfield, J. J. "Neural Networks and Physical Systems with Emergent Collective Computational Abilities", *Proceedings of the National Academy of Science*, USA, Vol. 79, pp. 2554-2558, April 1982.

Jones, W. P. and Hoskins, J., "Back-Propagation", *BYTE*, pp. 155-162, October 1987.

CONTRIBUTORS

T. Ae, *Univ. of Hiroshima (Japan)*
A. Ahmed, *SUNY-Binghamton (USA)*
R. Aibara, *Univ. of Hiroshima (Japan)*
H. Aida, *Univ. of Tokyo (Japan)*
J. Austin, *Univ. of York (UK)*
H. Bacha, *Int. Computer Services (USA)*
D. J. Baxter, *Univ. of Edinburgh (UK)*
J-L. Bechennec, *Univ. Paris-Sud (France)*
E. Belhaire, *Univ. de Paris-Sud (France)*
D. L. Bisset, *Univ. of Kent (UK)*
F. Blayo, *Lausanne (Switzerland)*
M. J. Brownlow, *Univ. of Oxford (UK)*
M. Cannataro, *CRAI (Italy)*
H. Card, *Univ. of Manitoba (Canada)*
C. Chanussot, *Univ. Paris-Sud (France)*
T. Chikayama, *ICOT (Japan)*
S. Churcher, *Univ. of Edinburgh (UK)*
P. L. Civera, *Politecnico di Torino (Italy)*
J. G. Cleary, *Calgary Univ. (Canada)*
W. P. Cockshott, *Strathclyde Univ. (UK)*
R. I. Damper, *Southampton Univ.(UK)*
P. M. Daniell, *Univ. of Kent (UK)*
P. Dasiewicz, *Waterloo Univ. (Canada)*
A. De Gloria, *Univ. of Genoa (Italy)*
P. De Wilde, *Imperial College (UK)*
J. Delgado-Frias, *SUNY Binghamton (USA)*
M. DeYong, *New Mexico State Univ (USA)*
F. Distante, *Polytechnic of Milan (Italy)*
D. Etiemble, *Univ. de Paris-Sud (France)*
P. Faraboschi, *Univ. of Genoa (Italy)*
B. Faure, *IMAG (France)*
C. Fields, *New Mexico State Univ. (USA)*
R. Findley, *New Mexico State Univ. (USA)*
M. Friedman, *TC Hartford (USA)*
S. Fujita, *Univ. of Hiroshima (Japan)*
P. Garda, *Université de Paris-Sud (France)*
M. Glesner, *Univ. of Darmstadt (Germany)*
F. Gomez-Castaneda, *Edinburgh Univ. (UK)*
K. Goser, *Univ. of Dortmund (Germany)*
A. Goto, *ICOT (Japan)*
M. Groezinger, *Aspex Microsystems (UK)*
E. Guidetti, *Univ. of Genoa (Italy)*
C. Hafer, *Siemens AG (Germany)*
D. Hamerstrom, *Adaptive Solutions (USA)*
A. Hamilton, *Univ. of Edinburgh (UK)*
T. Jackson, *Univ. of York (UK)*
P. Jeavons, *Univ. of London (UK)*
S. R. Jones, *Nottingham Univ. (UK)*

Y. Kimura, *Fujitsu Laboratories (Japan)*
C. Kleerbaum, *Univ. of Dortmund (Germany)*
A. Krall, *Univ. of Vienna (Austria)*
A. Krikelis, *Aspex Microsystems (UK)*
E. Lamma, *Univ. of Bologna (Italy)*
S. H. Lavington, *Univ. of Essex (UK)*
C. Lehmann, *Lausanne (Switzerland)*
S. Leinwand, *SRI International (USA)*
S. Lucas, *Univ. of Southampton (UK)*
T. Markussen, *Technical Univ. (Denmark)*
G. Marshall, *Univ. of Oxford (UK)*
G. Masera, *Politecnico di Torino (Italy)*
G. Mazare, *IMAG (France)*
P. Mello, *Politecnico di Torino (Italy)*
J. Meseguer, *SRI International (USA)*
G. Milne, *Univ. of Strathclyde (UK)*
Y. Mitsui, *Univ. of Hiroshima (Japan)*
A. F. Murray, *Univ. of Edinburgh (UK)*
A. Natali, *Univ. of Bologna (Italy)*
V. Neri, *Université de Paris-Sud (France)*
C. D. Nielsen, *Technical Univ. (Denmark)*
R. Payne, *SUNY-Binghamton (USA)*
G. L. Piccinini, *Politecnico di Torino (Italy)*
J. Plankl, *Siemens AG (Germany)*
W. Poechmueller, *Darmstadt Univ. (Germany)*
Pratibha, *Univ. of Waterloo (Canada)*
H. M. Reekie, *Univ. of Edinburgh (UK)*
U. Ruckert, *Dortmund (Germany)*
M. Ruo Roch, *Politecnico di Torino (Italy)*
M. G. Sami, *Polytechnic of Milan (Italy)*
P. Sapaty, *Ukranian Academic of Sc. (USSR)*
F. J. Schmitt, *Siemens AG (Germany)*
C. Schneider, *Manitoba (Canada)*
J. Shawe-Taylor, *Univ. of London (UK)*
T. Shinogi, *Fujitsu Laboratories (Japan)*
G. S. Sohi, *Univ. of Wisconsin (USA)*
G. Spezzano, *CRAI (Italy)*
J. Staunstrup, *Technical Univ. (Denmark)*
R. Stefaneili, *Polytechnic of Milan (Italy)*
G. Storti-Gajani, *Polytechnic of Milan (Italy)*
D. Talia, *CRAI (Italy)*
L. Tarassenko, *Univ. of Oxford (UK)*
M. Van Daalen, *Univ. of London (UK)*
W. A. J. Waller, *Univ. of Kent (UK)*
C. J. Wang, *Univ. of Essex (UK)*
S. R. Williams, *Univ. of Calgary (Canada)*
A. Wood, *Univ. of York (UK)*
M. Zamboni, *Politecnico di Torino (Italy)*